MW00397762

Capital Navy

The Men, Ships, and Operations of the James River Squadron

John M. Coski

Savas Publishing Company
1475 S. Bascom Ave., Suite 204, Campbell, California 95008
(800) 848-6585

Manufactured in the United States of America

Capital Navy:
The Men, Ships and Operations of the James River Squadron

by John M. Coski

Savas Publishing Company
1475 S. Bascom Avenue, Suite 204,
Campbell, California 95008 (800) 848-6585

Includes bibliographic references and index

Printing Number
10 9 8 7 6 5 4 3 2

ISBN 1-882810-03-1

This book is printed on 50-lb. Glatfelter acid-free paper

The paper in this book meets or exceeds the guidelines for permanence and durability of the Committee on Production Guidelines for Book Longevity of the Council on Library Resources

Grateful acknowledgment is made to U.S. Naval Institute Press, Annapolis, Maryland, for permission to quote from *Aboard the U.S.S. Monitor: 1862*, edited by Robert W. Daly (1964), and to the University of South Carolina Press, Columbia, for permission to quote from *An Irishman in Dixie: Thomas Conolly's Diary of the Fall of the Confederacy*, edited by Nelson D. Lankford (1987). Unless otherwise noted, all images reproduced herein are from the collections of the Eleanor S. Brockenbrough Library, The Museum of the Confederacy.

To my parents

Linda Willoughby Coski and
Bernard J. Coski (U.S. Naval Academy, class of 1952),
a pair of old salts long accustomed to clearing obstructions
and "damning the torpedoes."

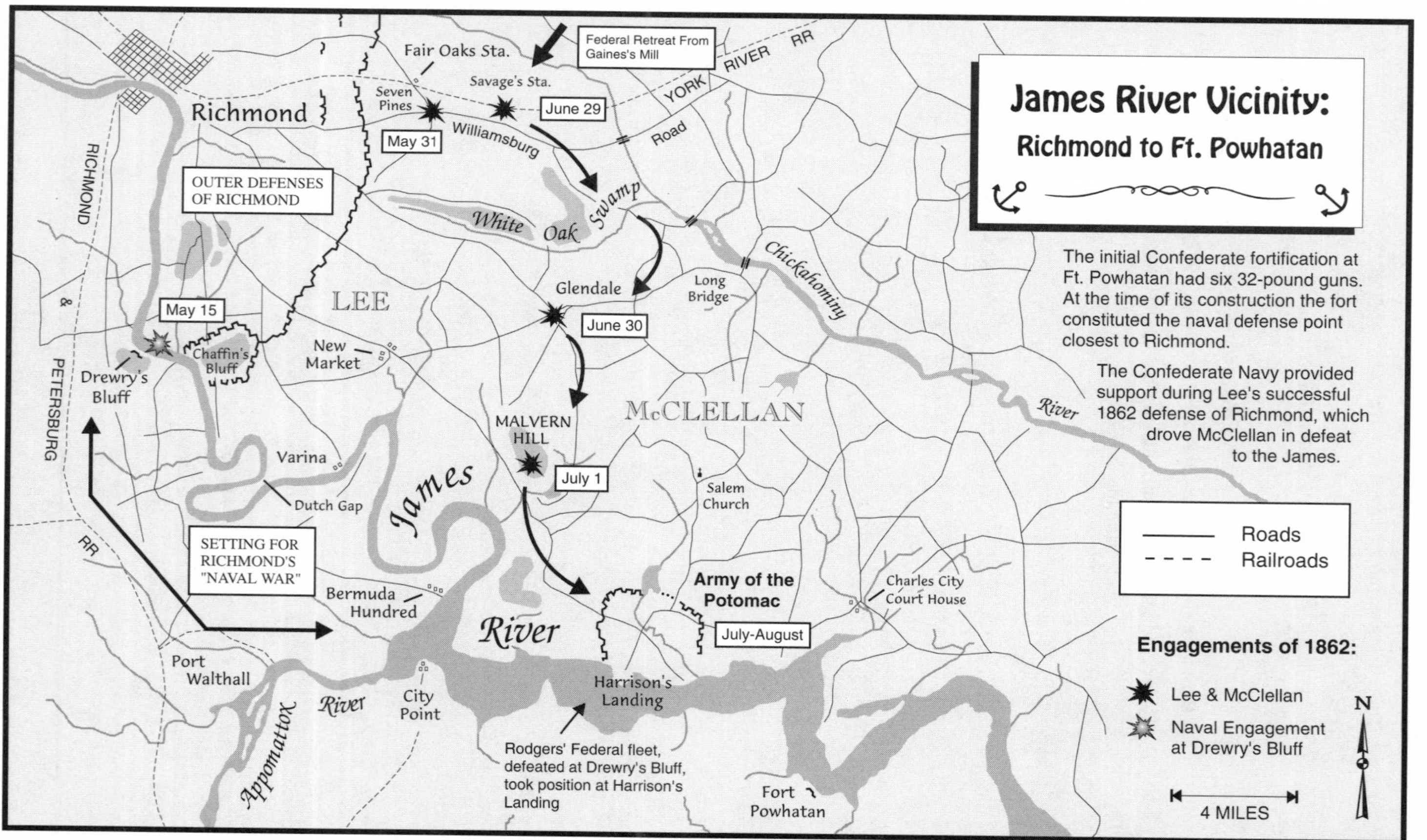
James River Vicinity:
Richmond to Ft. Powhatan
The initial Confederate fortification at Ft. Powhatan had six 32-pound guns. At the time of its construction the fort constituted the naval defense point closest to Richmond.
The Confederate Navy provided support during Lee's successful 1862 defense of Richmond, which drove McClellan in defeat to the James.
Roads
Railroads
Engagements of 1862:
Lee & McClellan
Naval Engagement at Drewry's Bluff
N
4 MILES
Federal Retreat From Gaines's Mill
Fair Oaks Sta.
Savage's Sta.
Seven Pines
June 29
May 31
Williamsburg
Road
YORK RIVER RR
Richmond
OUTER DEFENSES OF RICHMOND
White Oak Swamp
Chickahominy
River
Glendale
Long Bridge
June 30
LEE
May 15
Chaffin's Bluff
Drewry's Bluff
New Market
RICHMOND & PETERSBURG RR
McCLELLAN
MALVERN HILL
July 1
Varina
Dutch Gap
James
River
Salem Church
SETTING FOR RICHMOND'S "NAVAL WAR"
Bermuda Hundred
Army of the Potomac
July-August
Charles City Court House
Port Walthall
Harrison's Landing
City Point
River
Appomattox
Rodgers' Federal fleet, defeated at Drewry's Bluff, took position at Harrison's Landing
Fort Powhatan
Mark A. Moore

Table of Contents

continued. . .

Maps & Illustrations

Maps

Photographs & Illustrations

Photograph and illustration sections follow every chapter

Preface

To drive—or run, as I often do—down Richmond's famed Monument Avenue is to confront heroic statues of larger-than-life figures from the city's Confederate past: J.E.B. Stuart, Robert E. Lee, Jefferson Davis, Thomas "Stonewall" Jackson. . .and Matthew Fontaine Maury. Matthew Fontaine Maury? Many residents and visitors alike must wonder why Maury is among the men honored on Monument Avenue. The statue depicts the lame and grizzled naval scientist seated before a huge bronze globe and speaks to Maury's fame as "pathfinder of the seas." Why he is on an avenue of Confederates is not clear from either the monument itself or from its inscription. To understand why Maury is on Monument Avenue is to rediscover a virtually forgotten chapter in Richmond's history. *Capital Navy* is that forgotten chapter.

While there is much more to the city's history than the four years of the Civil War, Richmond will be forever identified as the capital of the Confederate States of America, 1861-1865. Historians have dubbed Richmond "Mr. Davis' City," and "General Lee's City," after the president who resided here and the general whose army so ably defended it for so long.[1] Their stories have been told often and well and, through them, Richmond's political and military history is well-established.

In the name of equal time, perhaps this book ought to be entitled *Commander Maury's City*. But Richmond's Civil War naval history is too rich to be reduced to association with one man, however important he might have been. The story of the Confederate navy in Richmond and on the James River is a story with many facets and of many men. Some, like Secretary of the Navy Stephen Mallory and Adm. Raphael Semmes, are familiar and need little or no introduction. Others, even more obscure than Matthew Fontaine Maury despite their contributions to the naval presence in Richmond, include John K. Mitchell, John M. Brooke, William A. Graves, Hunter Davidson, Francis Shepperd and Robert Dabney Minor. These and other men shaped the city's naval history. To defend the city, they helped create a naval force of several ironclads and wooden support ships that was among the most formidable in the South. *Capital Navy* is both the story of ships, people, industries and operations that constituted Richmond's life as the Southern naval capital, and the story of the capital navy—the James River Squadron based in Richmond from 1862 until the end of the war.

While I have attempted to place the role of naval Richmond and the squadron that defended her within the overall context of the war, especially the naval war, it was not my intention to write a thorough history of Richmond during the war or of the Confederate States Navy.[2] Rather, *Capital Navy* attempts to strike a balance between the technological details that are the stuff of naval history and the historical narrative that makes the story interesting and intelligible for the general reader.

I am confident Civil War enthusiasts and local historians will be surprised by the scope, variety and importance of the story held within these pages, and that they will share my pleasure in discovering a new dimension of Confederate history.

Acknowledgments

This is a book with many authors and contributors. First, I had the assistance of several interns with The Museum of the Confederacy. Frank White, a veteran of the United States Navy, conducted the initial research at the National Archives and in secondary sources. Frank produced a paper that was the first effort to translate the research into a coherent story. Keith Jessup and Ben Vig drew the eye-straining assignment of poring over Civil War newspapers in search of articles and notices. Keith also proved his proficiency with onion-skin paper and faded ink in the voluminous Tredegar Iron Works records.

As research progressed, I found myself following the footsteps of others and soon became acquainted with the small network of people working around this topic. Bob Holcombe, director of the James Woodruff Confederate Naval Museum in Columbus, Georgia, and Bill Still, formerly director of the Program in Underwater Archaeology, East Carolina University, were especially knowledgeable about sources and contacts. Bob patiently offered his technical expertise to this naval novice. Both men read and made valuable comments on an initial draft of the manuscript. One of Still's students, Dan Blair, provided his unpublished work on the *CSS Virginia II*. Taft Kiser and Dan Mouer, of the Virginia Commonwealth University archaeology program, shared resources and ideas. Their student and intern, Mark Joseph, likewise shared with me his research on Rocketts. Through discussions with John Townley of the Confederate Naval Historical Society I found a mutual friend, Sam Margolin, was an authority on the James River shipwrecks, and was able to secure from Sam a copy of his report. Jeff Johnston, secretary of the non-profit reenactment group, the James River Squadron, lent his expertise on torpedo warfare and ships of the squadron. To Patrick D. Harris, an energetic historian of Richmond's larger naval history, I owe my education on the mysterious submarine project and insights on the Trigg shipyard, as well as last-minute research assistance. Beginning in the early 1990s, Richmond historian and writer David Ryan and I began a happy camaraderie of working on thematically related projects. Fortunately for David, he has left me in his dust and published numerous fine works in the time that it has taken me to finish this one.

Mark Greenough and Dick Cheatham of Richmond's Living History Associates, and Jim Richrmond, U.S.N.–retired and friend of The Museum of the Confederacy, shared their knowledge and enthusiasm and also read and critiqued the manuscript. Don Pierce, Civil War historian and free-lance journalist and publisher, supported and promoted the book through all available means. Cliff Dickinson, the authority on the Richmond defenses, shared his resources and expertise. The historians at Richmond National Battlefield Park, especially David Ruth and Mike Andrus, made available the park's voluminous research files. Edwin C. Bearss, author of the most detailed study of the 1862 Drewry's Bluff battle, read and critiqued my chapter on the battle and its aftermath. Alice Creighton, head of the Special Collections and Archives at the United States Naval Academy, came through with some eleventh-hour biographical information.

After working several years in public history, I have come to appreciate the value of making history interesting and accessible to the general public as well as to experts and hardcore students of the conflict. Consequently, I envisaged this book having many features of a good museum exhibition or catalog, especially photographs with descriptive captions. My publisher shared this vision and even extended it in a new direction.

Theodore P. "Ted" Savas, lawyer, historian and publisher (not necessarily in that order), has a self-declared weakness for the Confederate navy and to that weakness this book owes its existence. He assisted with the manuscript as only a multi-talented publisher/historian/cartographer can. Ted also suggested the inclusion of detailed ship plans and put me in contact with David Meagher, of Meridianville, Alabama, to whom I am greatly indebted for his enthusiasm, knowledge and skill. Also through Ted's good offices, Mark Moore, of Wilson, North Carolina, has furnished the fine maps for this book; Connie L. Perkins and Stephen C. Wetlesen assisted in proofreading the manuscript; David Lang provided time and money-saving scanning services; and Lee Merideth provided the index. Their services were all greatly appreciated.

I am also deeply indebted to Dr. Charles Peery, M.D., who offered to share images from his extensive collection of Confederate navy items, the value of which is exceeded only by his unparalleled knowledge of and enthusiasm for his own and other collections.

My colleagues at The Museum of the Confederacy, past and present—especially Ruth Ann Coski, Lindsay Gray, Tucker Hill, Rick Pougher, and Guy Swanson—helped cut, slash, pound and massage the manuscript into proper submission. Photograph curator Cory Hudgins, assisted by Louise Hall, performed the leg work of identifying portraits of men in the James River Squadron and securing copies for the book. Former executive director Lou Gorr and current executive director Robin Reed gave to the project their support and encouragement, without which my work was not possible. Ruth Ann, colleague and co-habitor at the White House and at our house, like so many women before her, often gave up her man to the navy—so to speak.

The entire project is the brainchild of Paul Murphy, of Charles City County, Virginia, a Reynolds Metals retiree and now a formidable and persistent patron of preservation in downtown Richmond. A World War II veteran of the United States Navy, Paul has long tried to interest others in the untold naval history of Richmond. Working through the Historic Richmond Foundation and the William Byrd branch of the Association for the Preservation of Virginia Antiquities, Paul also contributed to The Museum of the Confederacy the funds for the initial research into this topic. *Capital Navy* is a testament to Paul's efforts, and, I hope, we are all the richer for them.

John M. Coski
Richmond, Virginia

Introduction: April 1865

On the evening of April 2, 1865, President Abraham Lincoln and Rear Adm. David Dixon Porter, United States Navy, sat on the deck of Porter's squadron flagship, *U.S.S. Malvern.* The warship was anchored in the James River near City Point (modern-day Hopewell). Nearby, the Federal army under Gen. Ulysses S. Grant had broken through the Richmond-Petersburg defenses, held for so many months by Gen. Robert E. Lee's Army of Northern Virginia. Within a short time Grant's soldiers would occupy the Confederate capital of Richmond.

"Can't the navy do something at this particular moment to make history?" Lincoln queried Porter.

"Not much," Porter replied. "The navy is doing its best just now holding in utter uselessness the rebel navy, consisting of four heavy ironclads. If these should get down to City Point they would commit great havoc."

At Lincoln's request, Porter ordered his fleet of gunboats to make "a noise" and fire across the neck of land that separated the Union and Confederate squadrons.

"In twenty minutes," Porter recalled, "there was a loud explosion which shook the vessel."

"The President jumped from his chair. 'I hope to Heaven one of them has not blown up!' he exclaimed.

"No sir!" I replied. "My ear detects that the sound was at least two miles further up the river; it was one of the rebel ironclads. You will hear another in a minute."

""Well," he said, "our noise has done some good; that's a cheap way of getting rid of ironclads. . . ." Just then there was a second explosion, and two more followed soon after.

"That is all of them," I said; "no doubt the forts are all evacuated, and tomorrow we can go up to Richmond."

"At daybreak," Porter later wrote in his memoirs, "it was discovered that all the forts had been set on fire and evacuated, and nothing was to be seen of the ironclads but their black hulls partly out of the water."[1]

As Porter predicted, the destruction of the Confederate forts and ironclads cleared the way for the Federal army to occupy the Confederate capital on the morning of April 3. With the self-destruction of the Confederate fleet, Porter's task was simple. "I sent the officers and men to work removing the obstructions from the channel in hopes of getting up to Richmond as soon as the army," he wrote in his private journal, "taking at the same time due precautions not to have anything blown up by the enemy's torpedoes." The following day, April 4, Porter and President Lincoln ascended the river to Richmond and toured the conquered city.[2]

Among the ruins of Richmond which Porter, Lincoln, and an army of Northern reporters viewed in the ensuing days were the city's river defenses, together with the remains of the Confederate States Navy. Eight miles downriver from Richmond were the Confederate fortifications at Drewry's Bluff and Chaffin's Bluff. The defenses there, wrote *New York World* correspondents George Alfred Townsend and Jerome B. Stillson, were "the most formidable" they had seen. "They are monuments of patient labor, and make of themselves hills as great as nature's." Townsend and Stillson were awed at the maze of obstructions and submarine mines (referred to as "torpedoes") which littered the James River at Drewry's Bluff. "We think it absolutely impossible," the correspondents concluded, "under any circumstances, that our fleet could have got to Richmond so long as the rebels contested the passage;

each step forward finds new and greater obstacles." Steaming up the James on April 4, *New York Times* reporter Lorenzo L. Crounse grew nervous as his vessel approached the lines of torpedoes below Drewry's Bluff. "It is readily admitted," Crounse wrote, "that this was the impassable barrier to the naval advance on Richmond." Before any of the vessels could ascend the river, the Federal Navy had cleared the channel of the much-dreaded torpedoes. Laid out on the banks, the torpedoes looked to Admiral Porter "like so many queer fish basking in the sun, of all sizes and shapes."[3]

The wrecks of the vessels in the Confederate navy's James River Squadron lay in the river bed near Drewry's Bluff. One reporter spotted the unfinished ironclad *Texas*—one of two Confederate vessels not destroyed and seized by the U.S. Navy. Visible above the water line just upriver from Drewry's Bluff were the iron sides of a ship assumed to be the *C.S.S. Virginia II*, late flagship of the Confederate James River Squadron.[4]

After passing the dangers at Drewry's Bluff and ascending further upriver than Federal ships had been able to ascend in four years, Crounse felt his "very pardonable trepidation" giving way to

> a feeling that just now is a moment in our lives, the significance, importance and sublimity of which cannot be justly appreciated. The City of Richmond is in view. The spires pointing heavenward; the smoke still rising from the conflagration's awful ruin, and the Stars and Stripes floating from a hundred house-tops and mastheads all form a picture so sublimely grand and inspiring that the human mind is lost in mute contemplation.[5]

Closer to the city, a *New York Herald* reporter spotted "a new ram on the stocks below Richmond. . . burning to this hour. . . ." Thus perishes, he mused, "the last of the formidable iron-clads which the Confederates have built, but which have had the singular fatality of ill-luck."[6]

That still-burning hulk lay on the ways of the Confederate navy yard which was located on both sides of the James River adjacent to the city at the landing known as Rocketts. "In the navy yard there is a heavy amount of lumber, and the kind needed in shipbuilding," wrote *New*

York Herald correspondent Theodore C. Wilson. "On the ways there is a seven hundred and fifty ton ship, two thirds finished. Work was commenced on it in 1860 [sic.] There is also a canal lighter, nearly finished, and four canal boats [sic. torpedo boats] in course of construction."[7]

The greater part of Richmond's commercial and warehouse district downtown was burned by the Confederates on the night of April 2. Located there was the seat of the Confederate bureaucracy. On the corner of 9th and Main, noted reporter Richard T. Colburn, "stood a handsome brick building, now in smoking ruins, which was known as the Mechanics' Hall, and has since been occupied as the rebel war departments [army and navy]."[8]

After extinguishing the evacuation fire, the Federal army secured possession of the city and its many government facilities, assembled captured arms and equipment, and discovered the extent of what might be called Richmond's "naval-industrial complex." The most vital industrial establishments in that complex escaped destruction in the evacuation fire. Chief Engineer Alexander Henderson, U.S.N., filed an extensive report of "the machinery and material found at the 'Confederate Naval Works' formerly known as 'Shockoe Iron Works' of Messrs. Talbot[t] and Brothers." Henderson found engines, propellers, and shafts for the unfinished ironclad ram, *Texas*, and an enormous quantity of spare propellers, boilers, torpedo boat machinery, boiler plate, iron plates, and tools. Admiral Porter reported that two other facilities vital to the Confederate States Navy, the Tredegar Iron Works and the Naval Ordnance Works, "remain untouched."[9]

The ruins of Richmond dramatized to Federal officers and the Northern public the extent to which Richmond had become a military city. Chosen as the Confederate capital in large part because it was the South's most important industrial city, Richmond evolved into the administrative and industrial heart of the nation. As Northern armies and navies occupied Southern territory and ports, more resources, industries, and people were relocated to the surviving cities. In December 1864, Savannah, Georgia, together with its naval squadron fell to the advancing Federals. Wilmington, North Carolina, followed in February 1865, as did Charleston, South Carolina, and by the beginning of April 1865, the only naval force remaining on the Confederacy's eastern seaboard belonged to the capital city. On April 3, 1865, the James River Squadron—the capital navy—hastened its own demise with torches and explosives. Its end heralded the loss of the Confederate navy capital, and with it, the end of the Confederate navy on the Atlantic seaboard.

Derrick built by the U.S. Military Railroad Construction Corps for unloading cars and engines, Richmond, April 1865

The victorious Federal forces used Rocketts—the port of Richmond—to stockpile captured Confederate war material, to transport it to the North, and to unload heavy equipment. The photographs on these facing pages afford rare close-up views of the busy Rocketts waterfront. This Andrew Joseph Russell photograph (above) was taken from

Captured Confederate artillery at Rocketts, 1865

across the James, while the image of the captured artillery (above) offers the best ground-level view of the Rocketts Navy Yard. The line of open sheds along the water pre-dated the war. The smokestacks and wheels visible in the background belonged to Federal ships docked at the wharves. Both photos courtesy of the Library of Congress.

Stephen Russell Mallory, Secretary of the Navy

In 1864, Stephen Mallory (1813-1872) and a delegation from the Confederate Congress were visiting the naval encampment at Drewry's Bluff, when the chairman of the House Committee on Naval Affairs proposed a toast to "Two great ideas: Ironclads and Torpedoes, and Mr. Mallory, their great patron, or introducer." Having been for more than seven years the chairman of the U.S. Senate Committee on Naval Affairs, Mallory was familiar with advances in naval technology and realized the Confederacy's need to innovate. While haunted by the "premature" destruction of almost all of the Confederacy's ironclads, Mallory nevertheless was justly proud of his department's accomplishments. Carte-de-visite.

The Making of a Navy Capital, 1861-1862

The Confederate States Navy arrived formally in Richmond in the person of Stephen Russell Mallory, secretary of the navy, on the evening of Monday, June 3, 1861. "Worked at navy matters in temporary quarters until 4 P.M—wrote to my charming wife.—Met several navy men," Mallory penned in his diary the day after his first full day in the new Confederate capital. Separated by distance from his beloved, but temperamental, wife Angela and his children, Mallory had a difficult time adjusting emotionally to his new situation. Along with many other newly-arrived Confederate leaders, including President Jefferson Davis, Mallory found temporary quarters in the Spotswood Hotel, where he dined with other cabinet members at the president's often contentious table. While settling in to his new surroundings, his navy department found temporary headquarters in the former U.S. Customs House, sharing that large stone building with the Treasury, Justice and War Departments and executive offices.[1]

The city into which Mallory settled in June of 1861 had just been designated the capital of the Confederacy. Richmond and Virginia had not even been part of the Confederacy when the newly-minted naval secretary assumed his duties more than two months before, or when war erupted between the North and South in April 1861. The Confederate government was already an ongoing institution by the time Mallory and his colleagues relocated to Richmond, though the war had not yet seen its first real battle.

The navy over which Mallory would preside came into existence on February 21, 1861, by an act of the week-old Provisional Congress of the Confederate States of America.[2] Representatives of six Southern states, which that winter had seceded from the old Federal Union, met in Montgomery, Alabama, to form a new confederacy. The government they created closely resembled the one just abandoned, and the men they appointed to lead the government had been prominent leaders in the old union. Jefferson Davis, inaugurated provisional president on February 18, had been a United States senator from Mississippi and secretary of war in the cabinet of President Franklin Pierce (1853-1857). Davis' vice-president, Alexander H. Stephens, had been a representative from Georgia.

Stephen Russell Mallory, the man whom Davis chose to head the fledgling Confederate navy, had been United States senator from Florida and for over seven years the chairman of the Senate Committee on Naval Affairs. While that experience fitted Mallory for his new post, it also sowed the seeds of discord within the Confederate navy. One of Senator Mallory's accomplishments had been the creation of the Retiring Board, (nick-named the "plucking board") which attempted to force the retirement from active duty of many officers, most notably the physically infirm but highly acclaimed naval scientist Matthew Fontaine Maury. Rather than enjoying a fresh start, the amiable Confederate naval secretary found himself facing a coterie of avowed enemies. Described by a contemporary as a "stumpy, 'roly poly' little fellow. . . for all the world like one of the squat 'gentleman farmers' you find in the south of England," and by another as "a little round bellied man who looks like a prosperous shoemaker," Mallory was an easy man to underestimate. Another contemporary noted that Mallory was respected for his "quick perception, decided cultivation, and especially his wit, genial nature and frank courtesy." His enemies machinated against him, even orchestrating a critical investigation of the department in 1862-1863. Mallory often did not get the appropriations or the manpower he needed and requested. President Davis did not always show him respect. Davis, observed Confederate army ordnance chief Josiah Gorgas in August 1863 "sneers continually at Mr. Mallory and his navy, and is at no pains to conceal his opinions before that secretary." Nevertheless, Mallory was one of only two Confederate cabinet officers to serve in one post the entire war.[3]

Anticipating that the United States would not allow the Southern Confederacy to secede in peace, the fathers of the new Confederacy began immediately to create a military establishment. Mallory and the navy began with an embarrassing richness of officers (eventually totalling almost 400) who had resigned commissions in the U.S. Navy, and an equally embarrassing paucity of vessels for them to command. The original seceding states seized or impounded ten U.S. Navy ships carrying a total of 15 guns. The states also seized private Northern vessels in Southern harbors and purchased others from Southern merchants. To this tiny fleet fell the task of defending the South's harbors, rivers, long Atlantic and Gulf coastlines and shipping against a Federal fleet of 90 warships—42 of which were in commission. The U.S. Navy also had hundreds of private vessels available for conversion into warships.[4]

For over three months the Confederate government was headquartered in the temporary capital at Montgomery, and it was there Mallory organized his department, formulating the policies which eventually created a viable navy. Even before the Confederate Provisional Congress confirmed Mallory on March 4, it passed an act dividing the Navy Department into four bureaus or offices that constituted the basic structure of the department for the Confederacy's entire life. During those early months in Alabama, Mallory initiated efforts to assemble a navy. The Confederacy assumed control of the several small fleets of converted civilian vessels the individual states had created following their secession from the Union. Those fleets were the genesis of the squadrons that later defended the South's Atlantic and Gulf of Mexico ports and rivers.[5] To supplement those weak assemblages of virtually unarmed ships, Mallory dispatched special agents to New York, Philadelphia, Baltimore, and Canada to purchase ships. This avenue of navy building was available only as long as the uneasy peace prevailed between the North and South.

Secession led to civil war when Confederate artillery began bombarding Fort Sumter on April 12, 1861. Seven days later, on April 19, President Lincoln declared a naval blockade on the coasts of the seceded states. Although diplomats then and scholars today have argued the legality, wisdom, and effectivness of the blockade, it had the potential effect of strangling the new Confederacy economically. The blockade meant that the Confederate States Navy had to defend the South's rivers and harbors against attack, and protect Southern shipping while preserving the South's seaborn lifeline to Europe.

In those first months—and throughout the war—the Confederate navy devoted substantial diplomatic effort and money to acquiring vessels overseas. In May, Mallory dispatched special agents James D. Bulloch and James North to England to purchase much-needed ships. Their mission succeeded in acquiring and fitting out the steam-powered ocean-going commerce raiders whose adventures dominate Confederate naval history: the *Alabama*, *Florida*, and the *Shenandoah.* They failed, however, to secure the ironclad warships Mallory wanted for the defense of the South's rivers and ports. By 1863, however, United States diplomatic pressure compelled the British and French to enforce neutrality laws forbidding construction and fitting out of warships for belligerents. Despite the Southern agents' best efforts, only one European-built ironclad, the *Stonewall*, was delivered to the Confederacy. Unfortunately for the South, the *Stonewall* only made it as far as Cuba before the war ended in 1865.[6] This failure meant the Confederacy had to rely on its own resources to create fleets of ironclads.

In addition to spurring the acquisition of naval vessels overseas, the beginning of the war in April, 1861, led to the relocation of the Confederate capital to Richmond a month later. President Abraham Lincoln on April 15 called on the states to provide a total of 75,000 volunteers to crush the Southern rebellion. Faced with the demand they take up arms against sister states, four Southern states (Virginia, Arkansas, Tennessee and North Carolina) that had initially declined to secede left the Union. All four seceded in April or May and joined the Confederacy.

Although the people of Virginia did not ratify the vote of the state convention until May 23, passage of the ordinance of secession on April 17 precipitated a flurry of military activity in the state. Virginia authorities claimed Federal property within the state's boundaries. As the state's militia moved on Norfolk, U.S. authorities hastened to destroy, then abandon, the valuable naval facilities located there. Virginia's lawmakers began immediately to prepare for the state's defense and to cooperate with the Confederate government. Confederate Vice President Alexander H. Stephens visited Richmond on April 25, and arranged a military convention between the Confederacy and Virginia. At that meeting, Stephens held out the prospect of moving the Confederate capital to Richmond. The new Southern government approved the relocation on May 21, and within days began the move north. By the terms of the April 25 convention, Virginia placed its army and navy under the "chief control" of the Confederate president, pending completion of the union between Virginia and the Confederate States of America.[7]

The Virginia State Navy, April-June, 1861

Between late April and mid-June 1861, Virginia created its own armed forces. Though the state navy was based at Norfolk, military preparations also laid the foundations for transforming Richmond into a naval city. Overseeing Virginia's military preparations was a three-man advisory council that included Cdr. Matthew Fontaine Maury, late of the United States Navy. One of the council's first actions was to recommend the appointment of Robert E. Lee as commander in chief of the Military and Naval forces of Virginia. Four days later the council appointed several army and navy officers, including naval captains Sidney Smith Lee (Robert E. Lee's older brother) and Samuel Barron, to a Joint Commission of army and navy officers "to name all efficient and worthy Virginians and Residents of Virginia in the Army and Navy of the United States; for the purpose of inviting them into the service of Virginia. . . ."[8]

Within a week of Virginia's secession, the council and the secession convention had assembled the nucleus of a state navy. Commodore French Forrest, U.S.N., accepted appointment as flag officer of the state navy and assumed command at the Norfolk Navy Yard. Several former U.S. naval officers destined to become important figures in the Confederate navy accepted state commissions as early as April 18: John Randolph Tucker, Robert B. Pegram, Catesby Ap R. Jones, John Mercer Brooke, James H. Rochelle, William C. Whittle, Thomas J. Page, and William F. Lynch. Pegram, Rochelle, and Jones were assigned to Norfolk and ordered to "assume command of the naval station, with authority to organize naval defences, enroll and enlist seamen and marines, and temporarily to appoint war officers, and do and perform whatever may be necessary to preserve and protect the property of the Commonwealth and the citizens of Virginia." The council advised officers assigned to naval defenses of the James, York, Rappahannock and Potomac rivers and their tributaries to inspect vessels seized and determine which should be retained and used for the public defenses.[9]

Many officers of the Virginia State Navy subsquently became the first leaders of the Confederate States Navy. Typical of the Confederate navy's founding officers, those men had been highly-placed veterans of the loyal fraternity that was the nineteenth-century United States Navy. Samuel Barron, French Forrest, Sidney Smith Lee, and William Lynch all had risen to the rank of captain in the old navy. Forrest and Barron were veterans of the War of 1812, while Lee and Lynch entered the service before 1820. Forrest had commanded the naval forces in the landing at Vera Cruz, Mexico, in 1847; Lee had been commander of a ship on Commodore Matthew C. Perry's legendary 1853 voyage to Japan. Another Virginia-born senior officer, John Randolph Tucker, joined the U.S. Navy at age 14 in 1826, and rose to the rank of commander in 1855. At the time of Virginia's secession, he was ordnance officer at the Norfolk Navy Yard.[10]

Along with those living navy legends were younger officers who later drew the more active roles in Confederate service in Richmond and elsewhere. Robert Pegram, James Rochelle and Thomas R. Rootes, United States Navy veterans, commanded ships in the James River Squadron based in Richmond, while Capt. Thomas Page commanded Confederate artillery at Chaffin's and Drewry's Bluffs in 1862-1863 before leaving for Europe on special assignment. Although John Brooke never commanded a Confederate vessel, he, like his mentor Matthew Maury, contributed to the Confederacy expertise in ordnance and naval technology and was arguably the Confederate navy's most valuable officer. Catesby Jones, another junior officer, became executive officer of the *Virginia* (*Merrimack*), held *de facto* command of that vessel during her epic battle with the *Monitor* and, like Brooke, subsequently made his mark in the development of naval ordnance.

Virginia enjoyed not only a wealth of trained naval officers, but also brought to the Confederacy a wealth of naval resources. The Norfolk Navy Yard, also known as the Gosport Navy Yard (and located actually on the Portsmouth side of the Elizabeth River), was the largest naval facility in the South. Because of indecision and hesitation, U.S. Navy officers failed to remove or destroy all of the yard's assets before they abandoned Norfolk on April 20, 1861. The result was a windfall for the Confederates: nearly 1,200 heavy guns (most without carriages), other heavy ordnance equipment, 300,000 pounds of powder, tools, small arms, a dry dock, and a handful of half-destroyed ships. Confederate authorities soon distributed the guns to defense works in five states.[11]

Ten U.S. Navy ships were at the Norfolk yard when the Federals abandoned and burned it. Six of them, ships of the line *Columbus*, *Delaware* and *Pennsylvania*, frigates *Columbia* and *Raritan*, and brig *Dolphin*, could not be raised and salvaged. The Confederates raised the 20-gun sloops *Germantown* and *Plymouth*, but ultimately could not use them. The U.S. Navy did not even try to destroy the frigate *United States*, originally commissioned in 1797 and one of the oldest vessels in service. Since there was little hope of making the *United States* seaworthy, Virginia authorities armed her with 19 guns for harbor defense and considered transforming her into a school ship under the command of Cdr. Thomas R. Rootes. Instead, she became the receiving ship *Confederate States*, and served in that capacity until sunk in April 1862. The *U.S.S. Merrimack*, a 40-gun frigate that probably should have steamed safely out of Norfolk before the city's abandonment, was instead fired by her owners. Although burned down to the water line, the vessel's hull and engines were not destroyed, and by early June, Virginia authorities raised her and put her in dry dock.[12]

In addition to the U.S. Navy ships salvaged at Norfolk, the Commonwealth of Virginia built a small navy through the purchase and seizure of vessels. The state purchased the steamers *George Page* (sometimes called the *Richmond*), *Virginia*, *Logan*, and *Northampton* for service on Aquia Creek, and the Rappahannock, York, and James rivers, respectively.[13] The Baltimore-built *Northampton* became a cargo ship in the service of the James River Squadron. The state also purchased the Philadelphia-built *Teaser*, formerly the Georgetown, D.C., screw tug *York River*. The only warship put into commission by the Virginia State Navy, the *Teaser* was given a battery of two 32-pound rifles, one fore and one aft. Her first commander was Lt. James Rochelle, a Virginia native and 20-year U.S. Navy veteran. Rochelle was soon transferred, and another U.S. Naval Academy graduate from Virginia, Lt. Robert Randolph Carter, of Shirley Plantation, followed with an equally brief command. Destined to play a role in the development of mine warfare on the James, the *Teaser* was an unimpressive little warship. At the time of her transfer to the Confederate navy in June 1861, the *Teaser* had a crew of seven men and was under the *de facto* command of its boatswain. Several crew members deserted, taking with them articles from the ship's stores.[14]

Two other vessels seized by Virginia authorities eventually joined the *Teaser* in the nascent James River Squadron. The *Jamestown* and the *Yorktown* were wooden side wheel steamships built in New York and used as passenger and packet vessels between New York City and Virginia. The *Jamestown* was renamed *Thomas Jefferson* (a name almost never used for her) and given a battery of two 32-pound rifles. She was put in service under Confederate authority in July 1861. Another accomplished U.S. Navy veteran, Lt. Joseph Nicholson Barney, of Maryland, was her first and only commander.[15]

Virginia and the Confederacy had bigger plans for the *Yorktown*, soon renamed the *Patrick Henry*. Built in 1859, the *Yorktown* was 250 feet long and 34 feet wide at beam. Capt. Samuel Barron saw the potential of transforming her into a first-class warship. In early June, Barron ordered Cdr. John Randolph Tucker to take command of the ship and superintend her preparation for service. The work was to be done at Richmond by Master Carpenter Joseph Pierce, who was ordered from Norfolk to Richmond. The conversion of the *Yorktown* was the beginning of Richmond's extensive industrial involvement with the Confederate navy. Several firms, including merchants Faherty & Walsh, G. A. Bargamin, and Rocketts shipping supplier Richard Haskins, provided bolts, washers, nails, and padlocks for the ship. The state, meanwhile, paid individual carpenters and laborers for their work. Under Tucker's command and Pierce's direction, the *Yorktown* received an iron shield to protect her boilers—and became in effect the Confederacy's first iron-clad warship. She was also, Barron reported, to be fitted out "with as heavy a battery as she will bear." Carrying between 10 and 12 guns, she was the most heavily armed active warship in Virginia waters until the commissioning of the *Virginia* (*Merrimack*) in February, 1862. Once fitted out, the rechristened *Patrick Henry* became the flagship of the James River Squadron under Tucker's command.[16]

So impressed with the *Patrick Henry* was Secretary Mallory that in July, upon assuming control over the Virginia Navy, he ordered Tucker to take the vessel out of the James "at the earliest practicable moment and make an active cruise at sea against the enemy." Mallory believed the *Patrick Henry* faster than any of the U.S. ships stationed in Hampton Roads and the Chesapeake Bay; she could, therefore, avoid the enemy's finest vessels and prey upon the second-class ones. Tucker was not able to test his ship's capabilities at sea, however, and instead the *Patrick Henry* served for over six months as the Confederacy's primary naval sentinel on the James River. Anchored off Mulberry Island (today the site of Fort Eustis), she steamed downriver and fired on enemy ships near Newport News in September and December 1861. On the second occasion, Tucker took the *Patrick Henry* downriver after dark in hopes of surprising a small fleet of weakly-armed steamships. In a two-hour period the Confederate ship fired 28 shell and 13 solid shot, but did no damage to the enemy. Those attacks were the most significant naval actions in the James River above Hampton Roads before the advent of the ironclad *Virginia* in early 1862.[17]

Along with acquiring, fitting out, and crewing vessels, the Virginia State Navy prepared land defenses for the state's rivers and coastline. The state navy employed 217 of the captured heavy guns in land fortifications, and assigned naval officers to command the 21 batteries. "The rivers of Virginia being undefended and exposed to attack, it is due to the naval forces of Virginia to say that they went to work to defend them with zeal proportionate to the necessities of the case," Samuel Barron, head of the Virginia Navy's Office of Detail and Equipment, wrote to

Virginia governor John Letcher in June. Those defenses are, Barron assured his commander-in-chief, "so far completed as to justify the belief that they will be able to drive off any naval force that the U.S. Government can bring against them."[18] Indeed, Virginia's coastal and river defenses were strong enough to deter Federal attack for nearly one year. The Potomac River batteries constituted an effective naval blockade on Washington, D.C., greatly embarrassing the Lincoln administration.

Charged with the duty of establishing defenses along the James River was Harrison Henry Cocke, a 67-year-old former U.S. naval officer who had been in the Battle of Lake Erie in the War of 1812. Too old for active service, Cocke was made a captain on the reserve list of the Virginia State Navy and assigned to special duty on the James. Most of the river's defenses were located on the lower part of the stream, just above its mouth at Newport News Point. Under the direct supervision of lieutenants John Brooke and Catesby Jones, and using the enforced labor of hundreds of impressed slaves and free blacks, Virginia constructed a strong fortification on historic Jamestown Island. To defend the river between Jamestown and Richmond, Cocke recommended a site on the south side of the river approximately halfway between the two points. Identified on period maps as "Hood's," it had been the purported site of an old Indian fort and was appropriately rechristened Fort Powhatan. There, not far from his own Prince George County estate, Cocke supervised the erection of an earthen fort protecting a battery of six 32-pound guns. Robert Pegram assumed command of the post in May. Fort Powhatan was not a very impressive work. Area resident, farmer and secessionist leader Edmund Ruffin, worried about the fort's weakness and expressed his concerns to Pegram.[19] The Confederate navy shared Ruffin's concerns, and, by the end of the summer, dismantled its battery.

Weak and short-lived though it was, Fort Powhatan was nevertheless the naval defense point closest to Richmond. The state organized a "naval battery" for the defense of the capital, but the battery was to consist of six 12-pound howitzers—land guns—and was intended to be used in conjunction with the army, not in river defense. Lieutenant William H. Parker, the officer assigned to organize the battery, eventually "[gave] up all hope of getting my howitzers into action," and happily accepted command of a vessel in North Carolina.[20] Though Samuel Barron was justly proud of the work which the Virginia State Navy accomplished in May and June 1861, the failure to establish better naval defenses for the Richmond was a notable oversight. Only quick action in the spring of 1862, prevented it from becoming a fatal oversight.

Richmond: Seaport on the James

Richmond did not figure prominently in the state's initial naval preparations. Virginia's naval "frontiers" were the estuaries of the state's major rivers, and its naval nerve center was Norfolk. With the Federal abandonment of Norfolk and its valuable facilities, Virginia gained almost complete control of its own territory. Only Arlington County and the city of Alexandria, across the Potomac River from Washington, D.C., and Fort Monroe, on the tip of the peninsula, remained in Federal hands. Richmond was, for the time being, well behind the naval lines.

Between Richmond and the naval front lines were over 100 miles of navigable waterway. Upstream from Norfolk was Hampton Roads, the estuary formed by the convergence of several rivers. One of those rivers was the James, Virginia's birthplace and Richmond's *raison d'être*. The capital city lay at the fall line of the James—the furthest point of navigability for seagoing vessels—90 miles upstream from Hampton Roads. No dramatic cataracts announce the fall line at Richmond. Instead, the river at and above the city is wild, rocky and divided by small islands, including Belle Isle (also known as Broad Rock Island), site of a prisoner-of-war camp. Almost imperceptibly, over a seven-mile stretch ending just below the city's 1860 eastern boundary, the James River falls 90 feet.[21]

From the capital downstream 16 miles to City Point (now Hopewell), where the Appomattox River joins the James, lay the stretch of river which was the truncated setting for Richmond's naval war. Varying in width from 1/8 to 1/3 of a mile, and in depth (at low water) from 13 to 42 feet, the channel of the James between Richmond and City Point was (and still is) difficult to navigate. Three bars, one over a mile long, were virtually impassable for larger vessels at low water. The river twisted and turned for 38 miles, more than double the distance as the crow flies. Although an east-west river, the James runs from Richmond nearly due south for eight miles to Drewry's Bluff. Shortly below, it enters a succession of five dramatic loops (two of which have since been cut off by canals)—features destined to complicate naval war on the river in 1864-1865.[22] From Richmond to the hamlet of Varina in Henrico County, the river is flanked on both sides by low, broad plains, punctuated by hills on which sat "Ampthill," "Wilton" and other seats of Virginia's first families. Below the dominating 90-foot rise at Drewry's Bluff, the land along the river is alternately more rugged and more swampy.

Situated at the fall line, Richmond is a natural inland port. Early nineteenth-century city leaders enhanced its commercial advantages by constructing the James River and Kanawha Canal. Though the canal itself never breached the Appalachian Mountain barrier to the Kanawha and Ohio River system, it linked Richmond with the rich agricultural region around Lynchburg, and connecting roads reached to the Kanawha Valley. The canal's Richmond terminus was the great turning basin, a six-square-block inland lake between Cary and Canal and 8th and 11th streets. In 1854, the James River and Kanawha Canal Company fulfilled its charter by completing the tidewater connecting locks, which linked the canal at the turning basin to the port for ocean-going vessels located downstream from the city. The canal company also owned and operated the city's commercial hub, a 3,450-foot dock fronting the canal east of the turning basin and extending from 17th St. to the Great Ship Lock. With those facilities, ocean-going vessels and ships of war (up to 35 feet in width, or beam) could come up the river as far as 17th St.[23]

Richmond, in 1861, boasted the resources to make it a valuable naval center. The city was enjoying a prosperity based in large part on its waterborn commerce. On the eve of the war, Richmond was the center of a substantial passenger and merchant shipping industry. Regular daily and weekly steamship and packet service connected Richmond with Boston, New York, Philadelphia, Baltimore, and Norfolk.[24] Before they were seized and transformed into warships, the *Yorktown* and the *Jamestown* carried passengers and merchandise between Richmond and New York. Many businessmen, such as commission merchant Richard Haskins and Joseph Anderson (owner of the Tredegar Iron Works) owned small fleets of canal barges, brigs and sloops. A boatyard for construction of such smaller vessels was located in a slip off the canal, adjacent to the Tredegar Iron Works.

Commercial statistics reveal the vitality of Richmond on the eve of war. Richmond was not only a center of the nation's tobacco industry and the South's most important iron industry, but was one of America's major flour milling cities. A handful of Richmond area mills produced as much flour as 50 Baltimore mills. The Gallego mills (reputed to be physically the world's largest), along with mills operated by the Haxall and Crenshaw families, opened a substantial flour for coffee trade with South America in the 1840s, and maintained a fleet of sailing vessels. The five years before the war saw the volume of shipping at the Richmond dock nearly double. In 1855, 1,217 vessels entered the dock and 1,377 departed. In 1860, 2,133 ships and boats arrived at the Richmond dock carrying such items as coal, fish, guano, hay, pig and scrap iron, salt, tar, and rosin, while 2,337 departed carrying 423,194 barrels of flour, 56,367 packages of tobacco, and 143,000 bushels of wheat. Even as late as December 1861, with the Federal blockade of the Southern coast in force, 109 commercial vessels entered the Richmond dock.[25]

Until the Federals occupied Norfolk in May 1862, and choked off shipping through Hampton Roads, Richmond continued its role as one of Virginia's major ports. The traditional port of Richmond was located on the eastern edge of the city at Rocketts landing (in the present-day Fulton neighborhood). Lying just below the falls of the James, Rocketts had served as Richmond's port since the city's founding. The area derived its name from Robert Rockett, who, in 1730, received authority to operate a ferry there. In 1781, a tobacco warehouse and inspection station were established, making Rocketts the center of a thriving international tobacco trade. By 1860, Rocketts boasted several wharves, dock equipment, storage sheds and innumerable warehouses.[26]

Surrounding the wharves and extending westward along the dock were businesses associated with Richmond's shipping industry. The city's 1860 directory listed five ship chandlers, or suppliers, including Richard Haskins and Edward Cunningham at Rocketts, and Luther Libby, whose warehouse on Cary St. between 20th and 21st streets became the infamous Libby prison. Eleven shipping agents and brokers, including four members of the Currie family, also maintained offices in the neighborhood. Richard Haskins was a member of the city council, as well as the most prominent businessman in Rocketts. He had one of the first businesses in Rocketts, and kept his business there even after his last partner, Luther Libby, moved upriver. On the eve of war, Haskins and Libby together owned six small ships, three of which were seized by Federal authorities and three by the Confederacy.[27]

Described as a "rickety suburb," Rocketts had by 1860 become a somewhat dingy working-class neighborhood, home to many of Richmond's immigrants and free blacks, and other men who worked in Richmond's shipping industry. Up the hill a few blocks away was one of the two plants that converted coal into gas for lighting the streets and homes of Richmond. Nestled amid the warehouses and large establishments on the main streets of Rocketts—Lester, Bloody Run, Pear, Peach, Ash, Maple, Elm, and Poplar—were small businesses and artisan shops. The grocers, blacksmiths, carpenters, and tailors of Rocketts usually lived behind or over their shops, often boarding other men with them.[28]

When Federal forces occupied Norfolk in May 1862, and effectively closed off commercial shipping up the James River, the Rocketts waterfront was given over to the Confederate navy and army. Not schooners and packets, but ironclads, steamships, and gunboats moored at the wharves of Rocketts. The warehouses held not only flour and tobacco destined for foreign ports, but food and clothing for the ships of the Confederacy's James River Squadron based at Richmond. The sheds and equipment at Rocketts were integrated into one of the Confederacy's most prolific and longest-lived shipyards.

Richmond: Headquarters of the Confederate States Navy

For the first year of the war, until the Federals reoccupied Norfolk, Richmond remained primarily an administrative headquarters for the Confederate navy, while Norfolk served as the primary shipyard and home port for the newly-created James River Squadron. Even as an administrative center, Richmond played a dual role. The city was both home to the bureaucrats who created a naval establishment throughout the Confederacy and one of the economic and industrial centers of that establishment. Naturally, the South's major port cities—Norfolk, Wilmington, Charleston, Savannah, Pensacola, Mobile, and Galveston—were the initial centers of naval activity. But as Federal forces captured and threatened those ports, inland cities like Richmond, Charlotte, North Carolina, Selma, Alabama, and Columbus, Georgia, became the centers of supply, production, and shipbuilding. Only in Richmond, however, did the Confederacy concentrate every facet of naval activity: assembling and manufacturing materials to construct ships, their engines and their ordnance; constructing and fitting out the vessels; repairing vessels; supplying a fleet; recruiting sailors and educating officers; providing medical care for naval and marine personnel; and administering the entire naval establishment.

Finding offices for an entirely new government bureaucracy and housing for its people was no easy task, but Richmond had enough public buildings and hotels to accommodate the government—at least in 1861. Richmond in 1860 was a city of 38,000 people, including almost 12,000 slaves and over 2,500 free blacks, and was enjoying a burst of prosperity. The prosperity and civic pride could be seen in the city's built environment. The equestrian statue of George Washington on Capitol Square was dedicated on February 22, 1858. Several important new public structures were completed on the eve of the war: the Spotswood Hotel, the alms house on the city's northern edge, the U.S. customs house on Main St. just below the capitol and the Mechanics Institute across 9th St. from the capitol. The state capitol building, a bright white temple perched on the brow of one of Richmond's many hills, was the center of governmental power. Sharing the sloped, landscaped confines of Capitol Square with the capitol were the governor's mansion, the general courts building and a bell tower. On the blocks surrounding Capitol Square were offices of the state government, newspaper offices, churches, residences and a wealth of fine hotels. The city's financial district was along Main St., one block below Capitol Square. Commission merchants and other businesses proliferated in the blocks southeast of the capitol, centered around the canal turning basin and Shockoe Slip on Cary St. Along the waterfront downtown were the city's iron manufacturers and flour mills. The tobacco factories and warehouses that gave

Civil War Richmond:

Naval Facilities and Government Offices

A. **Confederate Executive Mansion**

B. **Maury House**, where Matthew Fontaine Maury experimented with torpedo fuses

C. **Marine Corps Headquarters** (Sword & Thaw Dry Goods)

D. **Mechanics Institute,** home of the Confederate Navy Department and its constituent offices (The War Department was also housed here)

E. **Spotswood Hotel**

F. **Naval Rendezvous #3**: 9th St. between Cary and Main

G. **U. S. Customs House,** home of the Confederate State and Treasury Departments, as well as the executive offices of the president

H. **Confederate Naval Hospital** (William Ritter House)

I. **Gallego Mills**

J. **Naval Ordnance Works** (Ettenger & Edmond Machine Shops)

K. **Naval Works** (Talbott Brothers' Shockoe Foundry)

L. **Naval Rendezvous #2**: at Shockoe Bottom, on Franklin St. between 17th & 18th

M. **Naval Redezvous #1**: Luther Libby's ship chandlery (Libby Prison)

N. **Navy Supply and Provision Warehouse**, in Rocketts (Ludlam & Watson warehouse)

O. **City Gas Works**

Mark A. Moore

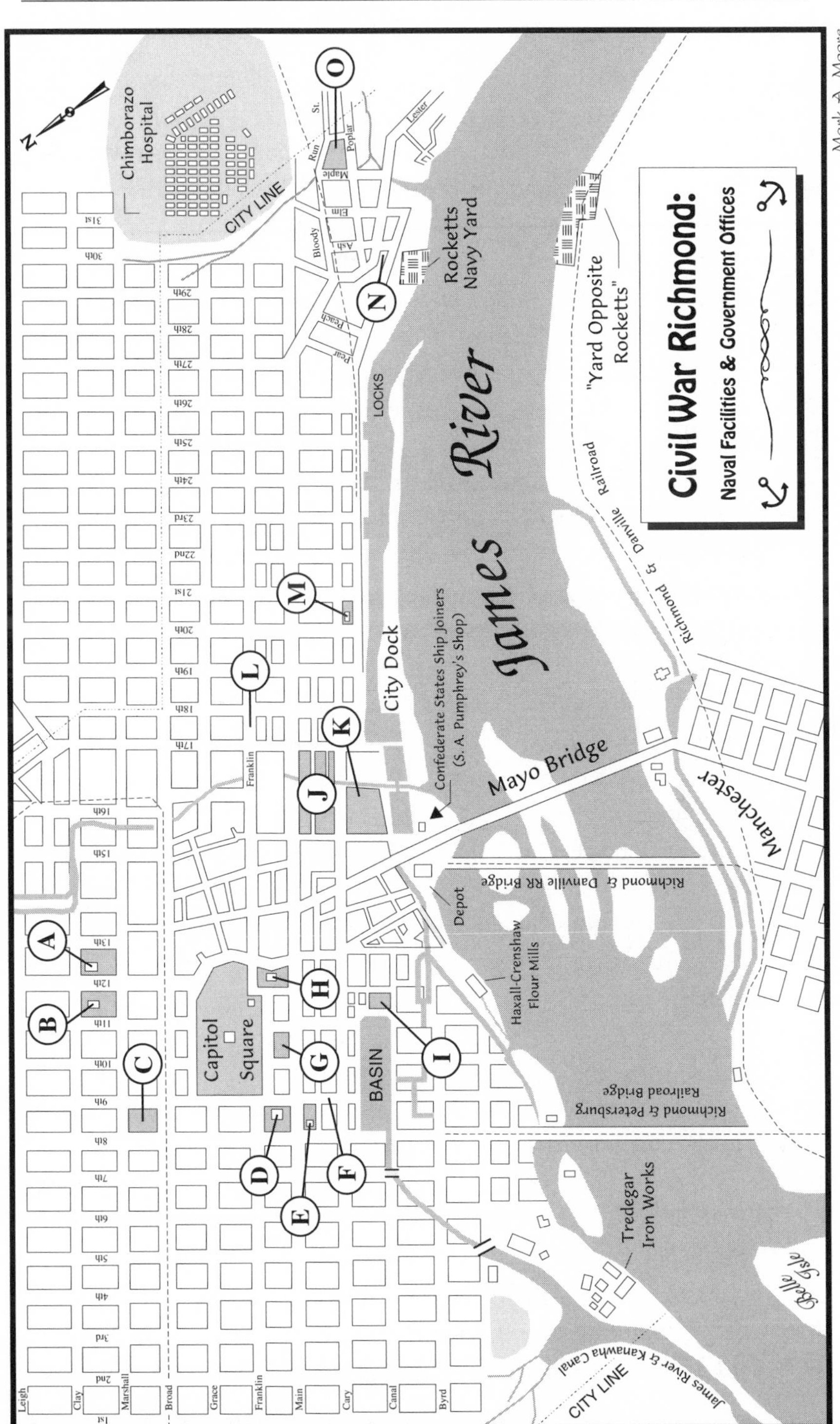
Civil War Richmond:
Naval Facilities & Government Offices
Mark A. Moore
James River
Chimborazo Hospital
CITY LINE
Rocketts Navy Yard
"Yard Opposite Rocketts"
LOCKS
City Dock
Confederate States Ship Joiners (S. A. Pumphrey's Shop)
Mayo Bridge
Manchester
Richmond & Danville Railroad
Richmond & Danville RR Bridge
Depot
Haxall-Crenshaw Flour Mills
BASIN
Capitol Square
Richmond & Petersburg Railroad Bridge
Tredegar Iron Works
Belle Isle
James River & Kanawha Canal
CITY LINE
Leigh
Clay
Marshall
Broad
Grace
Franklin
Main
Cary
Canal
Byrd
1st
2nd
3rd
4th
5th
6th
7th
8th
9th
10th
11th
12th
13th
15th
16th
17th
18th
19th
20th
21st
22nd
23rd
24th
25th
26th
27th
28th
29th
30th
31st
Bloody Run St.
Maple
Elm
Ash
Peach
Pear
Poplar
Lester
N
A
B
C
D
E
F
G
H
I
J
K
L
M
N
O

Richmond its distinctive odor and and color lay along Cary and Main streets east of downtown in the region known as Shockoe Bottom.[29]

Typical of nineteenth-century cities, the residential areas were not segregated completely from the commercial and the industrial. Several blocks of fine row houses lay to the west of Capitol Square along Grace, Franklin and Main streets. After he moved out of his room in the Spotswood Hotel (where many high-ranking government officials first settled), Navy Secretary Mallory rented a house on Main St. between 3rd and 4th streets. North of Broad Street in the neighborhood known as Court End were some of the most prestigious homes, including the house which became Jefferson Davis's executive mansion. By late 1863, Mallory had moved into a house on the fringe of Court End on 10th St. north of Leigh.[30] The oldest residential district in Richmond was Church Hill (named after St. Johns Church), which lay across the Shockoe Creek Valley from Capitol Hill, and looked down one side to the tobacco factories and the other to Rocketts. By 1865, the growth of the bureaucracy and the loss of much of the Virginia hinterland to Federal armies swelled Richmond's population from 38,000 to over 100,000 (some estimates are as high as 150,000). This influx of humanity overwhelmed the city, but in 1861, Richmond seemed well prepared for its role as a national capital.

During its four-year life, the Confederate government constructed no public buildings of any significance in Richmond, but continued to occupy former Federal government buildings, share spaces with the Virginia state government, and lease halls and warehouses from local businesses. During the war, the state General Assembly shared the capitol building with the Confederate Congress. The Confederate Treasury and State departments and the president's executive offices occupied the former U.S. customs house. After a short stay in the same building, the Navy Department and its four constituent offices were headquartered in the Mechanics Institute Hall, which also housed the War Department. Completed just a few years before the war, the four-story brick building on 9th Street between Main and Franklin Streets was one of Richmond's civic show pieces. Its primary purpose was to be headquarters for the Mechanics Institute, an organization of artisans dedicated to "the Promotion of the Mechanic Arts." The building also housed businesses, such as the architectural firm of Grant and Nenning and John W. Davies's marble works. A department directory, or "strangers guide," published in 1861 by a man who was himself a Navy Department messenger, clarified where the new government offices were located and where important officials resided. Secretary Mallory's office was located in the Mechanics Institute, "2d story, right-hand side"; he maintained public office hours from noon to 2:00. "Persons are notified not to enter any of the offices without addressing the messengers," the directory warned. "Positively no persons, on or without business, received in the offices after 3 o'clock, P.M." The four bureaus of the Navy Department shared the fourth floor of the Mechanics Institute with the Army Engineers and the Lighthouse Bureau of the Treasury Department.[31]

By current standards, the bureaucracy of the Confederate navy, and indeed of the entire government, was almost comically quaint. Mallory's chief clerk and right-hand man for the entire war was Edward M. Tidball, of Winchester, Virginia, formerly a clerk in the United States Navy's Ordnance and Hydrography Bureau. Tidball was, observed Mallory's biographer, "a handsome, dapper little robot, seldom guilty of an original thought, but a tireless and entirely reliable weaver of red tape." Serving under Tidball were four subordinate clerks.[32]

Another efficient long-time bureaucrat, Paymaster John DeBree, headed the Office of Provisions and Clothing. A 44-year veteran of the United States Navy, DeBree was able, but ancient, and increasingly dependent upon his assistant, Paymaster James A. Semple, who assumed control of the office in the last year of the war. The office's responsibility was enormous: manufacturing, acquiring and distributing uniforms and equipment, and administering the payment of every man in the service. Eventually the office negotiated contracts with textile manufacturers throughout the South to manufacture uniforms and cloth.[33] In port cities the office leased warehouses for storing uniforms, supplies, and provisions.

The chief surgeon of the Confederate States Navy and head of the Office of Medicine and Surgery, William Alexander W. Spotswood, maintained his office in room 35, fourth floor, of the Mechanics Hall. A 33-year navy veteran from an old Virginia family, Spotswood oversaw a staff of 89 medical officers distributed throughout the South. Major naval hospitals and apothecaries were established in several cities.[34] The naval hospital in Richmond was the largest in the Confederacy. The Navy Department leased William Ritter's home on the west side of Governor St. between Franklin and Main for $158.33 a month, and contracted with Richmond artisans to add walls and doors and outfit the large brick house with a water closet and gas light fixtures. In direct supervision of the naval hospital for most of the war was Surgeon James F. Harrison. During the first year of the war the hospital purchased thousands of dollars of supplies from several area druggists, especially the Main St. firm of Purcell & Ladd, and from Edward T. Robinson at 4th and Franklin streets. The department eventually established a naval apothecary shop, under the supervision of Spotswood's subordinate, Purveyor Robert Lecky, near the corner of 12th and Clay streets.[35]

Traditionally the most prestigious bureau of the navy, the Office of Orders and Detail, oversaw the department's paperwork and personnel. Initially limited by statute to a total of 3,000 officers and men, the Confederate navy grew in 1863 to a peak strength of 753 officers and 4,460 men (500 of whom were on stations abroad). Heading the Confederacy's office was a succession of high-ranking officers, most of whom also served stints as commander of the navy's James River Squadron. The first office chief was Captain Samuel Barron, a 60-year-old Virginian and fourth-generation navy officer who had served in the same capacity in the Virginia State Navy. Barron was one of several officers whose seniority and prestige created a dilemma for the Navy Department; ironically, one of the chief accomplishments of the office Barron headed was to promote the advancement of younger officers and essentially shelve older officers like himself. Congress, in May 1863, accomplished this by approving the creation of a more exclusive "Provisional Navy" (distinct from the "Regular Navy")—an administrative designation which allowed Mallory to exclude older ineffective officers and promote younger ones. Ultimately, nearly all officers were assigned to the Provisional Navy, but it did weed out infirm officers from active commands.[36]

Another of the office's responsibilities was the recruitment of sailors for the navy. The Confederacy followed the time-honored tradition of establishing naval rendezvous, or recruiting stations, in major seaport cities, where sailors were enlisted and processed. Even before the final incorporation of the Virginia Navy into the Confederate navy, a naval rendezvous was located in Richmond at the Cary Street warehouse of Luther Libby & Son, a building soon to be converted into a prison for Northern officers. The Naval Rendezvous continued to operate for the duration of the war, first in Shockoe Bottom on Franklin St. between 17th and 18th streets, then in a building on 9th St. between Cary and Main, just downhill from the Navy Department headquarters.[37]

Destined to have the greatest impact on Richmond was the fourth department bureau, the Office of Ordnance and Hydrography. Charged with arming naval vessels, the office became even more vital with the decisions to build a fleet of ironclad ships and experiment with new technologies. Even before the fall of Norfolk, the office began to create a kind of naval-industrial complex in Richmond and other areas of the South. Captain Duncan N. Ingraham, an old-line Charlestonian who had spent nearly a half-century in the United States Navy and five years in charge of its Ordnance and Hydrography Bureau, was the Confederacy's first office chief. Succeeding Ingraham in late 1861, was another venerable United States Navy veteran, Virginian George B. Minor.[38] And though Minor served capably in that post for 15 months, it was his assistant, Lt. (later Commander) John Mercer Brooke and Minor's younger brother, Lt. Robert Dabney Minor, who gave the office its energy and direction. The two younger officers oversaw the creation of ordnance works in Richmond, Selma, Charlotte, Atlanta, Augusta and Charleston.

John Mercer Brooke stands as a pivotal figure in the history of the Confederacy's naval technological revolution. Most famous for developing a banded rifled artillery piece, the Brooke Rifle, Brooke was also chief designer of the *C.S.S. Virginia* and an inveterate experimenter with naval armor. Born in Florida in 1826, Brooke was the son of an army general and the descendant of several prominent Virginia families. Joining the United States Navy in 1841, Brooke graduated subsequently from the United States Naval Academy and served several years with Matthew Fontaine Maury at the United States Naval Observatory in Washington, D.C. There Brooke developed an expertise in marine survey and a reputation as a naval scientist.[39]

Upon his resignation from the United States Navy, Brooke was accepted into the Virginia Navy and assigned by the Advisory Council to duty with General Robert E. Lee. For Virginia's commander-in-chief, the young naval lieutenant traveled the state inspecting the fortifications at Jamestown and Fort Powhatan, securing percussion caps and other ordnance supplies, "machine making, etc." On June 24, 1861, he was assigned to the Office of Ordnance and Hydrography with an office in the Mechanics Hall, and reported directly to Secretary Mallory.

Within days of his appointment, Brooke began to haunt the foundries and factories of Richmond assisting him with his work. On June 28, he visited the foundry of Thomas Sampson and James Pae, on the corner of Byrd and Fifth streets, "to have a projectile of my invention cast." While there, he also examined a Dahlgren rifled shell.[40] Not coincidentally, Brooke's appointment to the ordnance office came days after the Confederate navy embarked on a bold technological adventure.

Richmond and the C.S.S. Virginia

Late in the war, Navy Secretary Stephen Mallory and a Congressional delegation were visiting a naval encampment outside Richmond. The chair of the House Committee on Naval Affairs proposed a toast: "Two great new ideas: Ironclads and Torpedoes, and Mr. Secretary Mallory, their great patron, or introducer." Though Mallory was not responsible personally for causing a revolution in naval technology, he did champion the use of new technology and thus helped determine the course of naval affairs during the American Civil War.[41]

Hopelessly outnumbered in ships and in shipbuilding capacity, and threatened with a blockade of the nation's coastline, the Confederate navy was in an unenviable position in 1861. The dilemma facing Secretary Mallory was how he could best use his resources to defend most effectively the Confederacy's coastline, rivers and harbors against a stronger enemy. Although the United States Navy had fallen into serious disrepair in the decades before the Civil War, it still outnumbered and outgunned any force that the Confederacy could put to sea.

Even before the government moved from Montgomery to Richmond, Mallory indicated his response to this challenge: acquiring and building ironclad vessels. From his vantage point as chairman of the Senate Naval Affairs Committee in the 1850s, Mallory knew of the ironclad vessels developed in Europe in response to revolutions in naval ordnance.[42] In a report to the Confederate Congress on May 8, 1861, Mallory described the evolution of ironclad vessels, especially the French ship, *La Gloire*, and argued that the Confederacy concentrate on acquiring ironclads:

> I regard the possession of an iron-armored ship, as a matter of the first necessity. Such a vessel at this time could traverse the entire coast of the United States, prevent all blockades, and encounter, with a fair prospect of success, their entire Navy.
>
> If to cope with them upon the sea we follow their example and build wooden ships, we shall have to construct several at one time, for one or two ships would fall an easy prey to her comparatively numerous steam frigates. But inequality of numbers may be compensated by invulnerability, and thus not only does economy, but naval success, dictate the wisdom and expediency of fighting with iron against wood without regard to first cost. Naval engagements between wooden frigates as they are now built and armed will prove to be the forlorn hopes of the sea, simply contests in which the question, not of victory, but who shall go the bottom first, is to be solved.
>
> Should the committee deem it expedient to begin at once the construction of such a ship, not a moment should be lost.[43]

Mallory's recommendation led directly to the building of a Confederate ironclad fleet, beginning with the conversion of the frigate *U.S.S. Merrimack* into the *C.S.S. Virginia* in 1861-1862. Before the end of 1861, the Navy Department had also contracted with private shipbuilders in Memphis and New Orleans to construct four ironclad vessels for Mississippi River defense.[44]

On June 22, 1861, Mallory met at the Navy Department with Lt. John Brooke, Engineer William P. Williamson, and Constructor John L. Porter to discuss the construction of an "iron plated gunboat." From this meeting emerged tangible plans for realizing Mallory's vision of constructing a fleet of ironclad vessels. The meeting helped determine the course of Civil War navy history; it also committed the Confederacy to a policy of technological innovation, magnifying Richmond's importance as an industrial center.

William P. Williamson and John L. Porter, along with John Brooke, were key figures in the Confederacy's ironclad program. Each headed what subsequently became an autonomous office in the Navy Department. Both men worked before the war in the shipbuilding industry of the Norfolk area. Williamson had worked as an engineer with the United States Navy at the Gosport Navy Yard, and Porter, a native of Portsmouth, Virginia, had learned his trade in his father's shipyard. Porter supervised the construction of United States Navy ships in Washington and Pittsburgh before becoming a constructor with the United States Navy in Pensacola, Florida, on the eve of the war. He offered his services to the Confederacy in June 1861.[45]

Mallory assigned Brooke the task of drafting a preliminary design for an ironclad warship, then summoned Porter and Williamson to discuss Brooke's ideas. Porter brought to the meeting a model of an ironclad ram apparently based on Brooke's proposal. The four men inspected the model and approved Porter's design for a casemate shaped armor shield. They also approved Brooke's modification to submerge both ends of the deck. Attached to the bow of the ship was a "V"-shaped iron ram. Williamson apparently suggested that the ironclad be built upon the hull of the *Merrimack*.[46] The conversion of the *Merrimac* into the *Virginia* occurred entirely at Norfolk, and the vessel never saw Richmond, but the capital city played a vital role in the process. After their June 22 meeting, Brooke, Porter, and Williamson walked a few blocks south and west to Tredegar Iron Works, a business that was, in a real sense, the birthplace of the Confederacy's ironclad program.

Located between the James River and the James River & Kanawha Canal, adjacent to Nielson's (present-day Brown's) Island, Tredegar Iron Works was founded in 1836. Originally a joint-stock company, it became in 1848 the property of Joseph Reid Anderson and Associates and long remained an Anderson family business. In the 1850s, railroad expansion and United States Army contracts helped Tredegar become the South's largest industrial establishment. Tredegar even dabbled in naval contracts, constructing boilers for two Norfolk-built frigates in 1854. In 1846, the company built the iron-sided revenue cutter, *James K. Polk*, for the U.S. Treasury Department. Shortly after her completion, the *Polk* was transferred to the Navy Department, fitted out with three guns, and ordered into service in the war with Mexico. The ship barely made it out of port, and proved a complete failure in all respects.[47]

Tredegar was by no means the only iron manufacturer in the South, or even in Richmond. Iron manufacturing was a far-flung, and often small-scale, enterprise in the antebellum South. What distinguished Tredegar was the scale of its operations, the scope of its capabilities, and its experience in producing heavy ordnance for the army and navy. A strong Southern nationalist as well as a shrewd businessman, Anderson, in the 1850s, began to pursue contracts with Southern state governments. He was in a good position in 1861 to provide ordnance to the seceded states and to the new Confederacy. In addition to casting guns, Tredegar was one of only five rolling mills in the South, and one of the few capable of rolling plate for ironclad naval vessels. During the war, Anderson pledged to give production for the Confederate military precedence over all other production. He even offered to turn over his establishment to the government. Although the relationship between Anderson and the Confederate government was sometimes strained, Tredegar was a vital component of the navy's ironclad and ordnance production—in Richmond and throughout the South.[48]

Tredegar received the contract to produce iron plate for the armor shield of the *Virginia*. The contract between Tredegar and the Confederate government was signed in September 1861, and for six months, producing the two-inch thick iron plates and delivering them to the shipyard in Norfolk was one of the Richmond factory's top priorities. Rails stripped from the Baltimore & Ohio Railroad in Union-held western Virginia provided the raw materials for the plate of the *Virginia*.[49]

The construction of the *Virginia*, and of all the Confederacy's ironclads, was labor-intensive and slower than expected. Some officials worried that Mallory had put all the navy's eggs in the ironclad basket. Foremost among the skeptics was the recognized authority in naval science, Matthew Fontaine Maury. While Maury was himself responsible for development of the Confederacy's mine warfare—for which Mallory later was toasted—the "pathfinder of the seas" did not share the secretary's confidence in ironclads. His dissent was not to be dismissed easily. Maury was one of the most prominent men in American naval history. Born in Virginia in 1806, Maury entered the United States Navy in 1825. Lame since an 1839 accident, and thus unavailable for active service, Maury established a reputation as the service's leading scientific mind. As superintendent of the depot of charts and instruments, Maury mapped the world's oceans. His *Physical Geography of the Seas*, published in 1855, was a landmark in the field, and the sea charts he developed for the United States Navy are still in use today. At the outbreak of war in 1861, Maury was serving at the United States Naval Observatory in Washington, D.C. Undeniably talented and visionary, the well-connected and highly-respected scientist had a tendency to express his strong opinions freely. Convinced that Mallory—the creator of the U.S. Navy's "plucking board" which Maury believed had tried to crucify him in the 1850s—was still out to get him, and that his policies were calculated to ruin the service, Maury made himself a thorn in the secretary's side. Before his inevitable exile out of Richmond in 1862, he played a major role in shaping naval warfare on the James.[50]

In the fall of 1861, as work on the *Virginia* stalled, Maury began lobbying for a proposal he dubbed "Big guns and Little ships." Maury argued that a large fleet of small steam-powered wooden gunboats, each armed with two guns, offered the best defense for the South's rivers and harbors. This "hornet's nest" of gunboats could attack and destroy even the biggest ships that the Federals sent against the South, Maury insisted. The most attractive feature of the plan, Maury argued, was that a hundred gunboats could be completed quickly, cheaply, and in complete secrecy. Tidewater Virginia alone could furnish enough lumber, artisans, and makeshift shipyards to finish the gunboats by the spring of 1862.[51]

Maury tried in vain to sell the idea to Gov. John Letcher and the Virginia legislature. But in the last days of 1861, the Confederate Congress, with the apparent support of Secretary Mallory, authorized $2,000,000 for the construction of 100 gunboats. Contracts were signed and work began almost immediately on 15 gunboats. The vessels presumably conformed closely to Maury's prescription: approximately 106-112 feet long and 21 feet beam (wide) with approximately 170 tons draft. Two of the ships, the *Hampton* and the *Nansemond*, built at yards in Norfolk, were completed and became part of the James River Squadron.[52] None of the gunboats were built in Richmond, but the city's industrial establishment received thousands of dollars from the "100 gunboats fund" for material and services provided. Thus, as 1862 dawned, Richmond's industries and Virginia's shipyards labored upon potentially rival projects: small wooden gunboats and a large ironclad ram.

The ironclad was finished first. In the last days of February 1862, Lt. Catesby Jones hurried the completion and fitting out of the *Virginia*, while the vessel's newly assigned commander, Capt. Franklin Buchanan, grew anxious to put her to the test. Accompanied by the other ships of the James River Squadron—*Patrick Henry*, *Jamestown*, *Teaser*, and two ships brought from coastal North Carolina, *Beaufort* and *Raleigh*—the *Virginia* on March 8 steamed out from Norfolk to take on the Federal blockading fleet in Hampton Roads. She rammed and sank the 24-gun sloop *Cumberland*, caused the *Minnesota* to run aground, and crippled the *Congress*. The officers of the *Congress* were in the process of surrendering their ship to officers of the *Raleigh* and *Beaufort* when infantrymen and batteries on the Newport News shore opened fire, killing Northern and Southern sailors alike and compelling the Confederate vessels to fall back. Flag Lt. Robert Dabney Minor led the party from the *Virginia* to accept the surrender of the *Congress*, but was wounded by a volley of small arms fire. The boarding party retreated to the *Virginia*, which opened fire on the *Congress*, setting her ablaze. During the battle, Captain Buchanan was wounded in the leg and Lt. Catesby Jones assumed command.[53] The day's work vindicated beyond expectation Mallory's faith in the ironclad warship.

Undisputed Confederate naval supremacy proved short-lived. At 9:00 p.m. on the day of the battle, a strange-looking vessel, described by sailors as a cheese-box on a shingle, steamed into Hampton Roads and anchored among the beleaguered Federal wooden ships. A month after Mallory had inaugurated the Confederacy's ironclad building program, his U.S. counterpart, Secretary Gideon Welles, had obtained an appropriation for ironclad warships. One of the contracts was awarded in October 1861 to the Swedish-born inventor John Ericsson. His contribution to the history of naval technology was the *Monitor*. Considered revolutionary and outlandish, the *Monitor* became the prototype for the

Federal Navy's ironclad warship, just as the *Virginia* did for the Confederacy. On March 9, the two vessels fought their epochal standoff in Hampton Roads.[54]

The day after the battle, Lt. John Taylor Wood, an officer on the *Virginia*, traveled to Richmond to brief Secretary Mallory and President Davis and present a trophy: the flag of the *Congress*. "The news had preceded me and at every station I was warmly received and to listening crowds was forced to repeat the story of the fight," Wood remembered. In contrast to the public euphoria, Wood delivered to the Confederate leadership a report of the damage which the *Virginia* incurred, and a sober prediction that "in the *Monitor* we had met our match."[55]

Regardless of whether the *Virginia* proved superior to the *Monitor*, the battle at Hampton Roads proved the superiority of iron ships to wooden ships and thus clarified the future of naval construction in the Confederacy. Matthew Fontaine Maury's daughter Betty wrote in her diary on March 18: "We fear that the result of the battle will be that the enemy will plate all of his vessels with iron and that Papa's gun boats will be of no avail." In fact, the day before, the Confederate House of Representatives voted to suspend the construction of wooden gunboats. By the end of March, funds appropriated for Maury's "Little ships" were diverted to the construction of ironclads.[56]

The *Virginia* and the *Monitor* meanwhile underwent repairs and faced each other in Hampton Roads. On two occasions the *Virginia* challenged the *Monitor*, but the Federal warship was under orders to avoid battle. Despite her bold challenges, the *Virginia* continued to suffer mechanical problems and was forced to spend most of her short life in the Norfolk dry dock. The stalemate between the two revolutionary vessels ended in May, but not as a result of any naval activity.

Richmond became the target of a massive Federal land and sea campaign in the spring of 1862. In late March, Maj. Gen. George Brinton McClellan transported his 100,000-man Army of the Potomac down the Chesapeake Bay to Fort Monroe to begin a march up the peninsula between the James and York rivers. The presence of the *Virginia* prevented McClellan from using the James as a marine supply line, so he instead established his base of operations on the York River, and subsequently on its tributary, the Pamunkey River. McClellan squandered most of April preparing to besiege the Confederate lines around Yorktown, and when siege preparations were completed, the Confederate army under Gen. Joseph Eggleston Johnston abandoned the line. After a sharp battle outside Williamsburg on May 5, the Confederate army fell back to a new line just a few miles east of Richmond.

The army's abandonment of the peninsula led directly to the Confederate loss of Norfolk and most of the James River below Richmond. It also doomed the *Virginia.* On May 10, Confederate troops fired the Gosport Navy Yard and abandoned the city. Even when lightened to the extent that her unprotected hull was exposed, the huge (275 feet in length) *Virginia* drew too much water to be towed over the several sand bars that punctuated the channel of the James River between Hampton Roads and Richmond. Shortly after midnight May 11, off Craney Island in the lower James, the nation's first ironclad warship was destroyed by her crew.[57] The unfinished hull of another iron warship, which would eventually become the *C.S.S. Richmond*, was towed upriver to her namesake city.

Ironically, the destruction of the *Virginia* also sent up in flames Matthew Maury's dream of a "hornet's nest" of wooden gunboats. A dozen of the unfinished craft lying on the ways along the Rappahannock, York, and Pamunkey Rivers were set ablaze to prevent their capture by the advancing Federals. As enemy land and sea forces menaced Richmond from the east, the Confederacy had neither an ironclad ram nor a fleet of gunboats available to help defend the capital. After nearly a year as the South's navy capital, Richmond was still without a capital navy.

Chief Constructor John Luke Porter

Born into the shipbuilding trade in Portsmouth, Virginia, Porter (1813-1893) constructed ships for the U.S. Navy for two decades before the Civil War. While working for the U.S. Navy in Pittsburgh in 1846, Porter had submitted a plan for an ironclad vessel. The navy rejected that design, but Porter saw his idea realized in the form of the *C.S.S. Virginia*. Along with Norfolk shipbuilder William A. Graves, Porter designed and constructed the warship sat the Richmond shipyards. Oil portrait by John P. Walker, 1924. Courtesy of the Virginia Historical Society, Richmond.

The Mechanics' Institute

The Confederate Navy Department shared this new and substantial building with the Confederate War Department. Located a block west of capitol square, the Mechanics Institute burned in the April 1865 evacuation fire. *Richmond Dispatch*, June 30, 1896.

View from Libby Prison

Looking westward from Libby Prison, located on Cary Street between 20th and 21st Streets, this 1863 sketch shows the Richmond dock, the center of the city's waterborne commerce. *Harper's Weekly*, October 24, 1865.

The James River and Kanawha Canal, Richmond, Virginia

"Our artist has represented the scene at the Packet office on the departure of the boat which leaves on alternate days at five o'clock in the evening. It is a busy and characteristic scene, quite peculiar to the city of Richmond." *Harper's Weekly*, October 14, 1865.

Tredegar Iron Works

Sprawled along the James River on the edge of downtown Richmond, Tredegar Iron Works was the largest industrial establishment in the Confederacy. Already a primary source of ordnance for the army and the navy, Tredegar became even more vital to the Confederate navy when it began building ironclad warships. Courtesy of the Library of Congress.

"Off Chaffin's Bluff, C. S. Steamer 'Nansemond,' James River Squadron, March 22, 1865."

This pencil sketch is the only known image of a "Maury gunboat." The artist, Lt. Walter R. Butt, commanded both the *Hampton* and the *Nansemond* in the closing months of the war. Measuring approximately 106 feet in length and 21 in beam and carrying two guns, the *Nansemond* and the *Hampton* were to be two among 100 such gunboats. Instead, they were the only ones completed and commissioned. Courtesy of the Naval Historical Center.

Lt. Charles M. Fauntleroy

Formerly a lieutenant in the United States Navy, Fauntleroy was one of the officers of the short-lived Virginia State Navy, in which he commanded the naval forces on the Potomac River at Harper's Ferry. Stationed in Richmond briefly in 1862, Fauntleroy spent most of the year abroad on the cruisers *Nashville* and *Rappahannock* and the blockade runner *Economist*. Carte-de-visite by Ferrando, 11 Boca di Leone, Rome. Courtesy of Charles V. Peery.

Assistant Surgeon Charles M. Morfit

The Maryland-born Morfit began his Confederate naval service in Norfolk aboard the receiving ship *United States* in 1861. He returned to Virginia in 1864 after service in New Orleans, Mississippi, South Carolina, Georgia, and North Carolina. Carte-de-visite by Bendann, Baltimore, Maryland. Courtesy of Charles V. Peery.

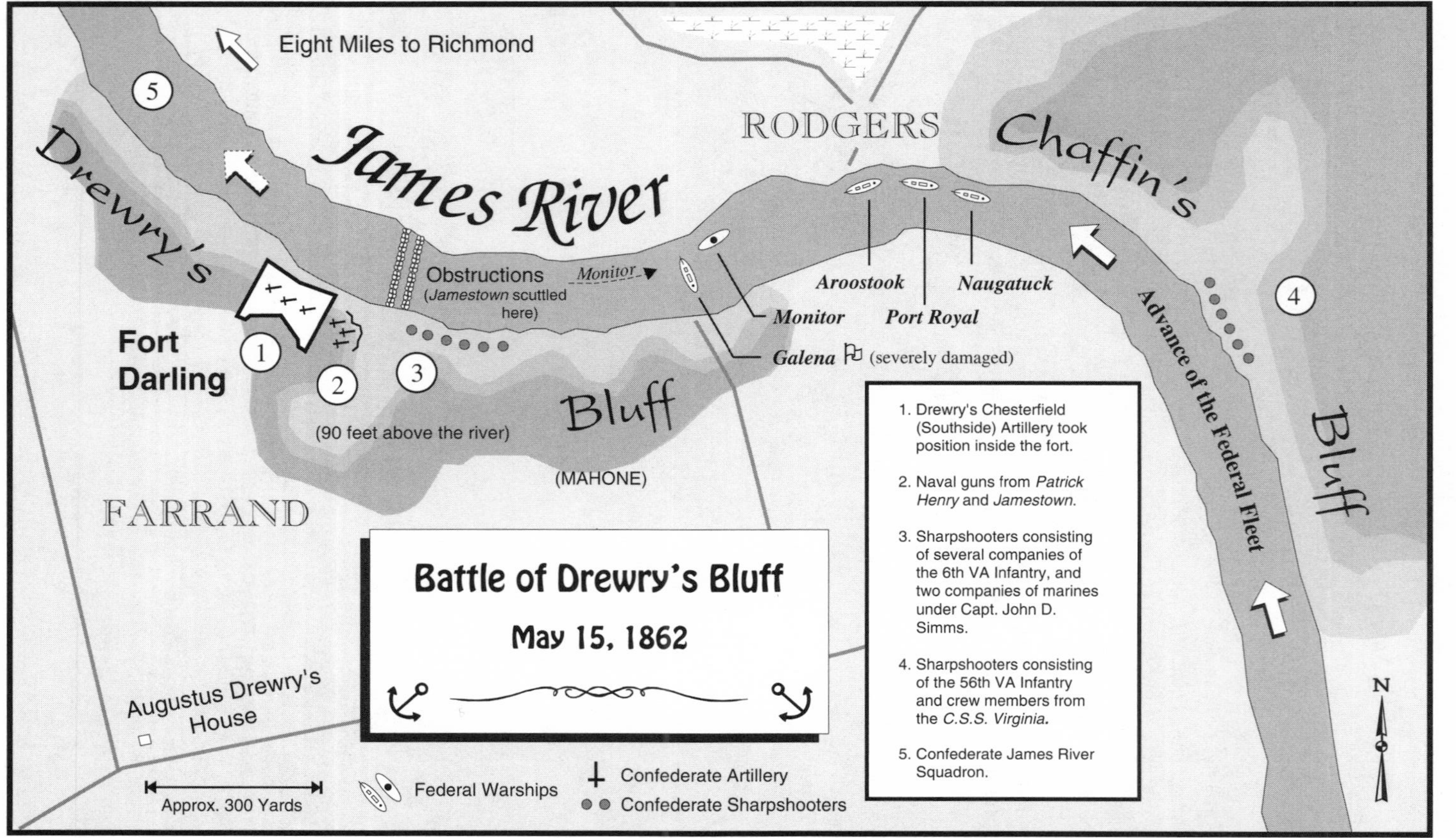
Battle of Drewry's Bluff
May 15, 1862
Eight Miles to Richmond
James River
Drewry's
Bluff
Chaffin's
Bluff
RODGERS
FARRAND
(MAHONE)
Fort
Darling
(90 feet above the river)
Obstructions
(Jamestown scuttled here)
Monitor
Aroostook
Naugatuck
Monitor
Port Royal
Galena (severely damaged)
Advance of the Federal Fleet
Augustus Drewry's House
Approx. 300 Yards
Federal Warships
Confederate Artillery
Confederate Sharpshooters
N
1. Drewry's Chesterfield (Southside) Artillery took position inside the fort.
2. Naval guns from Patrick Henry and Jamestown.
3. Sharpshooters consisting of several companies of the 6th VA Infantry, and two companies of marines under Capt. John D. Simms.
4. Sharpshooters consisting of the 56th VA Infantry and crew members from the C.S.S. Virginia.
5. Confederate James River Squadron.
Mark A. Moore

Chapter 2

"I Feel Very Anxious for the Fate of Richmond": Drewry's Bluff and the Defense of Richmond

With the *Virginia* destroyed, little stood between the Federal navy and the Confederate capital. Northern officers planned immediately to take advantage of this vulnerability. The Federal fleet ascended the James River on May 8, engaged the Confederate battery at Fort Boykin, then passed by it and by Fort Huger, the next Confederate strongpoint upstream. The advance of McClellan's Federal army from Williamsburg toward Richmond further complicated matters for the Confederates, compelling the abandonment of the Southern works on Mulberry and Jamestown Islands. Lieutenant Joseph Barney, commanding the *C.S.S. Jamestown,* notified the Confederate commander at Drewry's Bluff near Richmond that the vessels of the James River Squadron were steaming up the river ahead of the Federal fleet. "The river is then open to their passage to this point," Barney warned, "so that they may be expected up at any time."[1]

Over the next seven days, the Federals moved cautiously, but inexorably, toward Richmond. Admiral Louis M. Goldsborough, flag officer of the United States North Atlantic Blockading Squadron (which encompassed the Virginia coast and James River), on May 15, instructed Cdr. John Rodgers, commanding the Federal fleet on the James River, to move against the Southern capital as quickly as possible. "Sir, I presume," Goldsborough notified Rodgers, "that Lieutenant Commanding Jeffers . . told you of my wishes that our vessels in [the] James River, especially the *Monitor*, should push on up to Richmond, if possible, without any unnecessary delay, and shell the place into a surrender." The admiral knew that opposition would be encountered upriver. "The enemy, from what I gather, is placing obstructions in the way, of sunken vessels, about 10 or 12 miles this side of Richmond," he wrote Rodgers, "and his vessels are above that point, within, they say, 5 miles of the city." Goldsborough, confident that the Federal fleet could ascend the river, assured Rodgers that "The *Monitor*, *Aroostook*, *Port Royal,* and *Stevens* can, I am informed, all get over the bar just this side of Rocketts, and even to Richmond itself. The *Galena* can not do so, but the rest will be force enough. As the obstructions have been put down very hurriedly, and consist, I am told, of nothing but vessels, there will be no great difficulty, I take it, in clearing a passageway. . . .Should Richmond fall into our possession, inform me of the fact at the earliest possible moment. . . ."[2]

Panic seized the city as it had a year earlier when the bell tower in Capitol Square rang the alarm for the rumored approach of the *U.S.S. Pawnee*. While the "Pawnee scare" proved an almost comical false alarm, the situation in May 1862, was all too real. The news of the *Virginia*'s destruction caused Richmonders to cast their eyes to the naval defenses of the James River. They were aghast to discover just how inadequate those defenses were. The city's newspapers chastised Confederate officials for their failure to fortify the river banks and block the channel, and for the obvious over-reliance upon the *Virginia* to defend the river against the enemy's navy. "It will be to all the most gratifying news that the gunboats cannot pass our barriers and the greatest credit will be awarded to those who have built them," editorialized the *Richmond Daily Dispatch* on May 13. "If this proves so, however, it will have been a matter of very recent achievement."[3]

From mid-summer of 1861, until late February 1862, there had been no river fortification closer to Richmond than Jamestown Island. Shortly after Fort Powhatan was established on the south bank of the James in Prince George County, Confederate forces transferred its guns to Mulberry Island, downriver from Jamestown. The Federal naval forces that landed at Fort Powhatan in May and June of 1862, were not overly impressed with their opponent's preparations. According to one Federal source, there were "no bombproofs, only earthworks, [n]o guns, gun carriages, or platforms for guns"; and the interior was "overgrown with weeds."[4]

The weakness of Richmond's river defenses had been an issue for several months, attracting attention at the highest levels of government. The Virginia House of Delegates on February 21, had appointed a committee "to inquire into the state of the defences of the James river." Not coincidentally, on the following day, Lt. Charles T. Mason, an army engineer working on the defenses at Jamestown Island, received an urgent message from his superior, Capt. Alfred L. Rives: "I have absolute need of your assistance higher up the River & write to request you to come to Richmond without delay." Following the Virginia Assembly's initiative, the Confederate House of Representatives on February 24, passed a resolution asking President Jefferson Davis to furnish information about the James River defenses. In response, Davis provided a March 12 report by Captain Rives, endorsing Rives' conclusion that the best place to obstruct the river and construct a battery was Drewry's Bluff. The bluff, Davis wrote, "has intimate relations with the defenses proper of this city."[5]

Between the time of the House request and Rives's report, officers of the navy and army hurriedly examined the river, determined that Drewry's Bluff was the ideal site for the defense of Richmond, and prepared to construct a fortified battery on the heights overlooking the twisting river. Located eight miles downstream from Richmond at a point where the river flowed north to south, Drewry's Bluff loomed 90 feet above the water and commanded the river approach to the Confederate capital. On February 23, Brig. Gen. Raleigh E. Colston, commanding troops in Smithfield, south of the James, wrote to Capt. John Randolph Tucker, the commander of the *Patrick Henry* and newly-appointed commander of naval forces on the James. Colston inquired about "the practicability of obstructing James River at some point commanded by the guns of our forts." In response to Colston's inquiry, Tucker suggested that a point "higher up" toward Richmond offered the capital the greatest security. By the time President Davis assured the Confederate Congress that "the work is being rapidly completed" at Drewry's Bluff, Confederate navy, army, and engineering officers began transforming the site into a major point of defense for the capital. As late as April 28, however, an inspection report estimated that the works would not be completed for three to four months.[6]

Among the army officers to work at Drewry's Bluff was the owner of the property, Capt. Augustus H. Drewry of Chesterfield County. Drewry claimed after the war that he actually chose the site of the fort. His command, the Chesterfield (or Southside) Heavy Artillery, had been ordered to assist in building a land fortification on the Richmond-Petersburg turnpike when Drewry offered his property as a fortification site. While Drewry may well have suggested his property as the site for a river defense battery, the initiative for defending the bluff lay with other officers, and the work began before the arrival of the Southside Artillery on March 17.[7]

Lieutenant Mason, of the Army Engineer Department, supervised the construction of the earthen fort on Drewry's Bluff and, assisted by the navy, went to work blocking the channel. Sinking obstructions in the channel would force the enemy's ironclad fleet into a narrow passage, where the ships would be easy prey for Confederate artillery and sharpshooters on the bluffs above the river. Commander Tucker urged that the navy secure several masted vessels, "similar in size to vessels now in the Richmond docks belonging to Messrs. David Currie & Co.," load them with stone and have them ready to sink at a moment's notice. Although put down in haste, the obstructions were more formidable than Admiral Goldsborough believed. Log piles and cribs of stones were already in place in the river. To reinforce those obstructions the Confederates sank several small vessels—including two schooners formerly belonging to Rocketts merchant Richard Haskins—secured together with iron chains. As the Confederate fleet retreated up the river from Norfolk, Tucker warned the engineers at Drewry's Bluff that the passage through the obstructions had to be at least 56 feet wide, or his ship, the *Patrick Henry*, as well as the *Jamestown*, would have to be destroyed. Mason assured Tucker that the passage was 100 feet wide and the Confederate vessels could pass safely. Tucker's relief soon turned to distress upon his arrival at Drewry's Bluff on May 8, where he witnessed the continued unpreparedness of the defenses. "I feel very anxious for the fate of Richmond," he wrote to the newly-appointed commander of the defenses, Capt. Ebenezer Farrand, "and would be happy to see you about the obstruction placed here—I think no time should be lost in making this point impassable."[8]

The Confederate navy heeded Tucker's warning, but paid a dear price to make the channel impassable, sinking one of the few warships of the pitifully small James River Squadron. The *Jamestown*, one of the original vessels in the Virginia State Navy, had participated in the Battle of Hampton Roads on March 8-9, 1862. The crew's gallant conduct and bearing in that battle elicited praise from the Confederate Congress and won promotion for her commander, Lt. Joseph Barney. After the removal of her guns, the *Jamestown* was steamed out into the river below Drewry's Bluff. Robert Wright and Midshipman Daniel M. Lee were given the assignment of remaining on the ship and pulling the plug of the sea cock, a fatal course of action that quickly sent the *Jamestown* to the bottom of the river.[9]

The Battle of Drewry's Bluff, May 15, 1862

As black laborers completed the earthen fortifications at Drewry's Bluff, Confederate army and naval forces converged to defend the fort against the Federal fleet that was expected to steam up the river. On May 8, Ebenezer Farrand, a career naval officer from Alabama, was assigned to command the combined forces at Drewry's Bluff and ordered to "lose not a moment in adopting and perfecting measures to prevent the enemy's vessels from passing the river." Aside from Drewry's Southside Artillery battery, Farrand also had at his disposal the men (but not the guns) of eight other Virginia heavy artillery batteries. Several infantry regiments (6th Virginia, 56th Virginia, and 3rd Alabama) from Brig.

Gen. William Mahone's brigade arrived at the bluff on the day of the battle.[10]

"[T]he Navy for the time has been destroyed," a former officer of the *Virginia*, Lt. John Taylor Wood, lamented to his wife, "& we must seek other ways of rendering ourselves useful." While the squadron may have suffered a severe setback with the dual loss of the *Virginia* and *Jamestown*, the men of the Confederate States Navy (as well as the Marine Corps), made themselves useful fighting on land during the May 15, 1862, Battle of Drewry's Bluff.

Despite the loss of the warships, the navy was not actually destroyed. As many as six ships—the *Patrick Henry*, *Teaser*, *Beaufort*, *Raleigh*, the newly-completed Maury gunboat *Nansemond* (and possibly the *Hampton*)—were still available for use. Tucker and Farrand, however, wisely decided against using them to fight against enemy ironclads and sent them upstream out of enemy range. Not wanting to waste the value of the manpower on those ships, Farrand chose instead to employ most of his sailors as land forces. Along with Confederate infantry and engineers, the crews of the ships pitched in by digging rifle pits at the foot of Drewry's Bluff and across the river at Chaffin's Bluff. Stationed as sharpshooters on the Drewry's Bluff side were two companies of marines, under Capt. John D. Simms, and several companies of the 6th Virginia Infantry, while sailors from the crew of the *Virginia* and the 56th Virginia Infantry were deployed on the opposite side of the river at Chaffin's Bluff.[11]

While some sailors wielded picks and shovels, other members of the grounded crews of the squadron spent the better part of two days removing guns (five in all) from the *Jamestown* and the *Patrick Henry*, dragging them up the bluff and preparing them for action. How many and what kinds of guns were landed and mounted is not entirely clear. The *Jamestown's* two 32-pound rifles were certainly taken ashore, while at least one, and probably two, 8-inch guns (which fired 64-pound solid shot or shells), and either one or two 32-pound rifles were taken from the *Patrick Henry*.[12] According to Lt. James Rochelle, executive officer of the *Patrick Henry* and one of the naval officers present on the bluff during the battle, the guns from the ship "were mounted in pits dug in the brow of the bluff." One of the guns, an 8-inch Columbiad, was reported to have been mounted near the entrance of the fort crowning the bluff. The artillery pieces were well placed and skillfully protected, the crews shielding each of them with casemates constructed of earth, logs and sandbags.[13]

As the Confederates labored on the river defenses, the Federal fleet ascended the James River haltingly and not entirely confident that the way to Richmond was clear and safe. Intelligence from Confederate prisoners warned on May 5, that "[a] new iron clad steamer superior to the *Virginia*, to be called the *Brandywine* was launched at Norfolk some eighteen days since," and, incorrectly, that she "is thought to be nearly ready." Although marred by errors in detail, this report was one of the earliest alarms regarding the much-delayed progress of ironclad *C.S.S. Richmond*, then under construction in Richmond. During the afternoon of the 14th, the Federal ships fitfully ascended the river and fired into the woods two miles downstream from Drewry's Bluff, but advanced no further.[14] As Goldsborough sent orders to shell Richmond into submission, Rodgers was testing the Drewry's Bluff defenses.

The respite, put to good use by the Confederates, came to an end when the Federal fleet drew within sight of Drewry's Bluff at 6:30 a.m. on May 15, 1862, the flagship *Galena* in the lead. There was much curiosity in the Federal navy how the experimental *Galena*, with her relatively light armor, would hold up under enemy fire. "I am anxious to know your opinion of this new vessel now under your command," wrote a member of the U.S. Navy's Ironclad Board to John Rodgers in early May. While others may have been optimistic about *Galena's* capabilities, Rodgers was not. The sailor's pessimism about his new flagship proved to be well-founded.[15]

As the Union warships steamed up the river, Rodgers gracefully maneuvered the *Galena* into position perpendicular to the flow of the river approximately 600 yards from the enemy position, where he dropped anchor. At his order, the wooden vessels anchored 1,300 yards down river. At about 9:00 a.m. the *Monitor* steamed upriver above the *Galena*, but she could not elevate her guns enough to fire at the Confederate stronghold. Useless that far upriver, the single-turreted ironclad assumed a position below the *Galena* and joined the battle. Confederate sailors and officers, many of them former comrades and friends of John Rodgers (Catesby Jones, of the *Virginia*, was a cousin), watched this display of seamanship in admiration.[16]

At 7:45 a.m., the *Galena* fired upon the Confederate works on Drewry's Bluff, and the Battle for Richmond was under way. George Tucker Brooke, acting midshipman aboard the *Nansemond*, claimed later that his ship and the other small wooden vessels in the squadron were stationed just beyond the bend in the river, ready to mount a desperate defense should the Federal fleet pass the land batteries. He and Midshipman Wyndham Robinson Mayo each commanded one of the ship's 8-inch guns. Brooke recalled giving the command "cast loose" and prepared for action, but "the command 'fire' was never given," he later wrote. As a consequence, the small wooden warships did not participate in the action. "The little fleet never fired a shot," Brooke proudly wrote, "although every man stood at his guns ready for battle."[17]

A defense by the wooden ships was unnecessary because the battle turned out to be surprisingly one-sided. According to a member of the Southside Artillery, the *Galena* anchored "within point-blank range," making her an easy target, "so we wasted very few shots." Farrand, who supervised the work of the guns in the fort, agreed. The Confederate guns, he wrote in his report, concentrated their fire on the *Galena*, "nearly every one of our shots telling upon her iron surface." At 11:00 a.m., a solid shot fired by the 8-inch gun taken from the *Patrick Henry* passed through the *Galena's* bow port, and smoke billowed from the crippled ship. "We gave her three hearty cheers as she slipped her cables and moved down the river," Farrand wrote. Southern pickets lining the river bank overheard the *Galena's* captain say that she was "in a sinking condition." Throughout the action, the Confederate marines and sailors acting as sharpshooters annoyed all of the vessels, inflicting casualties on their crews. The shipless crewman continually harassed the retreating Federal ships for about a mile before giving up and returning to the bluff. John Taylor Wood, who commanded the former crew members of the destroyed *Virginia* serving as sharpshooters on the north bank, yelled out to his former U.S. Naval Academy colleague, Lt. William N. Jeffers of the *Monitor*: "Tell Capt. Jeffers that is not the way to Richmond."[18]

William F. Keeler, a paymaster aboard the *Monitor*, vividly described in his diary the effects of the bombardment upon the Federal fleet. For four hours the squadron endured "a perfect tempest of iron raining down upon & around us to say nothing of the rifle balls which pattered upon the decks like rain." Fortunately for Keeler and the men inside her, the *Monitor* was not the primary target of enemy gunners. The crew "suffered terribly for the want of fresh air," Keeler noted, but their suffering paled before that of the crew of the *Galena*, upon which the Confederate gunners concentrated their fire. According to Keeler, Rodgers' flagship was ripped apart by the Southern artillery:

> Her iron sides were pierced through & through by the heavy shot, apparently offering no more resistance than an egg shell, verifying the Commodore's opinion that 'she was beneath naval criticism.' Their guns were manned by sailors, probably from the Merrimac and the Jamestown & Yorktown, which last two [sic.] had been sunk with the other obstructions. It became evident after a time that it was useless for us to contend against the terrific strength & accuracy of their fire. . . .Suddenly volumes of smoke were seen issuing from the Galena's ports & hatches & the cry went through us that she was on fire, or a shot had penetrated her boiler—her men poured out of her open ports on the side opposite the batteries, clinging to the anchor, to loose ropes, and dropping into boats. We at once raised our anchor to go to her assistance but found she did not need it.

The next day Keeler went aboard the *Galena* lying at anchor off City Point. She looked, he wrote, "like a slaughter house. . . of human beings." Death had carpeted the interior. "The sides & ceiling overhead, the ropes & guns were spattered with blood & brains & lumps of flesh, while the decks were covered with large pools of half coagulated blood & strewn with portions of skulls, fragments of shells, arms, legs, hands, pieces of flesh & iron, splinters of wood & broken weapons were mixed in one confused, horrible mass."[19]

Rodgers, perhaps embarrassed by the drubbing his ship suffered, denied newspaper reports that *Galena* had caught on fire, and maintained he broke off the action only because his ammunition was nearly exhausted. He was, however, forthright in describing to his wife the rough handling of his fleet. "The batteries on the Rebel side were beautifully served and put their shots through our side with great precision," Rodgers penned. "The *Galena* did most of the fighting—her sides look as though she had an attack of smallpox." With considerable understatement, he reported to his superior officers that the battle demonstrated that the lightly-armored *Galena* "is not shot proof; balls came through, and many men were killed by fragments of her own iron." The casualty reports for the engagement bear out both Keeler's graphic description of the ship's interior, and Rodgers' summary of her performance under the Southern guns. The *Galena's* executive officer reported that the ship was hit by 44 shots and casualties were 13 dead and 11 wounded. Other Federal ships also suffered during the one-sided affair. The wooden gunboat *Naugatuck* (also known as *Stevens Battery*) was disabled by the explosion of her 100-pound gun, while the *Port Royal* received two shots below the water line and had to break off action to repair the damage and avoid sinking. The *Monitor* suffered only three hits and no casualties. Summarizing the battle and the Confederate defenses at Drewry's Bluff, Rodgers dryly concluded that it would be "impossible to reduce such works except by the aid of a land force."[20]

While she suffered greatly in the exchange of iron, the *Galena* managed to inflict a few casualties upon the triumphant Confederates. Eight of the defenders were wounded and seven killed, apparently all in the final moments of the fight when a bombardment by the *Galena* caught Confederate naval gunners making repairs to their positions. Among those killed was Farrand's aide, Midshipman Daniel Carroll. One soldier from the 3rd Alabama Infantry, Brig. Gen. William Mahone's Brigade, described the grisly scene at the battery: "One [man] had his head blown off, one lost his leg and two had their bodies torn open."[21]

The Battle of Drewry's Bluff was understandably considered a stunning Confederate triumph, and a great relief after expectations of disaster. "Joyful tidings!" exclaimed Richmond war clerk John B. Jones in his diary, "the gunboats have been repulsed!" On the day of the battle, before its outcome was known, Virginia Governor John Letcher had issued a proclamation pledging to defend Richmond to the last and calling upon the citizens to organize in preparation for the worst. A large defense meeting was held in City Hall at 5:00 p.m., and the citizens were asked to prepare meals to send down to the heroic defenders of Drewry's Bluff. "The people of Richmond seemed to realize that we had saved the city from capture, and early in the after-noon wagon-loads of good things came down,—cakes and pies and confections of all sorts accompanied by a delegation of Richmond ladies," wrote Midshipman Hardin Littlepage, formerly of the *Virginia*. Gazing upon the "beautifully spread table," Littlepage and his comrades ventured to say that they needed "something more substantial," and were soon rewarded with "real food for soldiers." Another soldier praised the resulting repast: "O, what a feast we had!" remembered Midshipman William F. Clayton. "Surely, from the quantity and quality, the markets must have been raked clean and the dear girls sat up all night cooking."[22]

While the Confederate States Congress showed its appreciation for the victory by voting a resolution of thanks to Farrand and Drewry, others celebrated the victory with poetry:

The *Monitor* was astonished,
And the *Galena* admonished,
And their efforts to ascend the stream
We're mocked at.
While the dreaded *Naugatuck*,
With the hardest kind of luck,
Was very nearly knocked
Into a cocked-hat.[23]

But was Drewry's Bluff a *naval* victory? Initial reports of the battle credited the crew of the *Virginia* with playing the most important role, and U.S. naval officers assumed that only the participation of those skilled sailors could have inflicted such a defeat upon them. Eyewitness Pvt. William Heirs, of the 3rd Alabama Infantry, wrote a day after the battle that a company of heavy artillery "fled as soon as the shells commenced falling around them" and in their stead rushed part of the "Merrimack's" crew who "stood their posts like men." An editorial in the *Richmond Examiner* noted that it was fortunate that the guns were manned by the crew of the *Merrimac* (a name which Southerners continued to use interchangeably with *Virginia*), "and not Yahoos ignorant of discipline and command."[24]

In response to such accounts, a correspondent with the pseudonym "TRUTH," asserted that "The crew of the *Merrimac* had no more to do with [the Confederate guns] than the man in the moon." The writer, likely a member or associate of one of the land-based artillery units, offered the first of what would become dozens of conflicting accounts on the number and effectiveness of Confederate guns on Drewry's Bluff. The three most effective guns, he argued, were manned by army artillery crews, especially that of Augustus Drewry's Southside Artillery. One naval 8-inch Columbiad, commanded by Tucker, entered the action late, but served "with good effect," while a second naval piece, manned by the crew of the *Virginia*, was not mounted or effective. The *Whig* answered the "Yahoo" slur with the proud assertion that the heroes of Drewry's Bluff were men from "the peaceful avocations of life." Saluting both service branches, a correspondent to the *Whig* wrote that "it is no empty honor to have been mistaken, by either friend or foe, for the officers and men of the *Merrimac*."[25]

The argument over the navy's role at Drewry's Bluff raged on long after the war. Former Navy Department clerk and postwar chronicler of the Confederacy, Thomas Cooper DeLeon, in 1890, waxed poetical on "that splendid defense of Drewry's Bluff by Farrand, *which alone saved* Richmond!" Resentful that the navy men "have always claimed the almost entire credit for the victory," however, veterans of the Southside Artillery sought to minimize the navy's role in the success at the bluff, and their arguments carry some weight. There is little doubt the two 8-inch Columbiads (produced at Bellona arsenal in Chesterfield County) of the Southside Artillery delivered the most shots against the Federal fleet (the Southside Artillery's other piece—a 10-inch Columbiad produced in Richmond—rolled off its carriage and was out of action for most of the battle). Federal records validate this claim, as a detailed report of the projectiles which riddled the *Galena* reveals that almost all were solid shot and shell from 8-inch guns. The Southside Artillery's 8-inch guns were most favorably placed to inflict the damage.[26] The unit's veterans maintained adamantly that the army, not the navy, worked those guns. Artillerist Samuel Mann conceded that Captain Farrand "rendered valuable aid" in assisting Drewry with directing the artillery battery. The presence of the *Virginia's* crew boosted morale, Mann noted, even if they did not participate actively in the battle. While Augustus Drewry acknowledged Farrand was in command, and that other officers, specifically, Lt. Catesby Jones, were stationed at the Southside Artillery's guns, he was merciless in denigrating the navy's contributions. "I am not aware that any man connected with the navy put his hand upon any gun in the fort during that engagement," he wrote to one of his former lieutenants. Farrand "would occasionally sally out to look after his defunct navy," Drewry caustically commented, but his presence at Drewry's Bluff was "more of an accident than otherwise."[27]

In his effort to deny the navy played a role in the victory, Augustus Drewry all but ignored the work of the navy's own artillery. He specified repeatedly that no naval personnel "*in the fort*" took part in the fight. All but one of the naval guns were, of course, not in the fort but on the brow of the bluff. And while they were more vulnerable and less advantageously positioned, those guns reportedly fired throughout the battle—even when Farrand ordered that the guns in the fort cease firing to preserve ammunition. The lone gun near the fort—Tucker's 8-inch gun from the *Patrick Henry*—was crippled early in the battle by the collapse of its log casemate, but its crew reconstructed the fortification, put the gun in action late in the battle, and apparently delivered the *coup de grace* against the *Galena.* It was that gun which Lt. Rochelle claimed was "[t]he most effective gun on the Bluff." An infantryman in Mahone's Brigade contended later that he saw not only Farrand, but also members of the *Virginia's* crew in the fort during the battle.[28]

Regardless of how credit for the victory is apportioned, the effect of the battle was decisive. The Federals were forced to abandon any hope of a quick dash up the James River with their ironclads to bombard Richmond into submission. Although no one could have forseen it, nearly three more years of war would be waged before the Federal fleet would progress up the James as far as it had on May 15, 1862.

The Federal army was equally unsuccessful in its land campaign against Richmond. As he had before Yorktown in April, Maj. Gen. George B. McClellan spent May 1862, cautiously and deliberately preparing his assault against the Richmond defenses. The Confederate army opposing McClellan, commanded by Gen. Joseph E. Johnston, precipitated the action by attacking the Federals on the last day of May in the Battle of Seven Pines (Fair Oaks). While the bloody two-day tactical stalemate achieved little, Johnston was wounded during the first day's fighting and was temporarily succeeded in command by Maj. Gen. Gustavus Smith, his senior lieutenant. Smith proved unable to bear the rigors of field command, however, and control of the army was turned over to Gen. Robert E. Lee the following day.

During the ensuing campaign, the Confederate navy again made its men, facilities, and vessels useful to the defense of the capital. As Lee prepared a strategy to drive McClellan away from Richmond, he solicited the assistance of Mallory's department. "Is there a possibility of constructing an iron-plated battery, mounting a heavy gun, on trucks, the whole covered with iron, to move along the York River Railroad?" Lee asked the army's ordnance chief on June 5. "Please see what can be done. See the Navy Department and officers," Lee suggested. Within three weeks, naval ordnance chief George Minor wrote Lee that the iron-plated battery was completed. Designed by John Brooke, the railroad battery had sloped sides—not unlike the casemate of an ironclad vessel—plated with iron rolled at Tredegar and originally intended for the *C.S.S. Richmond.* The battery was armed with a single 32-pound rifled gun, mounted and equipped by Brooke's assistant, Lt. Robert Minor. This unique railroad battery saw action in the Battle of Savage's Station, which occurred along the York River Railroad east of Richmond on June 29, 1862. The army officer in command of that part of the battlefield noted "the decided success of the experiment" with a prototype of armored land warfare. [29]

The Battle of Savage's Station was but one in a series of bitterly-contested actions comprising the Seven Days Battles. During the last week of June, Lee threw his Army of Northern Virginia against McClellan's army and drove it back from the outskirts of Richmond to the James River, 25 miles downstream. McClellan's weary and bloodied Army of the Potomac spent six weeks recovering at Harrison's Landing before withdrawing down the peninsula and abandoning the campaign against Richmond.

The Confederate navy further aided Lee's army as it pursued McClellan's retreat from Richmond, when the gunboat *Teaser* became what some historians tout as the first "aircraft carrier." Confederate and Federal armies had employed stationary reconnaissance balloons from fixed land positions during the Peninsula Campaign and Seven Days Battles. The Confederate balloon was filled with gas at the city gas works overlooking Rocketts and transported to the front lines east of the city on the Richmond & York River Railroad. When McClellan moved his army south and east of Richmond, the rail line no longer served as a useful vantage point for observing enemy movements. Colonel (later brigader general) Edward Porter Alexander, the officer charged with making the balloon ascents, accordingly shifted operations to the James River. Alexander had the ballon filled at Rocketts and transported on the *Teaser* to Drewry's Bluff. Just after midnight on the morning of June 30, 1862, Alexander made his first ascent from the vessel's deck. The balloon was sent back for more gas, and Alexander made a second airborne sortie later that day. His career as a balloonist ended without fireworks on the Fourth of July after only a few more nocturnal flights when the *Teaser* ran aground and was captured.[30]

Just as the Confederate navy assisted Lee, so too did the Federal navy help McClellan. Though soundly repulsed at Drewry's Bluff, John Rodgers' fleet was a welcome sight to the Army of the Potomac camped at Harrison's Landing. Anchored just off shore, the navy provided protection and confidence for McClellan's army—and especially for McClellan himself. A barbed story, popular in both the North and the South, claimed that when desperate Federal soldiers arrived at Harrison's Landing and saw the menacing vessels in the river channel, they threw their arms around the nearest navy man and exclaimed, "There ought to be a gun boat in every family!"[31]

The immediate military threat to Richmond passed with McClellan's retreat from Harrison's Landing. Lee, together with his lieutenants James Longstreet and Thomas J. "Stonewall" Jackson, carried the war into Northern Virginia and across the Potomac River. During the remainder of 1862 and throughout 1863, Lee's army kept the Federal forces far distant from the Confederate capital by waging some of the most celebrated battles of the Civil War: Second Manassas, Antietam (Sharpsburg), Fredericksburg, Chancellorsville, and Gettysburg. Not until the spring of 1864 did the Federal army—and the Federal navy—again threaten Richmond in force. Lee's victories (and stalemates) bought desperately-needed time to perfect the defenses of the capital city and the James River.

"A Perfect Gibraltar": Drewry's Bluff and the Defense of Richmond

Only in hindsight was it clear that the victory of May 15, 1862, ended the naval threat to Richmond. On the evening of the battle, Secretary Mallory wrote in his diary that Richmond was saved "only by the poor & temporary obstructions at Drury's Bluff, which the first freshet may destroy.—God only knows what his providence may yet subject us to. The hour is dark & gloomy for our beloved South."[32] With the enemy's army still menacing Richmond, Confederate forces spent the ensuing weeks in frenzied activity strengthening the defenses at Drewry's Bluff.

Ebenezer Farrand, the putative hero of the battle, did not enjoy the limelight very long. Orders were issued on the day of the battle for Farrand to surrender naval command at Drewry's Bluff to Sidney Smith Lee, Robert's brother. Lee waited until a few days after the battle, however, to supplant Farrand. In the meantime, overall command of the forces at the post was given to an army officer, Brig. Gen. William Mahone, whose infantry brigade had arrived just in time to witness the battle. Within a week, as Mahone prepared for a new naval attack rumored to be in the making, the Confederates had seven heavy guns mounted at the bluff, more on the way, and a growing garrison of land troops. Edmund Ruffin noted on May 20, that 11 guns had been mounted at the bluff.[33]

Vital to the land and river defense of Richmond, Drewry's Bluff quickly became one of the most important inter-service command posts in the Confederacy, and remained so until the end of the war. Virtually by definition, however, "inter-service commands" translated into friction and resentment. Admiral Franklin Buchanan wrote from North Carolina to his former first officer, Catesby Jones, to congratulate him and the crew of the *Virginia* for their victory at Drewry's Bluff and to express regret over "the subordinate position you are placed in." Echoing the belief that the navy had won the battle of Drewry's Bluff, Buchanan wrote belligerently that "had I been ordered there, it should have been a naval command or I would not have gone. . . .Naval officers command there, and men of the Navy work the guns, and marines are associated with them. No soldier should have anything to do with the batteries, officers or men." Obviously anticipating potential difficulties, Robert E. Lee (who immediately following the battle was a military assistant to President Davis), endeavored to prevent inter-service friction. On May 17, he assured the new commander of the naval forces, his brother Smith Lee, "that there will be no interference with the naval forces under your command by the land forces serving in conjunction with you." Lee further hoped "that the two services will harmonize perfectly in the duties that have been assigned them." Lee was serious when he wrote that there would be "no interference" with the naval command. When Gen. Joseph Johnston asked about army engineers assisting the navy engineers supervising the fortifications, Lee explained that President Davis was "unwilling to disturb the arrangement with the Navy Department now existing, further than is necessary to insure the general control of the military operations now exercised by General Mahone, who is of course subject to your orders." Mahone himself said he "would not be responsible for any co-partnership authority," and soon yielded command to his superior, Maj. Gen. Benjamin Huger.[34]

With such policies in place, naval officers were again ascendant at Drewry's Bluff within a few months of the May battle. Navy captain Thomas J. Page received a concurrent rank as army colonel, and was put in charge of the batteries at Drewry's and Chaffin's Bluffs. When Mahone and his brigade rejoined the army in August 1862, Captain Lee assumed command of the Drewry's Bluff post, which became primarily a navy and marine garrison. This state of affairs grieved the ambitious young officer in charge of the army artillery at Drewry's Bluff. Captain Francis W. Smith complained of being stuck with "a set of naval people who are first rate fellows, but commanded by an octogenarian imbecile, Capt. S. S. Lee, brother of the General, but utterly unlike him." Sidney Lee, Smith continued, "is the poorest excuse of an officer I ever saw and worst of all, he gets all the credit for my work." The disillusioned young artillerist later appealed to "Stonewall" Jackson for a position on his staff. "A garrison consisting of mixed command of soldiers and sailors of which the senior officer is naval presents an anomalous state of military organization with which it is unpleasant and unprofitable to be connected." Jackson refused Smith's application, dooming him to spend another two years in the inter-service garrison.[35]

Awkward as its command may have been, Drewry's Bluff matured into a strong, permanent, and reasonably comfortable outpost of the Richmond defenses. An extensive and elaborate earthen fort, sometimes called Fort Darling and sometimes Fort Drewry, secured the position against land as well as naval attack.[36] Drewry's Bluff, and especially Chaffin's Bluff across the James, were incorporated into a series of works which constituted Richmond's outer defenses. The troops rushed to Drewry's Bluff in mid-May endured the wet spring without shelter or regular provisions. Soon, however, tents and provisions arrived. A small steamship in the service of the navy provided twice-daily mail and transportation between Drewry's Bluff and Richmond.

Navy and marine personnel were stationed permanently at the bluff, transforming it into a sizable hilltop village. A small contingent of sailors unattached to any naval vessel remained there until the spring of 1864, when they joined the crew of the ironclad *Fredericksburg*. Beginning in the summer of 1863, midshipmen from the Confederate States Naval Academy who could not be accommodated on the school ship, *Patrick Henry*, were quartered in barracks on the bluff. Drewry's Bluff was an especially important post for the Confederate States Marine Corps. Three companies of Confederate marines—the largest concentration of marines anywhere in the South were stationed there, and a marine officer assumed command of the post in 1864.

Drewry's Bluff was not merely an outpost for the navy in Richmond, but also the *de facto* headquarters for the James River Squadron. Though based in Richmond, the squadron usually lay anchored off the precipice or a short distance downriver at Chaffin's Bluff. Smith Lee, in addition to commanding the Drewry's Bluff garrison, was commander of the James River Squadron.

Part and parcel to the squadron's presence at Drewry's Bluff were the river obstructions, which needed to be bolstered in order to deter the enemy. In the days and weeks following the battle of May 15, Edmund Ruffin watched government tugs carrying stone downriver to complete the barrier. Rock was not the only chosen impediment to Federal intrusion, and by the end of the summer, the *Jamestown* was joined on the channel bottom by two other ships, the unarmed steam transport *Curtis Peck* and cargo ship *Northampton*.[37]

Although the river obstructions were primarily for naval defense, they were controlled by the Army Engineers Department. This division of authority bred disagreement and ill-will among those involved in the affairs of the bluff. Captain Charles Mason, commander of the engineers at Drewry's Bluff for the entire war, had little respect for the navy's vision of properly constructed and regulated obstructions. In June 1862, he complained to his superior, Capt. Alfred Rives, about having to pay the bill for schooners sunk to obstruct the river. He had told Ebenezer Farrand he did not think the schooners should be sunk there, and protested against having to pay for them out of his limited budget. Instead of sunken vessels, Mason and the engineers preferred wooden cribs filled with stone to a level which allowed the passage of Confederate light, shallow draft vessels, but prevented the passage of enemy warships. By the summer of 1863, Mason and the army engineers had created three new lines of obstructions, each line consisting of 12 stone-filled cribs. A few of the cribs were filled up to the water line (at low water); most, however, were between two and six feet below the water's surface—too shallow to allow the safe passage of any sizable warship. Using smaller civilian vessels leased from Richmond businesses, primarily the *David Currie*, the engineers plied the waters of the James, mapping, monitoring and regulating the level of the stone-filled cribs.[38]

The engineers employed additional small vessels to build the first of several pontoon bridges across the James just below Drewry's Bluff. In the last days of May, Capt. William W. Blackford, who would later gain fame as a cavalryman and chronicler of Maj. General James Ewell Brown (JEB) Stuart, was given the task of constructing a bridge out of canal boats and schooners ("of which there were many" in Richmond, he recalled), and the abundant lumber supplies then in the city. Within a few days, Blackford had organized a small fleet of vessels and an army of 500 laborers, mostly black; five steamers towed the loaded vessels to the bridge site. By the end of the day, the bridge was finished.[39]

By the end of the summer of 1862, Drewry's Bluff had indeed become what a marine officer called "a perfect Gibraltar," which, he boasted, could "never be taken by gunboats." The 90-foot bluff was crowned with a strong earthen fortification defending against both river and land assault. Arrayed along the bluff were as many as 15 heavy guns on naval pivot carriages. Three of the guns were in the fort where the *Drewry's* guns had been on May 15, and another was placed just outside the fort where the Columbiad from the *Patrick Henry* had rested. Another trio of large pieces were deployed in an experimental earthwork protected by a specially-constructed shield made of railroad iron. Although formidable in appearance, the "iron battery" at Drewry's—and a second one at Chaffin's Bluff—would eventually be judged too weak and be dismantled in February 1864. Seven more guns were placed along the bluff upriver from the fort, staggered so as to command the entire stretch of river. The entire stronghold was defended by naval, marine and army personnel. Sunken vessels, stone-filled cribs and submarine mines blocked the channel, while a growing squadron of warships was under construction at the Richmond shipyards. As many as three bridges, all built on piles high enough to allow passage of the ships, allowed movement of land troops across the river. Drewry's Bluff was a naturally strong position, made even more formidable by Confederate defenses and by the experiences of May 15, 1862.[40]

Capt. John Randolph Tucker

A descendant of old Virginia families, John Randolph Tucker (1812-1883) served the Confederate navy in Richmond in the first and last stages of the war. Under his supervision, the steamer *Yorktown* was transformed into the formidable warship *Patrick Henry* and participated in the battle of Hampton Roads. After playing a major role in the defense of Richmond at Drewry's Bluff in May 1862, Tucker transferred to the Charleston Squadron, where he served for over two years and was promoted captain. Early in 1865, he resumed command of the James River defenses, having at his disposal the hundreds of sailors previously stationed at Charleston, Savannah and Wilmington. Tucker commanded the "Naval Brigade" during the Appomattox campaign of 1865. Scharf, *Confederate States Navy.*

Cdr. Ebenezer Farrand

The naval hero of Drewry's Bluff has fallen into obscurity despite his long and important service in the U.S. and Confederate navies. Born in New York in 1803, Farrand entered the U.S. Navy in 1823 and rose to the rank of commander. He resigned in January 1861 upon the secession of his adopted state of Florida. Stationed at Pensacola, he was instrumental in the Confederate takeover of the Pensacola Navy Yard. For much of the war, Farrand's specialty was supervising the construction of ships at Jacksonville, FL., Savannah, GA., Richmond (where he was briefly commandant of the Rocketts yard), and Selma, AL. Aside from his short and eventful command at Drewry's Bluff, Farrand also served as commander of the naval forces in Mobile harbor from 1863 until the surrender of the city in May 1865. Carte-de-visite courtesy of Charles V. Peery.

Capt. Sidney Smith Lee

Sidney (1805-1869), the eldest brother of Robert E. Lee, was known in his youth as "Rose," and in his prime as "Smith." Described by a Confederate soldier as "a splendid-looking man with a heavy black mustache," he was reputed to be the most handsome of the Lee brothers. After a long and active career in the United States Navy, Smith Lee served the Confederacy for two years as commander of the James River Squadron and of the inter-service command at Drewry's Bluff, then left active command to be chief of the Office of Orders and Detail in Richmond. Courtesy of the Library of Congress.

Lt. Francis Lyell Hoge

Salt print, Class of 1860, United States Naval Academy album. Courtesy of Charles V. Peery.

(Above) Francis Hoge, a native Virginian, attended the U.S. Naval Academy before the war and became a midshipman in the Confederate Academy. He spent the first part of the war in the James River Squadron on the *Patrick Henry*, and was stationed subsequently at the fortified post atop Drewry's Bluff, and later on the ironclad *Richmond.* (Below) Thomas Harrison, a classmate of Hoge's at the Academy, was briefly assigned to service with the James River Squadron on the *Jamestown* in 1861, before being transferred to the *Alabama* for the remainder of the war.

Lt. Thomas Locke Harrison

Salt print, Class of 1860, United States Naval Academy album. Courtesy of Charles V. Peery.

Balloon View of the Attack on Fort Darling

Looking upriver toward Richmond, this sketch shows the *Galena* in front of the line bearing the brunt of the attack and the *Monitor* close behind. The *Harper's* correspondent conceded that the battle was an "unequal conflict." The Federal vessels were "exposed to a heavy plunging fire" from Fort Darling, which, he wrote, "is located on a bluff 200 feet high"—more than double its actual elevation. Nevertheless, he predicted with excessive optimism, "it is believed [Adm. Goldsborough] will soon be able to take Fort Darling and clear the way to Richmond." *Harper's Weekly*, May 31, 1862.

The C.S.S. Richmond

Official Records

Chapter 3

The New Norfolk:
Richmond as a Naval Center

Francis W. Dawson was a 20-year-old Englishman whose sympathy with the Confederacy was so strong he joined its military service. He enlisted as a landsman on the commerce raider *C.S.S. Nashville*, the first warship to show the stars and bars in England, and became clerk to the ship's captain, Cdr. Robert Pegram. Arriving safely in his adopted land in late February 1862, Dawson was rewarded with a promotion to master's mate, and ordered to Norfolk. There he went aboard the receiving ship *Confederate States* (formerly *United States*), volunteered for service with the James River Squadron, and was assigned to the gunboat *Beaufort*.

His new ship and the other converted gunboats in the squadron did not impress Dawson. "An ordinary rifle ball would have perforated the boiler of the war-tugs," he later lamented, "and a shell from a field-peice, if it hit at all, would be tolerably sure to send any one of them to the bottom." Shortly after Dawson went on board, the *Beaufort* and the other tugs accompanied the *Virginia* in going out to challenge the *Monitor* in Hampton Roads, but the Federal ironclad declined the challenge. The young Englishman's friendship with Pegram soon delivered him from the weak "war-tug," and he was selected to be part of the crew of the new ironclad (eventually named the *Richmond*), then under construction at Norfolk. Until she was finished, however, Pegram and his young protégé were detailed to New Orleans. The "Crescent City" fell to the enemy before Dawson arrived, so he was ordered back to Richmond.[1]

Dawson reported to Richmond shortly after the Battle at Drewry's Bluff and was assigned again to the James River Squadron. Much to Dawson's delight, his commander was William Parker, the officer under whom he had served on the *Beaufort*. Dawson went down to Rocketts to find his new ship, the *Drewry*, and begin his service aboard her. "I had fancied she was a vessel of the same class as the Virginia," he later remembered, "and when I went down to the place where she lay I looked about vainly for the vessel. Hailing a man who was at work on what I supposed to be a dredge, I asked which was the *Drewry*. 'This is she,' said he. I was both disappointed and disgusted."

Not yet equipped with engines or sails, the *Drewry* was, in Dawson's words, "a large flat, with a shield heavily plated with iron in front." She was "really a lighter," he wrote, "about eighty feet long and fifteen feed broad," and carrying a single heavy gun. Unhappy with his prospects for active service, Dawson transferred to the army soon afterwards. The adopted son of the South had the unfortunate timing to join the James River Squadron at the nadir of its size and strength.[2]

When Dawson was first with the squadron in March 1862, it was based in Norfolk, operated in Hampton Roads and was in close proximity to the enemy. Thanks to the already legendary exploits of the *Virginia*, the squadron enjoyed a reputation for *elan*. During the Battle of Hampton Roads on March 8-9, 1862, the smaller vessels let the *Virginia* engage the enemy warships directly while they poured in a destructive fire from a safer distance. With the Confederate abandonment of Norfolk on May 10, and the *Virginia's* destruction the following day, the squadron no longer seemed quite so formidable. The only ships constructed as warships were the two recently-commissioned, Norfolk-built Maury gunboats, *Nansemond* and *Hampton*. Otherwise, the squadron consisted of the flagship *Patrick Henry* (reduced to six guns), and several lightly-armed converted vessels: the two-gun tug *Teaser*, and two ships brought to Virginia from North Carolina, the single-gun *Beaufort*, built of thin iron for use on the Dismal Swamp Canal, and the tug *Raleigh* (later converted into the gunboat *Roanoke*). Dawson's new ship, the Richmond-built armed tender *Drewry*, was completed but not fitted out, and lay at Rocketts for months awaiting her engines.[3]

One of the most impressive achievements of the Confederate navy in Richmond was to transform the small, ersatz fleet that retreated up the James in May 1862 into one of the most powerful wartime naval squadrons. Richmond inherited from Norfolk not only the squadron, but also the responsibilities and some of the equipment of the Norfolk shipyards. Between 1862 and 1865, the Richmond naval yards completed three ironclad warships, four specialized torpedo boats, and an unarmed all-purpose vessel. To the Navy Department facilities and civilian industries of Richmond fell the task of constructing, fitting out, maintaining, and manning a squadron capable of defending the capital city.

Richmond's Naval-Industrial Complex: Shipbuilding, 1862-1865

The creation of two large-scale, labor-intensive shipbuilding operations in Richmond was the greatest consequence of the fall of Norfolk. Prior to the spring of 1862, the waterfront at Rocketts was the site of a limited shipyard operation. It was at the port of Rocketts in the late spring and summer of 1861 that Acting Naval Constructor Joseph Pierce, with a few mechanics from the Norfolk shipyard, transformed the passenger ship *Yorktown* into the warship *Patrick Henry.* It was also at Rocketts in 1861 that Master Carpenter J. H. Wyatt supervised alterations to the *Jamestown.* When Joseph Barney joined his ill-fated vessel at Richmond in late December 1861, he found an account had been opened with Rocketts merchant Richard Haskins to supply all the articles Wyatt and his employees needed for their work.[4] In late March 1862, even before the fall of Norfolk, preparations were underway to establish a second shipyard directly across from Rocketts, adjacent to the city of Manchester. By the summer of 1862 hundreds of laborers were constructing ships of war at Rocketts and at the yard across the river.

The establishment of shipbuilding facilities in Richmond was not difficult since the construction of ironclads did not require elaborate drydocks or deepwater ports. With the loss of Norfolk, New Orleans and Memphis in the first 14 months of war, the most powerful vessels in the Confederate navy were constructed on riverfront beaches and mudflats in such unlikely places as Edward's Ferry, North Carolina; Pee Dee, South Carolina; Oven Bluff, Alabama; and Yazoo City, Mississippi. The most essential attribute of a shipyard was access to the enormous supply of timber, iron, and labor that ironclads required.[5] Despite occasional shortages of each of those commodities, Richmond—with its industries, nearby coal mines, and connections with western Virginia iron mines—proved itself as one of the Confederacy's most well-endowed and most urban shipbuilding locations.

Shipbuilding required the coordination of several government departments, countless private businesses and thousands of skilled and unskilled laborers. At the center of the network were the navy yards facing each other across the James River just below the city. Despite what would eventually be accomplished along the banks of the James River, Rocketts was not an impressive facility. Francis Dawson described the place as little more than "a shed and 200 or 300 carpenters."[6] Surviving photographs of the site provide few additional details. Several open air sheds and numerous pre-war warehouses are the only visible structures in the navy yard vicinity. Accounts of the work conducted at Rocketts and at the yard across the river indicate that both possessed elevated ways essential for shipbuilding, together with support facilities such as saw mills and blacksmith shops.

Responsible for coordinating operations at the Rocketts yard was the commandant, a post filled first in 1862 by Cdr. Ebenezer Farrand and for most of the war by Virginia-born Cdr. Robert Gilchrist Robb. Navy regulations specified that the commandant shall "exercise entire control over every department in the navy yard, and will be considered responsible for the due preservation of all buildings and stores contained therein, and of all vessels in ordinary or repairing, and for the judicious application of all labor." Under the commandant's supervision were constructors, master workmen, engineers, storekeepers, paymasters and a small army of laborers who not only constructed new vessels, but also repaired and maintained warships and civilian vessels used by the navy. The commandant was also responsible for security, fire prevention and the care of public property.[7]

No commandant was assigned to the yard opposite Rocketts. The facility apparently was initially under the command of Rocketts commandant Farrand, but subsequently fell under the supervision of other authorities. Acting Master (subsequently lieutenant) Maxwell T. Clarke exercised command in 1862. By early the following year, the yard was under the control of the Office of Special Service (OSS). Created originally in December 1861 to coordinate the construction of wooden gunboats, the OSS became an adjunct to the shipyards, securing men and material. With its office in a building adjacent to the Mechanics Institute on 9th St., the OSS was commanded initially by gunboat champion Matthew Fontaine Maury, for a short spell by Cdr. Thomas R. Rootes, and for most of the war by Lt. John Henry Parker, a Virginia-born former United States Navy officer. The October 1863 city guide listed Parker as "in charge" of the shipyard opposite Rocketts.[8]

Regardless of who commanded the shipyard, design of the Confederacy's warships and direct supervision of ship construction fell to naval constructors and their assistants—usually master carpenters and builders. John L. Porter, the man who became the Confederate navy's chief constructor in 1863, designed the ships built at the Rocketts yard and may have supervised work there. Performing and overseeing the skilled work at Rocketts for most of the war (and occasionally listed as "superintendent") was Master Builder James Meads. Although he initially held a naval rank as carpenter, Meads resigned that rank to assume the civilian position of master builder, or master carpenter. Another key individual in the development of the shipyard was Acting Constructor and Norfolk shipbuilder William A. Graves, who was so closely associated with the yard opposite Rocketts it was often referred to as "Graves' Yard." Although Graves, like Porter, designed ships to be built elsewhere in the Confederacy, traveled widely, and supervised shipbuilding projects in several other states, he was the primary naval architect for the yard opposite Rocketts. The highest paid and ranked civilian employee at that facility was Master Builder Daniel Constantine, who occupied a position analogous to that of James Meads at Rocketts.[9]

All of the ships built at Richmond were steam-powered, and thus demanded machinery and mechanical expertise as well as raw materials and traditional shipwright skills. For this reason, the Confederate Navy Department established links with dozens of area businesses, suppliers, artisans, and mechanics. John Parker and the OSS often advertised for a wide range of materials essential for naval operations. On several occasions the demand for supplies was all-encompassing, and, in the supply-starved Confederacy, difficult to come by: "Block and sheet lead, copper, zinc, tin and brass; wire of different metals, sheet iron, window glass, cast steel and bar iron, chain rope and all other articles for Naval purposes." In addition to all the supplies, lumber, and iron, ship construction required enormous numbers of skilled and unskilled laborers, both black and white. Construction of the *Virginia*, for instance, required the labor of over 1,500 men. Monthly payrolls for Rocketts and the yard opposite each typically listed between 125 and 250 civilian employees, mostly ship and house carpenters, joiners, smiths, bolt drivers, caulkers and laborers. The kind of laborers in demand depended on the stage of construction. Axemen, carpenters and joiners were in heavy demand when ships were being framed; bolt drivers, fasteners and blacksmiths when iron plating was being attached. For example, in November 1863, when the yard was finishing the placement of iron plates on the *Fredericksburg* and still framing the *Texas*, almost 250 men were employed at Rocketts.[10]

To fill those positions, the Navy Department tapped into skilled labor in Richmond and throughout the region. Men with engineering and mechanical knowledge who had joined the army were sometimes detailed to service at the navy yards, since their individual contributions to the Confederate war effort would be much larger wielding tools than muskets. The ranks of the 1st and 12th Virginia Infantry regiments, raised largely in Virginia's urban centers, included many carpenters, boilermakers, and ironmolders who were eventually detailed for naval construction projects. In July and August 1862, a total of 21 carpenters and joiners serving in a variety of regiments and a Louisiana artillery battery were detailed to work at Rocketts. Eight other soldier-carpenters were detailed at the same time to the yard opposite Rocketts. Logical as this policy was, it was not always followed. More often, Mallory found himself complaining in futility to the War Department against the drafting of skilled laborers impressed into the army. "The President refuses to permit a man to leave the army to work on gunboats or for the navy," Mallory confided in disgust to his diary in August 1862.[11]

A vital source of labor were the hundreds of blacks, both slave and free, who worked at the Richmond yards. Indeed, Virginia's military mobilization depended upon black labor. Accordingly, the state goverment (followed by the Confederate government) passed laws to facilitate the impressment of slaves and conscription of free blacks for work on fortifications and at military facilities. In December 1862, for example, 87 blacks worked at (or in association with) the Rocketts yard. They included 32 axemen, 17 yard hands, 15 carpenters, 11 sawyers, four caulkers, three whitewashers, and two cooks. That same month the navy advertised for "150 able bodied Negro men with axes to cut and hew timber near Richmond for the Confederate States Navy Department," a telling announcement suggesting the frenzied level of activity in Richmond. A total of 122 blacks, including 67 skilled artisans (joiners, blacksmiths, caulkers, carpenters, machinists), worked at the navy yard in 1863. The free blacks received daily wages, though they were paid less than white counterparts working in the same positions.[12]

Among the blacks working in Richmond's naval facilities were slaves impressed or hired from white artisans and from naval officers also employed in the city. Randolph and Billy, slaves of Lt. Robert Minor, superintendent of the Naval Ordnance Works, worked as axemen at Rocketts. Master Builder Meads and Master Blacksmith James A. Farmer each hired out to Rocketts yard six slaves. The owners received the wages earned by the slaves, though the slaves themselves received pay for any "extra time" they worked. Under this arrangement Meads collected $273.50 for the labor of his six slaves in February 1863. Farmer owned, and presumably had trained, blacksmith Joe Thomas, one of the highest paid black laborers at the Rocketts yard. In 1864, the Confederate government authorized the conscription of free blacks for labor in government facilities. During the last year of the war, the navy yards employed 36 such men.[13]

The first stages of shipbuilding were the same for all mid-nineteenth-century vessels, including ironclads. Sitting on an elevated platform, called a slip or way, the keel was laid and the structure framed and planked (or skinned). The typical Confederate ironclad had a hull that was either flat or sloped gently upward toward a rounded bilge, and sides sloped at a 35-40 degree angle to form a protective casemate. Wood for the framing and skinning was pine and oak, and in places was 24 inches thick. While the bottom layer of the planking was horizontal and merely fitted and dovetailed, the top layer was vertical and caulked. The resources required for framing and skinning an ironclad were tremendous. In April 1862, as he began to build the *Virginia II*, William Graves advertised for 200 carpenters and a total of 152,000 feet and 610 pieces of pine and oak timber and planking of lengths up to 50 feet. The Navy Department was forced to periodically dispatch officers into the counties surrounding Richmond to locate "gunboat timber" and forward it to the Richmond yards.[14]

After the ships were framed and planked, they were "launched," meaning they were slid from the elevated ways into the water. The ways, constructed of smooth-faced hardwood, were greased before the launching and fitted with "drags" which absorbed the friction from the slide into the water. Although the record is unclear, the Richmond-built ironclads were possibly side-launched into the James rather than launched stern first, as they would have been in a larger, deep water port.[15]

By the time an ironclad was launched, the only part of the craft that had received its armor was the "knuckle"—the small ridge near the waterline where the sloped casemate met the hull. Confederate shipbuilders determined to put armor on both the upper side of the knuckle (continuing the line of the casemate) and on the lower side, well below the water line. The iron plating below the knuckle offered protection against artillery shot and against attacks from enemy rams. The armor was attached to the casemate and the flush deck (the deck fore and aft of the casemate) as the vessel sat in a berth or a sheltered area of the river. Attached with iron spikes onto the framing and planking was an armor of between four and eight inches of rolled railroad iron applied in two-inch layers. The iron, like the wood planking, was placed in alternating layers, horizontal underneath and vertical on the surface. Those tiers, combined with the slope of the casemate, caused most artillery shells to glance harmlessly off the ship.

Despite the proximity of Tredegar and Richmond's other iron manufacturers, shortages of iron were the greatest cause of delays in the completion of the Confederacy's ironclad vessels. Each ironclad required an average of 1,000 tons of iron. Tredegar, a private operation, agreed in late 1861 to provide the navy with at least 4,500 tons of armor plate each year. While a laudable goal, this proved to be an impossible task. Indeed, the amount required for just two vessels strained the firm's capacity. Demands for various forms of ordnance from both the army and navy competed with ironclads for an increasingly sparse supply of metal, and placed an ever-growing strain on the operators of Tredegar. For example, it took seven months to roll the iron for the gunboat *Richmond*, twice as long as it had for the *Virginia*. While the massive Tredegar works contined to survive and thrive as long as Richmond held out, the supply of raw materials in western Virginia fell into Federal hands in 1862, further hampering efforts to satisfy the seemingly insatiable demands streaming in from various points around the Southern nation.[16]

Other factors hampered the completion of the inland navy. Former general and entrepreneur Joseph Anderson, the owner of Tredegar, explained to Navy Secretary Mallory in March 1863 that a breakdown in machinery and a labor shortage had caused delay in the completion of iron for the ships. "[A]ll we ask," Anderson pleaded, "is that the Department will give us all the facilities in their power. We have a prospect of a larger production this year at our furnaces if not interfered with by the Enemy." Anderson promised the completion of specific plates later that week, and predicted "[a]fter this the vessel [the *C.S.S. Fredericksburg*] may be launched. Then we propose to go on with Mr. Graves' order for the other vessel, but if you can turn over to us the material we will be able to hasten its completion." The following week, Anderson informed Mallory: "We regret to state that we shall be compelled to suspend the operation of Making Gun Boat iron after today for want of Materials."[17]

After the ships were framed, planked and clad in iron, they were "fitted out." This time-consuming process entailed the installation of the ship's engines, boilers, steering apparatus, propellers and other machinery, as well as equipping the ship with supplies, stores, and crew. Essential to this process were "shears," the hoisting apparatus used to lift and lower engines and guns into the ships. While the Rocketts yard was equipped with this lifting mechanism, it is unknown whether the yard across from Rocketts possessed the device. As with plating the vessels, fitting out Confederate ironclads was dependent also upon the acquisition or manufacture of complex machinery, as well as the assembling of men and supplies. The entire process proved lengthy, expensive and frustrating.[18]

The Confederacy usually had to rely on its own skilled mechanics to build the engines, boilers, and other machinery that ended up in their naval vessels. Each ironclad had two paired engines which powered a central drive shaft and propeller. Providing steam to the engines were two furnaces, each about 22 feet long, nine feet high and eight feet wide. The Navy Department occasionally salvaged engines from captured ships—as it did for the *Richmond* (and possibly the *Virginia II.*) Surviving records suggest the Tredegar Iron Works produced the engines for the *Fredericksburg* and probably the *Virginia II.* as well.[19]

In February 1862, the Navy Department leased the Shockoe Foundry and Machine Shops, at 17th and Cary streets, from its owners, Charles and James M. Talbott. Among other things, the Talbott Brothers manufactured steam engines for saw mills, pumps, tobacco factories and other industrial purposes. Their establishment was immense, stretching over a block of three and four-story structures arranged in a hollowed square and consisting of a fitting up shop, turning shop, smith's shop, foundry, drying oven, boiler room, and flash room. The government intended originally to build the engines for Maury's 100 gunboats at Shockoe Foundry. As the Confederacy's naval building strategy shifted from small gunboats to larger, more powerful ironclads, the Shockoe Foundry's role similarly changed. Federal naval officers in 1865, rummaging about in the foundry, came across the engines, boilers and shaft for the uncompleted Confederate ironclad *Texas*. So important was the Talbott Brothers Foundry to the Navy Department that it became known formally as the "Confederate Naval Works," and operated under the supervision of Thomas W. Smith. In early 1863, the Naval Works employed nearly 150 men, including 47 machinists, 34 boiler makers, 22 blacksmiths and 12 moulders.[20]

In addition to machinery needed to operate these mammoth ships, the fitting out process also required the acquisition or production of heavy guns, or ordnance. Confederate ironclads typically carried batteries of two, four, or six guns of different weights and types—some smoothbores, some rifles, some firing solid shot, some firing shells, and some capable of firing any kind of projectile. Guns firing solid shot were designated by the weight of their shot, while guns designed to fire exploding shells (preferred by Confederate authorities) were designated by the diameter of their bores. Thus, the same piece could be called a 6.4-inch gun or 32-pounder, an 8-inch or a 64-pounder, depending on the projectile it fired. The Richmond-built ironclads typically carried batteries consisting of 11-inch smoothbores and 8-inch and 6.4-inch rifles.[21]

The capture of the Norfolk Navy Yard in April 1861 provided almost 1,100 artillery pieces for the Confederate navy. These guns, which included a variety of types and sizes, were put to good use in river and harbor defense, mounted in naval vessels and saw service in artillery batteries. For most of the war, however, the Confederacy relied on its own gun production. Richmond and Selma emerged as the centers of Confederate naval ordnance. Tredegar Iron Works contracted with the government to produce heavy guns for the navy and, during the course of the war, manufactured almost as many guns as the Confederacy captured at Norfolk. The manufacturing process was laborious and expensive. It took, for example, nearly 900 hours to simply bore each 7-inch rifle.[22]

John Brooke, the Confederate navy's ordnance chief, fashioned Richmond into not only a center of gun manufacturing, but also of research, development and experimentation in guns, projectiles and explosives. The primary fruit of his labors was the so-called Brooke Rifle, an innovative artillery piece rifled (grooved) in the barrel and reinforced with a double iron band shrunken onto the gun at its breech. This band strengthened the piece at the point where the explosion of the powder created the greatest stress on the gun tube, thereby reducing the number of burst guns. The Brooke rifle was designed originally for use on the *Virginia*, but Brooke continued his experimentation and produced several sizes of this design, including 6.4-inch, 7-inch, 8-inch, 10-inch and 11-inch versions. Brooke made daily visits to Tredegar and to other

Richmond foundries contracted to produce the weapons. Always at work on new designs, Brooke became discouraged at what he described as the "want of mechanics" that delayed progress in transforming his designs into reality. "The Tredegar turns out guns so very slowly that I lose patience," he confided to his diary in February 1863.[23]

In addition to relying upon the resources of Tredegar to cast and bore guns, the Navy Department established its own extensive ordnance works. The central figure in the development of these facilities was Lt. Robert Minor, younger brother of George Minor, chief of the Office of Ordnance and Hydrography. Born near Fredericksburg, Virginia, in 1827, Minor enjoyed an eventful prewar career. He entered the United States Navy in 1841, and served as a lieutenant aboard Commodore Matthew C. Perry's flagship *Lexington* on the fabled voyage to Japan in 1853. Thereafter, he worked with Matthew Fontaine Maury at the U.S. Naval Observatory, and rose to the rank of lieutenant commander before the outbreak of the Civil War. The popular "Bob" Minor was related to many of the prominent men in the Confederate navy and army. He was, remembered his classmate John McIntosh Kell, "one of those large-hearted men with life and face all brimming over with the sunshine of a happy heart. A very 'Nathaniel in whom there was no guile.'" His popularity and his convenient location in Richmond for most of the war made his rented rooms a kind of naval officers' salon.[24]

Before coming to Richmond in 1862, Minor enjoyed a little swashbuckling adventure and some duty as an ordnance specialist. The native Virginian was among the officers who in June 1861 seized a U.S. civilian ship, the *St. Nicholas*, on the Potomac River, and used that vessel to capture other river vessels before destroying her. After his brief career as a privateer, Minor served for a few months assisting Maury's torpedo experiments, and then a few more months as ordnance specialist assisting Gen. Robert E. Lee in constructing coastal defenses in South Carolina. The naval ordnance officer traveled twice to New Orleans to inspect ironclads under construction. As Admiral Buchanan's flag lieutenant aboard the *C.S.S. Virginia* during her historic clash with the *Monitor* in Hampton Roads, Minor was shot through the chest while leading a party to burn the crippled *U.S.S. Congress*. After his recovery at Norfolk

Naval Hospital, Minor was assigned to the Office of Ordnance and Hydrography.[25]

On September 1, 1862, Minor received instructions from his older brother George to "take charge of the establishment of Mess. Ettenger & Edmond in this City which has been rented by this office for ordnance purposes and cause to be removed thereto from the present store house, all the stores and property belonging to this office, and have the same stored in some suitable place in that establishment." The younger Minor's duties included the "manufacture of gun carriages and other ordnance articles." For the remainder of the war, the Cary Street shop of Ettenger & Edmond, "Builders of Portable and Stationary Engines," was the core of the Naval Ordnance Works.[26]

A few weeks before the Navy Department took control of Ettenger & Edmond, George Minor gave a detailed report on the works:

> From the ordnance store the guns are equipped for service. At the laboratory, shells are strapped, fuzed, fitted, and prepared for use, fuzes are driven, friction primers are made, and charges prepared for heavy guns. At the gun-carriage shop, carriages have been made for vessels at Charleston and Savannah, for the batteries at Drewry's and Chapin's [Chaffin's] Bluffs, and are now being made for the *Richmond* and other vessels. The work is progressing as well as the limited numbers of mechanics (blacksmiths especially) will admit.[27]

With the new facility, the ordnance works began rifling and banding heavy guns and constructing machinery for those tasks. Divided into a gun carriage makers shop, a finishing shop, a blacksmith shop and pattern making shop, each headed by a foreman and staffed with skilled artisans and unskilled laborers, the ordnance works employed nearly 100 men.[28]

John Brooke, soon to succeed the elder Minor as head of the office, wrote in his diary on November 1, 1862: "I visited the Naval Ordnance Works of which Robert Minor is superintendent, everything well regulated, work of the best character executed there." Bob Minor himself penned for his wife an admittedly "egotistical," yet honest, description of his operation:

> I wish you could spend an hour or so at the Works and see how busy we are and how much efficient work we turn out in the heavy ordnance line. I am my own Inspecting Officer, or at least Mr. [shop superintendent Richard B.] Wright is, and of course as we do not care to make money for the Gov't we only let the best work leave the shops unlike the contractors who have to make money for their own support, and thus our work will stand the test better than theirs. . .[29]

Not only did the Office of Ordnance and Hydrography completely subsume into the navy's operations such businesses as Ettenger & Edmond and the Shockoe Foundry, it also used the services of Philip Rahm's Eagle Foundry on Cary Street between 14th and 15th streets, and the Sampson and Pae Foundry at Byrd and 5th streets. The Dock Street shop of S. A. Pumphrey in late 1862 became the Confederate States Ship Joiners Shop. Surviving Navy Department records are replete with dozens of Richmond businesses and artisans that provided simply small quantities of material and skilled labor to the government.[30]

Though an inevitable part of any successful war effort, the growth of the Confederacy's naval-industrial complex was rich in irony. The demands of a war originally fought to defend an agrarian way of life precipitated an economic transformation one historian termed "revolutionary." Various industries developed in Selma, Atlanta, Augusta, and in other small inland cities.[31] Richmond of course was no stranger to industry, and the demands of naval shipbuilding simply confirmed that city's value to the Confederacy.

The Construction of the James River Ironclads

In three years of operation, the yards at Richmond completed one ironclad begun at Norfolk, constructed two ironclads start to finish, nearly completed a third, and were working on a fourth at war's end. The yards also completed five smaller, specialized vessels, and were working on two more. This praiseworthy record ranks the Richmond facilities among the busiest and most prolific of all Confederate navy yards.

Consuming by far the most time and resources were the ironclad warships. The ironclads constructed at Richmond represented a microcosm of the evolution in Confederate ironclad design and construction—testimony to ongoing experimentation and the effort to learn from experience. The Richmond vessels, and those built for the North Carolina, Charleston, Savannah, Mobile and Red River squadrons, imitated the basic design of the *Virginia*, and thus presented an easily distinguishable profile: a raft-like base on which sat a box-like casemate (that portion resting on the deck above the waterline) pierced on port, starboard, fore and aft by gunports and topped by a large iron smokestack. Within the menacing iron hulk was a traditional arrangement of decks: a gun deck at the water line, a berth deck (housing living quarters, galley, storage rooms, the magazine and the engines) under the water line, and a spar deck (also called the shield deck or casemate deck), which was simply the top of the casemate. These vessels, like the original *Virginia*, were armed not only with rifled guns and smoothbores, but also carried iron rams on their bows. All were technically "ironclad steam sloops," or ironclad vessels powered by steam engines and having their guns on a single deck.

Even the ships of that general description were not uniform in design or appearance. They varied in the configuration of their hulls, the size and shape of their casemates and in such details as the location of their pilot houses. All of the ironclad vessels constructed at Richmond (and almost all Confederate vessels) were smaller than the *Virginia*, whose 275-foot length—built as she was on the hull of a wooden frigate—and 23-foot draft contributed to her own demise. When Norfolk was abandoned, the *Virginia's* deep draft made it impossible for her to move upstream, and her crew was forced to scuttle her. While an expensive lesson, ship designers learned from it. As Confederate authorities surrendered the dream of sending a seaworthy ironclad warship up the coast to threaten Northern cities, Southern shipbuilders designed lighter draft vessels that drew between eight and 14 feet of water—a significant improvement that made them more suitable for operating on shallow southern rivers. To achieve the lighter draft, designers created smaller vessels with shortened casemates (sometimes called citadels) in proportion to overall length. The *Richmond*, which was the prototype of the first post-*Virginia* class of Confederate ironclads, measured approximately 180 feet with a 105-foot casemate. Her companion ironclads in the James River Squadron, the *Fredericksburg* and *Virginia II*, measured 188 feet with a 89-foot casemate, and 201 feet with a 74-foot casemate, respectively. The *Texas*, not completed before the war came to an end, exemplified the later tendency of Confederate ironclad design: its casemate extended just over 60 feet on a deck that measured 217 feet overall.[32] As the James River Squadron discovered in 1865, however, the sacrifices in casemate size did not result in vessels capable of reliably navigating rivers.

The crucible of war also demonstrated the need for heavier armor to withstand the impact of the U.S. Navy's large caliber guns—as well as the Confederate's need to develop heavier guns in their own armament. The original *Virginia* was most vulnerable at and below her waterline because her knuckle (where the casemate joined the deck) received only one inch of the planned three inches of plate before the Battle of Hampton Roads. The *Richmond* class vessels, and all subsequent Confederate ironclads, carried two inches of armor on the underside of the knuckle and for several feet below the waterline. The *Texas*, usually considered the best hull in the James River Squadron, carried a full six inches of armor on her dramatically shortened casemate. The *Virginia II*, constructed earlier than the *Texas*, reportedly carried eight inches of iron on each end of her casemate in an attempt to add extra protection to the bow and stern sections of the ship. This extra iron significantly increased her draft, but made her the strongest vessel in the squadron.[33] The *Fredericksburg*, however, was designed with lighter armor at and below the waterline and no armor on top of the casemate (the spar deck) to lighten her draft.

While keels were laid in the spring of 1862 for the *Fredericksburg* and the *Virginia II*, the first ship completed at the Richmond yards was the *C.S.S. Richmond*. In May 1862, the yard at Rocketts assumed the urgent assignment of completing that vessel, which had just been launched at Norfolk. The ironclad ram slid into the river on May 6, and was towed up the river to Richmond that same day by the *Jamestown* and *Patrick Henry*. Ironically, the most detailed surviving reports on the progress of the ship came from informants for the Federal government, which was keeping close tabs on the progress of the vessel. Throughout the summer of 1862 the Federal navy and army anticipated with dread the completion of the ship they called the "Merrimac No. 2." Much to the dismay of Confederate officials, detailed plans of the ship fell into enemy hands in July 1862 with the capture of the *Teaser* on the James River.[34]

T. S. Seybolt, a member of the secret service corps with the Federal Army of the Potomac, warned United States Secretary of State William Seward that he had received "a very valuable piece of information" from "a reliable source":

> It is to the effect that a second Merrimac, more formidable than the first, has just been completed at Richmond, and is daily expected by the citizens there to come out and clear James River. This vessel, it seems, was commenced at Norfolk before the evacuation of that place, and on the evacuation was taken with other craft to Richmond. She is said to be of smaller dimensions and much lighter draught than the old Merrimac, but similar in her construction and much more formidable, combining as she does all the improvements suggested by experience. . . . A peculiar kind of shot have been cast expressly for her at the Tredegar Iron Works in Richmond, and, as I have said, it is daily expected by the most knowing citizens there to come out and clear James River.

Hours after sending this alarmist report, however, Seybolt forwarded further intelligence that the new ironclad was actually far from finished.[35]

Northern and Southern sources detailed the slow progress of the new ship. Exchanged Union prisoners of war who had been held on Belle Isle in the James River upstream from Rocketts reported in late July that, while its wood work was done, the ship had not yet received either her engines or iron plating. A different account was passed along to a Federal general in Suffolk, Virginia, that specified that the ship received her boilers on July 26, was at that time receiving her engines, but did not yet have her guns. Two Southern soldiers stationed in Richmond, one an infantryman and the other a marine, each noted that the ship was "1/2 finished" in the late summer and fall of 1862.[36]

In contrast to Federal fears of the "secesh monster," the "Merrimac No. 2," Confederate observers found much to criticize about the new vessel, especially her engines, which had been pirated from the civilian lightship *Arctic.* "The Richmond comes on slowly," wrote navy Lt. John Taylor Wood on August 30. "She will not be ready before the 1st of October." Wood was skeptical not only of the ship's progress but also of her capacity. "I doubt very much if she goes below the barrier [at Drewry's Bluff], for with her very weak engine (80 horse) she would be mobbed and forced out of the channel. She will not steam more than 5 knots, if that." Writing at almost the same time, George Weber, a sailor aboard the *Patrick Henry,* similarly remarked that "the worst thing" about the *Richmond* "is that she carries bad engines."[37]

Federal informants were inconsistent in relating where the new ironclad was being built. One of Seybolt's informants, an Irish-born printer who had worked for several Richmond newspapers, claimed to have been aboard the vessel "since the completion of her wood work, before she was taken across to the Manchester side of the river to be iron clad." A 14-year-old boy told Seybolt that he witnessed the ship "lying at the Rocketts, below Richmond, day before yesterday, receiving her iron plating. . . .he saw about fifteen hands working on her, but the plating did not seem to be very far advanced yet. . ."[38] There was no advantage to taking the vessel across the river to the Manchester (Graves) yard, however, since the iron plating to sheath her came from Tredegar, located on the north bank of the river. Thus it is reasonable to conclude that the work on the *Richmond* was almost certainly done entirely at the northside (Rocketts) yard, Seybolt's informant notwithstanding.

Designed and constructed under the supervision of chief constructor John Porter, the *Richmond* was the prototype of the Confederacy's most common class of ironclads. One hundred feet shorter than the *Virginia,* Richmond class vessels also had a shallower draft—13 feet, ten feet less than that of the *Virginia*—a casemate sloped at 35 degrees, and four inches of iron plating. Their batteries consisted of four guns, one in each broadside and one pivot-mounted gun at each end, fore and aft. The Richmond prototype was completed and commissioned in November 1862. Her original battery consisted of one double-banded 7-inch Brooke rifle and three single-banded 7-inch Brookes.[39]

As the *Richmond* was being commissioned into service, work progressed on several other ironclads. By the summer of 1862, Federal authorities were well aware that the Southern capital was being transformed into a Confederate shipbuilding center. Brigadier General Joseph Mansfield on August 3 warned Commodore Charles Wilkes that the Confederates in Richmond "are laying the blocks to build four more [ironclads], for which the boilers are already made." Indeed, keels had been laid for the two ironclads built entirely at the Richmond yards: the *Fredericksburg* and the *Virginia II*.[40]

The work Mansfield noted had actually begun before the arrival of the hull of the *Richmond*. By late March 1862, Confederate authorities established an entirely new shipyard across the river from Rocketts. The first evidence of this southside shipyard was a pair of advertisements placed by William Graves beginning in the April 1, 1862, *Richmond Daily Dispatch*. These notices requested large quantities of lumber to be "delivered at the ship yard, opposite Rocketts" and 200 ship carpenters "to work at Richmond." Four days earlier, John Brooke noted in his diary that he was "at work on [a shield] to be built by Mr. Graves who is to start a ship yard at Richmond." The yard was established directly across the river from Rocketts (at what is now the public boat landing), and was usually known simply as the "Yard opposite Rocketts." Although no records survive, the Confederate Navy probably leased the site from Joseph Marx or from the Richmond & Danville Railroad, and made use of the coal wharves and other facilities on the site. There, on the eastern edge of the industrial suburb called Manchester, William Graves created a complete shipyard capable of all phases of ship construction and repair, complete with ways, a blacksmith shop and other improvements.[41]

William A. (possibly Armistead) Graves was the man whose name eventually became synonymous with the southside shipyard. Born about 1820 in Norfolk, Graves was well-schooled in the art of naval construction. He served first as an apprentice in shipbuilding under William H. Hunter, and by the beginning of the Civil War, maintained his own business as "shipwright, sparmaker and caulker" on Water St. in Norfolk. During the first year of the war, the Confederate government contracted with Graves and two other private Norfolk shipbuilders for the repair and construction of naval vessels. In the winter and spring of 1862, Graves' yard was at work on one of the Maury gunboats for the Confederate navy. The vessel (apparently named the *Dixie*) was launched and in the process of fitting out when the Confederates destroyed her during the evacuation of Norfolk. The Navy Department in November 1862 belatedly paid Graves $7,718.25 on his contract for construction of three gunboats at his Norfolk yard.[42]

Until he was appointed as a naval constructor in March 1862, however, Graves served in the Virginia Militia. Evidence suggests that he was a private in the 54th Virginia Militia, a Norfolk-based unit that included several men listed as ship yard employees. Someone deemed his skills too valuable to squander as a militiaman, however, and he was relieved from the service for "Govt work." Upon his arrival in Richmond, Graves began assembling materiel and workers to build an ironclad of his own design that was to become the *Virginia II*. On November 1, 1862, John Brooke described "Mr. Graves vessel" as "pretty well advanced, frames up, clamps in etc. . . She will be a strong and fine vessel."[43]

The construction of the *Virginia II* benefited from the contributions of the "Ladies Aid and Defense Society," usually called the Ladies Defense Association and best known as the Ladies Gunboat Association—one of the most fascinating chapters in Confederate naval history. Citizens on the Confederate homefront sought ways to assist the war effort, and as early as December 1861, the women of New Orleans organized in order to raise funds to build ironclad vessels. As a result of the exploits of the *Virginia*, "gunboat associations" sprang up throughout the South in the spring of 1862. The formation of groups in South Carolina and Georgia in March inspired the mobilization of the citizens, especially the ladies, of Richmond and Virginia generally. The patriotic fervor to assist in the construction of ironclads was not the exclusive domain of females. In a letter published in the *Daily Dispatch* on March 18, 1862, exiled Kentucky secessionist Blanton Duncan challenged the "old men" of Virginia to give of their money as the young men were giving of their blood. Prominent men, primarily those living along the James River—including agriculturalist and celebrated Southern patriot

Edmund Ruffin—pledged money for a gunboat which project sponsors proposed to call the *Richmond*.[44]

The sudden interest in self-defense and civic responsibility inspired the Richmond city council on March 26 to appoint a committee to "enquire into the expediency of building one or more boats or vessels for the defence of the City on James River, and report the cost of said boat or other vessels, and the earliest time the said vessels can be ready for service." The committee apparently never reported its findings, if there were any to report, probably because the immediate crisis of May 1862 precluded any long-term project like the building of an ironclad ship.[45]

While the local government's efforts dissipated, private efforts intensified, and on March 24, 1862, the "National Defense Association" was founded at a meeting held in the Broad Street Methodist Episcopal Church. The organization's purpose was "to raise funds for the building of gunboats, or other means for the protection and defence of the city of Richmond." Although it was an organization of Richmond ladies, the National Defense Association encouraged the formation of "auxiliary associations" in other cities and towns, and invited the participation of "the old men who are unfit for military duty." Chaired by Maria Gaitskell Clopton, the energetic and diminutive English-born wife of prominent judge John Bacon Clopton, the association quickly got down to business. By the end of March it had appointed members to collect funds in 16 specified districts in the city. On April 4, Mrs. Clopton led a committee that met with President Davis and Navy Secretary Mallory. The secretary, reported the *Daily Dispatch*, "with the approval of the President, tendered to the Association the gunboat now in the process of construction by the Government [presumably the *Virginia II*], which will facilitate the consummation of their project very much, and enable the ladies to afford the Confederate capital a most formidable defence." Secretary Mallory offered Mrs. Clopton and the association a choice of which ship they wished to sponsor. Responding to Mallory's invitation, Mrs. Clopton consulted with a few of her associates and concluded "that the Boat on the Chesterfield side of the river would be the one preferred by the majority of the Assoc[iation]." Mallory concurred.[46]

On April 11, 1862, the association published an address by Capt. Richard Maury, the association's unofficial mentor, describing the work on the new ship:

> The Association has the further pleasure to announce to its friends that in a few days the keel of their vessel will be laid. Capt. Farrand, an experienced officer of the Navy, has been placed in charge of the work. He is to be assisted in the construction by one of the most celebrated ship builders of the country—Mr. Graves—who is also on the ground. Advertisements are out for two hundred mechanics—a considerable force of them has already been engaged—and vessels have been sent down the river to fetch up timber ready cut to our hands by the enemy.[47]

Ten days later, the association announced "that their gunboat is now in the process of building on James river, on the Chesterfield side, opposite to Rocketts, under the superintendence of Commander Farrand, a well-known and efficient officer of the navy." The government has, the announcement continued, "detailed the best workmen in the Confederacy for the construction of the boat, Mr. Graves being the master carpenter, and we have every assurance of the speedy completion of the work." The news excited Mrs. Clopton, who wrote to her daughter on April 8 that "We are now fully organized, and have our arrangements in such forwardness that we expect to lay the keel of the Gun Boat next week. Commander Farrand is superintendent and promises every exertion shall be made to have the Boat in ninety days ready for the Engines."[48]

Despite Farrand's promises and Mrs. Clopton's hopes, it was two years before the *Virginia II* was completed. None of the responsibility of the lengthy delay rested with the Defense Association and its many auxiliaries, for contributions of money, jewelry and plate were sent to the association treasurer, tools and building materials were sent to Cdr. Farrand or Richard Haskins at Rocketts, iron and metals to the Tredegar Iron Works, and grain, flour, and produce to Samuel Hicks on Cary Street. Indeed, individuals and auxiliary organizations from Goochland, Louisa, Orange, Albemarle, and Prince Edward counties, the city of Lynchburg, and as far away as eastern Tennessee responded to the association's appeal with money and materials. Contributions of iron and other metals were so prolific that Tredegar's owner expressed pleasant surprise at the result.[49]

In the spring of 1863, however, the activities of the association stalled. On April 9, the board met and voted to turn over all available iron and money to Secretary Mallory "and request Mr. Mallory to act for the Society." Later that month, the association turned over to the naval secretary nearly $18,000 in funds. Mallory told a committee that, although work on the ship was proceeding rapidly, iron was "wanting," and he appealed for further donations of the metal. By the end of the following month, the association agreed weekly meetings were "useless," and the board decided to meet only when called. According to one estimate, the Richmond "gunboat association" raised over $30,000 toward the construction of the *Virginia II*, a worthy sum that assisted materially in the construction of the ship.[50]

Work progressed just as slowly on the *Fredericksburg*, a vessel designed and supervised by Chief Constructor John Porter. Despite the advantageous location of the Richmond yards, the chronic shortage of raw materials and labor, occasional transportation snafus, and natural disasters delayed completion of the ships. A Confederate soldier in Richmond in early March 1863 wrote of the "urgency" and the constancy of labor at the ship yards and other "Government shops" in Richmond: "they do not stop for Sunday down in the dock at Rocketts, but continue to hammer away on the ironclads on that day as earnestly as upon any other day."[51]

Despite delays experienced by both work crews, the *Fredericksburg* and *Virginia II* were ready for launching in June of 1863. It was not an auspicious beginning for the former ship. Lieutenants Robert Minor and Hunter Davidson rushed back from Drewry's Bluff on June 6 to the yard at Rocketts "just in time," Minor wrote, "to see the "'Fredericksburg' refuse to enter her proper element and after trying for two hours to get her into the water, the attempt was abandoned for the present. . . . Mallory was on board [expressly] to be launched in her but as it was 'no go' he had to give up his idea of adding importance to the ceremony." A week later on June 11, however, the second attempt to launch went smoothly, and Minor was there to participate and describe it:

> The "Fredericksburg" (iron clad steamer) was launched beautifully today from the Navy Yard at Rocketts and as a native of the dear old place I christened her on touching the water while the spectators greeted her entrance upon her proper element with cheer upon cheer. 'Twas a beautiful sight, as she glided majestically into the river with her flags flying amid the plaudits of [those] who thus witnessed the launching of the first man-of-war on the waters of the James river.[52]

While the birth of the recalcitrant *Fredericksburg* proved troublesome, the launching of the *Virginia II* was, according to the *Richmond Whig*, "accomplished without delay or difficulty at the time appointed" on June 29. "She glided into the water 'like a thing of life' amid the prolonged cheers of the spectators."[53]

As they had with the *Richmond*, Federal informants reported accurately on the launching of the two new ironclads. Typical of the information provided by these informants, much of it was in error. The names of the ships were incorrectly transmitted (the *Fredericksburg* was described as the *Chickahominy*, and the *Virginia II* as the *Lady Davis*), and the information estimated one of them would be ready for service soon. The reality of the situation, however, was considerably different. Even though they had been launched, both ships were still far from serviceable. The primary reason for the lengthy delay was the chronic shortage of iron. As the ships were still being framed and skinned on the ways, Tredegar was producing large quantities of iron, spikes, and boiler plate and transporting them to the "Richmond Navy Yard" for the *Fredericksburg,* and across the toll bridge over the James for the "Ladies Gun Boat." By the spring of 1863, however, Anderson was forced to inform Secretary Mallory that work on armor plate had ceased because no iron was available. With Tredegar unable to produce iron for both ships simultaneously, navy officials apparently opted to finish the *Fredericksburg* first, and she was fully clad by the end of autumn 1863. The *Virginia II* demanded substantially more iron, however, since she was designed for up to eight inches of plating on the ends of her casemate.[54]

Early 1864 found Richmond's naval yards and industries struggling to finish both vessels. A Confederate deserter reported as of late January that the *Fredericksburg* was "lying under the shears," presumably receiving her guns, while the *Virginia*, known in some quarters as the *Lady Davis*, still awaited her battery and "mail" (iron plates). In early March 1864, Joseph Anderson wrote Mallory that Graves had visited Tredegar that morning inquiring about the 65 tons of eight-by-one-inch iron still required for the *Virginia*. Anderson promised that Tredegar would finish half the next week, and the last of it the week thereafter. Other problems continued to plague the completion of the boats. The rainy spring months of 1864 flooded the James River, further disrupting work on the ships. "All the new wharves at Rocketts and the new Navy Yard were under water," reported the *Daily Dispatch*, "and at the latter place great quantities of valuable lumber was in danger of being washed away." Robert Minor returned to his office in the Naval Ordnance works to find more than a foot of water. "[A] double banded VII inch Brooke gun looked like a great whale lying as it did nearly submerged in the water, in which boxes, plank, timbers, etc., etc., were floating about in the most admirable disorder."[55]

Though the *Fredericksburg* and the *Virginia II* were the last ironclads completed at the Richmond yards, work progressed until the last days of the Confederacy on several other vessels, particularly the *Texas*. Described by a Federal naval officer as "[o]ne of the best and most valuable hulls built by the Rebels," the *Texas* benefited from the growing experience of Confederate ship designers and builders. Mallory reported in the fall of 1864 on the progress of the ships under construction at Richmond. The *Texas*, which Mallory described as an ironclad steamer "216 feet in length, to mount four heavy guns under a short citadel [casemate] which is to be plated with an armor 6 inches thick," had just been launched. "The engines and boilers for this vessel are all in readiness and of the best kind," reported Mallory, "and from her fine model there is no doubt but she will prove an excellent vessel, with good speed, etc." Also on the stocks at Richmond, reported the naval secretary, "was an ironclad ram with a short citadel and one gun. This vessel is intended for light draft, has four propellers, two in each end, with four engines. She is also fitted with a ram on both ends and is intended to move either way. Her machinery is being constructed at the Naval Works in this place also." Designed and constructed by William Graves, the unnamed ironclad ram remained unfinished and was burned on the stocks (presumably at the southside shipyard) when Richmond fell to the enemy in April 1865. Four torpedo boats, in addition to ironclad ships, were under construction in Richmond at the time of Mallory's report. He described them as "well advanced in their hulls and machinery." Two other torpedo boats of the same class (the *Hornet* and *Wasp*), had been put in service earlier in 1864.[56]

In addition to shortages of iron and other logistical problems, the requirement that Richmond's shipyard workers serve in local defense forces further delayed construction of ships already in progress in 1863 and 1864. In June 1863 employees of the yards and supporting works were organized as the 4th (Naval) Battalion of Virginia Local Defense Troops. As commander of the five-company battalion, Lt. Robert Minor held the concurrent rank of army major. The additional time and effort required in organizing, outfitting, drilling, and calling these units into service further drained valuable time and energy away from the business at hand. Secretary Mallory complained a few months later that "The frequent calls upon the workmen employed by the Navy Department to defend the city against the Yankees have greatly retarded the work for several months past, and which is still the case."[57] Unfortunately for the Confederate cause, the situation only worsened when later in 1864 Federal forces arrived at the gates of Richmond.

Despite the myriad of problems, the construction of ironclad vessels represented both the greatest triumph for the Confederate navy—and its greatest tragedy. During the war the Confederacy laid down over 50 ironclad vessels, but completed only 22.[58] Though it invariably took longer than anticipated, mobilizing the raw materials and resources for that many vessels was no mean feat. But, as Stephen Mallory, John Brooke and the officers of the Confederate navy were painfully aware, most of the ironclads suffered from fatal flaws, usually weak and unreliable engines or excessive draft. The ultimate tragedy (and bitter irony) for the Confederates, however, was that most of their ironclads were destroyed by Southern torches in order to keep them out of enemy hands. Only one of the 22 completed and commissioned Confederate ironclads, the *C.S.S. Albemarle*, was destroyed by the enemy. Several others, most notably the much-bloodied Mississippi River ram *Arkan-*

sas, were all but destroyed in action by the time their crews destroyed them. Three others were surrendered, while the remaining ships were scuttled or blown up by retreating Confederate forces. Many other ironclads were in the final stages of construction when they were destroyed by their creators.

Secretary Mallory was rudely reminded of these unpleasant facts by Maggie Howell, the saucy-tongued young sister-in-law of President Davis. The story of the Howell-Mallory exchange was recorded by War Department clerk and *bon vivant* Thomas Cooper DeLeon: "Invited to inspection and lunch aboard a new ironclad, in the James, near 'Rocketts,' full praise was given by all. As we left the side the genial host said: 'Well, ladies, I have shown you everything about them.' 'Everything but one,' Miss Howell replied demurely, and to the Secretary's surprised stare, she added: 'The place where you blow them up.'"[59] It was small comfort to Mallory that most of the blowing up of Confederate vessels occurred because Federal armies captured Southern port cities, not because the Federal navy succeeded in defeating the Confederate squadrons.

The James River Squadron, 1862-1864

The Confederate navy was fortunate to have nearly two years of uninterrupted opportunity to build a squadron capable of defending the capital. As it turned out—and as the authorities could not have predicted—the shipyards in Richmond needed every day of that time to complete the ships laid down in 1862. Meanwhile, as black workers—both slave and free, skilled and unskilled—and white artisans worked all week long, and ironmakers worked when they could, ships already in the squadron pursued a dull routine plying the waters of their universe: an eight-mile stretch of the James River below the Southern capital. Only in the spring of 1864, as the two Richmond-built ironclads were fitting out and a new Federal fleet steamed upriver, was that routine finally broken.

Reflecting the city's expanded naval role, the Navy Department designated Richmond as a separate administrative unit, or station. The commander of the station, typically a senior officer, handled administrative and logistical functions in support of the squadron, but, according to navy regulations, had no authority over individual shore installations. According to some sources, command of the Richmond Naval Station became independent of the James River Squadron in April 1862, but it is not clear who exercised command of the station for most of the war. Evidence suggests that command of the station and command of the squadron often remained synonymous. Since Confederate navy regulations provided the commandant of a navy yard could also serve as station commander, it is possible Rocketts Navy Yard commandant Cdr. Robert G. Robb (about whom information is exceedingly scarce) may have been station commander for much of the war.[60]

The men who commanded the James River Squadron during the quiescent years were among the most prestigious and senior officers in the service: Capt. Sidney Smith Lee (May-November 1862), Capt. Samuel Barron (November 1862-March 1863), and Capt. French Forrest (March 1863-May 1864). The squadron commanders divided their time between Drewry's Bluff, where the ships were usually anchored, an office in Richmond, and aboard the squadron's flagship (first the *Patrick Henry*, and then the ironclad *Richmond*). Forrest apparently spent most of his time in Richmond, but came down to Drewry's Bluff several times a week to inspect the squadron.[61]

The "squadron" that these men, especially Lee, commanded in 1862 existed more on the builder's blueprints than in reality. With the sinking of the *Jamestown* in May and the Federal capture of the *Teaser* in July, the squadron was weaker than ever. The remaining ships experienced various mechanical and structural troubles that made a mockery of efforts to keep the squadron in a state of readiness. Smith Lee asked Lt. James Rochelle to make sure repairs to his ship, the *Nansemond*, were finished as soon as possible. With obvious disgust, Lee explained to Rochelle that the *Beaufort* was "broken down" and that "I never expect to see the 'Hampton' return when she goes up to Richmond." The sad state of the squadron's plight was confirmed by one of its sailors. "We are of no earthly use," Midshipman John T. Mason, of the *Hampton*, confided to a relative, and "would be of no protection to Richmond if the enemy were to force the barricade, but would share the same fate that attends all our war vessels." Mason sketched a pessimistic hypothetical scenario of the *Hampton* retreating up the James River & Kanawha Canal only to be torched by her own crew.[62] During the summer of 1862, two small vessels, the *Drewry* (which Francis Dawson had mistaken for a dredge) and the *Torpedo* (used by the navy's Submarine Battery Service) augmented the squadron's numbers if not its strength.

Only with the commissioning of the *Richmond* in early November did the squadron again possess a formidable ironclad. Because of the delays in plating and fitting out the *Fredericksburg* and *Virginia II*, the *Richmond* remained the only ironclad in operation on the James for 16 months. The only ships to join the *Richmond* in the meantime were small vessels, most notably a trio of wooden boats designed to carry and launch submarine mines, or torpedoes. Appropriately, the first ironclad warship ever to visit its namesake city, the *Richmond*, was a source of great interest. Among the first visitors to the ship was Mary Custis Lee, the wife of Gen. Robert E. Lee, who accompanied her brother-in-law, Smith Lee, to Rocketts. She went on board and later wrote to her daughter that she, "saw for the first time an ironclad ship & some Gun Boats." Despite her formidable appearance, the *Richmond* never enjoyed great respect in military circles. John Taylor Wood's skepticism over the strength of her engines proved widespread and prescient. War Department official Robert G. H. Kean went so far as to dismiss the *Richmond* as "a stupid failure." She drew too much water to clear the river obstructions and her defective machinery made her unsafe.[63]

Although the *Richmond* was not widely respected, the man assigned to command her was one of the most accomplished naval officers produced by Virginia during the mid-nineteenth century. Commander Robert Baker Pegram was a 32-year U.S. Navy veteran who had won fame in August 1855 when he rescued a British vessel from pirates in the South China Sea, an action that prompted Virginia's legislature to present him with an engraved sword. After service in Norfolk in the Virginia State Navy, Pegram commanded the cruiser *Nashville*. Although Pegram brought prestige to the James River Squadron, the bottled-up fleet was not able to make much use of his extensive experience.[64]

Even after the commissioning of the *Richmond*, however, neither the squadron nor its activity (or inactivity) impressed the naval professional.

Assistant Engineer John Horry Dent, Jr., who came to Richmond in June 1863 from the Chattahoochee River in Georgia, was made chief engineer on the gunboat *Hampton.* Dent expressed his displeasure at being assigned to the ship, which he dismissed as "nothing more than a small Tug Boat." The engine "is represented as being a regular old saw mill affair. In fact it is a miserable affair." Echoing the words of John T. Mason a year earlier, Dent wondered whether the *Hampton* would ever be of any use, aside from taking "His Majesty" (Mallory) on a "pleasure excursion" between Richmond and Drewry's Bluff. "I think our Navy is a perfect farce," Dent concluded in disgust. He later upgraded his estimate of the *Hampton*'s engines to "rather common" and "plain and simple," confessing the squadron was "one of the easiest berths I ever had."[65] The latter statement is revealing, coming as it does from a man who had just come from duty on a river nowhere near the enemy.

In 1863, the James River Squadron was able to achieve some semblance of routine, albeit a lazy routine. The vessels were anchored at Drewry's Bluff and a mile downriver at Chaffin's Bluff. Two small and unarmed steamships, the *Shrapnel* and the *A. H. Schultz*, traveled between the city and the squadron delivering mail and supplies. When those vessels were undergoing repairs, the small warships of the squadron, the *Drewry*, *Roanoke*, *Hampton* and *Nansemond*, were detailed for the duty. Although the squadron was stationed near the capital and day-to-day operations did not entail much in the way of hostile encounters, its sailors and most of its officers did not spend much time in Richmond except when in the hospital. John T. Mason, on board the *Hampton*, complained to his mother in 1862 that "I cannot even get permission to go to Richmond eight miles off. I have not been there now for a month." At least a few of the officers, however, spent most of their time in Richmond. Dent complained that the commander of the *Hampton*, Lt. John S. Maury, was "never on board more than ten minutes a day." He came down to Drewry's Bluff on the tug and returned with it to Richmond, where his wife resided.[66]

After an inauspicious beginning, the Navy Department succeeded in creating an efficient supply system for the James River Squadron. The hurried transfer of the squadron from Norfolk to Richmond created conditions bordering on chaotic. The heroes of Drewry's Bluff depended upon the citizens of Richmond for their meals. When Rochelle appealed to the Office of Provisions and Clothing for supplies in June 1862, the reply revealed just how overwhelmed the supply system was. The assistant paymaster told Rochelle there were no stores at hand, and that the nearest stores were in Charlotte, North Carolina, where they would remain until the navy found a suitable store room in Richmond. The clothing was at a local depot but, for the same reason, could not yet be stored or distributed. In the meantime, the only provisions available were requisitioned locally. Within a few days, however, the office managed to secure the warehouse of the firm Ludlam & Watson, at the corner of Lester and Ash streets in Rocketts, and made it the chief warehouse in Richmond.[67] Within a few months, food supplies in the squadron were plentiful enough to create the general impression that men in the navy ate better than their counterparts in the army.

The supply system was also efficient enough to provide officers and sailors with regulation uniforms. Despite the persistent image of Confederate soldiers and sailors dressed in makeshift, often mix-and-match uniforms, sailors in the squadron received issues of regulation Confederate naval uniforms. The Confederate navy in late 1861 adopted a regulation uniform of steel gray. Depending on the occasion, officers were to wear gray frock coats or gray jackets, and steel gray or white vests and pantaloons. Sailors' uniforms were to consist of "gray cloth jackets and trousers, or gray woolen frocks with white duck cuffs and collar, black hats, black silk handkerchiefs and shoes, or boots in cold weather." During the summer, sailors could wear white frocks, and commanders were instructed to prescribe uniforms with "proper regard for the comfort of the crew. . . ."[68]

Navy blue was the traditional color for seamen the world over, and Confederate officers were reluctant to depart from it even in the name of Southern nationalism. Officers "kicked like steers when they were afterwards compelled to don the gray, contemptuously demanding to know, 'Who had ever seen a gray sailor, no matter what nationality he served,'" remembered Midshipman James M. Morgan. As early as 1862, sailors in Richmond were nevertheless wearing the gray. Upon joining the navy in Richmond in June 1862, Francis Dawson described his uniform as gray, "with any quantity of buttons, gold lace band, etc." Dawson's future brother-in-law, Midshipman Morgan, received a cold welcome when he arrived in Richmond in May 1862 still wearing blue. As late as February 1863, the government still issued blue jackets to men in the James River Squadron. However, an April 1863 order from the Office of Orders and Detail forbade officers in Richmond from departing "from the prescribed uniform" without "sufficient reason."[69]

Along with uniform requirements came orders mandating routines for exercises, drills and inspections for the ships of the squadron. Navy regulations charged ship commanders with a vast array of responsibilities for preserving the health, safety and efficiency of their vessels, equipment and men. Captain Lee ordered the crews of every vessel to drill for a half-hour each day with the heavy guns and small arms. On Wednesdays the crews performed a full hour of small arms drill and, from 9:00 to 10:00 a.m., an hour of "General Exercise." Lee designated Mondays, Wednesdays, and Fridays as "Wash Days," and scheduled weekly inspections of the gunboats. At the behest of the Navy Department, Capt. French Forrest in July 1863 began quarterly ordnance inspections of each vessel in the squadron, while the chief engineer of the squadron, Charles Schroeder, made weekly inspections of the vessels' engines and machinery. Commanders of steam vessels had the additional responsibility of conducting their routines in a way that minimized the possibility of fire, explosion or accident. To each ship's executive officer (usually a lieutenant) fell the daily inspection of the ship and receiving reports from the master, boatswain, gunner, carpenter and sailmaker—the officers who supervised the ship's specialized jobs.[70]

Although not part of its daily routine, the squadron assisted John Brooke and the ordnance office with the testing of new guns, projectiles and armor. In the summer of 1862, Robert Minor, Lt. John R. Eggleston, and Midshipman John T. Mason conducted experiments to test the usefulness of cotton bales as armor for vessels. After firing small arms and shell guns at cotton bales placed along the foot of Drewry's Bluff, Minor concluded cotton "was among the poorest of all materials for defensive works."[71]

The routine in 1863 was that of a squadron safely out of contact with the enemy. Only on two occasions during that summer did the Federal navy venture up the James River to the vicinity of City Point, where the Appomattox flows into the James. On one of those occasions, the Federal navy learned the hard way of the effectiveness of one of the Confederate navy's latest weapons of defense. Even if the Confederate navy had wanted to engage the enemy during its rare ascents up the James, it could not have done so. The obstructions below Drewry's Bluff not only sealed out the enemy, but, in the words of a Federal officer, "hermetically sealed in" the Confederate gunboats and ironclads. While the obstructions effectively sealed in the largest warships of the squadron, the smaller vessels, *Schultz* and *Shrapnel*, along with schooners and canal lighters in the service of the navy and the army engineers, were light enough to pass over the obstructions and provide river transportation to City Point and, via the Appomattox River, to Petersburg.[72]

Conscious that the obstructions limited the squadron's usefulness, navy officials wanted to clear a passage through which the *Richmond* could proceed downriver. Thus began, as early as September 1862, a long-running, bitter feud between the Navy Department and the army engineers over the status of the river obstructions. Part of the problem was caused by the navy's own ambivalence over the relative importance of the obstructions' two purposes: to prevent the passage of the enemy but also to allow the passage of friendly vessels. Another problem was inter-service disagreement. The engineers were both skeptical of the wisdom of opening a passage, and of the navy's commitment to it. Mallory's first request, in September 1862, to clear a passage in anticipation of the *Richmond*'s completion dramatized the dilemma. Alfred Rives, of the Engineer Department, assured Chief Engineer Jeremy Gilmer an adequate passage could be cleared with 10 days notice, but noted "There is some difference of opinion as to the propriety of making the passageway, and it would certainly seem of doubtful policy to send below an ironclad vessel with inferior single-acting engine, at least if we are to form any judgment from recent disasters."[73]

In response to Mallory's second request (in April 1863) to clear an opening, Gilmer observed that even if the *Richmond* could pass the obstructions, there were two bars in the James River she could pass only in flood stage. Furthermore, Gilmer wrote, the *Richmond's* speed and engines were "defective," and thus he recommended opening a passage only when a second ironclad was completed. Though many naval officers shared Gilmer's assessment of the *Richmond*, Mallory was understandably perturbed to learn a year later why the engineers had delayed opening a passage. Captain Charles Mason, commanding the engineers at Drewry's Bluff, revealed not a little contempt for the navy when in August 1863 he observed to his commander, Col. Walter H. Stevens that "the Excitement on the part of the navy with regard to [the obstructions] is periodical." At that point, the "excitement" was a fear the obstructions were not adequate to prevent passage upriver by enemy vessels. Mason assured Stevens they were sufficient, but for the sake of appearances, he ordered more stones added to a few of the cribs.[74]

The war of words escalated with the coming of the new year and the near completion of the *Fredericksburg*. In response to Mallory's repeated requests to open a passage, Secretary of War James Seddon queried the engineers and learned work toward that end was proceeding as quickly as winter floods allowed. The continued delays in fitting out the *Fredericksburg* and plating the *Virginia II* undermined the Navy Department's effort to coordinate the opening of a passage with the completion of the ships. Finally, Mallory informed the engineers in March 1864, that the *Virginia II* would be finished in six weeks and that a passage sufficient for that vessel must be opened by that time. According to her builder, William Graves, the *Virginia II* had "the greatest breadth of any vessel we have at this time" (47 feet), and he asked Charles Mason to make sure that the passage would be large enough for her. Still worried over premature opening of a passage, the engineers offered to construct a "'caisson'" which could plug the gap if necessary, and kept the towing vessel *Falconer* available for that purpose. Acutely aware there would be hell to pay if the passage were not ready, Stevens told Mason a few weeks later the gap should be finished a week before the target date, and urged him to "put it through at once and as fast as possible." May 1864 found the obstructions still impassable for Confederate ironclads.[75]

Cdr. John Mercer Brooke

"[W]hatever success attended the efforts of the Confederate Navy was, in no small degree due to your skill and ability," wrote Secretary Mallory after the war to John Brooke (1826-1906). It was Brooke who convinced Mallory that the South had the capacity to construct its own ironclad ships of war. Proving his point, Brooke oversaw the conversion of the *USS Merrimack* into the *CSS Virginia*. A dispute with John L. Porter over credit for the design, however, dampened his enthusiasm for the entire ironclad program. Energetic and intense but with a tendency to brood, Brooke suffered numerous personal problems during the war, including the death of his wife. In addition to his achievements with the *Virginia*, he designed, tested and perfected several naval artillery guns and projectiles, and armored shields for ships and land batteries. Courtesy of The University Press of Virginia and The Library of Virginia.

A view of Rocketts from Libby Hill, April 1865

(Opposite page). The only Civil War-era photographs of the Confederate navy yards were taken—by Mathew Brady or his assistant, or Levy & Cohen of Philadelphia—after the Federal capture of the city. On the near (north) side of the James River is Rocketts. A few residences and businesses of the Rocketts neighborhood are visible in the left foreground. The Rocketts landing, with its permanent sheds or shelters, can be seen near the right edge of the photo. Visible in middle of the photo is the captured Confederate artillery shown on page xiii.

Across the river is the yard (usually called the "Yard opposite Rocketts") where the *C.S.S. Virginia II* was constructed. On the point of land to the left are ways used for constructing the wooden frame of vessels. The unfinished vessel on the ways was probably an unnamed ironclad warship designed by William A. Graves. On the beach directly across the river are additional ways where a smaller vessel (probably a torpedo boat) was under construction. Archaeologists have recently discovered the foundations of the substantial building near the right side of the photograph. To the right of that structure (just beyond the frame of the photograph) were buildings and tents which were probably used by the laborers at the southside yard.

The vessels in the river are Federal ships. The sunken ship visible at the far left of both photographs is probably the Confederate school ship *Patrick Henry*. Courtesy of the Library of Congress.

Lt. Robert Dabney Minor

While he spent most of the war as superintendent of the Richmond Naval Ordnance Works, "Bob" Minor (1826-1871) saw active service as flag lieutenant aboard the *Virginia* (*Merrimac*) in 1862 and the *Virginia II* in 1864. As an ordnance specialist, he traveled throughout the Confederacy on inspection trips. Detached from the ordnance works in 1863 for special assignment, Minor was to be second-in-command of the aborted expedition from Canada to rescue Confederate prisoners of war at Johnson's Island, Ohio. Described as "a real Christian. . .gay as a lark," Minor was one of the most popular officers in the Confederate Navy. Crayon drawing by McMethvin.

Lt. John Henry Parker

Virginian John Parker (1822-1905) had to wait eight months before he could offer his services to his native state. A career naval officer since 1836, Parker was on board the *U.S.S. Dacotah* in the Far East when the war broke out. His entire Confederate service was spent on special assignment in Richmond, most of it as chief of the Office of Special Services and in charge of the navy yard opposite Rocketts. From an ambrotype.

Capt. French Forrest

Captain French Forrest (1796-1866) was a distinguished U.S. Navy officer, who, according to a brother officer, "literally did not know the meaning of the word fear." As a high-ranking Confederate officer, Forrest had little opportunity to show his fearlessness. Forrest commanded the Norfolk Navy Yard under Virginia and Confederate authority and held dual command of the Richmond Station and the James River Squadron during a prolonged period of inactivity. Library of Congress.

Although he never commanded a major vessel in the James River Squadron, Rochelle (1826-1889) commanded the ironclad *Palmetto State* in the Charleston Squadron and served on the James as commander of the *Teaser* and gunboat *Nansemond*. A protégé of John Randolph Tucker, Rochelle was Tucker's executive officer on the *Patrick Henry* during the battle of Hampton Roads. In the last days of Confederate Richmond, Rochelle was again aboard the *Patrick Henry* as commandant of midshipmen. Scharf, *Confederate States Navy*.

Lt. James H. Rochelle

Cdr. Robert Baker Pegram

Famed for his 1855 rescue of a British ship from pirates in the South China Seas, Pegram (1811-1894) made his mark in the Confederacy as commander of the commerce raider *Nashville*. As commander of the first Richmond-built ironclad, *C.S.S. Richmond*, during the quiet period between the fall of 1862 and the spring of 1864, Pegram had little opportunity to further burnish his reputation. He left the James River in the late summer of 1864 for England, where he acted as agent for the Virginia Volunteer Navy Association, a joint-stock venture. Pre-war ambrotype.

Capt. Frederick Chatard

Marylander Frederick Chatard was a commander in the United States Navy with 37 years experience when he decided to cast his lot with the Confederacy in 1861. Appointed to the rank of captain, Chatard spent most of his Confederate service on land. He was considered an expert in heavy artillery, and was accordingly given command of the batteries on the Potomac River in 1862, and at Drewry's Bluff in 1862-1864. His last assignment was in Richmond as chief of the naval recruiting service. Carte-de-visite published by Bendann Brothers, Baltimore, Maryland.

Officers of the James River Squadron, 1862-1863

All of the officers on this and the following pages served at Richmond Station or on ships in the James River Squadron during its two-year period of inactivity. Like many of the images throughout this book, these photographs are reproduced here for the first time.

Midshipman Irvine Stephen Bulloch served on the *Nansemond* in 1862; Midshipman James H. Dyke on the school ship *Patrick Henry* and ironclad *Richmond* in 1862; Passed Assistant Surgeon James W. Herty served on the ironclad *Richmond* in 1862; Assistant Surgeon George Weldon Claiborne at Richmond Station in 1863; Midshipmen Orris A. Browne on the *Patrick Henry* in 1862-1863; Midshipman John Thompson Mason on the *Hampton* in 1862-1863; Asst. Engineer William Hutchinson Jackson, Midshipman William C. Whittle, Jr., and Engineer's Mate E. G. Whitney all saw service at Richmond Station in 1862.

After their months of inactive service, these men (all but Claiborne) went on to spend the latter years of their Confederate service on commerce raiders: Bulloch on the *Alabama*; Dyke on the *Florida* and *Rappahannock*; Herty on the *Rappahannock* and *Stonewall*; Jackson on the *Florida*, *Rappahannock*, and *Stonewall*; Browne, Mason and Whittle on the *Shenandoah*. Lieutenant William H. Murdaugh commanded the *B*eaufort in 1862-1863 before he, too, went on service abroad. The photographs of all these officers were made while stationed abroad.

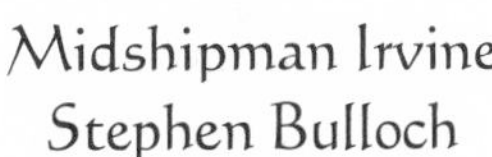

Midshipman Irvine Stephen Bulloch

Carte-de-visite, ca. 1863-1865.

Midshipman James H. Dyke

Carte-de-visite by Mage Freres, Rue de Siam, Brest, France, ca. 1863-1865.

Passed Asst. Surgeon James W. Herty

Carte-de-visite by De La Chaperonniere, Calais, France, ca. 1863-1865.

Asst. Surgeon
George Weldon Claiborne

Carte-de-visite courtesy of Charles V. Peery.

Asst. Engineer
William H. Jackson

Carte-de-visite
courtesy of Charles V. Peery.

Midshipmen
Orris A. Browne,
John Thompson Mason,
and William C. Whittle, Jr.,
serving aboard the
Shenandoah

Carte-de-visite, ca. 1865.

Engineer's Mate
E. G. Whitney

Carte-de-visite by Quayle & Gault, Hamilton, Bermuda, 1864, signed on reverse: "Your affectionate friend E. G. Whitney—Charleston, S.C./Fort "Lafayette." N. Y. Harbor/Sept. 18, 1864. Courtesy of Charles V. Peery.

Midshipman John Thompson Mason

Carte-de-visite by C. Ferranti, Photographer, Liverpool, England, ca. 1865.

Lt. William H. Murdaugh

Carte-de-visite by "A," 10, Rue Villedo, Paris, France, ca. 1863-1865.

DEFENSIVE.

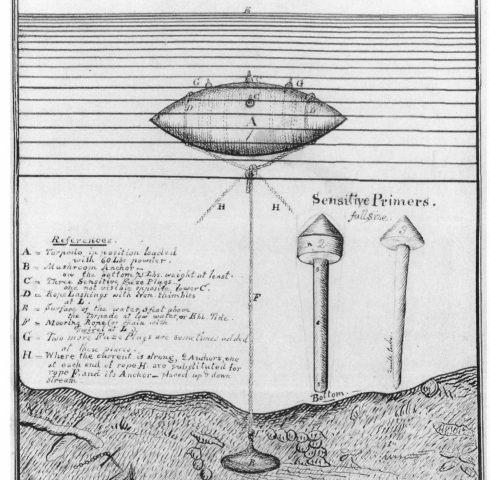

Sensitive Primers.

full size.

References.

A = Torpedo in position loaded with 60 Lbs powder.

B = Mushroom Anchor — on the bottom 75 Lbs. weight at least.

C = Three Sensitive Fuze Plugs — one not visible opposite lower C.

D = Rope Lashings with iron thimbles at L.

E = Surface of the water, 3 feet above the Torpedo at low water, or Ebb Tide.

F = Mooring Rope (or chain with swivel at L.)

G = Two more Fuze Plugs are sometimes added at these places.

H = Where the current is strong, 2 Anchors, one at each end of rope H. are substituted for rope F, and its Anchor — placed up & down stream.

Chapter 4

Marines, Mines and Midshipmen in Confederate Richmond

When Richmond inherited Norfolk's naval mantle in the spring of 1862, the capital city became the center not only for the shipyard facilities and the James River Squadron, but for other branches of naval service, including the Confederate States Marine Corps. The headquarters for the corps and its primary recruiting center were already located in Richmond, and in 1862, the city—specifically Drewry's Bluff—became the largest and most important marine post in the Confederacy.

Established by an act of Congress on March 16, 1861, the Confederate States Marine Corps was intended, like its Federal counterpart, to be an adjunct to the navy. Although authorized up to 990 men and officers, for a variety of reasons the corps never reached a strength of more than 600. The marines were distributed in small contingents to naval installations and aboard vessels of squadrons throughout the South.[1]

Upon the Confederate abandonment of Norfolk in May 1862, two 80-man companies of marines that recently had been assigned to Norfolk made their way to Richmond. They accompanied sailors from the *Virginia*, and with them participated in the defense of Drewry's Bluff.

The two companies, organized into a battalion under the command of Capt. John D. Simms, acted as sharpshooters on the south bank of the James River during the battle of May 15. A third company of marines (out of a total of six in the entire corps) transferred to the post from Georgia in the summer of 1862.[2] Thus, a station established primarily out of expedience soon became the permanent post for over half of the Confederate States Marine Corps.

With the establishment of the station came tangible signs of permanence. The marines called their home on Drewry's Bluff "Camp Beall," named after the Marine Corps commandant, Col. Lloyd Beall. For several months the camp consisted of nothing more than tents, and was, Beall himself complained, a "bleak and exposed position." By autumn of 1862, Beall had secured permission to build permanent barracks. As winter approached, the barracks were still not finished, so the men dug pits in which to place their tents to provide shelter from the stiff winds blowing off the river. Completed by January 1863, the Marine Corps barracks were the main structures of what a naval midshipman later described as "quite a little village" at Drewry's Bluff. That "village" included not only barracks, but two small chapels, and such facilities as a "government shoemaker." Camp Beall, with its white-washed cabins, walkways, and flower and vegetable gardens, was by all accounts one of the most pleasant and comfortable stations in the South.[3]

The marines at Drewry's Bluff were not simply a static garrison for the defense of that post, but constituted instead a pool that was drawn upon for other existing needs. Beginning with the commissioning of the *Richmond* in the fall of 1862, scores of the marines were assigned to vessels and facilities in Richmond. In February 1863, a guard of about 20 men was assigned to the navy yard opposite Rocketts, while a slightly larger contingent was assigned to the Rocketts yard in September 1863. Those transferred to Rocketts were under the authority of the navy yard commandant, Robert Robb.[4]

Consistent with their traditional roles, most of the marines stationed in and around the Southern capital were assigned to Confederate warships as they were commissioned into service. The original *Virginia* carried a large contingent consisting of 54 marines, while her companion vessels in the early James River Squadron, the *Patrick Henry* and the

Jamestown, carried 20 and 46 marines, respectively. The marine guards aboard the three James River Squadron ironclads—*Richmond*, *Fredericksburg* and *Virginia II*—were considerably smaller, consisting of approximately 20-25 officers and men each.[5] The squadron never fought a pitched naval battle which required the boarding of enemy vessels or the defense of friendly ships with small arms. Thus, the role of the squadron's marines, much like that of its sailors, was often as an auxiliary land force, and its routine consisted of preparation for battles that never came.

Those Damned Torpedoes: Mine and Submarine Warfare

"Iron-clads are said to master the world, but torpedoes master the iron-clads."

—Brig. Gen. Gabriel Rains[6]

In the summer and autumn of 1861, in a house just a block west of the Confederate Executive Mansion, Cdr. Matthew Fontaine Maury devoted hours to setting off small explosions in a metal children's washtub filled with water. As he carried tub after tub of water up to Maury's bedroom, the family butler warned that "Marse Mat" was going to blow up the whole house. In that tub, Maury experimented with fuses and triggers developed with the assistance of Richmond industries and the best scientific minds in Virginia. The entire undertaking would have been absurd had not the purpose been so deadly serious. "It is a business," Maury wrote, "this thing of blowing up men while asleep that I don't glory in, and nothing but the implacability of the enemy would induce me to undertake it. . . ."[7] Indeed it was a business. Maury's experiments were part of a concentrated effort to perfect explosive "submarine torpedoes"—mines in today's parlance—as a means of defending the South's vulnerable rivers and harbors. Much of that experimentation occurred in Richmond, and took advantage of the city's industrial, scientific and military resources. The Confederate navy embraced torpedo warfare, along with the development and construction of ironclad ships, as a means of compensating for its severe disadvantage in warships and naval resources.

Maury's work on torpedoes and related scientific applications began immediately upon his resignation from the United States Navy and his joining the Virginia and Confederate navies. On April 22, 1861, Maury sent to New York for insulated wire to be used in his experiments. The formal severing of Virginia's ties with the old Union soon made even small orders impossible, so he had to depend upon Confederate blockade runners and divine providence for obtaining the precious cable. Maury made generous use of his contacts with local industries and scientists. The Tredegar Iron Works and the Talbott Brothers' Shockoe Foundry furnished mechanical equipment for his experiments. He established at the University of Virginia, in Charlottesville, "a laboratory in connection with the Ordnance Department" of Virginia and worked closely with a former Richmonder, Professor Socrates Maupin. The Richmond Medical College (the forerunner of the Medical College of Virginia) allowed Maury to use its laboratories, located in the same neighborhood as his Richmond residence.[8]

Maury's experiments bore fruit with a successful demonstration of a torpedo in the James River off Rocketts in early August 1861. Before a special audience consisting of Virginia's governor, John Letcher, and selected Confederate congressmen, Maury, along with his son Richard, used a gig borrowed from the *Patrick Henry* to deploy an oak keg packed with powder. Standing in the gig, the younger Maury pulled the lanyard, and later described the results: "The explosion was instantaneous; up went a column of water fifteen or twenty feet; many stunned or dead fish floated around; the officials on the wharf applauded. . . ." More important than the applause was the immediate result, for the witnesses were able to convince the Confederate Congress to appropriate $50,000 for Maury's torpedo experiments.[9]

While the Confederacy was not the first nation to experiment with torpedoes or employ them in warfare, it was—as with ironclads—the first to pioneer the effective use of torpedoes as a central element of naval strategy. The experiences of other nations had revealed imperfections in both delivery and detonation that rendered torpedoes of dubious practical value by 1861. It was in that context the Confederacy's experimentation was such a breakthrough in torpedo technology. Mid-nineteenth-century torpedoes, relatively simple devices, consisted of explosive powder-filled cylinders with conical ends. Sometimes these metal cylinders had outer shells of wood that protected the powder, but more often than not the exterior hull was made of tin. Anchored to the sea or river bottom by heavy weights, these torpedoes could be made to explode on contact with an enemy vessel. Confederate authorities were justifiably dissatisfied with this arbitrary and inefficient method of detonation, however, and determined to create torpedoes that could be used against specific ships.[10]

Two Confederate failures in July 1861, demonstrated the practical difficulties of using torpedoes. A team of sailors tried to sink United States ships in the Potomac River with a crude variety of torpedo that consisted of two iron cylinders loaded with powder and suspended from floating barrels tethered together with a 500-foot rope. The fuses failed to ignite, and the "infernal machine" was recovered by the Federal fleet. "The idea was a wicked one, but the execution clumsy," wrote the fortunate commander of the intended target, who sent the recovered torpedo to the United States Navy Yard in Washington for a "close and thorough examination."[11]

So strongly did Maury believe in the promise of torpedo warfare, he determined to lead expeditions personally. "I have acquired an influence for good in a certain way," he confided to a friend, "but in this our greatest trial," he found himself quite "powerless." All he needed was an opportunity to prove the merit of his work and undermine the baneful influence of those men (especially Stephen Mallory) whom he held responsible for his powerlessness, and for retarding development of the Confederate navy. "Papa," Maury's daughter Betty wrote in her diary in June 1861, "has a scheme to blow up the enemy vessels in the different rivers by submarine works of some kind. I do not know whether he will be able to carry it out. It is a great secret now." Maury got his chance, and on the night of July 7, 1861, led an expedition to explode torpedoes against the Federal fleet in Hampton Roads. Five small boats rowed out from Sewell's Point with a device consisting of two barrels, each containing 200 pounds of powder, connected by a 500-foot rope and held laterally stable by weights 20 feet below the surface. The Confederates set loose the barrels so that they would drift alongside a Federal ship, and set off the fuse when the rope grew taut. The party waited in vain for the explosion. The disappointed Maury later discovered that while the fuse would burn 15 feet below the water's surface, the pressure at 20 feet was too great to allow ignition.[12]

These failures led Maury to further washtub experiments designed to explode torpedoes with either a lanyard, or a battery and electric wire operated from shore. The challenge was to develop insulation and a fuse that could operate under water. Though still without an adequate supply of wire, Maury developed fuses capable of functioning underwater, and in October 1861, the Confederate navy attempted to put his device to a practical test. The expedition, led by Maury's assistant Robert Minor, resembled Maury's July failure off Sewell's Point. Minor and a few volunteers rowed close enough to the Federal warships anchored off Newport News to hear voices on the shore, and set loose barrels of powder connected by a rope. Despite Maury's careful planning, the torpedoes yet again failed to detonate. Maury, who resented not being able to lead the expedition himself, was privately "much disappointed" at this failure and blamed it on Minor for not getting close enough to the enemy ships.[13]

The James River Submarine Mystery

The problem of effective delivery of torpedoes drove Confederate naval authorities to experiment with, and successfully develop, man-powered submarine boats. Possibly with the support of Maury, New Orleans mechanics James McClintock and Baxter Watson constructed the submarine torpedo boat *Pioneer* in late 1861 and early 1862. Unfortunately for the South, however, that boat was scuttled upon the unexpected capture of New Orleans in April 1862. McClintock and Watson continued their labors in Mobile, Alabama, where they built a second version of the *Pioneer*, also known as *American Diver*, which sank in Mobile Bay in February 1863. The inventors labored on despite these setbacks, and, with the official encouragement and assistance of the Confederate navy, designed and assembled the submarine that eventually bore the name of one of her sponsors, *H. L. Hunley*. After her transport to Charleston, South Carolina, the *Hunley* became the first submarine to sink an enemy war vessel when, in February 1864, she cruised out from Breach Inlet and sent the *U.S.S. Housatonic* to the bottom. Her success was not without great cost to her operators, however, for Horace Hunley and at least 20 others went down with the vessel in at least three different accidents, including her final and only successful mission, from which no one returned.[14]

Despite widespread popular belief, Confederate submarine experiments were not confined to the *Hunley* and McClintock's earlier efforts. In late 1861, similar vessels were developed in Richmond and tested in the James River. William G. Cheeney, a New York-born former United States Navy officer subsequently commissioned in the Confederate navy, worked in the Southern capital from the late summer of 1861 through the late spring of 1862, on what was described as a "submarine boat." Records reveal that Tredegar Iron Works provided him with boiler plate, castings, bolts, cloth, timber, an air pump and articles for "diving bells." Robert Minor's notebook contains a sketch dated September 25, 1861, of a "Propeller for sub-marine Boat." Tredegar performed substantial work on this project in November, charging Cheeney's account over $3,000 for labor and over $2,000 for materials. John Brooke, who had already had several arguments with Maury over torpedoes, recorded in his diary on November 8, 1861, that "Cheeney will be ready to start on his submarine expedition soon. I fear that Com. Maury will alarm the enemy by his attempts—which have already proved unsuccessful." Whatever his reservations, Brooke authorized payment to Tredegar from the navy's "appropriation for Submarine Batteries."[15]

It was difficult to keep such a major undertaking under wraps, however, and United States secret service chief Allen Pinkerton soon caught wind of the Confederate experiment. In early November 1861, Pinkerton dispatched a female undercover operative to Richmond to investigate the river-based submarine. Later that month, "Mrs. Baker," as Pinkerton called her, was among the group of ladies and military men who witnessed a test of the submarine in the James River below Rocketts. Pinkerton related her report of the test in his postwar book, *The Spy of the Rebellion*:

> A large scow had been towed into the middle of the river, and the submarine vessel was to approach it and attach a magazine, containing nearly

> half a bushel of powder, to which was attached several deadly projectiles, and this was to be fired by a peculiarly constructed fuse, connected by a long wire coiled on board the submarine vessel.
>
> At a given signal the boat was sunk into the river, about half a mile below the scow, and shortly afterwards it began to make its way under the water towards it. The only visible sign of its existence was a large float that rested on the surface of the water, and which was connected with the vessel below, designed to supply the men that operated it with air. The float was painted a dark green, to imitate the color of the water, and could only be noticed by the most careful observer. . . .It was learned that this vessel was but a small working model of a much larger one, that was now nearly completed, and would be finished in about two weeks, and would then be taken to the mouth of the James River, to operate on the war vessels guarding that port. . . .[M]y operative was closely watching, by the aid of her glass, the movements of the boat, and she now noticed that having approached to within a few rods of the scow, it stopped, and the water 'float' which indicated its position remained motionless. After remaining in this position for a few minutes, it slowly began to recede from the scow, in the direction from whence it came.
>
> It moved steadily away some hundreds of yards, and Mrs. Baker was wondering at the seemingly long delay, when suddenly, and without any previous warning whatever, there was a terrific explosion, and the scow seemed lifted bodily out of the water and thrown high into the air. Her destruction was complete, and there was no longer any doubt that the submarine battery could be used with deadly and telling effect on the ships constituting the Federal blockading squadron.[16]

Pinkerton claimed Mrs. Baker's intelligence allowed Federal ships to take precautions and avoid the destruction which otherwise would have been their fates. Apparently in corroboration of Pinkerton's claim, *Harper's Weekly* (quoting the *New York Herald*) reported that the Federal flagship, *Minnesota*, in Hampton Roads, caught in its grappling a Rebel man-powered "infernal machine" shaped like a cigar boat and equipped with propeller and breathing apparatus, which had apparently been sent down to blow up the Federal fleet.[17]

Whether Cheeney's man-powered submarine was actually used against the Federal fleet is unclear because of discrepancies in dates. The *New York Herald* report was made on October 12—over a month before

"Mrs. Baker's" account of the Confederate "submarine battery" test, and weeks before Brooke reported that Cheeney was about to embark on his submarine expedition. Complicating the situation, is that the *New York Herald* account coincided with Robert Minor's October 9 attack using buoys and magazines. Correspondence among Federal navy officers suggests, however, the attack of that date was made by a man-powered machine. Admiral Louis M. Goldsborough, flag officer of the Federal Atlantic Blockading Squadron, reported to Navy Secretary Gideon Welles that on October 9 that "an attempt, no doubt, was made by the insurgents to get an infernal machine among our shipping here [Hampton Roads], but it was happily foiled by the alertness of the 'Lockwood.'" Goldsborough did not imply anything unusual about the October 9 attack, but, in reply to Goldsborough's warning about "submarine infernal machines," Cdr. William Smith of the ill-fated *Congress* described in detail the precautions he had taken to deal with an attack. "Should such a machine as the one that attacked the *Minnesota* approach us and come near the cable," he assured Goldsborough,

> it must be caught in the net and held there until we relieve it. Or should it pass outside the net, the tube which floats on the surface to supply the inmates with fresh air would be caught on the A spars, and the supply of fresh air cut off, causing suffocation, and if it should pass outside of the spars it would go entirely clear of the ship, doing no harm. I think this arrangement will secure us against such torpedoes.[18]

Perhaps coincidentally, as Federal officials discussed the Confederate "infernal machines," Goldsborough expressed concern about the presence in Virginia waters of a Northern-built experimental tank which, if lost, "could be so easily converted into an instrument of destruction if possessed by the enemy. . . ." The tank, remarkably similar to the submarine which allegedly attacked the *Minnesota*, had been made from a semi-submersible "cigar boat" built before the war by Baltimore inventor Ross Winans. Since Winans was suspected of secessionist sympathies, Goldsborough was nervous about his intentions. Confederate records do not clarify what variety of torpedo was used against the *Minnesota*, or whether one of the attacks were actually conducted by a manned submarine boat. It is feasible the Federals imagined that ordinary torpedoes used in Minor's attack were a man-powered submarine, and Minor himself may have omitted important details. The confusion could also be a result of more than one October 1861 submarine attack.[19]

Regardless of whether a submarine attack was actually launched against Federal ships in Hampton Roads, it is clear that Cheeney continued to work on a James River-based submarine, either the prototype or a new model. His ongoing project employed five men—one of whom can be identified as a Richmond carpenter—in December 1861 on "Submarine Batteries." An invoice from Tredegar dated May 13, 1862 (payment on which was again approved by John Brooke), listed a wide variety of supplies and services "For alterations to Submarine Boat." Among the items charged to the account were "Brass Casting for air Pump. . .Propeller & castings for gas furnace. . ." False Bows put on Boat . . .Grinding Glass for sight. . .Boiler makers making Furnace [and] Painters Painting Boat." Since the invoice also charged for work performed on the sheds at Rocketts, however, it cannot be definitively concluded all the materials listed were for the submarine boat. Despite its conclusive existence as demonstrated by both Confederate and Federal sources, the James River submarine inexplicably disappeared from the historical record.[20]

While submarine warfare in the Civil War era struck many as a violation of the rules of war, this ethical ambivalence did not prevent former Confederates from arguing over who deserved credit for developing torpedoes and submarines. Yet, despite the numerous accounts of the *Pioneer*, *Hunley* and "Davids" (semi-submersible torpedo boats in Charleston) that appeared in newspapers and magazines after the war, no one stepped forward and claimed credit for the Cheeney submarine, which apparently preceded them all. This silence invites all sorts of speculation. The most likely answer is the Cheeney submarine was, ultimately, a failure, and thus an embarrassment to its inventors. Few people wish to draw attention to personal embarrassments. William Cheeney himself became an embarrassment for the Confederate navy. After spending a few months in the Submarine Battery Service along the James, Acting Master Cheeney, C.S.N., defected to the United States in September 1862, and told the United States Government of his work.

With his defection, submarine experiments in the James River apparently ended.[21]

The Establishment of the James River Torpedo Defenses

Electric, or "galvanic," torpedoes, however, did become a mainstay of the defenses of the James River and of other Southern rivers and harbors. Matthew Maury, with the assistance of lieutenants Hunter Davidson and Robert Minor, devised by trial and error a system capable of detonating reliably to a depth of 15 feet. The technology could not initially be exploited, however, because there was not enough wire for a comprehensive galvanic torpedo system. Just as Confederate land armies benefited from captured enemy supplies, so too did Maury's Submarine bureau. On May 1, 1862, he reported that "a godsend of about 10 miles of insulated submarine wire that was lost by the enemy in the Chesapeake" fell into Confederate hands and was on its way to Richmond. The indefatigable inventor immediately put the wire to good use. Weeks after the fall of Norfolk, the destruction of the *Virginia*, the repulse of the Federal fleet at Drewry's Bluff, and the relocation of the James River squadron to Richmond, Maury was at last prepared to bolster the capital's river defenses with torpedoes.[22]

Maury personally supervised the laying of torpedoes in the James River at Chaffin's Bluff, just downstream from Drewry's Bluff. On June 19 he described the torpedo defenses in detail to Secretary Mallory. Fifteen "tanks," as he called them, made of boiler plate and each filled with between 70 and 160 pounds of powder, were arranged in three rows about 30 feet apart. These containers were in watertight wooden kegs anchored several feet below the surface by pieces of iron shell. The torpedoes in each row were to be detonated simultaneously using Wollaston electrical batteries manned on the shore. Four larger torpedoes—totalling 6,000 lbs. of gunpowder—were placed upstream, but these sank to the bottom and were to be redeployed. Maury had available materials for an additional 11 back-up torpedoes. The navy contracted subsequently with Tredegar to produce larger wrought iron mines holding up to 1,800 pounds of gunpowder.[23]

Sowing torpedos was an arduous task that required, in addition to patience and personal faith in the explosive devices, a ship suited for the assignment. Maury utilized the small gunboat *Teaser*, Lt. Hunter Davidson commanding, aided by his assistants, submarine designer and Acting Master (and soon to be deserter) Cheeney, and his own nephew, Lt. William L. Maury.

The *Teaser's* career as a torpedo boat proved short-lived. On the morning of July 4, 1862, while serving in its other novel capacity as "aircraft carrier," the vessel grounded on a mud bank near Haxall's Landing, a few miles above Harrison's Landing. As the *Teaser* waited for the water level to rise and free her from her stick anchorage, she was confronted by a Federal warship, the *Maratanza*, which promptly put a shot through the lightly-armed *Teaser's* boiler. That single shot convinced the crew that a duel with the *Maratanza* would prove one-sided, and they quickly abandoned her. The loss was crippling for the South. In their haste to abandon ship, the crew left behind the reconnaissance balloon, a supply of valuable insulated wire, and other instruments for setting out torpedoes. In addition to these important items, complete descriptions of the construction and locations of the recently-laid torpedoes (including the June 19 letter to Mallory cited above), were left behind, together with details on the construction of the ironclad *Richmond.* Replacing the *Teaser* a few months later was the *Torpedo*, a 70-foot vessel which was in essence the floating headquarters for the navy's submarine service for the remainder of the war.[24]

The sowing of torpedoes in the James marked the coming of age of Confederate torpedo technology. The Confederate government recognized the potential of torpedoes for river and harbor defense, and in 1862 created bureaus for research and development. On June 18, 1862, Brig. Gen. Gabriel J. Rains was appointed commander of the "submarine defenses of the James and Appomattox Rivers," and two days later Secretary Mallory informed Hunter Davidson that he was to "relieve Commander Maury in the charge of devising, placing, and superintending submarine batteries in the James River. . . ." Rains, an army officer and graduate of West Point, was in command of the James River torpedo defenses until relieved by Davidson in September 1862. The Confederate Congress also passed that October legislation creating a Torpedo

Bureau for the army and the Submarine Battery Service within the navy's Office of Ordnance and Hydrography.[25]

The Submarine Battery Service was a naval equivalent to partisan, or guerrilla, warfare. As Maury himself worried privately, there was something vaguely dishonorable about blowing up ships with torpedoes. So that they would not be treated as spies or guerrillas, men who joined the service were given letters signed by Secretary Mallory and President Davis identifying them as members of the Confederate States Navy who, if captured, would be exchanged for a Federal general officer.[26]

Conversely, because the effectiveness of submarine torpedoes depended upon the secrecy of their location, members of the service, upon enlistment, swore "Under no circumstances now, or hereafter, to make known to any one not employed on this service, anything regarding the methods used for arranging, or exploding its submarine batteries, excepting only, by permission of the Hon. Secy of the Navy or the Commdg. officer of said service." Sailors detailed from the navy to the Submarine Battery Service were stationed at observation posts and detonators along the banks of the James River for several miles below Chaffin's Bluff. They were responsible for monitoring the torpedoes and the networks of wires connecting them to the shore, and for preparing smaller keg mines and detonator devices.[27]

Ironically, the establishment of the Submarine Battery Service marked the passing of Matthew Fontaine Maury from the story of the Confederate navy on the James River. The man immortalized on Richmond's Monument Avenue was a thorn in the side of the Confederate government, especially for Secretary Mallory. The two men had been feuding since the 1850s when then-Senator Mallory endeavored to retire Maury from the United States Navy. The feud was heightened by Maury's political maneuvering on behalf of his "Big guns, Little ships" proposal, and by Maury's criticism of the government in newspaper articles published under the pseudonym "Ben Bow." Maury's stature in naval circles presented Mallory with the challenge of finding an appropriate role for him within the evolving military structure of the Confederacy. In June 1862, Mallory decided to send Maury to Europe, where he could use his international reputation and contacts to acquire materials for torpedo work and for other naval purposes. He sailed for Europe in

October 1862 as his protégé, Hunter Davidson, assumed command of the new Submarine Battery Service. Maury did not return to America until after the end of the war.[28]

Though Maury was out of country and out of the riverine torpedo picture, his work was carried on by Davidson, and his faith in the usefulness of torpedoes was soon vindicated. Maury's successor was well suited to the task. A native of Georgetown, District of Columbia, Hunter Davidson entered the U.S. Navy as a midshipman in 1841 and served on the *U.S.S. Preble* with several of his future Confederate compatriots, most notably Robert Minor. At the time of the South's secession, Davidson was an instructor at the U.S. Naval Academy. As a lieutenant in the Confederate navy, Davidson had commanded one of *Virginia*'s guns during the battles of Hampton Roads. With his friends, Bob Minor and Catesby Jones, Davidson subsequently drew specialty assignments in ordnance technology. From the summer of 1862 until late 1864, when he went to Europe to serve with the French-built ironclad *Stonewall*, Hunter Davidson and the Submarine Battery Service were virtually synonymous.[29]

Davidson was confident as long as his battery service had a sufficient supply of powder he could obstruct Southern rivers against any enemy. He was especially pleased with an improved electrical battery devised by the service's electrical expert, R. O. Crowley. Davidson tested the Crowley-Boynton galvanic battery on the James River in late 1862 by exploding tanks holding 75 and 200 pounds of powder under 10-ton sloops. The larger tank sent up a 75-foot column of water and fragments of the sloop 100 feet into the air. "I don't believe you can find a Yankee to risk a blowing up," he wrote to his friend and late *Virginia* comrade, Catesby Jones.[30]

Davidson's bravado notwithstanding, in the summer of 1863, a few "Yankee" vessels did take the risk and ascend the James. Unlike 1862, the Federal fleet did not ascend the river with the expectation of bombarding Richmond into submission, but with orders from the Federal Navy Secretary "to make such a demonstration up the James River as in your judgment would be advisable, in view of the desire of the Government to threaten Richmond by that approach to assist military movements in the vicinity." An expedition in July ascended only to Fort

Powhatan, 25 miles below Richmond. A second expedition in early August ventured past Powhatan to the stretch downriver from Drewry's Bluff which meanders through a series of bends and necks. The Federal ships exchanged fire with Confederate infantry on shore before continuing upriver.[31]

The Confederate torpedo stations on the James consisted of pairs of tanks, each filled with 1,000 pounds of powder. These receptacles were submerged in 12 feet of water, and connected by wire to a galvanic battery stored in a small hut on shore, and thence by wire to a lookout station on high ground. The man stationed as lookout was able to sight the torpedoes using posts set in the water and aligned on the shore. In what can only be described as a stroke of great fortune, the ascent of the Federal fleet on August 5, 1863, took place with the entire Confederate torpedo service away on business in Richmond—save for one inexperienced lookout. The spotter apparently crossed the wires and exploded the mines prematurely. According to the senior Federal fleet's officer, the torpedoes exploded under the starboard bow of the gunboat *Commodore Barney*, "producing a lively concussion and washing the decks with the agitated water." Twenty men were washed overboard and two of them apparently drowned, while an officer on board was killed and three other seamen wounded. The ship's steam pipe was severed, disabling it temporarily. Although disappointed at losing an opportunity to destroy an enemy vessel, Crowley believed disabling the *Commodore Barney* "established the reputation of the Torpedo Bureau." Apparently forgetting about the Confederate defenses at Drewry's Bluff, Crowley claimed later that "but for this explosion a Federal gunboat would have been moored at the wharf in Richmond that morning, and would have captured the city."[32]

By the last year of the war, the Submarine Battery Service also had at its disposal the service of several specially-designed "torpedo boats," in addition to the tender *Torpedo*. These "Squib class" torpedo boats, named after the first such vessel built under these specifications, were 46 feet long and just over six feet wide. Four vessels of this class, the *Squib*, *Hornet*, *Scorpion*, and *Wasp*, were constructed at Richmond and put into service in the James River Squadron. Two others were still being constructed at the Richmond yards in April 1865. These small ships were armed with a single torpedo suspended from a 16-foot-long oak boom, or spar, which the crew raised and lowered using a chain and tackle. Equipped with sensitive tubes which exploded on contact, spar torpedoes could be placed against the hull of an enemy vessel and exploded after the attacking ship had withdrawn sufficiently to avoid being destroyed by its own charge. Lieutenant William Parker took a spin in the *Squib* not long after she was completed. He was impressed when the vessel traveled at 3/4 speed (about 10 miles per hour), she "made absolutely no noise."[33]

Hunter Davidson himself commanded the *Squib* in an attack on what seemed the Confederates' favorite target, the *U.S.S. Minnesota*, anchored off Newport News on April 9, 1864. In contrast to the earlier failure of floating barrels and of the mystery submarine, the *Squib* succeeded in exploding a torpedo with 53 pounds of powder against the Federal warship. Ignoring cries to halt from sailors aboard the *U.S.S. Roanoke*, Davidson and his crew of seven men lowered the spar six feet under water and steamed toward the *Minnesota*. "I never beheld such a sight before, nor since," recalled one of the *Squib's* crewmen, Acting Master John Curtis. "The air was filled with port shutters and water from the explosion, and the heavy ship was rolling to the starboard." The *Squib* was dragged under by the roll, but escaped when the *Minnesota* rolled back to port, badly damaged but still afloat. Although the dangerous mission won Davidson promotion to commander "for gallant and meritorious conduct," he did not believe he received proper recognition for this and other deeds.[34]

The spar torpedo became the weapon of choice for both navies in the last years of the war. More spectacular than the *Squib's* minor success against the *Minnesota* were the crippling of the Federal ironclad *New Ironsides* by the Confederate torpedo boat *David* in Charleston in October 1863, and the sinking of the feared Confederate ironclad *Albemarle* in North Carolina in October 1864 by Lt. William B. Cushing. Acting Constructor William Graves, an authority in the design of torpedo vessels, also became an expert in designing protective rigging, which anchored Confederate vessels utilized to avoid a repetition of the *Albemarle* disaster. By 1864, when opposing fleets again confronted each other on the James River, torpedoes had transformed the landscape of river warfare. The river channel between the fleets was littered with such weapons and defenses—the naval equivalent of entrenchments and abatis. Sunken vessels, piles, and torpedoes lurked in the channel just below the water line, while outriggings, nets, chains, and spars extended from and between the ships themselves.[35]

The last two years of the war proved the effectiveness of torpedoes, both as weapons of destruction and as deterrents to the Federal fleet on the James River and throughout the South. The Confederates used electrically-detonated torpedoes only in the James River and in the Cape Fear River, Wilmington, North Carolina, and employed other kinds of torpedoes in the Confederacy's surviving port cities. Roving torpedo expert Gabriel Rains was assigned to Charleston in September 1863, and working with Gen. P. G. T. Beauregard, made the waters and beaches of Charleston harbor the most heavily mined in the South. A year later, Rains was given ultimate charge of all torpedo operations in the Confederacy. Mobile, Alabama, one of the last major Southern cities to fall to the Federals, was protected by a formidable barrier of torpedoes even after the defeat of the Confederate squadron at the Battle of Mobile Bay in August 1864. Confederate torpedoes sank nine United States Navy ships in the waters around Mobile. Federal ships in the James experienced firsthand the deadly effect of Confederate torpedoes when they ascended the river in May 1864.[36]

Annapolis on the James: The Confederate States Naval Academy

If the Submarine Battery Service exemplified the Confederate navy's dedication to technological innovation, its officers revealed their commitment to service tradition with the creation of a naval academy. Not only were Confederate officers familiar with the U.S. Navy's system of education, but nearly all had experienced it firsthand, and many had been instrumental in establishing it. Before 1836, education for U.S. naval officers was procured in the field. During that year, a naval training school was founded at the Naval Asylum in Philadelphia, the establishment of a permanent U.S. Naval Academy in Annapolis, Maryland, following nine years later in 1845. Its organizer and first superintendent was Capt. Franklin Buchanan, a Maryland native who subsequently cast his lot with the South and commanded the *Virginia* during her epic battle in Hampton Roads. In addition to Buchanan, the academy's commandant for three of its first six years was Capt. Sidney Smith Lee, Robert E. Lee's brother. Midshipmen who entered the service after 1840 were assigned to Annapolis for formal education. The first class entered in 1846, and upon successful completion of their studies received the rank of "passed midshipman" in 1847. Just as the officers that had passed through West Point developed close ties, so too did those men trained in the rigors of the Naval Academy at Annapolis after 1846. Despite the forged links of friendship that bound them from their Annapolis days, many later found themselves confronting former comrades in naval combat.[37]

Realizing the necessity of superior naval training, the Confederate Congress in December 1861 passed a bill mandating "that some form of education be established for midshipmen." A second law specified that a naval academy be established, and that 106 acting midshipmen be appointed. On the very day that her crew manned the guns in battle on May 15, 1862, at Drewry's Bluff, the passenger ship-turned-warship *Patrick Henry* was redesignated as the Confederate States Naval Academy school ship. The Academy was not formally established, however, until the late summer of 1863.[38]

In the meantime, midshipmen were trained much as they had been in the U.S. Navy before the opening of the academy at Annapolis: they were appointed, examined physically and academically, assigned to vessels throughout the South, and trained while on active duty. Evidencing Mallory's commitment to a naval academy, the Navy Department in the spring of 1862 sent what was described as a "roving board" of officers to Richmond and other Southern ports to examine midshipmen—many of whom were formerly midshipmen at the United States Naval Academy at Annapolis—now assigned to the Southern squadrons. Not all the midshipmen were pleased with Mallory's dedication. "I must say I think the Department might find some better occupation than examining Acting Mid[shipme]n," complained John T. Mason, a young midshipsman stationed aboard the *Hampton* on the James River.[39]

The task of organizing the academy fell to the Office of Ordnance and Hydrography, specifically to John Brooke, and to the academy's first and only superintendent, Lt. William Harwar Parker. Parker was fully suited to the task and brought an impressive resume to the position. Entering the U.S. Navy in 1841, he was among the midshipmen ordered to Annapolis in 1847 to receive formal instruction. After graduating from that institution the following year, he returned to the academy in 1855, while still a midshipsman to begin a three-year stint as instructor, a position that demonstrated his aptitude for naval matters. Although his older brother remained loyal to the Union, Parker resigned his commision in 1861 to serve in the virtually nonexistent Confederate navy. His baptism of fire arrived while in command of the gunboat *C.S.S. Beaufort* during an unsuccessful attempt to defend Roanoke Island in February 1862. He captained the same vessel on the James River during the battle of Hampton Roads, where he witnessed the clash between the *Virginia* and *Monitor*. Shortly afterward he was transferred to the Charleston Squadron, where he found himself executive officer of the ironclad *C.S.S. Palmetto State*. His sojourn in Charleston garnered invaluable firsthand experience in the handling of an ironclad in battle. Parker's warship, together with another ironclad, ventured forth on January 31, 1863, in a desperate sortie out of the harbor against the Federal blockading fleet. While at Charleston that June, Parker received a dispatch from Mallory directing him "to make out an estimate for books, apparatus, etc., necessary for the establishment of a naval school." After he prepared the estimate and sent it to the Confederate purchasing agent in England, he received orders "to report in person at the Navy Department in Richmond." Parker prepared regulations for the academy "school-ship," which Brooke and Mallory approved in late July. At the same time, the shipyard at Rocketts finished converting the interior of the *Patrick Henry* to serve as a floating school and dormitory. Midshipmen occupied its modified quarters in August 1863.[40]

A midshipman's formal education, usually divided between the training ship and the squadrons, could last as long as four years, although he could achieve graduation sooner. Midshipmen were examined semi-annually and, should cause exist, advanced more than one class at a time. As in the U.S. Navy, midshipmen who completed their course of study and passed their examinations graduated from the rank of acting midshipman to passed midshipman. By the spring of 1864, many of the midshipmen formerly at the United States Naval Academy (and 29 midshipmen appointed to the Confederate Academy) had graduated as passed midshipmen or as masters. Confederate Naval Academy midshipmen, much like their Federal counterparts, tended to be from elite families and from the naval establishment. The midshipmen at Richmond included sons of some of the Confederacy's most highly-placed individuals, including Secretary Mallory, Raphael Semmes, Thomas Rootes, Robert Pegram, and George Terry Sinclair, and the brother-in-law of President Jefferson Davis. As might be expected, given their background and family ties, midshipmen in the Confederate Navy—like all military school students—were expected to abide by high standards of conduct and honor.[41]

The Navy Department devised a rotation system whereby only 52 of the 106 midshipsmen were assigned to the school ship at one time. As a result, many of the young sailors received much of their education while on service with Confederate naval squadrons. The midshipmen apparently preferred the practical to the formal schooling, even though service with the squadrons meant that they had to find study time amid other duties. "I do not progress very rapidly in anything, the weather is so hot and I have so many interruptions, but every little bit helps," wrote Midshipman John Mason from his active duty station on the James River aboard the *Hampton*. Mason's "progress" may have been slow in many areas, but he did learn the finer points of navigation when a new acting master agreed to teach him the subject. Midshipman William F. Clayton, who spent his first two years in Wilmington, North Carolina, was not so fortunate. The midshipmen at his station received no formal teaching, "but were expected to fathom everything for ourselves, no lectures to explain or elucidate; in other words we must make the brick and furnish the straw."[42]

Whatever the pedagogical obstacles of squadron duty, Clayton resented being transferred to the school ship on the James. "The boys did not like this arrangement; they went into the war to fight and not to study aboard ship and be examined yearly by a roving board. . . ." Seconding this opinion was Midshipman J. Stevens Mason, who in September 1863 pleaded to accompany "Cousin Bob" Minor on special service to Canada. The school ship, Mason argued speciously, was for men whose health was too poor for active duty. "I ask this not because I feel dissatisfied with my very pleasant position here, or don't appreciate the kindness of yourself and other friends in procuring me this," he explained, "but that I do feel dissatisfied with myself for remaining in such a snug, lazy berth in these times." Another midshipman member of the extended Minor family, Hubbard Taylor Minor, hoped that "Cousin Robert's" special service could be a ticket off the school ship. On September 30, 1863, Midshipman Minor called upon Lieutenant Minor and asked whether he could accompany him to sea duty. "He said that there would be no chance for me until I had graduated so I have made up my mind to get thro' as soon as possible & then come what will I am prepared for it."[43]

In contrast to the frustrated Mason, by the time he set foot on the *Patrick Henry* in 1864, the boyish-looking, 17-year-old Midshipman James "Jimmie" Morgan was already a rakish, swashbuckling veteran of three-years experience. A native of Louisiana, Morgan had been in his first year at Annapolis when the war began. He commenced his Confederate service on the *McRae* in the Gulf of Mexico, and was an aide to Capt. George Hollins before the battle of New Orleans. After service aboard the ironclad *Chicora* in the Charleston Squadron, Morgan served aboard the commerce raider *Georgia* on her cruise in the Atlantic. When he finally returned to the Confederacy, one of his first acts was to ask George Trenholm, the new Confederate treasury secretary and one of the South's wealthiest men, for permission to marry his daughter. Trenholm at first did not even recognize "'*Little*' Morgan," the youth who had wooed his daughter in Charleston two years before. Recovering from his incredulity, Trenholm deferred to his daughter, who accepted Morgan's proposal. Fresh from his recent romantic triumph, Morgan traveled to Richmond and promptly failed his examination for passed midshipman. "I had not opened a schoolbook since I had left Annapolis," Morgan confessed, and "if there was one thing I needed more than anything else, it was a little schooling."[44]

Even when assigned to the school ship, Confederate naval midshipmen had occasional opportunities to engage the enemy, the most notable instance being the so-called *Underwriter* expedition. On February 2, 1864, Lt. John Taylor Wood took 33 men, including 10 midshipmen, from Richmond to the Neuse River near New Bern, North Carolina, to cooperate with the Confederate army against the Federal garrison. Lieutenant Benjamin P. Loyall, the academy's commandant of midshipmen, was Wood's second-in-command. Though the plan to surprise and storm Federal land batteries went awry, Wood's men succeeded in boarding and capturing the *Underwriter*, one of the largest Federal gunboats prowling North Carolina's waters. Before the Confederates could get the prize to safety, however, cannon from the Federal forts crippled her. Out of viable options, the Confederates fired the *Underwriter* and escaped in launches. Five men, including Midshipman Palmer Saunders, were killed in the hand-to-hand combat on board the captured ship. Midshipman Morgan—who was not on the expedition—learned later that Saunders, the academy's most famous martyr, "had his head cloven to his shoulders by a cutlass in the hand of a big sailor." Despite the failure of the expedition, Wood's men had acted with great gallantry and spirit, evidenced in part by Loyall's promotion to commander for his leadership in the affair.[45]

Raids similar to the *Underwriter* affair, however, were few and far between. More often than not, life for the 52 midshipmen assigned to the school ship consisted of the drudgery of formal education and endless drill. Part of this routine was based upon work that flowed from the superintendent's pen. In May 1864, Lieutenant Parker finished *Elements of Seamanship*, a textbook for use in teaching his midshipmen. Though Parker noted that the book was written without benefit of the sources he had at his disposal in Annapolis, the text is a detailed introduction to the anatomy of sailing vessels, naval science, naval organization and gunnery drills. Midshipmen endured a rigorous, structured regimen of practical seamanship, naval tactics, gunnery drills, infantry tactics, astronomy, navigation, mathematics, english, geography, political science, history, and romance languages taught by a faculty of navy lieutenants. A typical day on the school ship included over six hours of recitation, drill, and study. The ship boasted two "little pine box recitation rooms" located between paddle boxes on the hurricane deck, and a mess hall. Although steam-powered, the ship was outfitted with a foremast with a complete set of yards and sails. Lessons in "practical seamanship" included everyday experience with sails and steam engines. The ship was equipped with a variety of rifled and smoothbore guns for gunnery drills, as well as an armed launch. Fitted out in this manner, the *Patrick Henry*, Secretary Mallory declared approvingly, served as a school ship "without interfering with her efficiency as a vessel of war."[46]

Even when some of the midshipmen were called off for duty with ships in the James River Squadron, the school ship operated with a predictable academic routine. John Thomas Scharf, a midshipman who later wrote *History of the Confederate States Navy*, described that routine:

> The morning gun was fired at seven o'clock, and at eight a breakfast of hard-tack and a decoction of sweet potatoes or beans that masqueraded as coffee was served. Sick call, studies and recitations occupied the hours until two o'clock, and then came a dinner of salt-junk, perhaps a mess of vegetables, and the inevitable corn-meal that became a staple article of diet when wheat-flour climbed toward $1,200 per barrel in Confederate currency. School exercises and dress parade took up the remainder of the afternoon, and the day ended with tattoo at 9:30, and taps at ten o'clock.[49]

Echoing Scharf's description, Midshipman James Oliver ("Olly") Harrison related to his family his daily routine. "You have no idea how fully our time is occupied," Harrison wrote from the *Patrick Henry* in October 1864. "The majority of my Section rise at 4 in the morning & are busily engaged until 10 at night. We have 8 different branches to be examined on the 1st of December." Apparently mastering the academic demands, Harrison received good marks early in his service on the school ship. He was made leader of his section, and had nothing but good things to say about the Academy. "We have fine teachers, who demand a reason for everything. . . .I like the navy better and better every day." The euphoria did not last, however, for the December examinations in eight different branches proved too much for Olly Harrison. He failed the examinations, and anticipating his dismissal or resignation, Harrison's father inquired about positions for his son in the artillery.[48]

Hubbard Taylor Minor was in the first class assigned to the *Patrick Henry*. His diary described an eclectic daily drill with "great guns" and small arms, algebra lessons, periodic exams, night watch duty, and a personal "eternal war" with the commandant of midshipmen. He "went uptown"—into Richmond—often, socializing with the fashionable set of which his family was a part. Minor was, nevertheless, bored on the *Patrick Henry*, complaining in his diary that "the days all slip swiftly by here in the same monotonous way. . . . " Minor, who yearned to be off the school ship and among the midshipmen housed in cabins on Drewry's Bluff, in October 1863, received an opportunity to inspect the hilltop stronghold. "Obtained permission to go on shore & look around & was charmed with the place," Minor noted, "& only wish that I was in command of a piece of heavy ordnance and stationed there on the bluff." The camp on Drewry's Bluff had expanded significantly since its early days in 1862. "There is quite a little village here now & two churches in one of them," he wrote in his diary. I "took dinner on the Bluff with some midship men who are stationed there & in the evening walked down with them to the shore & hailed the Patrick Henry, which is lying out in the river opposite the Bluff[.]" His desire to command an artillery piece on the bluff was never fulfilled, for Minor left the school ship for a year of service in the Savannah Squadron.[49]

Had Minor been assigned to the school ship in 1864 when a strong enemy fleet was on the James, he also would have experienced more of the sense, which Scharf described, of being "school-boys one hour and fighting men the next." Even the seasoned Midshipman Morgan was impressed with what he later dubbed "the most realistic war college that ever existed." Morgan recalled studying in the recitation room while listening to the firing of shore guns, which were manned by other naval personnel. The professor asked a student to find out which battery had been fired before resuming instruction. The lesson was interrupted again, Morgan wrote, by a message from the captain requesting midshipman to assist with the batteries. "It was useless to call for volunteers," Morgan wrote, "as every midshipman clamored for permission to go: so these details were given as rewards."[50]

Though rotation between the school ship and the squadrons made for an adventurous life for the midshipmen, Secretary Mallory did not find it satisfactory. This rotation, he wrote in his April 1864 report, "is disadvantageous to the officer, who thus loses, or fails to acquire the habit of methodical and continuous study, and who, being uninformed upon the theory of his profession is unprepared to properly profit by the opportunity thus afforded him of participating in its practical duties." Mallory asked the Confederate Congress to increase the number of midshipmen from 106 to 150, and to provide funds to construct enough cabins at Drewry's Bluff to accommodate all of the midshipmen. For reasons that are not clear, Congress ignored Mallory's request. A week after Mallory submitted his report, a Federal fleet steamed up the James River toward Richmond. The training these young sailors had received in "the most realistic war college that ever existed" was about to undergo a rigorous examination.[51]

Cdr. Matthew Fontaine Maury

Celebrated in Europe as a result of his works on naval science and navigation, Matthew Fontaine Maury (1806-1873) managed to antagonize his superiors in both the United States and Confederate navies. Constantly at odds with Navy Secretary Stephen Mallory, Maury was also critical of President Davis. In October 1861, he told a friend that "a small man, Frank, a very small man is your president, & so are the men generally by whom he surrounds himself." Such criticism, coupled with his reputation abroad, earned Maury an assignment to Europe in the summer of 1862. Before he left Virginia, however, Maury had left his mark on naval warfare in the James River: the construction of two "Maury gunboats" and devising and implementing the first effective system of electric torpedo (mine) defenses. Photograph taken in Europe, 1863.

"Rebel Infernal Machine"

This speculative drawing was not the product of pure fantasy. While it is doubtful that a man-powered submarine attacked the U.S. flagship *Minnesota* in Hampton Roads in October 1861, it is clear that the Confederates developed a submarine in Richmond in 1861-1862—a year before the construction of the famed submarine *Hunley* in Mobile. William B. Cheeney, a Confederate naval officer, supervised workers and purchased materials and labor from Tredegar Iron Works (using a specially designated "submarine boat" fund) to build what may have been a steam-powered submarine. What became of Cheeney's submarine and why former Confederates said nothing about it after the war remains the greatest mystery of Richmond's naval history. *Harper's Weekly*, November 2, 1861.

Deck of the Confederate ship Teaser after her capture, July 1862.

(Above) A small converted tug boat armed with only two rifled guns, the *Teaser* was proved valuable to the Confederate navy in the conduct of torpedo warfare. Her crew abandoned her after she received a crippling shot through her boiler from the *U.S.S. Maratanzas* on July 4, 1862. Lost with the *Teaser* were tanks and powder for making torpedoes, a spool of telegraph wire used to explode the torpedoes, correspondence describing in detail their location in the James River, and a reconnaissance balloon. Photograph by James F. Gibson. Courtesy of the Library of Congress.

An illustration from "Torpedo Book" Brig. Gen. Gabriel J. Rains, postwar

(opposite page): "There is no fixed rule to determine the ethics of war—that legalized murder of our fellow man," wrote Gabriel Rains in 1877. "Each new weapon, in turn, when first introduced, was denounced as illegal and barbarous, yet each took its place according to its efficacy in human slaughter by the unanimous consent of nations." Though he initially believed the use of torpedoes to be barbarous, Rains warmed to his job as superintendent of the Confederate Army's Torpedo Bureau. He later earned Hunter Davidson's wrath by claiming credit for placing torpedoes in the James River. After the war, Rains compiled a book of clippings, detailed drawings, instructions on how to build different types of torpedoes and assessments of their performance.

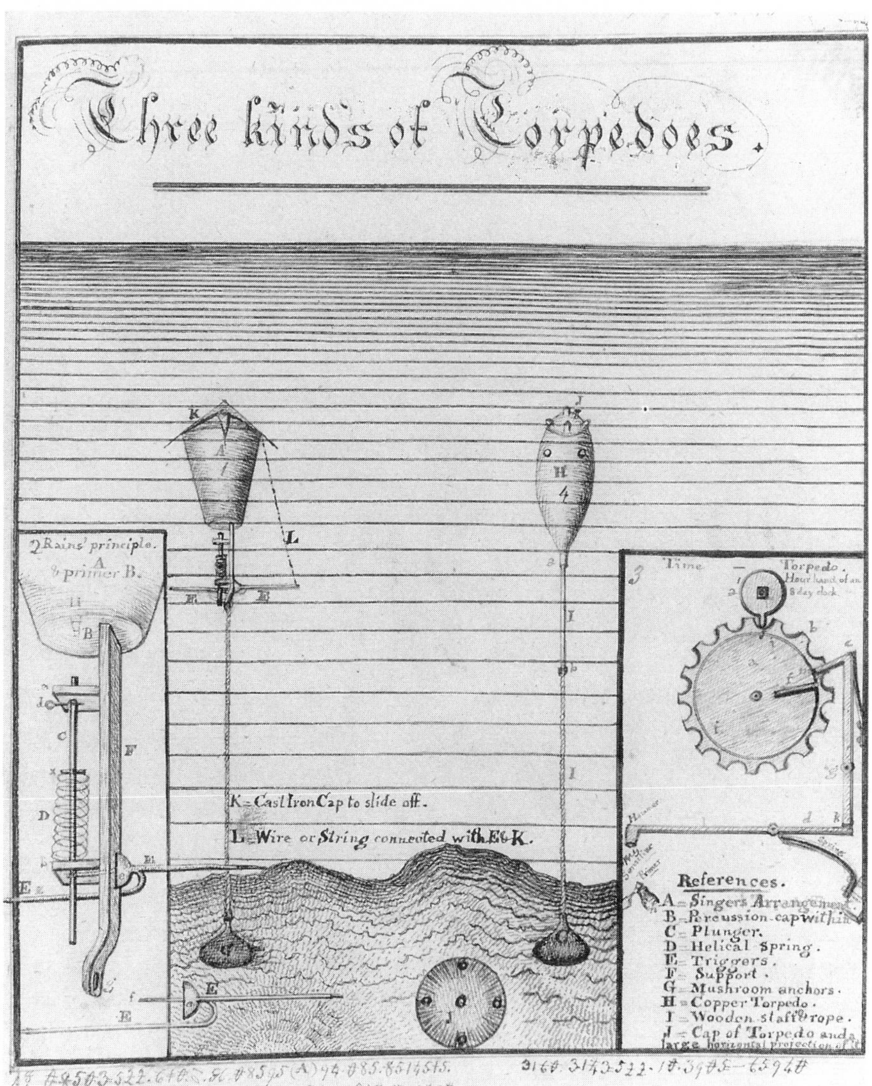
Three kinds of Torpedoes.
2 Rains' principle.
A
& primer B.
K = Cast Iron Cap to slide off.
L = Wire or String connected with E & K.
Time — Torpedo.
Hour hand of an 8 day clock.
Spring
References.
A = Singers Arrangement.
B = Percussion cap within
C = Plunger.
D = Helical Spring.
E = Triggers.
F = Support.
G = Mushroom anchors.
H = Copper Torpedo.
I = Wooden staff & rope.
J = Cap of Torpedo and a
large horizontal projection of it

Cdr. Hunter Davidson

Hunter Davidson (1826-1913) never entirely got over the "marked discourtesy" shown to him on two occasions by President Jefferson Davis. When Davidson wounded the U.S.S. *Minnesota* with the torpedo boat *Squib* in April 1864, Davis allegedly remarked: "'Humph, why didn't he blow her up?'" When Davidson's electric torpedoes sunk the *Commodore Jones* a month later, Davis remained silent. After the war from his home in South America, Davidson grew incensed when Davis' memoirs seemed to credit Gabriel Rains for the successes in torpedo warfare, and blame Davidson for all the failures. While praising Matthew Fontaine Maury and thanking John Brooke and R. O. Crowley for their assistance, Davidson claimed distinction for the "success" which entitled him "to be known as having made the first successful application of electrical torpedoes, or submarine mines in time of war, and as a system of defence." Salt print from Class of 1860 U.S. Naval Academy album. Courtesy of Charles V. Peery.

Cdr. William Harwar Parker

Typical of many Confederate naval officers, William Parker (1826-1896) was born into the service. His father and elder brother (both named Foxhall Parker) rose to the rank of commander in the U.S. Navy. Rather unusually, however, secession and civil war split the Parker family; ironically, only the New York-born William chose to cast his lot with Virginia and resign from the U.S. Navy. William entered the navy at age 14, graduated at the head of one of the U.S. Naval Academy's first classes and returned to Annapolis as a professor of mathematics. It was because of his academic status and authorship of several technical seamanship books that Parker was chosen to be commandant of the Confederate States Naval Academy in 1863. Scharf, *Confederate States Navy.*

Captured Confederate Torpedo Station along the James River

National Archives

"Commodore Barney, sunk in the James River"

Part of a Federal naval expedition that ventured up the James toward Chaffin's Bluff in August 1863, the *Barney* was only damaged, not sunk, by Confederate torpedoes. *Harper's Weekly*, August 29, 1863.

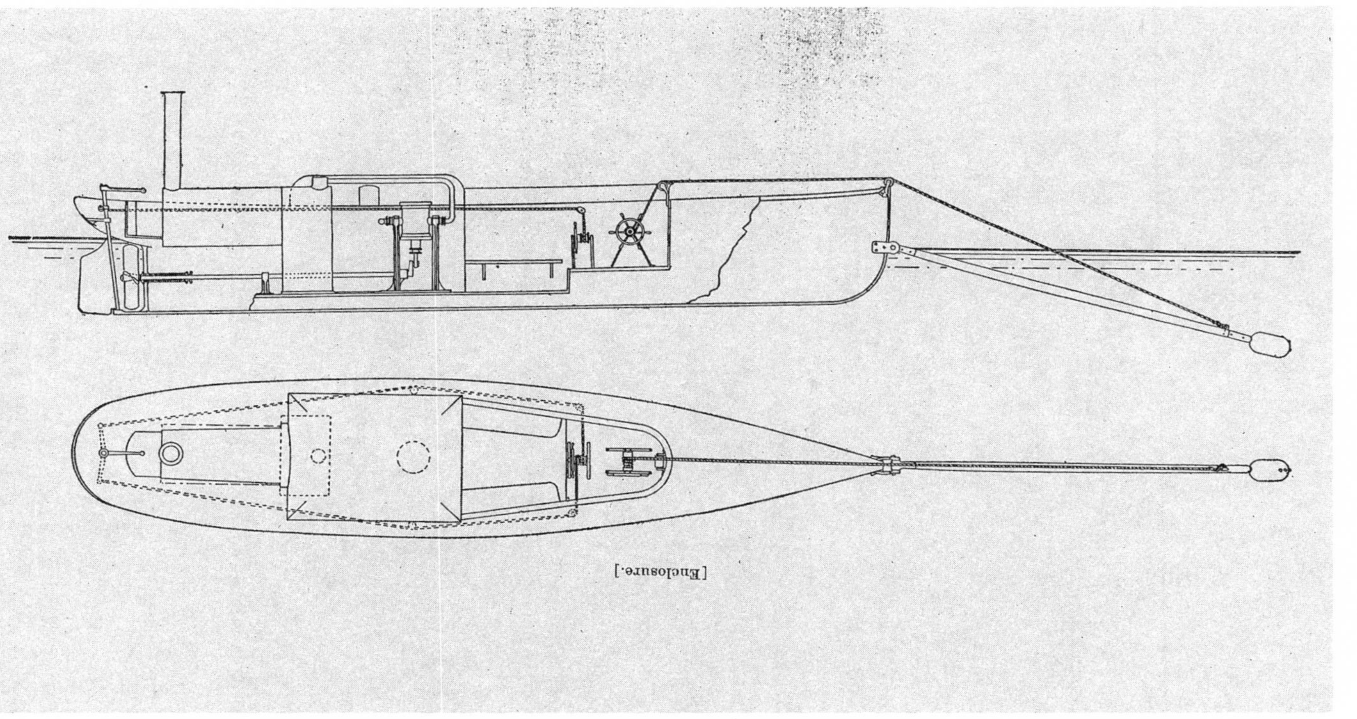

Squib Class Confederate Torpedo Boat

The Richmond navy yards constructed more torpedo boats than any other kind of vessel. Between 1863 and 1865, the yards completed the *Squib*, *Hornet*, *Wasp*, *Scorpion* and two other unnamed torpedo boats. Approximately 40 feet long, they were powered with strong quiet engines and equipped with a 16-foot-long spar for placing small torpedoes at the water line of enemy vessels. *The Official Records of the Union and Confederate Navies.*

Confederate States Naval Academy school ship Patrick Henry

Neither glamorous nor celebrated, the *Patrick Henry* was nevertheless the James River Squadron's most long-lived and versatile vessel. She was built in New York in 1859 as the passenger and packet ship *Yorktown.* Seized by Virginia authorities in 1861, she was converted at Rocketts into a strongly armed and partially ironclad warship and rechristened. After fighting in the battle of Hampton Roads, the *Patrick Henry* contributed several of her guns to the defense of Drewry's Bluff. In 1863, she went to the navy yard a second time for conversion into a floating naval academy—the role for which she is best remembered. Anchored with the James River Squadron near Drewry's Bluff, the *Patrick Henry* served at intervals as the squadron's flagship. Scharf, *Confederate States Navy.*

Midshipman James Morris Morgan

"What a dear little rascal he is! Such affectionate winning ways!" wrote Sarah Morgan of her brother, Midshipman James Morris Morgan (1845-1928) "Such a baby to mother and his sisters, such a noble little man to all the world besides!" Before he was 18, the noble little "Jimmie" Morgan had fought in the Battle of New Orleans, cruised the Atlantic on the *Georgia*, become a favorite of the Confederate first family, and become engaged to the daughter of the Confederate treasury secretary. Still, his sister wrote, "He would die if he had not somebody to hold his hand and rub his head, and kiss him occasionally." *Recollections of a Rebel Reefer.*

Midshipmen at the Confederate States Naval Academy

Pictured on these two pages are four of the young men who attended the Confederate Naval Academy. Reflecting the typical experience of a Confederate midshipmen, Pegram , Sinclair, Sterling, and Wilkinson each spent part of his service on warships and part of it abroad. All but Pegram also spent time on the school ship *Patrick Henry*. Wilkinson had been a U.S. Navy midshipman at Annapolis on the eve of the war, while Pegram, son of Cdr. Robert B. Pegram, first entered the short-lived Virginia State Navy. Pegram and Sinclair served on the elder Pegram's cruiser, the *Nashville*, in 1861-1862.

Midshipman William W. Wilkinson

Carte-de-visite, 1863-1865.

Midshipman
Neil H. Sterling

Carte-de-visite,
courtesy of Charles V. Peery.

Midshipman
William H. Sinclair

Carte-de-visite by E. Swift & Son, 126 Bold St., Liverpool, England, 1863-1864.

Midshipman
James W. Pegram

Carte-de-visite, 1863-1864.

Operations on the James

May-October 1864

1. Federal steamer *Commodore Jones* sunk by torpedo May 6.

JAMES RIVER SQUADRON, POSITIONS DURING:

2. Bombardment of the Federal fleet at Trent's Reach, June 21.
3. Bombardment of Dutch Gap, August 13.
4. The defense of Signal Hill, August 17.
5. Bombardment of Fort Harrison and the defense of Chaffin's Bluff, Sept. 29 - Oct. 1.
6. Squadron bombarded from Federal batteries on Signal Hill, Oct. 22.

* Trent's Reach
** Kingsland Reach

Federal Lines
Confederate Lines

2 MILES

MALVERN HILL
Fort Harrison
Fort Burnham
Chaffin's Bluff
Wilton Farm
(obstructions)
Drewry's Bluff
Deep Bottom
Jones' Neck
Strawberry Plains
Boulware's
SIGNAL HILL
Fort Brady
Graveyard
Varina
Cox's Ldg.
Battery Brooke
HOWLETT LINE
Bishop's Ldg.
Howlett's Farm
DUTCH GAP CANAL
Battery Semmes
Battery Sawyer
Battery Wood
FARRAR'S ISLAND
Battery Dantzler
(obstructions)
TURKEY ISLAND
CURLES NECK
James
Bermuda Hundred
BUTLER (Army of the James)
River
Chester Station
City Point (Federal Supply Base)
POINT OF ROCKS
Appomattox River
Port Walthall
N

Mark A. Moore

Chapter 5

"Prepare for Service Against the Enemy": The James River Squadron May-December 1864

On May 5, 1864, a telegram from Cdr. Hunter Davidson, chief of the Submarine Battery Service, arrived at the Navy Department in Richmond: "Four monitors, the *Atlanta*, 5 gunboats, 2 ironclads, 59 transports coming up the river; also 3 rafts have passed Fort Boykin."[1] Davidson's message was as ominous as it was brief. The news it communicated ushered in a new era for the capital navy. Between 1862 and 1864, Richmond had been a center of shipbuilding, war production, and administration. Since the late summer of 1862, the James River Squadron had not directly confronted any enemy vessels. From May 5, 1864 to the end of the war, however, Richmond was on an active military front, and the James River Squadron was in the constant presence of a strong enemy fleet.

The Federal Invasion of 1864

The naval war on the James mirrored the fighting between the opposing field armies in the Eastern Theater. For nearly two years, Gen. Robert E. Lee's Army of Northern Virginia had kept the Federal Army of the Potomac away from Richmond. After blunting George McClellan's cautious thrust against the capital city during the Peninsula Campaign in the summer of 1862, Lee moved his army north and thrashed Maj. Gen. John Pope's newly-organized Army of Virginia at Second Manassas. Lee exploited this victory by crossing the Potomac River into Maryland, where the Army of Northern Virginia narrowly averted complete destruction at Sharpsburg on September 17, 1862. While the navy yards in Richmond finished the *Richmond* and framed the *Virginia II* and *Fredericksburg* in late 1862 and early 1863, the tide of war in the East again turned in the Confederacy's favor when the Army of Northern Virginia defeated the Army of the Potomac at Fredericksburg in December. The campaigning season of 1863 opened with perhaps Lee's most spectacular success at Chancellorsville in May, but was followed by his second raid into the North and the bloody defeat at Gettysburg in July. Meanwhile, the *Virginia II* and the *Fredericksburg* were launched, and the *Texas* framed. The Army of Northern Virginia and the Army of the Potomac (commanded by Maj. Gen. George Gordon Meade from late June 1863 for the remainder of the war) maneuvered across the northern Virginia piedmont during the fall and winter of 1863, during which time the school ship *Patrick Henry* received her first midshipmen, and the Submarine Battery Service continued to create torpedo stations downriver from Chaffin's Bluff.

The movement of the United States Navy up the James River in early May 1864 was related directly to coordinated offensives by Federal military forces. In March 1864, Maj. Gen. Ulysses S. Grant was promoted to lieutenant general and took *de facto* command of the Army of the Potomac. On May 5 Grant moved his army against Lee's, beginning a relentless and bloody 11-month campaign against Richmond. One small army moved south up the Shenandoah Valley to threaten Richmond's communications to the west, while another force, the Army of the James under the command of Maj. Gen. Benjamin F. Butler, moved against Richmond from the southeast. Those simultaneous thrusts engaged Confederate forces throughout Virginia and prevented them from reinforcing themselves or the Richmond defenses. It was the advance of Butler's army that brought the United States Navy up the James River. The navy's mission was to transport and escort Butler's army up the

James to City Point, and cooperate with the army as it moved from City Point through the "back door" to Richmond.[2]

Unlike the ascent of the James in May 1862, the Federals in 1864 were not laboring under the illusion that they could disregard Confederate defenses and shell Richmond into surrender. Recalling the fate of the *Commodore Barney* in August 1863, Rear Adm. Samuel P. Lee, commander of the North Atlantic Blockading Squadron, was fully aware of the danger posed by Confederate torpedoes. Accordingly, on May 4, he issued detailed instructions to ships of the James River division: all ships were to "be fully prepared to drag for torpedoes. . . .As soon as a torpedo is discovered, the vessel making the discovery will at once signify it by hoisting the meal pennant, when every precaution will be taken by dragging with the boats and following slowly." So instructed, the ships of the Federal fleet began the ascent of the James from Newport News at 3:00 a.m. on May 5.[3]

Despite Lee's warnings, Hunter Davidson's Submarine Battery Service struck the blow that paralyzed the Federal navy in its attempt to ascend the James. Since Matthew Fontaine Maury first supervised the sowing of torpedoes in the James in June 1862, Davidson had worked to improve the torpedo defenses. By 1864, the battery service on the James consisted of what Davidson later described as "nine well-constructed stations. . . connected by telegraph, and with the office of the Secretary of the Navy." The Submarine Battery Service on the James in May 1864 employed 32 men: 24 at the batteries, six telegraph operators, and one signal man, all under the command of Thomas H. Friend. In the early afternoon of May 6, at one of the several stations located a few miles down river from Drewry's Bluff at Deep Bottom, three men of the Submarine Battery Service—Jervies Johnson, Acting Master Peter W. Smith and an unnamed third man, probably John Britton—waited at their detonator. Alerted by local slaves to the general location of the Confederate torpedo defenses, the Federal fleet bombarded the shore, smaller ships dragged the channel for torpedoes and parties of Federal marines combed the shore searching for torpedo stations. Ensconced in a pit and avoiding detection, the three men at Deep Bottom waited, hoping that the *Atlanta*, a Confederate-built vessel captured ignominiously in the Savannah River in June 1863 and converted to Federal use, would pass over one of their submerged torpedoes. Although the *Atlanta* did not venture close enough to the deadly torpedoes, one of the smaller vessels of the Federal fleet, the steamer *Commodore Jones*, was not as careful.[4]

At 2:00 p.m., Confederates at the Deep Bottom detonator crossed the wires and set off the torpedo. "It was," wrote an eyewitness, "as if the bottom of the river was torn up and blown through the vessel itself. The *Jones* was lifted almost entirely clear of the water, and she burst in the air like an exploding firecracker. She was in small pieces when she struck the water again." Sixty-nine men were killed in the explosion. The destruction occurred despite Federal precautions. Commander J. C. Beaumont of the *U.S.S. Mackinaw* warned the commanders of the *Commodore Jones* and *Commodore Morris* to stay back from the small boats dragging for torpedoes. Lieutenant Thomas F. Wade of the *Jones* reportedly disobeyed his orders, with fatal consequences.[5]

After the vessels located and traced the wires connecting torpedoes to shore, a landing party from the *Mackinaw* shot dead the unnamed Battery Service man and captured Smith and Johnson. Placed in the forward gunboat ascending the torpedo-strewn river, the prisoners reluctantly violated their enlistment oath and revealed the location of other torpedoes.[6] The destruction of the *Commodore Jones*, however, shocked Federal commanders and instilled in them a cautiousness which made the Federal fleet's presence in the James River almost purely defensive. A week after the destruction of the *Jones*, Admiral Lee appealed to General Butler for his forces to move up and occupy the south bank of the river. Without that assistance from the army, Lee argued, the U.S. fleet could not adequately defend itself from both shore-detonated torpedoes and roving Confederate artillery batteries, which had destroyed the gunboat *Shawsheen* the day after the *Jones* was destroyed.[7] Thanks to the Submarine Battery Service, the Federal fleet was put on the defensive. But could the Confederate navy exploit this cautiousness?

Behind the Torpedo Barrier: Preparing the Squadron for Action

Davidson's telegram to Mallory alerting him to the presence of Federal warships found the James River Squadron woefully unprepared to confront an enemy fleet. Although it was the most powerful in the South and featured three ironclad warships, the squadron was in reality not appreciably stronger than it had been in late 1862. Against the Federal squadron of four ironclad warships modeled after the original *Monitor* (and referred to as "monitors") and over a dozen wooden gunboats, the Confederates mustered only eight fully operational warships mounting a total of 19 guns: the ironclad *Richmond* (four guns); steam gunboats *Hampton*, *Nansemond*, *Roanoke* (formerly the *Raleigh*) and *Beaufort* (two guns each); school ship *Patrick Henry* (four guns); tender *Drewry* (two guns); and steamer *Torpedo* (one gun) used by the Submarine Battery Service.[8]

The arrival of the Federal fleet found Richmond's naval facilities working frantically to finish arming, fitting out, manning and maintaining the vessels of the James River Squadron. Owing to the shortage of iron plate and problems with their engines, the *Fredericksburg* and *Virginia II* lay for months half-finished at the Richmond shipyards. The *Fredericksburg* at Rocketts and the *Virginia II* at the yard opposite Rocketts had been laid down in the spring of 1862 and framed that summer and fall. Both ships were launched in June 1863, and fitted out in the 11 months afterward. But by March 1864, neither ship had her guns, and the *Virginia II* had not yet received her iron plating. Secretary Mallory reported on November 30, 1863 that the *Fredericksburg* was "completed and waiting her armament," and the *Virginia II* was "now receiving her machinery and armor, [and] will soon be ready for service." Five months later, on April 30, 1864, both vessels were reported "in commission" but still "awaiting their armaments, which are nearly ready."[9] The *Virginia II* was not fully in commission until May 18.

At the beginning of 1864, the squadron's ironclads were also without adequate crews, and the Navy Department scrambled at the eleventh hour to find suitable sailors to man them. Sailors stationed at Drewry's Bluff were reassigned to crew the *Fredericksburg*, which was commissioned in March but did not have her crew in place until May 12. Adjutant General Samuel Cooper, on March 22, 1864, sent instructions to nine Confederate generals throughout the Confederacy ordering the immediate transfer of a total of 1,200 men "[t]o man efficiently, and at once, the vessels of the Navy. . . ."[10] Several hundred of those transfers were earmarked for the James River ironclads.

Along with new crews, the squadron also had a new commander. The same day the *Commodore Jones* was destroyed, Stephen Mallory replaced the aging Capt. French Forrest with Capt. John Kirkwood Mitchell, then chief of the Office of Orders and Detail. Mitchell was to assume command of all naval vessels in the James River, except the *Patrick Henry*, "and prepare them for service against the enemy with all possible dispatch."

Born in 1811, Mitchell joined the United States Navy at age 14 and rose through the ranks to command his first vessel in 1859. He had been in the Pacific in 1861, and was ordered to San Francisco to protect United States interests there. Instead, Mitchell took his ship to Panama, where he resigned his commission and made his way to the Confederacy to offer his services. Though he earned a reputation for bravery in 35 years in the United States Navy, Mitchell was in 1864 under a cloud for his short and disastrous command of the naval defenses of New Orleans in April 1862. He had inherited the New Orleans command just days before Adm. David G. Farragut's U.S. Navy fleet fought its way past the forts that guarded the Mississippi River below the Crescent City. The strongest of the Confederacy's river defense vessels were a thousand miles away, guarding the northern approaches to Confederate territory, while the ironclad warships on which Southerners were relying for the defense of New Orleans had not been completed. The *Mississippi* had just been launched; the formidable *Louisiana* was still fitting out. She had virtually no motive power, and Mitchell used her essentially as a floating battery in the battle with Farragut's fleet. Engineers were working feverishly installing her propellers so she could at least escape to fight another day. As Farragut's fleet accepted the surrender of the Confederate forts and prepared to move on New Orleans, Mitchell held a council of war, then gave the order to destroy the ironclads.

The ignominious loss of the South's largest city, and of two uncompleted warships, provoked recriminations and investigations. While a formal navy investigation concluded that Mitchell "did all in his power to sustain the honor of the flag and prevent the enemy from ascending the Mississippi River," the episode was a blemish on his record.[11] After a few months as a prisoner of war at Fort Warren, Boston, Mitchell was exchanged and returned to Richmond in July 1862, where he was given charge of the Office of Orders and Detail. He was destined to command the James River Squadron during the ten months of its greatest promise and greatest frustration.

When he assumed command of the squadron on May 6, Mitchell could not help but note troubling parallels between his new situation and the one he faced in New Orleans two years earlier. Had Mitchell been entrusted with an important command only to preside over its destruction? Would the *Virginia II*, the *Fredericksburg* and *Texas* suffer the fate of the *Louisiana* and *Mississippi*? Fortunately for Mitchell and the Confederates, the Submarine Battery Service gave Mitchell time to prepare in Richmond—a luxury he had not enjoyed in New Orleans. Mitchell used the time to finish fitting out his two new ironclads and finish repairs to other vessels. In the first two weeks of May, both the *Fredericksburg* and the *Virginia II* received four-gun batteries consisting of double-banded Brooke rifles on the bow and broadsides and a single 10-inch smoothbore Columbiad at the stern. A day after assuming command, Mitchell asked Mallory to "Please hurry up [Assistant Constructor William] Graves with the Magazine, light room, steering apparatus, windlass and port shutters for the Virginia." Mallory had requested that Mitchell "[s]end the crew of the *Virginia* on board at once," but Mitchell demurred, explaining that work on the ship could be finished more quickly with her crew quartered temporarily on the *Patrick Henry*, moored nearby. In this way, working parties from the *Virginia II* and the *Richmond* could assist with the final fitting out, but not interfere with the mechanical work still going on. Mitchell ordered the gunboat *Hampton*, temporarily detained in Richmond for repairs, to get fitted out immediately with "coal, provisions, stores, etc.," and make ready "in all respects for active service." "While in Richmond," Mitchell directed her commander, to "make a diligent search for competent pilots for the ironclads and the gunboats."[12]

In order to complete the crews of the ironclads, Mitchell asked permission to borrow midshipmen from the *Patrick Henry*. On May 10, he asked Sidney Smith Lee, his replacement as chief of the Office of Orders and Detail, to transfer 11 sailors from the school ship to the squadron. A week later he requested the services of three specific midshipmen "on account of their acquaintance with the gun exercise." In all, 17 midshipmen spent over a month on active service with the squadron before transferring back to the *Patrick Henry*.[13]

On May 15 Mitchell reported that the *Fredericksburg* was "ready for service against the enemy at any moment" and that the *Virginia II* was ready except for the completion of her steering apparatus, which William Graves would finish the next day. Mitchell asked Mallory for a few days to test the *Virginia II* and train her crew before embarking on offensive action. The flag of commander Mitchell was transferred formally from the *Richmond* to the *Virginia II* on May 18, and the squadron prepared for battle.[14]

In addition to preparing the vessels for action, Mitchell also shuffled officers in an effort to give each ship an adequate number of seasoned and competent commanders. Transferring from the *Richmond* to command of the newly-commissioned *Virginia II* was Cdr. Robert Pegram, who had been acting squadron commander in the days before Mitchell's appointment. His transfer left the *Richmond* without an experienced officer, so Mitchell temporarily transferred William Parker from the school ship *Patrick Henry* to the *Richmond*. Another Virginian and career naval officer, Cdr. Thomas R. "Old Tom" Rootes, was taken off special assignment in Richmond (including a brief stint as head of the OSS) and given command of the *Fredericksburg*. Rootes's kinsman, Robert Minor, was similarly temporarily detached from the ordnance works to serve as Mitchell's flag lieutenant aboard the *Virginia II*.[15]

To command the smaller vessels, Mitchell depended upon a wealth of junior officers, mostly first lieutenants, many of whom were transferred to Richmond to outfit the new ironclads. Indeed, owing to attrition and sickness among senior officers, the smaller vessels and even the three ironclads were under command of junior officers during much of

1864 and 1865. All of those junior officers were trained at the U.S. Naval Academy and veterans of the U.S. Navy, and many had already acquired considerable experience as commanders of vessels. Virginian John S. Maury, commander of the *Hampton* in 1864, had held temporary command of the *Richmond* in 1863, while Lts. John W. Dunnington of Kentucky and Francis E. Shepperd of North Carolina, both of whom were destined to command James River ironclads in the squadron's only major engagement, were among the most experienced junior officers. Dunnington had commanded the steamers *Tuscarora* in the Gulf of Mexico and *Calhoun* on the Mississippi River, while Shepperd had held temporary command of several ships on the Mississippi River, as well as the Charleston ironclad, *Palmetto State*. Lieutenants Wilburn B. Hall (formerly commandant of midshipmen of the Confederate States Naval Academy), Charles W. Hays, William W. Read, Mortimer M. Benton (summoned to Richmond from Mobile in May), William H. Wall, Edward J. Means and Maxwell T. Clarke, all enjoyed opportunities to command vessels in the James River Squadron during its most active service. Means and Clarke commanded the *Roanoke* and *Beaufort*, respectively, for an extended time in 1863-1864 when the fleet was inactive. In June 1864, Mitchell—denying any intent to disparage the young officers—asked that they be replaced by men of greater professional experience.[16]

"Like Chained and Sulky Bulldogs": The James River Squadron Contemplates Attack

Placing experienced officers at the helms of all the ships was essential, since it seemed inevitable that the James River Squadron would at last see action against the enemy. In the days and weeks following the destruction of the *Commodore Jones*, the Federal flotilla advanced up the James at the painfully deliberate pace of a half-mile per day. Small tugboats dragged the channel for torpedoes, and landing parties searched out detonators and torpedo stations on shore. The monitors and gunboats followed behind at a safe distance. By May 17, Federal tug boats advanced upriver far enough to come under the fire of Confederate batteries at Chaffin's Bluff, raising the prospect the opposing fleets would soon confront each other near the Drewry's Bluff obstructions.[17]

The James River and the Confederate army stalled the advance of the Federal flotilla. When the Federal monitors reached Trent's Reach, an elbow-turn in the river several miles downstream from Drewry's Bluff, Admiral Lee decided his warships could advance no further. He feared the monitors could not negotiate the bar and shallow shoal waters there. The vessels would have to be lightened and needed the luxury of advancing through the reach deliberately without the worry of coming under enemy attack from the shore. Benjamin Butler's army would have to occupy the adjacent shore line, especially the high ground on the south bank.[18]

Instead of seizing and holding the river banks, however, on May 16-17—two years after the repulse of John Rodgers's flotilla by Confederate gunners—a Federal force again suffered a decisive defeat at Drewry's Bluff. With reinforcements from both the Richmond defenses and the Army of Northern Virginia, Gen. Pierre Gustave Toutant Beauregard assembled a force strong enough to attack Butler's army south of the James. Beauregard's forces, including the Confederate States Marines stationed at Drewry's Bluff, pushed Butler's army to a position adjacent to the Federal navy's anchorage at Trent's Reach. The Confederates threw up new lines which—in the popular imagery of the day—"bottled" effectively "Beast" Butler at Bermuda Hundred. Butler's defeat left Samuel Lee's naval flotilla similarly bottled.

Any gratitude the Confederate navy might have felt to the army for "bottling" Butler was mitigated by the belief that the Confederate army had also kept the James River Squadron bottled behind the obstructions at Drewry's Bluff. Since the autumn of 1862, the navy and the army had wrangled over the status of the river obstructions, which were controlled by army engineers. Mallory had asked Secretary of War James Seddon to have a channel cleared through the obstructions in September 1862 as the *Richmond* neared completion, and reiterated the request in the late winter of 1864, as the navy yards fitted out the new ironclads. The army engineers worked to remove stones from cribs blocking the channel, but a passage through the obstructions was not completed when the Federal flotilla appeared at City Point. After the *Commodore Jones* was destroyed and the Federals began using tugs to clear Confederate torpedoes, Mitchell's warships were unable to stop them. The two cabinet secretaries fired volleys of angry recriminations at each other, then aired their respective grievances in long letters to the president. "Mr. Mallory's usual red face turned purple," War Department clerk John Jones confided to his diary. "He has not yet got out the iron-clad *Richmond*, etc., which might have sunk General Butler's transports."[19]

Whatever colors Mallory's face might turn, the navy secretary could not deny his own service contributed to his frustration. Put simply, the navy had a credibility problem. Mallory requested clearings in the channel so that his ironclads could operate downriver. But army engineers had good reason to believe that the Confederate vessels would not be finished as soon as expected or be as strong as hoped. All the James River ironclads were months behind schedule. Experience throughout the South had taught painful lessons about the defects of Confederate ironclads, and Confederate naval officers had expressed private doubts about the James River vessels. Mallory later ruefully described the James River ironclads as "chained and sulky bulldogs," fierce and powerful, yet unable to get at their tormentors. But even during the tense days of May 1864, Confederate naval officers tended to treat those ships as cosseted lapdogs, potential prey for the enemy's "bulldogs." Mallory himself continued to betray uneasiness about the safety of his ironclads even as he railed at the army for not clearing the obstructions.[20]

At no time was the defensive mindset of Confederate naval officers more evident than after a passage was at last cleared through the Drewry's Bluff obstructions. The army engineers had removed enough stones from cribs to allow safe passage at high tide of vessels with no more than 14 feet draft. There were doubts whether this would be sufficient for the *Virginia II*, the heaviest of the ironclads, whose draft was estimated at just under 14 feet. Chief Constructor John Porter and Acting Constructor William Graves provided cross-sections which put that vessel's draft at between 13'4" and 13'9" (Graves, the ship's builder, insisted that the shallower draft was accurate). More stones were removed, and on May 23, the lightest ironclad, the *Fredericksburg*, passed. The *Richmond* and the *Virginia II* followed on the 24th. Secretary Mallory urged Mitchell to attack on the 25th.[21]

By this time, however, the Federal flotilla had ceased its slow advance up the James. The unchained Confederate bulldogs were not to be set on unarmed tugs dragging for torpedoes. If they were going to make use of their new freedom, they would have to battle Federal monitors in the narrow channel and shallow waters of Trent's Reach. Just as Admiral Lee had asked Butler to provide support for his advance up the James, Mitchell asked Beauregard to erect artillery positions along the south shore. Only then could the squadron advance. After a battery was put in position, the *Fredericksburg* on May 29, suffered an injury to an engine boiler and was out of service for a day undergoing repairs.[22]

Although he dutifully went through the motions of preparing for action, Mitchell was clearly reluctant to attack. Reports from forward observers informed Mitchell the Federals at Trent's Reach had five wooden gunboats, including the 10-gun flagship *Agawam*, one single-turreted and two double-turreted monitors, and another single-turreted monitor not far downstream. Additional protection for the Federal fleet was provided by a makeshift obstruction of nets and chains. Mitchell matter-of-factly described the likely scene of battle as a narrow channel in shallow water, which would make it almost impossible for the Confederate ironclads to turn or fight abreast of each other, and likely that they would run aground. On May 30, Mitchell laid out that scenario as part of a plan of attack submitted to the senior officers of his squadron. His plan was for a night attack using fire vessels (expendable brigs and schooners set aflame) preceding the gunboats and ironclads. Two days later, the officers responded unfavorably. Echoing Mitchell's pessimistic assessment of the situation, the officers expressed their preference for an early morning attack using fire vessels sent down well ahead of the ironclads (but keeping the vulnerable gunboats behind the ironclads), and making generous use of spar torpedoes as "a powerful auxiliary" against the enemy monitors.[23]

The prospect of undertaking what amounted to a suicidal mission mortified officers throughout the navy. Mitchell's flag lieutenant, Robert Minor, deprecated the public's "insane desire" to engage the enemy. From Charleston, Lt. James Rochelle, the former long-time commander of the *Nansemond*, assured Minor: "I have no doubt but that you will get a chance at the Yankees before they are driven away from Richmond and I am satisfied that the Squadron will do all that it is possible for vessels to do, none but fools will expect you to accomplish impossibilities."[24] One of the few recorded dissents from the counsels of caution came from Lt. Frank Shepperd, executive officer of the *Fredericksburg*. Shepperd continued to urge the use of fire vessels and volunteered personally to row down in a skiff at night and cut the protective rope that might prevent the fire vessels from reaching the Federal monitors. The former Annapolis ethics instructor offered little to convince Mitchell that an attack might succeed. Instead, he emphasized, whatever the odds against success, delay would likely increase those odds. Success, on the other hand, would result in the destruction of the enemy's fleet and the routing of Butler's army. Concluding with a flourish of bravado, Shepperd assured Mitchell that he was "ready and willing to run such a risk for the sake of our cause, and with a firm belief that a merciful and just God will crown our efforts with success."[25]

Mitchell and the other officers of the squadron rejected Shepperd's plea to take a calculated gamble. When on June 8 he again solicited the opinion of his officers, Mitchell clearly summarized the dilemma arising from the squadron's dual role:

> The great benefits to our cause that must necessarily follow any decided success in an attack upon the enemy's monitors in particular, and his naval forces and transports generally, will warrant the adoption of any plan of attack which may afford a reasonable prospect of a favorable result. On the other hand, the importance of the squadron to the defenses of Richmond and the extent to which these defenses would be imperiled in the event of any serious disaster to us will not escape your due consideration.

Upon due consideration, the other officers concurred with Mitchell's rather transparent preference for restraint. The officers recommended Mitchell avoid engaging the enemy fleet directly, and try instead to force him from his position with fire ships and floating torpedoes. "At some future time it may become necessary to make an attack, even though our entire squadron may be sacrificed, either for the good of the country or the honor of the Navy. When, in the opinion of his Excellency the President or other authority, such a course becomes incumbent upon us, we will most cheerfully adopt it, and will not be found recreant to the trust confided to us by the [country.]"[26]

Lieutenant Shepperd wrote an official letter lambasting the Confederate naval and army high command for the years-long string of failures that had brought about the stalemate:

> It has never appeared to me that the vigor with which the work of preparing our squadron for service has progressed was in consonance with the great objects in view, viz., the defense of our capital and with it the safety and independence of our country; for it must be admitted that any decided success of our fleet over that of the enemy must result in the total defeat of his army on either side of the James River.
>
> [W]hen the history of this war is written, and the capture of Richmond be a sad fact recorded in it, and the question be asked why the Navy took no active part in its defense, and why so much money and so much valuable time has been devoted to the building of three formidable ironclads, two of which can barely, under the most favorable tides, navigate the river, I, for one, desire that my conduct in the matter, however humble and unimportant it may be, shall appear above reproach, and that those who are directly responsible shall bear the burden of condemnation they deserve.[27]

Although Shepperd's rhetoric was shrill and self-serving, the substance of his charges was accurate and his predictions proved prescient. While the presence of the James River Squadron helped deter the Federal navy from assaulting Richmond, and the capital navy occasionally engaged Federal land and water forces, its role was primarily passive. The ships, in effect, became floating batteries and their fates tied almost entirely to the fortunes of the Confederate army.

Ironically, while Confederate naval officers were agonizing over whether to attack, U.S. authorities were having similar arguments about the Federal flotilla on the James. Generals Butler and Grant urged Admiral Lee to carry through the original plan of placing obstructions in the river above the Federal ships. Lee professed an eagerness to take on the Confederate warships, and a confidence that his flotilla would triumph in such a battle. "The Navy is not accustomed to putting down obstructions before it," Lee complained to Navy Secretary Gideon Welles on June 7, "and the act might be construed as implying an admission of superiority of resources on the part of the enemy." He reluctantly agreed to do so because the cost of a Confederate success—using what Butler denounced as "unchristian modes of warfare," such as of torpedo boats and fire ships—was too high to risk.[28]

This became even more of a consideration when the Army of the Potomac fought its way to the north bank of the James River a few days later. In May and early June 1864, the opposing armies had fought the bloody engagements of the Wilderness, Spotsylvania, North Anna River and Cold Harbor. Although the Federals suffered (and inflicted) staggering casualties, Grant followed each battle by moving progressively southward and eastward until the army arrived on the James in Charles City County 30 miles east of Richmond. Federal engineers built a pontoon bridge across the river at Weyanoke plantation, and massed transports at Wilcox Wharf. Grant could not afford to have Confederate ironclads and torpedo boats disrupting the army's crossing, so he urged that the obstructions be put down as soon as possible. At Admiral Lee's direction, the army brought up five small vessels and sank them on the Trent's Reach bar. The obstructions were in place late on June 15, as the Army of the Potomac furtively crossed the James and marched toward Petersburg.[29] The Federal army fumbled in its attempt to take Petersburg by assault, and instead settled in for a slow strangulation of that important rail center. From June 1864 to early April 1865, Grant methodically extended his lines south and westward to cut the railroads connecting Petersburg—and, ultimately, Richmond—to the remaining portions of the Confederacy. To supply the Army of the Potomac, Grant established at City Point, located at the confluence of the Appomattox and James Rivers, the largest logistical and supply base of the war. Protecting that base from Confederate naval attack became the primary function of the Federal navy.

When Admiral Lee agreed to cork his own bottle, the prospect of a naval dog fight on the James River faded. Over subsequent months, the Federal Navy seated the cork even tighter. It supplemented and reinforced obstructions in its front to make absolutely sure that no Confederate shipping could get below and attack Federal supply and communications lines at City Point. With the James River naval front completely inactive, the warships stationed there seemed wasted, and

Federal authorities hoped to transfer two monitors from the James River for service in the more active North Carolina waters. With support from Grant, Admiral Lee in July successfully delayed such a transfer. "There is no disguising the fact," Grant wrote, "that if the enemy should take the offensive on the water, although we probably would destroy his whole James River navy, such damage would be done our shipping and stores, all accumulated on the waters near where the conflict would begin, that our victory would be dearly bought." To guard against such an attack, the Federal Navy created a James River Division within the North Atlantic Blockading Squadron. Captain Melancton Smith was given a force consisting of the double-turreted monitor *Onondaga*, single-turreted *Saugus* and *Canonicus*, captured Confederate ironclad ram *Atlanta* and 20 wooden steam gunboats.[30]

Thus, the two fleets opposed each other across several wide, looping bends in the James, each protected by a wall of sunken logs and small vessels, content to prevent the other from attacking military targets in its rear. By early August 1864, the situation on the James had become so static Robert Minor assured a comrade overseas: "There is but a slim prospect of an action here, for the Yankees have penned us in and themselves out." The flag lieutenant asked for and received a transfer from the squadron back to the Naval Ordnance Works.[31]

Patrolling the James

After the James River Squadron declined to attack its enemy and the Federal flotilla erected obstructions in its front, the opposing navies assumed new roles in support of their respective land forces. The months between June 1864 and January 1865 saw an unprecedented number of combined operations (coordinated between armies and navies) by both Federal and Confederate forces.

The confused geography of the James River determined the nature of those operations. The river between Chaffin's Bluff and Trent's Reach was essentially a no-man's land, nominally controlled by Confederate forces, but exposed to the fire of Confederate and Federal land batteries. North of the James, the Confederate line was anchored at Chaffin's

Bluff, one mile downriver from Drewry's, and extended inland to a series of formidable earthen fortifications, most notably Fort Harrison. Until late September, the Confederates also maintained a battery several miles downriver on Signal Hill. On the south bank, the Confederates established the Howlett line, named for the family whose home occupied the hill overlooking the river. Anchoring the Howlett line at the James was a formidable fortified post called Battery Dantzler, commanded by Maj. Francis W. Smith, the army artillerist who had been so frustrated in the inter-service garrison at Drewry's Bluff. Though free of navy command, Smith was not free of the navy. During the first months of its existence, Dantzler was compelled to borrow a Brooke rifle and part of the crew from the *Drewry* to man the gun.[32] The Federal line north of the James was anchored several miles to the east of Signal Hill at Deep Bottom. On the south side, where Butler's troops were concentrated on the narrow neck of land between the James and Appomattox rivers, the opposing forces were less than three-quarters of a mile apart.

On June 21, the Confederate army and navy planned a combined attack on the Federal vessels at Trent's Reach. Smith's artillerists at Battery Dantzler were to open the bombardment, and Mitchell's ships would join the fray from a position at Cox's Wharf. From just before noon until nearly 6:30 p.m., the sound of heavy guns echoed over the James. From the navy's perspective, the bombardment was little more than a gunnery drill and ordnance test. The distance between the Confederate and Federal positions was nearly two miles—at or beyond the effective range of Confederate guns—and required sighting and firing over a wooded neck of land known as Farrar's Island.

Confederate vessels fired hundreds of shot, shell and projectiles. Robert Minor, still with the squadron as its ordnance officer, kept careful track of the performance of guns, projectiles and fuses. The results of the afternoon's work were not encouraging. According to deserters from the U.S. Navy, Confederate fire was accurate, but the Federal vessels were too well-protected by the intervening bank for the fire to do any damage. Most other reports claimed the Southern ships failed entirely to hit their targets. Despite having expended tons of powder and shot upon the Federal fleet, Confederate gunners inflicted only a few hits and no casualties. The *Virginia II* was hampered by a mechanical problem and the chain of the *Richmond* fouled her propeller, preventing her from participating at all. One of the two guns on the *Nansemond* burst, and the other Maury gunboat *Hampton* experienced continuing propeller shaft problems that required immediate attention. "The whole affair," William Parker later wrote, "was a *fiasco*." In making the attack, Parker confessed, the squadron was "yielding to the clamor of the army to 'do something.'"[33]

The Confederate guns at Battery Dantzler were far more dangerous to Federal forces than was the James River Squadron, and for that reason Butler determined to reduce or bypass that stronghold. The siege guns of the 1st Connecticut (Heavy) Artillery were stationed on promontories along the river. From the summer of 1864 to the end of the war, the Connecticut gunners dueled with their Confederate counterparts in Dantzler and elsewhere, and—when opportunities allowed—punished Southern vessels on the James. The 1st Connecticut was also charged with the task of providing cover fire for the building of the Dutch Gap Canal, Butler's attempt to bypass Dantzler. One look at a map of the meandering James suggested the possibility of digging a canal across the narrow (174 yards wide) neck of land at Dutch Gap. In early August, Federal forces began excavation on the proposed channel. After months of labor, Federal engineers exploded 12,000 pounds of powder on New Year's Day to blow open the last segment of the channel; the explosion instead threw dirt back into the canal.[34] The canal was not finished during the war.

Realizing the canal could circumvent their defensive works, the Confederates determined to prevent its completion. Major General George Pickett, immortalized by the charge of his division at the July 1863 Battle of Gettysburg, was in the summer of 1864 commander of Confederate troops manning the Howlett line. He and Maj. Gen. Charles Field, the commander of Confederate troops across the river at Chaffin's Bluff, solicited the help of the navy. On August 13, the three ironclads, along with the gunboats *Hampton*, *Nansemond* and *Drewry*, moved to within three-quarters of a mile of Dutch Gap and fired at intervals of 20 minutes from 6:00 a.m. to 6:00 p.m. At the same time, Confederate land forces similarly harassed the canal diggers and the Federal ships anchored nearby. The Federal ships suffered a few casualties from the land batteries and returned fire with their big guns. Mitchell reported forthrightly that he did not believe that the bombardment—an estimated 147 shots fired with the aid of spotters—inflicted much damage on the enemy. The shelling killed and wounded a handful of laborers, but had no effect on the progress of the canal. Enemy land batteries, he believed, had the advantage of being able to return accurate fire using the Confederate vessels' smokestacks as a guide. While the squadron suffered no casualties, several enemy shells hit the *Fredericksburg*, inflicting serious damage to her smokestack. "[T]he enemy struck the Ship 3 times in 5—good work," conceded the vessel's commander, Thomas Rootes, "and if I had not moved her she in my opinion would have been seriously injured."[35]

The squadron rendered more effective service in subsequent months in support of Confederate land forces. At 10:30 a.m. on August 17, Robert E. Lee asked for the navy's help in repelling an enemy sortie against Signal Hill. Mitchell was in the city that morning, and Rootes was the senior officer present. Rootes took the ironclads downriver, and at 3:00 p.m. began shelling the Federal forces. "[O]ur fire was elegant—" boasted Robert Minor, who had offered his services on board the *Fredericksburg*, "the shells exploded right in among them, and when the beggers tried to get out of the way of [the *Virginia's*] fire, they fell into the range of our guns and the *Richmond's*." For five hours, the ironclads pounded the hill at five, 10 and 15 minute intervals, then maintained a more desultory fire until 9:00 p.m. The following morning, Rootes learned the Federals had retreated and that Confederate forces reoccupied the stronghold. Rootes had nothing but praise for the men and officers, who for six hours on a hot August day had worked their guns in completely closed ironclad vessels. He especially praised the work of Minor and Frank Shepperd, the *Fredericksburg's* first officer.[36]

Mitchell was again away in Richmond, and Rootes in temporary command, when the navy received another, more important, summons to help the army block an enemy attack. In contrast to the Signal Hill sortie of August 17, the dawn assault on September 29 against New Market Heights and Fort Harrison was the largest military operation north of the James between the Battle of Cold Harbor on June 3 and the end of the war. The assault overwhelmed Fort Harrison and threatened the Confederate works at Chaffin's Bluff. Rootes brought down the three ironclads to Kingsland Reach, just above the bend in the river known as the graveyard, and began firing on the fort. Confederate marine officer Lt. E. T. Eggleston was stationed on shore to monitor the effect of the naval fire and reported that the shots were falling short. The target was an estimated two miles inland and required using the ironclads' extreme elevation of six to seven degrees. Sensing a situation of "extreme emergency and to Save Chaffins Bluff," Rootes gave the order to use high charges. Lieutenant John Maury, in temporary command of the *Richmond*, had her 7-inch rifles loaded with 14-pound charges. "Much to my satisfaction," wrote Rootes, "Eggleston signaled that the shells were finding their targets and scattering enemy troops in Fort Harrison." Mitchell soon arrived on the scene and assumed command of the squadron.[37]

For three days, September 29-October 1, the ironclads, together with the *Nansemond*, *Beaufort* and *Drewry* and the batteries on the south shore (manned by naval personnel), fired hundreds of rounds against Federal army forces in and around captured Fort Harrison. In contrast to most of the squadron's other encounters with the enemy, the ships suffered little damage and their fire was accurate and effective. The only mishap occurred as the *Virginia II*, Frank Shepperd commanding, prepared to join her sister ships. In the midst of the complicated process of receiving a new gun, the flagship was the least prepared for action. After unburdening her of derricks and skids and getting the gun carriage onto the gun deck, the engineers got up steam only to find the supply ship *Gallego* was fouled in her anchor chain. The *Gallego* sunk at her moorings and delayed the flagship's departure for another half hour. The large charges of powder used in the guns caused one of the few accidents suffered by any of the vessels when, on September 30, a 7-inch rifle on the *Fredericksburg* burst after firing two 12-pound and one 14-pound charges. The large consumption of powder and the risk of accident were necessary, Rootes explained to ordnance chief John Brooke, because Chaffin's Bluff was in real danger of falling to the enemy. Obviously proud of the work initiated under his command, Rootes declared he was "confident that this squadron saved Chaffin's Bluff," and claimed "a number of army officers gave the squadron credit of saving Chaffin's Bluff."[38]

Though Confederate forces successfully parried the Federal army's thrust against Richmond, the capture of Fort Harrison further complicated the strategic situation on the James River. The attack on the 29th overran and secured Signal Hill, and the Federals began erecting fortified batteries on that promontory dominating two bends in the river. Several miles of meandering river were no longer safe for Mitchell's ironclads. By early October the Federals had constructed Fort Brady on Signal Hill, thus anchoring a new Federal line running northwest to Fort Harrison, and located a little more than a mile from Chaffin's Bluff. The no-man's land between the two squadrons became more confused than ever. The Confederate squadron could not get downriver to the portion of the James dominated by Southern land fortifications without passing under the Federal guns—but neither could the Federal fleet get upriver to the cover of Fort Brady without passing by Battery Dantzler.

The Confederates constructed several new batteries on the south bank of the river both upstream and downstream from Fort Brady. Much to John Mitchell's dismay, he was asked to provide men and guns from his squadron for these new batteries. Battery Semmes, a position overlooking Cox's Landing and situated across a neck of land from Signal Hill, had been established in late September with Columbiads and Brooke rifles supplied by the navy and a garrison under the command of Lt. Matthew P. Goodwyn. Battery Semmes was something of a source of pride for the navy—a shore position consisting of navy ordnance crewed by naval officers and sailors with the paramount purpose of protecting the squadron. Mitchell was not so favorably disposed toward Battery Brooke, located upstream from Fort Brady at the southern end of Kingsland Reach, and Battery Wood, just upriver from Battery Dantzler near Osborne Landing. The army's request that the squadron man the batteries came as Mitchell was complaining to Secretary Mallory that his squadron could not perform its assigned roles without more officers and trained sailors. Mitchell found men for Battery Brooke among the crew of the *Virginia II*, and transferred Lt. Charles W. Hays from the *Nansemond* to command the position. He drew the line, however, in providing men for Battery Wood. "The *Beaufort*, *Roanoke*, and *Nansemond* are now without the officers and men necessary to man their guns and have barely sufficient on board to keep them in order and in a condition for service in other respects," Mitchell explained in declining to furnish men for Battery Wood. The arrival in Richmond on October 18 of exchanged prisoners—mostly men from the captured Savannah Squadron ironclad *Atlanta*—eased the officer shortage. Mitchell was able to free 45 men and Lt. John H. Ingraham for service at Battery Wood, though he was quick to point out the cost of the navy having to provide crews for land batteries.[39]

The new strategic situation along the James not only required the navy to erect additional shore batteries, but also made the squadron's routine patrols more important and more dangerous. Because of the twists and turns of the James between Chaffin's Bluff and Trent's Reach, and because Federal lines on the north side had been pushed so much farther forward than the lines on the south side, it was possible for Federal troops to cross the James River somewhere in that naval no-man's land to a point behind Confederate army lines. Only constant patrolling of that no-man's land by Confederate vessels could protect Battery Dantzler and other positions on the Howlett Line from surprise attack. Accordingly, the ironclads and the gunboats every night ventured downstream from their anchorage at Chaffin's Bluff and took positions in the relatively straight, three-mile section of river in Kingsland Reach as far as the friendly guns of Battery Brooke. The routine must have been a familiar one, for Mitchell issued orders "to perform the usual picket duty" under "the usual orders," and with instructions "to keep a strict watch on the river above, as well as below them, to detect and prevent any attempt the enemy might make to cross from Boulware's farm to the rear of our battery."[40]

The ships of the James River Squadron were still on their downriver patrol on the morning of October 22 when they learned the hard way that the Federals had, on the previous evening, completed a new fortified position on Cox Hill upstream from Fort Brady, and outfitted it with three 30-pound and four 20-pound Parrott rifles. Dawn on the 22nd found the gunboat *Drewry* in plain sight of the new battery, about a mile distant. The Federal gunners found their range and hit the little ship with an estimated 16 shells before she got up steam and moved out of range.

Lieutenant William Wall, the *Drewry*'s commander, admitted to being surprised by the bombardment and commended the effectiveness of the enemy's fire. Shells passed through the ship's smokestack and disabled the center pivot gun. Under orders not to return fire against land batteries unless necessary, Wall did not attempt to do so. The Southern ironclads also got up steam and beat a hasty retreat toward Chaffin's Bluff. The *Virginia II*, and especially the *Fredericksburg*, endured a heavy fire for nearly a half-hour. The Federal shells riddled those two ships' smokestacks and splintered the unarmored spar deck (casemate roof) of the *Fredericksburg*. That vessel answered with a few half-hearted rounds, but, consistent with his own orders, Mitchell did not attempt to engage the enemy. He left that task to the land batteries. After the Confederate ships were out of range, Batteries Semmes and Brooke, commanded by navy lieutenants Hilary Cenas and Charles Hays, respectively, punished the Federal batteries with an hour of heavy and effective firing from Brooke rifles and Columbiads.[41]

The unexpected encounter of October 22 dramatized for John Mitchell the tenuous condition of his squadron. In his report on the incident, Mitchell took another opportunity to complain about the deficiencies in officers and trained gun crews, owing in large part to "frequent changes" as well as sickness. "The importance of well-trained officers and guns' crews can not be overrated, especially respecting the heavy guns of the ironclads," Mitchell reminded Mallory. Deficiencies in their crews were the only problems commanders of the squadron's ships found in the quarterly inspection reports they were required to file. Officers of the gunboat *Hampton* and ironclads *Virginia II* and *Richmond* noted that "frequent changes" in personnel impaired the efficiency of their crews. The crew of the *Richmond* was "mostly composed of men recently transferred from the Army, and it is suggested that a change among either officers or men should be made only in case of emergency."[42]

Because of the continuing shortage of sailors and the damage sustained in the October 22 bombardment, the squadron was never able to muster its full complement of warships. The school ship *Patrick Henry* was not formally a part of the squadron, and in the fall of 1864, was sent upriver to guard one of the bridges across the James. When the majority of their crews were detailed to North Carolina in July for special assignment, the lightly-armed gunboats *Beaufort* and *Roanoke* were reduced to mail and packet duty. The remaining men could serve only as "ship keepers," Mitchell noted bitterly, until the arrival of the exchanged prisoners in October allowed them to assume picket duty. The *Drewry* suffered engine problems and was sent to the naval works for repairs in July, and unfortunately, the pounding of October 22 sent her back to Richmond for repair of her gun carriage. A month before, the *Nansemond* had been sent to Richmond for gun carriage repairs. Among the small gunboats, only *Nansemond's* sister ship *Hampton* was fully serviceable. In his report of November 1, Mitchell noted that she, too, required a trip to Richmond for work on her gun carriage. The squadron commander proposed to play musical crews between the ships while they underwent repairs.[43]

Of the three ironclads, the *Fredericksburg* spent the most time at the Richmond yards. "Temporarily disabled" by a boiler problem in May, the ram sustained considerable damage on October 22. At the suggestion of Commander Rootes, Mitchell, on October 24, ordered the *Fredericksburg* to the shears near the Rocketts navy yard. The vessel was to receive a new gun to replace a burst 10-inch Columbiad. More importantly, the ship's wooden shield deck was to receive a protective covering of iron bars. The iron, Mitchell informed Rootes, "is now at the yard already drilled for fastening and that the work of putting it on will not require over forty-eight hours."[44]

Despite the sobering lessons of the October 22 bombardment, the enemy's torpedoes, not his shore batteries, most concerned John Mitchell. The same twists and turns that made it possible to cross the river behind Confederate batteries made it possible for Federal parties in small boats to place torpedoes in the river behind the ships of the James River Squadron. The successes of the *Squib* against the *Minnesota*, the *David* against the *New Ironsides* and the *H. L. Hunley* against the *Housatonic* underscored the danger of attacks by small vessels armed with spar torpedoes. The Confederate navy pioneered this technology, but the Federals also adopted it and had several torpedo boats (numbered one through four) in the James River Division. When on patrol, the Confederate vessel furthest downstream extended a line to detect enemy ships and torpedoes. When at anchorage, the ships were outfitted with their own torpedoes and surrounded with an increasingly elaborate protective rigging made of logs, ropes and chains, and with wooden gratings suspended on spars ten feet below the water line. As early as the summer of 1864, squadron ordnance officer Robert Minor distributed to every vessel—including fire rafts—staffs, rigging, sensitive fuses, torpedo tanks, powder and sundry tools.[45]

Although Mitchell made the necessary nightly dispositions to patrol the river, he told General Lee that he preferred not to use his ironclads because of the exposure to torpedoes, and in late October solicited Lee's opinion. All the concern about enemy torpedoes made Lee wonder whether the navy had forgotten its primary responsibility: the defense of Richmond. The general foresaw disaster—including the loss of Richmond—should the Federal army succeed in crossing to the south side of the James behind Confederate lines. "I fully appreciate the importance of preserving our fleet, and deprecate any unnecessary exposure of it. But you will perceive the magnitude of the service which it is thought you can render, and determine whether it is sufficient to justify the risk." Lee recommended Mitchell send the ironclads downriver and patrol behind them with smaller ships and boats, while land forces patrolled the banks. "I can," Lee concluded, "foresee no state of circumstances in which the fleet can render more important aid in the defense of Richmond at present than by guarding the river below Chaffin's Bluff." Secretary Mallory agreed with this assessment, and with the reputation of the service at stake, cautioned Mitchell that "Ceaseless vigilance is essential."[46] And ceaseless vigilance it was.

Naturally prone to cautiousness, and all too aware of his squadron's deficiencies, Mitchell was given more reason to be cautious by an event that occurred on North Carolina's Roanoke River on October 27. In one of the Civil War's most celebrated acts of individual heroism, Lt. William B. Cushing, U.S.N., together with an eight-man crew, exploded a spar torpedo against the formidable Confederate ironclad *Albemarle*, which quickly sank to the bottom of the river.

The effect on naval warfare on the James River was almost immediate. A Confederate deserter told U.S. Navy officers the Confederates in November 1864 "were much frightened when the *Albemarle* was blown up." When they were not patrolling, the ironclads were surrounded by ropes and booms to obstruct the approach of an enemy torpedo boat. Within days, Mitchell arranged to have a new line of surface-level obstructions, consisting of logs and chains, placed in the river at the eastern end of Kingsland Reach to "to prevent [sic.] our vessels from a surprise by torpedo or other boat expeditions from the enemy. . . . " The obstructions allowed passage of Confederate gunboats and picket boats, but not the ironclads. In subsequent weeks and months, Mitchell worked with Colonel Stevens of the army engineers to reinforce that new line of obstructions. Two days after the sinking of the *Albemarle*, Mitchell also directed that a new field of torpedoes be sown in the river just below the Kingsland Reach obstructions. Lieutenant Beverly Kennon, a Virginia-born officer who had won a reputation for reckless bravery in command of the *Governor Moore* at New Orleans, supervised the placing of as many as 36 torpedoes.[47]

Mitchell's obsession with enemy torpedo boats worried at least one disgruntled subordinate. Thomas Rootes confided to Robert Minor that while he shared Mitchell's concern that enemy torpedo boats could destroy Confederate ironclads, he disagreed with his commander's response to the threat. Rootes preferred to keep the ironclads behind the obstructions at Drewry's Bluff (the passage of which could be closed off), away from the front lines but cleared of any booms and other apparatus that hampered their mobility, should it be necessary to confront enemy monitors. He expressed a fear "that by the time the Services of the Iron Clads are wanted they will be so securely fixed to prevent the torpedo boats of the enemy from getting at them that we shall be able to do with them but little. . . . "[48] But, as Rootes complained, Mitchell had his own way. The flag officer labored to reinforce the new obstructions at Kingsland Bar. He noted in his diary on December 17 that Charles Mason of the army engineers had begun working at night to sink small commercial vessels in the river just above the bar. By the 22nd, a half-dozen hulks had been placed in a line from the south shore to the channel.[49] Although there was a passage in the channel for friendly vessels, the message of Mitchell's actions was clear. He ended 1864 with the same defensive mindset which had convinced him not to engage the enemy in May and June.

Sailor Life on the James River

Active service, even when it did not involve pitched battles, took a toll on both the ships and crewmen of the James River Squadron. Ironically, the squadron reached its peak size and faced its most difficult duty when Confederate naval manpower was least able to handle the demands. The Navy Department struggled to find enough adequately trained men for the fleet and to provide them with adequate food, clothing and supplies. While the navy eventually met the latter challenge, it could not diminish the hardships of life aboard small cramped vessels or the effect of that life on morale. The men of the James River Squadron were relatively well fed and supplied until the last months of the war, but the crews were, nevertheless, plagued by sickness and desertion.

Ironclad vessels required a wide variety of skilled and unskilled crew members, though fewer men than required on equivalent wooden warships. Mitchell asserted that a minimum of 90 men were necessary for an ironclad steamer. By comparison, the original *Virginia* had carried a full complement of 230 officers and men. Though ironclads did not require sailors to work rigging and yard arms, they needed engineers and firemen instead. Manning the four guns carried by each of the James River ironclads required the most sailors. William Parker's manual for midshipmen described a gunnery drill for 17 men on a single 9-inch gun. Eleven men could work a 6.4-inch gun, while the heavy pivot guns required as many as 27. Most of the men on an ironclad crew were landsmen, ordinary seamen and boys (an official personnel title), but the ships also carried a host of administrative and technical officers (commissioned, warrant or petty): boatswains, surgeons, paymasters, quartermasters, yeomen, coopers, armorers, gunner's mates, boatswain's mates, firemen, and others. The most important skilled officers assigned to ironclads were the engineers. Working in stiflingly hot boiler rooms, the engineers maintained the ships' machinery and provided their motive power.[50]

By 1864 the James River Squadron was forced to tap into a variety of sources to man its ships adequately. The commissioning of two new ironclads strained the navy's manpower supply. "Where we are to get officers for the ironclads is beyond my ken," wrote Robert Minor in late

March 1864. The *Richmond* was able to maintain her crew at between 120 and 148 men, not including officers.[51] The *Fredericksburg* drew her crew from the sailors stationed at Drewry's Bluff.

Crews of Civil War vessels—South and North—were composed of men of diverse ethnic and national origins. The Confederate raiders that operated on the high seas were manned largely by foreign-born crews and Southern officers. The same diversity could be found in the home defense squadrons. An English sailor serving on the *Virginia II* late in the war reported most of the vessel's petty officers were foreigners. Oliver Hamilton, a young soldier transferred from the 38th North Carolina Infantry to the *Fredericksburg* in April 1864, told his father that the crew of that vessel was "very much mixed up—about half of us here just came from the army—and the others are all seamen some are English, some Irish some Dutch and I don't know what all—Some are very wicked too." George Weber, a sailor stationed aboard the *Patrick Henry* early in the war (before it became a school ship), similarly described some fellow sailors as "hard shells," or "wild and reckless fellows." The leader of the "hard shells" was Dan Williams, a man who "does not seem to care a straw for his life," observed Weber. Particularly impressive to Weber were the "india ink pictures"—including one of the Virgin Mary kneeling before the cross—which covered Dan Williams' body.[52]

Not surprisingly in a region whose population was one-third black, crews of Southern vessels were bi-racial. Slaves of officers and blacks hired for menial services were an integral part of a warship crew, just as they were on commercial vessels. As a rule, Confederate naval regulations forbade recruitment of free black or free colored (a distinction made in the regulations) persons as sailors, but allowed station commanders and the Navy Department to make exceptions. No more than 1/20 of a vessel's complement could, by regulation, consist of black or colored persons without written permission from the station commander. There is no evidence that free black or colored sailors served on ships in the James River Squadron in numbers approaching the regulation quota, but they did serve. On May 10, 1864, Mitchell, as he searched for seamen to crew the new ironclads, notified Commander Pegram that "two colored boys," David Green and Henry Leonard, were transferred from Drewry's Bluff to serve as landsmen on the *Virginia II*.[53]

The most important characteristic of the crews of the James River Squadron in 1864-1865 was the preponderance of men taken from Confederate armies. Early in the war, the navy plucked from the army men with skills which fitted them for naval service. Seafaring men from several units raised in Norfolk and elsewhere in Tidewater, Virginia—such as the 32nd Virginia Infantry regiment—were transferred to the navy. The original Company E, 41st Virginia Infantry, for example, became part of the crew of the *C.S.S. Virginia* in time to participate in the Battle of Hampton Roads. Although the Navy and War departments never overcame completely the friction between them, the War Department did issue several orders authorizing the transfer of men from the army to the navy, and the Confederate Congress in April 1862 and May 1863 passed acts facilitating this process. An army order of October 1862 specified that transfers must be forwarded through superior officers "who will certify whether the party whose transfer is sought is or is not a seafaring person." The process, in other words, required the approval of commanding army officers.[54]

Later transfers from the army were more numerous and less carefully selected than early in the war. So desperate was the navy for men the department made it known soldiers and civilians held in Richmond's prisons could shorten their sentences by transferring to the navy. Richmond's provost marshal, Brig. Gen. John H. Winder, received dozens of letters from men who were willing to take their chances in the navy rather than languish in prison. "I take pen in hand to inform you that I wish to join the navy," wrote Gideon Fellers, a soldier arrested for selling a captured pistol. "I am anxious to join the Navy," declared William Jones. "I am in Here for being Abscence [sic.] without Leave." Not surprisingly, men who joined the navy under such circumstances were not the most loyal recruits. "A great many men who are transferred never report themselves," complained Murray Mason, head of the naval rendezvous, to John Winder in January 1864, "and it would not be amiss if they were, when so transferred, sent under guard either to the Provost Marshall, or to this office."[55]

Most of the hundreds of men impressed unwillingly from the army in 1864 apparently had no previous naval experience. Deserters from the James River Squadron in late 1864 told Federal interrogators there were "not many seamen" among the crews of the ironclads. Soldier-turned-sailor Oliver Hamilton estimated half of the *Fredericksburg's* crew consisted of army transfers. According to one deserter who was himself plucked from Lee's army: "The conscripts are not supposed to be very good fighting men, as the balance of the crew kick them around." Though they found themselves with better food and more abundant supplies than they enjoyed in the army, most army transfers resented the change and did not adjust well to the monotony and the hardships of shipboard life. "There are about 150 men in this steamer and we are very much crowded," wrote Oliver Hamilton, "though I think we are going to have a Scooner [sic.] brought along side for some of the crew to stay in.—We get plenty to eat and of that which is tolerably good we get very near twice as much to eat as we did in camp." Despite the improved fare, Hamilton resented being separated from his army comrades. "I can't say yet how I like my transfer though I hope I shall be well pleased after I get used to it. . . . "[56]

In the war's final months, the squadron's flag officer reported that the crews of the squadron were on half-rations and dangerously demoralized. Surviving letters and records suggest, however, that until those final months the supply system for the James River Squadron worked with reasonable efficiency. Paymasters aboard each of the ships received allotments of food, small stores, and clothing from the Richmond warehouses of the Office of Provisions and Clothing. The men of the ironclad *Richmond* received a wide variety of regular rations, including beef, pork, biscuits, flour, rice, sugar, coffee, molasses, beans, tobacco, and soap. For the period of April-October 1864, for example, each member of the crew of the *Richmond* received one ration per day, including on average two-thirds of a pound of meat (usually beef) and a pound of biscuits or flour. This compared well with the rations issued in May 1861 to employees of the Gosport Navy Yard, with the recommended ration of 12 ounces of meat per man per day.[57] Perhaps erroneously, the vessel's commander, William Parker, recalled rations in the summer of 1864 were "pretty short," consisting of a half-pound of salt pork and three biscuits per man per day. The primary ration shortage in the autumn of 1864 was vegetables, which Mitchell not unreasonably believed a contributing factor to the illnesses plaguing the crews.[58]

There are also indications by the final year of war that the Navy Department was having difficulty supplying crews with adequate clothing of any description. In appealing to the Office of Provisions and Clothing for pea jackets and blankets, Captain Mitchell reminded the paymaster in Richmond:

> An adequate supply of winter clothing is all important at this time to make the men comfortable, and unless they are made so they must become discontented and unreliable in health and loyalty. It should be remembered that exposure to bad weather on shipboard is worse than in camp life, where the men can have the advantage of exercise and cheerful fires; hence the wants of the sailor in clothing are greater than those of the soldier in the field.[59]

Sailors on the James were reportedly wearing English-made clothing. A deserter from the *Virginia II* reported in January 1865, that the fall of Wilmington, North Carolina, the Confederacy's last port open to blockade runners—and thus to English clothing supplies—had created fears of a fabric shortage. Clothing, he said, was being issued very sparingly. Clothing records for the *Richmond* in 1864 reveal only blue and duck (white) cloth issued to the crews, but the ship's commander, John Kell, in January 1865 managed to draw seven yards of double-width gray cloth from the ship's supply.[60]

Even with adequate clothing, life on ironclad vessels was notoriously uncomfortable. Southern summers turned ironclads into ovens, forcing men to live in barges alongside or on shore. "The heat and close air are almost unbearable," Robert Minor wrote his wife from what he called his "hot hole of a cabin" on the *Virginia II* in July 1864. Because later war Confederate ironclads had shorter casemates, their flush decks (the decks fore and aft of the casemate just above the waterline) were longer and provided more space for men seeking quarters in the open air. Worried about the effect of the heat on the health of his crew, Mitchell in June 1864 appealed to Mallory for a supply of canvas from which the men could make awnings to shield the flush decks and tents to sleep on shore. In the winter, quarters aboard the *Virginia II* were "very cold and uncomfortable," complained one disgruntled sailor. "Do not like life on an iron-clad," wrote Capt. Edward Crenshaw, commander of the marine guard on the *Virginia II*, in his diary. "There is not air nor ventilation, nor light enough."[61]

Civil War ironclads had the same kind of accommodations as traditional warships, with living quarters located on a berth deck (located below the gun deck) and among the guns. Upon boarding a vessel, crew members were assigned to messes, given bags and hammocks, with racks and nettings in which to store them, and assigned berths which, ideally, were located near their stations.[62] One of the best descriptions of the living spaces of an ironclad comes from Irishman Thomas Conolly, who toured the *Virginia II* with Adm. Raphael Semmes just a week before the fall of Richmond in late March 1865. Conolly described in his diary being led:

> thro a small iron port hole where we saw the thickness of her iron-sides lined with oak about 4 feet [sic.] when inside the great guns one astern of gigantic proportion d[itt]o for'ad & 3 at either side light & air coming thro thick iron bars at top sloping inwards garnished with all the gun requisites tower tier filled with long steel soled shot about 12 inches each. Middle supports covered with racks of six & ten shotting rifles in fine order men & officers sauntering about quietly—Thence to mens quarters down a hatchway for'ad all in order with a cooking stove full of excellent dinner surrounded by mess boxes wh[ich] when opened had their tin plates, cups knives salt pepper &c in good array with the n[umber] of rations for each mess in middle! All as nice as any man of war hammocks all stowed along inside making a pleasant couch to lean against—Men all standing round at attention & all neatly clad in confed: grey shirts Then to engine room at other end—Thro wardroom & quarters Ad[mira]ls sleeping room all dark but bright & clean when lighted up. Back again to Adls Office in the barge after having a long talk with officers in Ward Room. . .[63]

The men of the squadron suffered enormously from heat, cold, and sickness, and, as Mitchell predicted, discomfort had a dramatic effect on morale. Sickness prevailed in the squadron from the summer of 1864 to the end of the war. The navy's chief surgeon, William Spotswood, identified the sickness as malaria, and attributed it to the low water level of the river. Sailors sent to the naval hospital in Richmond recovered quickly, "but very soon after their return to duty in the fleet, relapses invariably occurred, showing conclusively where the cause existed."

Spotswood admitted such sickness was, to a degree, inevitable and "there are no means of prevention, as to its general operation, except through the medium of strict attention, on the part of the officers, to the comfort of the crews, in regard to clothing, food, and a regimen, that will strengthen and fortify the system against attacks." Specifically, Spotswood suggested the men be given their daily spirit ration with their morning coffee "as a means of counteracting the effects of the damp and chilling draughts, so prevalent on all fresh water courses and malarial regions at the dawn of day." A board of navy surgeons inspected the vessels in August 1864 and blamed the prevailing sickness on not only the climate and diet, but also the shipboard environment and routine. The "heated atmosphere of the ironclads" affected men at quarters and in action, but the berth deck assigned to the crew was "uninhabitable" because of heat from the nearby galley (kitchen). When the men did not have to be in the ship, they remained on the flush decks, often exposed to the strong sun. In any case, patrol duty afforded little opportunity for proper exercise.[64]

"On an average about one half of the midshipmen went through this disagreeable experience [of chills and fever] every other day," recalled young Jimmie Morgan. The midshipmen were sent to the Richmond hospital and returned to duty "as soon as the paroxysm was over." In late August 1864, Mitchell reported 226 men in the squadron (not including the *Patrick Henry*) were ill, 157 of them in the naval hospital. One-third of the crew of each of the squadron's ironclads was sick and in the naval hospital. The annual report for the Office of Medicine and Surgery revealed 464 men were admitted to the Richmond Naval Hospital between July and September 1864, though only 13 died. No other station in the Confederate navy suffered as severely from disease.[65]

Sickness was the primary cause of what Mitchell described as "the crippled condition of the squadron from the want of officers and men." Mitchell warned in October 1864 that, because of sickness and because of orders to man land batteries, ironclad steamers and gunboats had few experienced officers on board, and the gunboat *Nansemond* did not have a crew adequate to man her guns.[66]

Though ships of the squadron anchored off Drewry's and Chaffin's bluffs eight miles downriver, Richmond was the squadron's home base.

The Southern capital was the focus of the squadron's social life, but most officers and men had few opportunities to enjoy shore leave. Although he was twice visiting in the city when his squadron was called into action, John Mitchell apparently spent little time there. On Christmas Day in 1864, he noted it was the first time he had spent a day and a night in the capital since September 28—the day before the attack on Fort Harrison. In response to his wife's query about his opportunities to visit the city, newly-appointed commander of the *Richmond* John McIntosh Kell replied that his duties confined him close to the ship. "For although but 9 miles from the city I have been up there but once on a special visit to see Capt Semmes & remained the night."[67] Writing under the pseudonym, "Iron-Clad," a disgruntled sailor who had transferred to the navy from the army, complained in a letter to the editor of the *Richmond Daily Dispatch* that sailors did not have the same furlough opportunities enjoyed by soldiers. The soldiers in Lee's army who had answered the navy's plea for seamen in April 1864 had done so out of patriotism, he wrote:

> But, if, in the exchange, we have made, we are to forfeit the privilege shown our former comrades in the army—I say, if we are to be denied the *dear* privilege of *occasionally* visiting the loved ones from whom we have been so long separated—we earnestly entreat the authorities at Richmond to return to our several commands in the field.[68]

"Iron-Clad's" complaint was apparently not uncommon, for desertion became a severe problem among crews of the squadron in 1865.

Naval Academy midshipmen enjoyed more privileges and more social opportunities than did crews of the vessels. During his two stints on the *Patrick Henry*, Hubbard Taylor Minor "went uptown" frequently between long study sessions. On consecutive nights in January 1865 Minor played billiards and attended "Miss Anna McCan's Party."[69]

More often than not, however, officers and sailors did not go to the city; the city came to them. The squadron was in constant communication with the capital through regular twice-daily mail ships and through periodic visits of cargo ships. Those midshipmen who lived in the cabins at Drewry's Bluff were especially fortunate. "Parties composed of ladies and gentlemen would frequently visit the Bluff and they made it quite gay," remembered Midshipman Morgan. Those river excursions to the furthest point of Confederate control of the river had by 1864 become a highlight of Richmond social life. Midshipman Clayton described Drewry's Bluff as "a regular picnic ground for the young people of Richmond and Petersburg, which we middies greatly enjoyed." Hubbard T. Minor wrote in his diary in November 1863 that "there was a party of young men & I was invited to be one of them who chartered the Str. Schultz & brought a nice party of young ladies most of whom I knew down to the Bluff. . . . " Among the people who visited Drewry's Bluff were the wife and sister-in-law of President Jefferson Davis. The Naval Academy midshipmen even issued invitations to a "Midshipman's Hop" aboard the *Patrick Henry* at Rocketts on December 27, 1864.[70]

The ships themselves entertained occasional visitors from the city. "A party of pretty ladies visited on ship from Richmond today," wrote Capt. Edward Crenshaw, commander of the Marine guard on the *Virginia II*, on March 18, 1865. "They dined on board the Richmond and returned to the city in the evening." A week later a party of Richmond ladies dined on both the *Richmond* and the flagship, *Virginia II*.[71]

When sailors, and even the more elite midshipmen, did get into Richmond, the result was often predictable. Midshipman Minor wrote in his diary in October 1863 that he and his six-man crew boat escorted Cdr. William Parker and his wife to Richmond. "I then allowed all of my crew to go on shore well knowing that they would be well intoxicated but determined never the less to gratify them knowing I could easily control them no matter in what state they were."[72]

Minor's self-confidence notwithstanding, midshipmen, sailors, and marines on liberty in Richmond often proved beyond control. Richmond newspapers carried reports of drunken sailors in trouble with the law. Samuel Keene, a riverboat pilot by trade serving as master's mate on the *Beaufort*, was sent into Richmond on February 2, 1864, in search of a deserter from the ship. By all accounts, wrote then-squadron commander French Forrest to Secretary Mallory, Keene "had indulged too freely in spiritous liquors." "When he was sober he was a good officer and a peaceable man," a newspaper observed, "but when intoxicated seemed bereft of reason." Although apprehended and taken back to the ship, Keene was dedicated to his duty, for he "sallied out" again at 10:00 p.m.

and arrested an Irishman "in no manner connected with the steamer." Police chased and caught Keene behind Castle Thunder prison and subdued him when he drew his cutlass. The story ended tragically when Keene again gained freedom and drew his weapon. Police shot him dead.[73] Others suffered similar fates. James Kelley, of the *Patrick Henry*, was robbed of a gold ring and $200 Confederate money on the night of February 15, 1864, then murdered the following evening at what a newspaper described as "the house of two white women of easy virtue."[74]

William F. Clayton, a young midshipman from Georgia who was in the Academy from 1861 to 1864, recalled his own participation in one of these "incidents." In early January 1864 Clayton returned with his class to the school ship and enjoyed a reunion with an old friend, boatswain Jim Smith. To celebrate their reunion, Clayton and Smith planned a night on the town. After a few drinks, the men went to the theater, where they found themselves seated behind a gentleman wearing a fashionably tall beaver hat. The hat, Clayton recalled, "cut off Jim's view of the stage, and he politely asked the individual to please 'douse the glim.'" To this request, Clayton wrote, the man "replied that he would not take in his royals—that is remove his hat."

"Now Jim was a tolerably large-sized man," Clayton continued, "and had on him the hand about the size of an ordinary spade, and letting fall his hand on the top of this beaver, it went down, with the rim resting on the owner's shoulders. Immediately, a cry was raised, 'Put 'em out.' The ludicrous attempt of the fellow to get his head out of that beaver would have made a saint laugh."

Transformed from spectators to fugitives, the two sailors made their escape from the theater. Several policeman gave chase, but, having been stationed there before, the sailors knew the streets and alleys of Richmond and found their way safely back to the American Hotel. "Of course," Clayton mused, "the Richmond Examiner gave an account headed: 'Some More Ruffianism of the Navy,' but we preferred to remain quiet and let Mr. Pollard soothe his wounded arm with any use he might care to make of printer's ink."[75]

For the men of the James River Squadron, such adventures were the exception and not the rule. Drudgery and routine, even when operating in close proximity to the enemy, were the norm. Living in physical discomfort in an unfamiliar shipboard environment, prone to frequent illness, and growing ever more demoralized, it is little wonder so many sailors of the squadron deserted. Hundreds of others, however, endured the privations, resisted the temptations to desert, and remained with the squadron to war's end. One of those was John T. Chappell, a veteran of the 10th Virginia Cavalry who transferred to the navy in the summer of 1864. The self-styled amateur poet of the *Virginia II*, Chappell on January 4, 1865, wrote "'Buddies' of 1865," a poem which stands as an anthem of sorts to the spirit of the Confederate sailor:

It was Tuesday night,
By an oil lamp light,
Sat Rankin, Chappell, and Paul;
It was a curious sight,
Say what you might,
As the lamp light fell on all.

They are three friends,
Each on the other depends
For comfort, consolation, and fun;
Their evenings are spent,
With each other's consent,
To enjoy their pleasures as one.

Their friendship dies not,
Like the flowers that rot,
When the frost shows its gleaming white eye,
But like the stout oak,
Which by storm is not broke,
Stands their friendship, as the years pass by.
May it ever be so,
'Till time is no more,
And death ends this world's wild career, and all;
May they ever agree,
That wonderful three,
Jack Chappell, Bob Rankin, and Paul.[76]

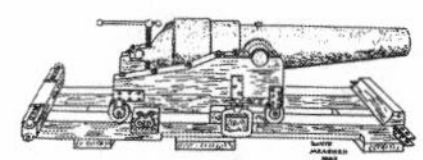

Capt. John Kirkwood Mitchell

Entering the Confederate navy with a reputation as a fighter, Mitchell (1811-1889) had the misfortune to twice demonstrate the incapacities of Confederate naval technology. In April 1862, he arrived in New Orleans in time to have his fleet (including the celebrated, but incomplete ironclad *Louisiana*) destroyed by Adm. David G. Farragut's Federal fleet. Two years later, Mitchell was given command of the James River Squadron as a strong Federal fleet ascended the river. Chastened by his New Orleans experience, Mitchell proved overly cautious, though he correctly judged that his own ships were flawed. Professional and gentlemanly, Mitchell accepted the consequences of his James River failure, but fought to his dying day the criticism he faced for the New Orleans debacle. Scharf, *Confederate States Navy.*

Officers in the James River Squadron, 1864-1865

On October 18, 1864, a large group of Confederate officers who had been held in prison at Ft. Warren, Boston, were exchanged at Aiken's Landing on the James River and brought to Richmond. Most had been captured in June 1863 aboard the Savannah-built ironclad *Atlanta*. Considered one of the Confederacy's best built vessels, the *Atlanta* ran aground on her maiden voyage and was forced to surrender. Following their exchange, the naval officers were assigned to vessels of the James River Squadron or to the river defense batteries. While in prison, the officers from the *Atlanta* took the opportunity to have their portraits made.

Lt. William A. Webb

A former lieutenant in the U.S. Navy, Webb commanded the *Teaser* during the Battle of Hampton Roads before assuming command of the *Atlanta*. He briefly held command of the *Richmond* shortly after his exchange. Carte-de-visite by W. Rattray, Liverpool, England [probably from another image].

Lt. George Henry Arledge

Arledge was stationed in Richmond briefly before joining the crew of the *Atlanta*. Upon his return to the Confederacy, he was assigned to the *Fredericksburg*. As illness swept through the officer ranks of the James River Squadron, Arledge held temporary command of the *Beaufort* in 1865. He surrendered and was paroled at Greensboro in May 1865. Carte-de-visite by J. W. Black, Boston, Massachusetts, ca. 1863-1864.

Lt. Alphonse Barbot

Barbot found himself "in charge" of the *Fredericksburg* temporarily in 1865 when illness incapacitated her senior officer. Before his service aboard the *Atlanta*, Bardot had been an officer on the *Arkansas* and was stationed at New Orleans and Charleston. Carte-de-visite by J. W. Black, Boston, Massachusetts, ca. 1863-1864.

Midshipman James A. Peters

Upon his return from prison, Peters served in the James River Squadron aboard the *Richmond* and *Virginia II*. Though still only an acting midshipman, Peters was temporarily "in charge" of the latter vessel in early 1865. Carte-de-visite by J. W. Black, Boston, Massachusetts, ca. 1863-1864.

Joining the Confederate navy from the Confederate Army, Wragg served throughout the war as master not in line of promotion. After returning to the South from prison in Boston, Wragg was assigned to the James River batteries, then to the crews of the James River ironclads *Fredericksburg* and *Richmond*. Carte-de-visite by J. W. Black, Boston, Massachusetts, ca. 1863-1864.

Master Thomas L. Wragg

Master's Mate William McBlair, Jr.

After his release from Fort Warren and exchange at Aiken's Landing, McBlair was assigned to the *Richmond*. Carte-de-visite by J. W. Black, Boston, Massachusetts.

Asst. Engineer Joseph Stanhope West

West joined the crew of the *Hampton* as engineer in late 1864. He served on that vessel until the evacuation of Richmond, then, with the other officers and sailors of the squadron, became part of Raphael Semmes' command in the Confederate army. Carte-de-visite by J. W. Black, Boston, Massachusetts.

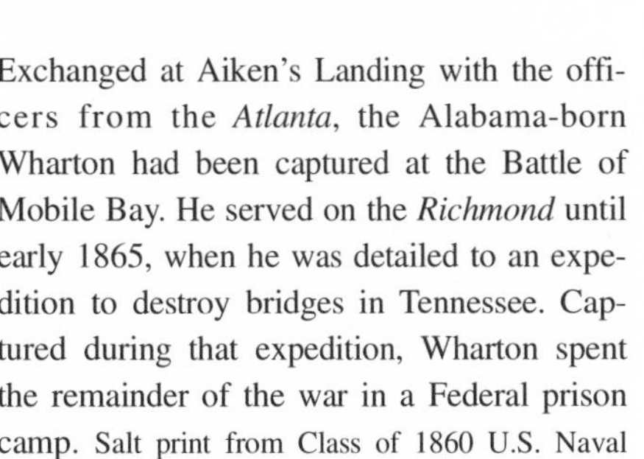

Exchanged at Aiken's Landing with the officers from the *Atlanta*, the Alabama-born Wharton had been captured at the Battle of Mobile Bay. He served on the *Richmond* until early 1865, when he was detailed to an expedition to destroy bridges in Tennessee. Captured during that expedition, Wharton spent the remainder of the war in a Federal prison camp. Salt print from Class of 1860 U.S. Naval Academy album. Courtesy of Charles V. Peery.

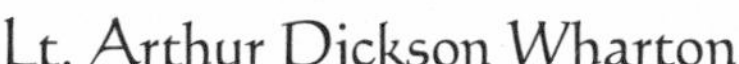

Lt. Arthur Dickson Wharton

Cdr. John McIntosh Kell

Formerly the executive officer of the commerce raider *Alabama*, Kell (1823-1900) arrived in Richmond in the last days of 1864 to assume command of his own vessel, the C.S.S. *Richmond*. Plagued by the chills and fever which felled many other men who served in the James River Squadron, Kell was only able to serve for a few months. During that time, he commanded the first of the Richmond-built ironclads during its only major engagement, at Trent's Reach in January 1865. Crayon sketch.

Lt. John W. Dunnington

Virtually unknown in Virginia waters before 1864, Dunnington commanded the flagship *Virginia II* during the Battle of Trent's Reach. A 12-year veteran of the United States Navy, the Kentucky-born Dunnington commanded vessels in New Orleans and on the Mississippi River for the first two years of the war. Captured at Arkansas Post in early 1863, Dunnington was exchanged and given command of the blockade runner, *Owl*, before his assignment to Richmond. Copy print of photograph taken in Paris, France, ca. 1861-1862, courtesy of Charles V. Peery.

Lt. Francis Edgar Shepperd

Impatient with the timidity and shortcomings of his superiors, the flinty-eyed North Carolinian proved his own mettle as commander of the *Fredericksburg* in the Battle of Trent's Reach. A graduate of and former instructor at the U.S. Naval Academy, Shepperd (1834-1887) resigned from the U.S. Navy in July 1861. He commanded a succession of Confederate vessels at New Orleans and Charleston. Transferred from command of the Charleston ironclad *Palmetto State* to Richmond station in 1864, Shepperd variously commanded the gunboat *Hampton* and the ironclads *Virginia II* and *Fredericksburg*. The persistent illness of the latter's commander, Capt. Thomas Rootes, gave Shepperd his opportunity to command a warship in action. Carte-de-visite courtesy of Charles V. Peery.

Lt. Joseph D. Wilson

A long-time compatriot of Raphael Semmes, Wilson served aboard both the *Sumter* and the *Alabama*, and was taken prisoner after the latter vessel was sunk off Cherbourg, France. Upon his return to the Confederacy, Wilson joined the crew of the *Virginia II*, and was in command of the *Hampton* during the winter of 1865. When the Confederates abandoned Richmond, Wilson accompanied Semmes to Danville, Virginia, and into North Carolina. From a wartime carte-de-visite.

One of the Confederate navy's many talented young officers, Butt (1839-1885) had been a midshipman in the U.S. Navy before the war. He was captured and held prisoner briefly aboard the U.S. warship *Congress* and at Fort Warren, Boston. He was exchanged in time to serve on the crew of the *Virginia* at the Battle of Hampton Roads, during which battle the *Congress* was destroyed. Butt was stationed at Drewry's Bluff in 1862-1863 and returned to Virginia in 1864 after service abroad. He commanded the gunboat *Nansemond* during the Battle of Trent's Reach and until the vessel's destruction in April 1865. Carte-de-visite by "Nadar" (Felix Tournechon), Paris, France, ca. 1863. Courtesy of Charles V. Peery.

Lt. Walter Raleigh Butt

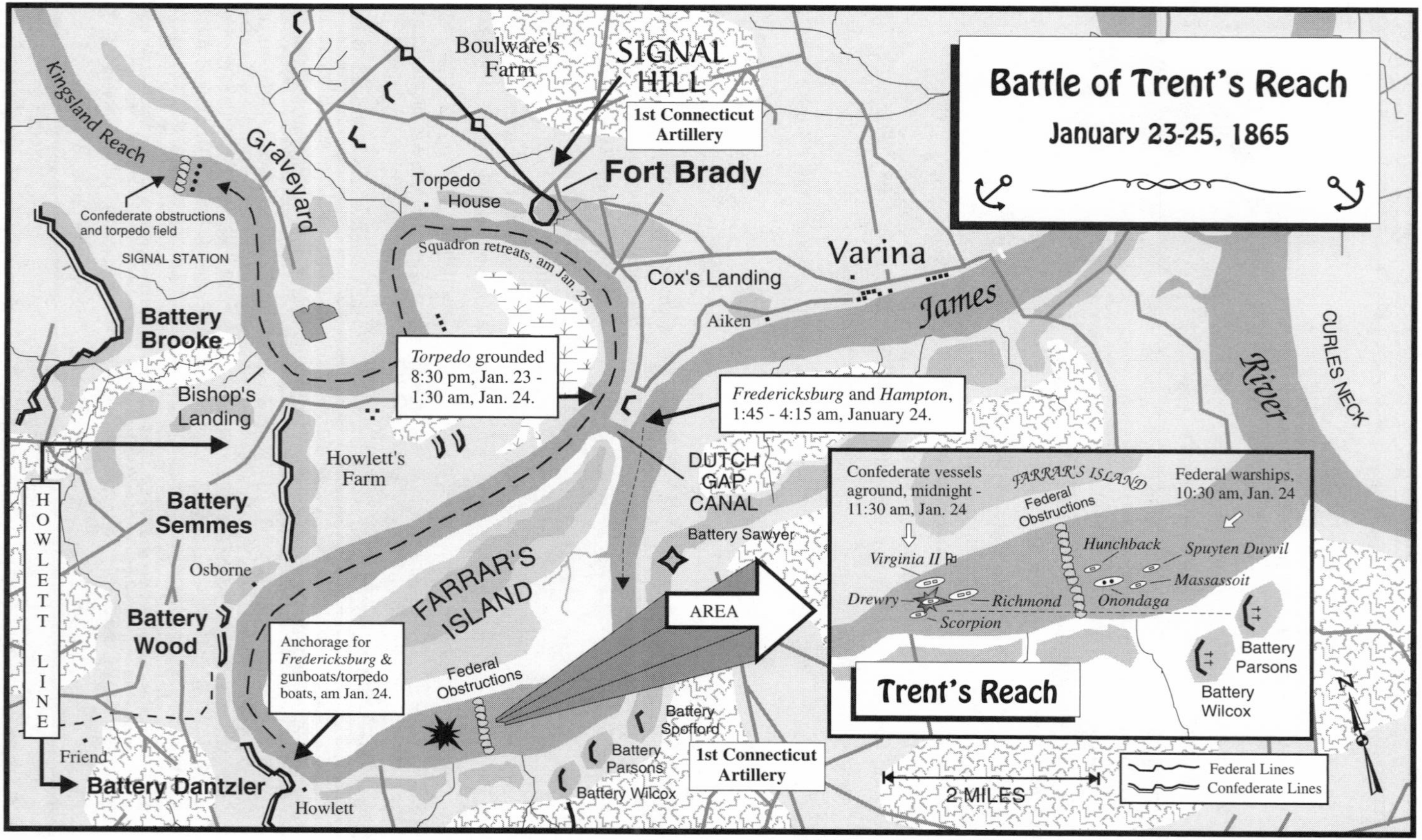

Battle of Trent's Reach

January 23-25, 1865

Boulware's Farm

SIGNAL HILL

1st Connecticut Artillery

Fort Brady

Torpedo House

Graveyard

Kingsland Reach

Confederate obstructions and torpedo field

SIGNAL STATION

Battery Brooke

Bishop's Landing

Squadron retreats, am Jan. 25

Torpedo grounded 8:30 pm, Jan. 23 - 1:30 am, Jan. 24.

Cox's Landing

Varina

Aiken

James River

CURLES NECK

Fredericksburg and *Hampton*, 1:45 - 4:15 am, January 24.

DUTCH GAP CANAL

Battery Sawyer

Howlett's Farm

Battery Semmes

Osborne

Battery Wood

FARRAR'S ISLAND

Anchorage for *Fredericksburg* & gunboats/torpedo boats, am Jan. 24.

Federal Obstructions

AREA

Battery Spofford

Battery Parsons

Battery Wilcox

1st Connecticut Artillery

HOWLETT LINE

Friend

Battery Dantzler

Howlett

Confederate vessels aground, midnight - 11:30 am, Jan. 24

FARRAR'S ISLAND

Federal Obstructions

Federal warships, 10:30 am, Jan. 24

Virginia II

Drewry

Richmond

Scorpion

Hunchback

Spuyten Duyvil

Massassoit

Onondaga

Battery Parsons

Battery Wilcox

Trent's Reach

2 MILES

Federal Lines

Confederate Lines

N

Mark A. Moore

Chapter 6

No Advance, No Retreat:
The Battle of Trent's Reach & the Final Months of the James River Squadron

The winter of 1864-1865 was "intensely cold," remembered Midshipman James Morgan, with several feet of snow on the ground. The new commander of the ironclad *Richmond*, John Kell, arrived on the James in January 1865 in the midst of the most bitter weather. "You must not think however I am quite frozen up on board of an Ironclad," the former first officer of the Confederate raider, *Alabama*, wrote his wife, "for with all the severe weather we have had, we make ourselves quite comfortable with a stove below."[1]

The weather proved of great concern to Kell and his comrades in the James River Squadron for reasons beyond personal comfort. Snow followed by rain in central Virginia created freshets (flooding) in the James that played havoc with both the Confederate and Federal squadrons. On January 15, 1865, Lt. Charles W. Read, commander of the Confederate torpedo boats on the James, ventured downstream to reconnoiter the enemy's position. He reported to Mitchell (and to Secretary Mallory) that the floods had apparently washed away the Federal obstructions at Trent's Reach.[2] The time for action had arrived.

The Battle of Trent's Reach

This was exciting news for Mallory, who had fretted for months over the impotence of the James River Squadron. "I deem the opportunity a favorable one for striking a blow at the enemy, if we are able to do so," Mallory wrote to Mitchell. "If we can block the river at or below City Point, Grant might be compelled to evacuate his position." Such an attack Mallory deemed "a movement of the first importance to the country, and one which should be accomplished if possible."[3] Time was of the essence. Not only were the Federal obstructions temporarily washed away, but most of the Federal flotilla that had steamed up the James in May 1864 was gone—participating in the massive sea and land operation against Fort Fisher, near Wilmington, North Carolina.

Once again, as in May 1864, Mitchell declined to act precipitously. Although informed that the enemy obstructions might be gone, the squadron commander was more concerned with the state of his own navy's obstructions. On the last day of 1864, the chief engineer of Lee's army had asked Mitchell whether it was necessary to retain the line of obstructions at Kingsland Reach just beyond Chaffin's Bluff. Somewhat peevishly, Mitchell offered the engineer a history lesson, pointing out how the Federal navy overwhelmed Confederate defenses in the Mississippi and in Mobile Bay. "Would he be likely to do less on the James in any naval enterprise he undertakes against us? Surely not, and we can never hope to encounter him on anything like equal terms, except from accident." It "behooves us," Mitchell concluded, to make full use of obstructions, torpedoes, and land batteries to defend the James." On the same day Read reported that freshets opened a gap in the Federal obstructions, Mitchell queried the squadron's ship commanders about the state of Confederate obstructions. He was relieved to learn that they had suffered no damage from the rising waters. Responding to Mallory's request for action, Mitchell asked for two days to inspect the Federal obstructions more closely. He also took the opportunity to ask that he be able to reclaim the men and officers lost to the manning of the shore batteries. Five days after receiving Read's intelligence, the squadron had not moved. Mallory persisted: "You have an opportunity, I am convinced, rarely presented to a naval officer, and one which may lead to the most glorious results to your country. I deplore that you did not start immediately after the freshet, and have deplored the loss of every day since."[4]

Fortunately for the Confederates, Mitchell's Federal counterpart was just as dilatory in acting on intelligence he had received. Commander William A. Parker had assumed command of the Fifth Division, North Atlantic Blockading Squadron, in late November 1864. The division was a shadow of its former self. Admiral David Dixon Porter, who had replaced Samuel Lee as squadron commander in October, concentrated his resources against Wilmington—the busiest port for Confederate blockade running vessels—and took with him the monitors *Saugus* and *Canonicus*. Barricaded behind its obstructions, Parker's flotilla mustered only one ironclad, the double-turreted monitor *Onondaga*, and a handful of wooden warships: the screw steamer *Daylight*, side-wheel steamers *Eutaw*, *Hunchback*, *Massassoit*, *Miami*, *William Putnam* and *Commodore Barney*, the side-wheel steamer that almost met her death against a James River torpedo in August 1863. All except the *Putnam* had as many or more guns of heavier weight than those carried by Confederate vessels. The *Onondaga* carried two 15-inch Dahlgren smoothbores and two 150-pound Parrott rifles—one of the strongest batteries of any vessel in service. Other war vessels on blockade duty 90 miles downstream at Hampton Roads were available to Parker if he needed them. Porter left Parker in command of the division, confident this force was sufficient to defend City Point *and* destroy the Confederate squadron if it were foolish enough to invite battle. Confederate warships were not, however, Porter's paramount concern. The James River Division's primary duty was to patrol the long stretch of water between Hampton Roads and Trent's Reach and prevent land attacks on Federal shore facilities and shipping. In the last days of 1864, Porter instructed Parker to "run no risks at present or while I am away." Insisting that Parker resist any temptation to diverge from routine, he ordered his subordinate: "Preserve your vessels until the right time comes. Keep most of the vessels on the river busy patrolling."[5]

Two days before the James River Squadron began its descent, the army informed Parker the Confederates were about to launch a desperate attack. General Grant's chief of staff, Brig. Gen. John Rawlins, told

Parker that the Confederates reasoned "that upon the return of our iron clads, theirs would be permanently shut up in the upper part of the James, and that even if the movement resulted in the loss of their vessels, it could be no worse than what would eventually be the case, and might inflict incalculable damage upon us." Despite this intelligence, Parker evidently did not believe that "the right time" had come for a change in his squadron's routine. Parker, like his Confederate counterpart Mitchell, was plagued by a defensive mindset, and had since early January resisted suggestions to attack the Confederate fleet. Informed by several sources of the impending attack, Parker fretted at the vulnerability of his position. "I do not consider our naval forces sufficient to prevent the possibility of coming down at high water, should they make the attempt."[6] Strangely fatalistic, Parker ignored warnings to be especially vigilant and did not monitor the obstructions.

Thus, the Confederate movement planned for the night of January 23-24, 1865, would meet minimal enemy resistance.[7] Although still not convinced that the Trent's Reach obstructions were entirely gone, Mitchell ordered the squadron to move at 6:00 p.m. and warned that it must pass Battery Semmes two and one-half hours later in order to arrive at Trent's Reach at high water. At low water, the river at the Trent's Reach bar was only eight feet deep, one to two feet *less* than the draft of the lightest Confederate ironclad. Maneuvering vessels through the narrow channel was fraught with dangers. To minimize the chance of collision, Mitchell ordered that the wooden vessels be lashed firmly to the ironclads: the gunboat *Hampton* and torpedo boat *Hornet* to the *Fredericksburg*; the gunboat *Beaufort* and armed tender *Drewry* (towing the torpedo boat *Wasp*) to the *Richmond*; and the gunboats *Nansemond* and *Torpedo* (towing the torpedo boat *Scorpion*) to the *Virginia II*. The lightest of the ironclads, the *Fredericksburg* led the flotilla. Her commander, Lieutenant Shepperd, had evidently suffered no punishment for his earlier blunt criticism of Mitchell's cautiousness, for he was still in command of his ram when the squadron lifted anchor for Trent's Reach.[8]

The journey down the river entailed several hazards, natural and man-made, friendly and otherwise. The first was the line of 36 torpedoes sowed recently by Beverly Kennon. Aided by coded stakes identifying the location of the torpedoes, the squadron negotiated that hazard successfully.[9]

After steaming through the Kingsland and Graveyard Reaches, the Confederate squadron drew under the enemy guns of Fort Brady on Signal Hill at approximately 8:00 p.m. The ships were steaming downriver completely darkened, the guns of each ironclad pulled inside and the port shutters sealed. Dark and silent, the squadron managed to approach the fort undetected, the Federal pickets on the opposite bank entirely unaware of their presence.[10]

As the squadron drew near, the commander of Fort Brady, Capt. Henry Pierce of the 1st Connecticut Heavy Artillery, reported his lookout stationed on the parapet "discovered the rams approaching, floating, not steaming, down the river. Thanks to the vigilance of my own officers and men. . .I was not surprised," he afterward insisted. As the ships closed with the fort and attempted to pass downstream toward Cox's Landing, Fort Brady opened fire with its guns, including 100-pounder Parrott Rifles. We "gave them in the neighborhood of twenty-five shots while floating a distance of thirty or forty rods," Pierce later wrote. Although the guns of the squadron remained silent, Confederate land batteries across the river directed their fire upon the fort. The 1st Connecticut's colonel later reported this exchange as "very severe." A fortuitous shot, the second delivered against the fort, disabled the left-most 100-pounder, "my best gun," lamented Pierce in his after-action report. Federal gunfire ceased as the ironclads passed Fort Brady because poor engineering prevented the occupants of the land battery from training their pieces downriver. "In consequence of the mal-construction of Fort Brady," Pierce reported, "was unable to fire down the river. . .the embrasures having been built with special reference to the enemy's land batteries, my left 100-pounder being destroyed, was prevented from injuring the boats after passing a certain point. . . ."[11]

While fire from Fort Brady failed to check the squadron, it did alert Federal batteries downstream that enemy vessels were approaching. This allowed the men of the 1st Connecticut Artillery, who also crewed the guns at Batteries Wilcox, Parsons, Spofford and Sawyer, overlooking Trent's Reach, to give the James River Squadron the most severe pounding it endured during the entire war. Before daylight, the batteries fired about 100 rounds into the darkness toward the obstructions and at the vessels passing to and fro, uncertain whether their shots were finding their marks.[12]

Shortly after passing by Fort Brady at some time after 8:00 p.m., the *Virginia II* steered perilously close to the shore, running the *Torpedo* aground near the western side of the Dutch Gap Canal. The *Nansemond*, commanded by Lt. Walter Raleigh Butt, cast loose from the *Virginia II* and attempted to free the *Torpedo*. Butt found the vessel not merely grounded, but, in the words of her commander, Lt. Thomas P. Bell, "high and dry in the bushes." Tying a hawser (rope) to the *Torpedo*, Butt tried in vain for a half-hour to free her. Preparing for the worst, Bell remained with the ship but transferred most of her crew to the *Nansemond* and destroyed the ship's ammunition and torpedo. Before long, the *Drewry*, commanded by Lt. William H. Wall, came to the *Torpedo's* rescue and freed her without difficulty, towing her downstream as far as Battery Dantzler.[13] Unfortunately for the Confederates, this would not be the last time that several vessels were diverted from the main purpose of the expedition to free sister ships. Throughout the ordeal of the next 24 hours, John Mitchell must have recalled with grim smugness his May 1864 warnings about the difficulties of navigating the James.

Those problems notwithstanding, success still seemed possible when the *Fredericksburg* cleared the channel in the Federal obstructions at 1:30 a.m., January 24. The lead vessels had arrived at the western end of Trent's Reach about 9:00 p.m. Since the squadron's presence was no longer a secret, the ships endured constant small arms fire from shore. As he was ordered to do, Shepperd anchored the *Fredericksburg* 50 yards short of the obstructions and had them inspected. Under steady small arms and mortar fire, Charles Read, commander of the squadron's torpedo boats, went forward in the *Scorpion* with a "Pilot Wood" from the *Virginia II* in order to sound the depth of the river and scrutinize the blockage. "We proceeded to sound the bar, but when we arrived at the obstructions the enemy opened upon us with musketry and a small mortar," Read later reported. "The pilot declined to sound farther, saying that he was satisfied that the channel was not open." The fire from the Federal gun emplacements may have unnerved the ironclad's pilot, for

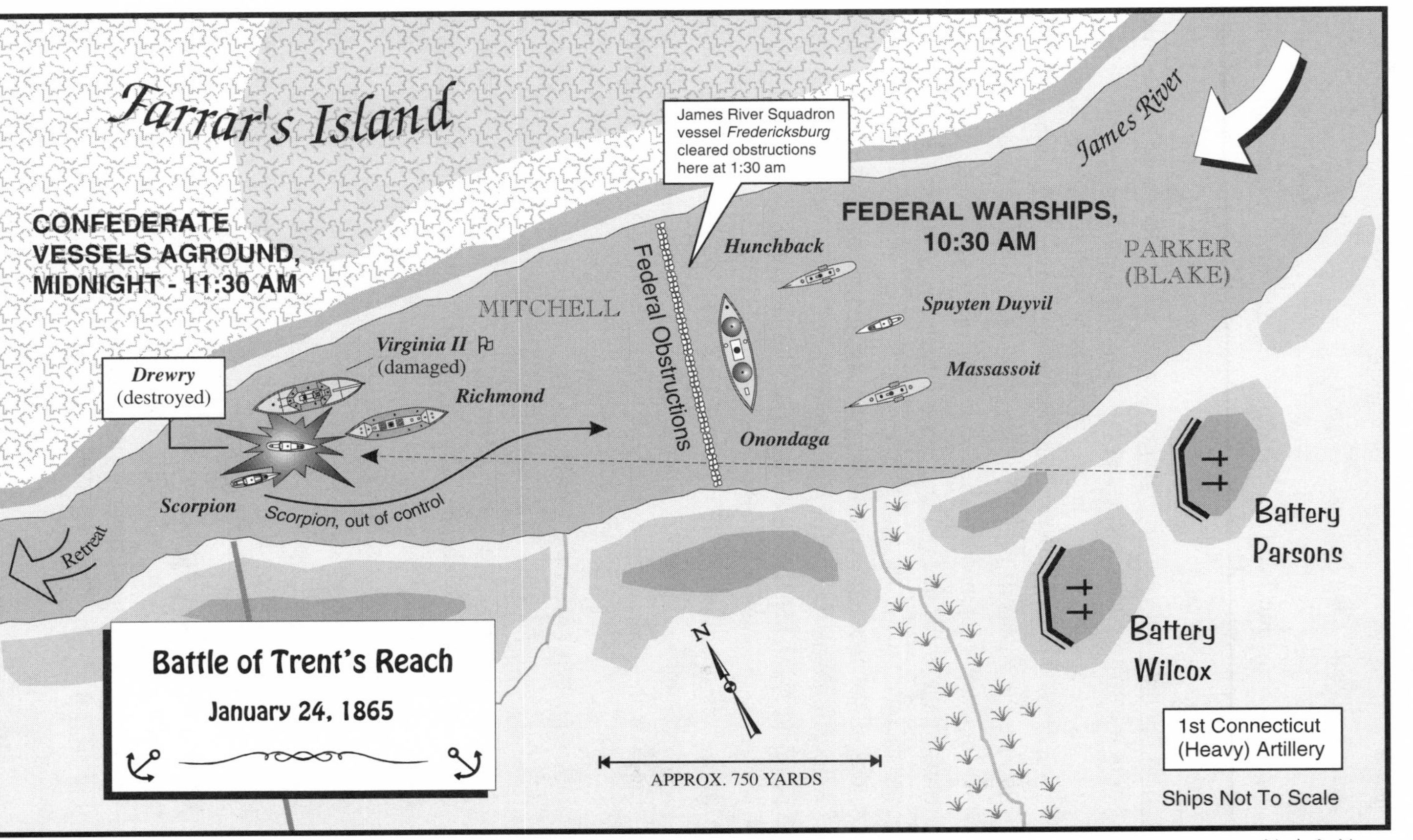
Farrar's Island
James River
James River Squadron vessel Fredericksburg cleared obstructions here at 1:30 am
CONFEDERATE VESSELS AGROUND, MIDNIGHT - 11:30 AM
FEDERAL WARSHIPS, 10:30 AM
PARKER (BLAKE)
Hunchback
Spuyten Duyvil
Massassoit
Onondaga
Federal Obstructions
MITCHELL
Virginia II (damaged)
Richmond
Drewry (destroyed)
Scorpion
Scorpion, out of control
Retreat
Battery Parsons
Battery Wilcox
1st Connecticut (Heavy) Artillery
Ships Not To Scale
N
APPROX. 750 YARDS
Battle of Trent's Reach
January 24, 1865
Mark A. Moore

Read noted that "he became very insubordinate because I would not send him back to the *Virginia*."

Read found there was 18 feet of water through the channel and a large spar running from the middle of the channel to the south shore, anchored on both ends. He informed Mitchell the obstructions could be cleared and communicated orders to Shepperd that he stand ready to pass through. Leaving his flagship and the *Richmond* about a half-mile from the obstructions, the squadron commander went in a small boat to join Read at the channel in the obstructions before joining Shepperd aboard the *Fredericksburg*. Read returned to the obstructions to cut through the chains that held the spar in place, but before he could finish, the impetuous Shepperd took the *Fredericksburg* through the obstructions on the north side of the channel where there was no spar. The bold commander paid a price for his haste, for the torpedo outriggers on both sides of the ironclad were torn away, apparently by sunken hulks that were as high as seven feet below water level. More importantly, Shepperd and several officers felt their ship's hull strike something below the waterline, and later discovered later she was leaking at the rate of two to three inches per hour.[14]

Meeting no resistance, Shepperd took the *Fredericksburg* past the range of the Federal shore batteries and anchored 100 yards below the eastern entrance to the Dutch Gap Canal. The gunboat *Hampton*, Lt. James D. Wilson commanding, was able to pass the obstructions and join the *Fredericksburg*. Although neither officer could have known it at the time, the anchorage of those two vessels was the "high water mark" of the capital navy's advance against the enemy. They waited in vain for the other ships of the squadron to join them for the attack on City Point. Critical of his fellow officers for their indecision in May and June 1864, Shepperd soon was given new cause for disillusionment. Why hadn't the other ironclads come through the barrier?[15]

The expedition had already suffered a fatal blow by the time the *Fredericksburg* cleared the enemy obstructions. After personally witnessing the passage and accompanying the *Fredericksburg* through the barricade, Mitchell at 1:45 a.m. returned to his flagship, *Virginia II*. "To my inexpressible mortification I found her aground," Mitchell wrote in his official report. The grounding had occurred at midnight. The *Nan-*

semond and the *Beaufort* tried in vain for three hours to free the ship widely considered the strongest of the three ironclads. The situation only grew worse. John Kell, commander of the *Richmond*, had dispatched the *Beaufort* and *Drewry* to the aid of the grounded *Virginia II* and the *Torpedo*, only to discover a little after midnight his own ship was aground. The *Drewry* returned from the fruitless effort to free the flagship to assist Kell's stranded ram, then ran aground herself on the ironclad's port side. While Kell and Mitchell tried to free their warships, the crew of the *Fredericksburg* continued waiting beyond the obstructions, unaware of the fiasco playing out upriver. Meanwhile, Read took the torpedo boat *Scorpion*, which he had used in channel-clearing work, and sought to locate the *Hampton*, which Mitchell had planned to use as a stationary beacon to mark the north side of the channel. Unable to locate the *Hampton*—he assumed in error she had passed through the obstructions—Read instead steamed to the *Virginia II* for a lantern to light the passage. Much to his chagrin, he found the flagship aground, and was informed by Mitchell "that the squadron would not go through that night." Coming alongside the ironclad, the *Scorpion* was pushed into the *Virginia II's* torpedo outriggers by a hawser which ran from the flagship to the *Beaufort*. A short while later, the *Scorpion* herself was grounded. Trying unsuccessfully to free the *Scorpion*, her sister ship *Hornet* ran aground temporarily as well.[16]

Faced with this tragi-comic chain of events, Mitchell reluctantly recalled the *Fredericksburg* and *Hampton* and began plotting a strategy to save the helpless ships once daylight brought them into full view of Federal gunners. As Mitchell later explained in his report:

> The tide having been at ebb for some hours, and it therefore being impossible to get the vessels afloat before the next flood, I directed the wooden vessels and torpedo boats to take up their anchorage before daylight opposite Battery Dantzler, under cover of a wooded point of land, which would secure them from the observation of the enemy, or at least afford some protection from his fire.

Mitchell initially asked Shepperd to keep the *Fredericksburg* nearby to cover her helpless sisters with her broadside gun, but apparently changed his mind, for the *Fredericksburg* joined the wooden ships at

Battery Dantzler before dawn. As the morning approached, the *Richmond* lay in the channel with the *Drewry* close by, and the *Virginia II* some distance nearer the north shore. All three were in easy range of the Federal batteries.[17]

Realizing the stranded *Drewry* "would suffer seriously without being able to return the fire," Kell ordered the ship abandoned and her crew brought aboard the *Richmond*. "This was at 6:55 a.m. of the 24th instant," Kell noted in his report. Dawn brought a punishing bombardment which the ships could only endure until the water rose enough to float them. The gunners of Battery Parsons were pleasantly surprised when the rising sun revealed the stranded enemy vessels roughly 1,500 yards upriver. The Federal gunners immediately loaded their 100-pound Parrott rifle with exploding percussion shell and trained it on the helpless *Drewry*. "As soon as the breech site could be used, I opened with long percussion shell," explained Lt. H. A. Pratt, commander of Batteries Parsons and Wilcox. "The second shell struck the wooden boat; the third, fired at an elevation of four degrees, penetrated it, causing a magnificient explosion." The fiery destruction of the *Drewry* at 7:10 a.m. came just a quarter-hour after the evacuation of her crew. Thereafter, the stranded ironclads suffered under a hail of shot and shell. According to Kell, both the blast from the *Drewry's* destruction and the continual pounding of his ironclad from the shore batteries was intense:

> The shock felt on board the *Richmond* was terrific. I ordered the crew to keep silence and remain at their quarters, which was observed with prompt obedience, the officers and crew exhibiting great coolness and presence of mind. Up to 11:10 a.m. the ship was struck so constantly by shot and shell that it was impossible to keep account of the number—three times with heavy shot, causing decided shocks and knocking off the heads of bolts, with slight indentures in the shield and starboard bow port and starboard side of stern port.

The shock from the *Drewry's* explosion sent the nearby *Scorpion* drifting downstream out of control, killing two men and washing overboard four others who had been attempting to free the torpedo vessel. Despite attempts to rescue her later that day, the *Scorpion* fell into enemy hands.[18]

From City Point, 18 miles downriver, Ulysses Grant heard the explosion of the *Drewry*. The commanding general of the Federal armies was as apoplectic as Mitchell was desperate. Where, he wondered, was Parker and the Federal flotilla? Grant realized if a Confederate ironclad steamed past the batteries and the flotilla she could wreak havoc with his supply base. But, since the Northern forces knew of Confederate intentions, Grant viewed the breakout attempt as an opportunity to destroy the James River Squadron. "What fleet have you collected or ordered to the front?" Grant anxiously telegrammed Parker. "You ought to have every gunboat you can get in the river up with you." Consistent with Porter's instructions in less extraordinary times, the wooden gunboats were on patrol duty farther downstream. Parker was holding the *Onondaga* downriver from the Federal obstructions, fearful of engaging her alone against the Confederate ironclads. He also believed it more advantageous to confront the enemy downriver where there was more room for maneuver, and less chance of coming under the fire of friendly shore batteries. Although Parker had ordered two torpedo boats, *Spuyten Duyvil* and *No. 4*, to attack the vessels that had come through the obstructions, by the time they arrived, the enemy had crossed back upriver.[19]

Infuriated with Parker's lack of initiative, Grant communicated directly with Assistant Navy Secretary Gustavus A. Fox, in Washington, to take action. Late on the 24th, Fox removed Parker from command and replace him temporarily with Lt. Cdr. Homer Blake of the *Eutaw*. Fox told Grant President Lincoln even suggested dispatching the U.S. Navy's most celebrated officer, Adm. David G. Farragut, to take command at City Point. Instead, Fox and Grant arranged for several warships in the Hampton Roads area, including the ironclad *New Ironsides*, monitor *Saugus* and the captured Confederate ram *Atlanta* to proceed immediately up the James. Commodore William B. Radford of the *Ironsides* was to assume command of the division upon his arrival.[20]

Those ships would not, of course, arrive in time to punish the stranded Confederate vessels. The gunners of the 1st Connecticut had no difficulty finding their targets in the daylight. The unit's commander counted as hits nearly 50% of the 140 projectiles fired from the 30-pound and 100-pound Parrotts. After destroying the *Drewry*, the gunners trained on the ironclads, but found that most of their projectiles glanced off the casemates. While John Kell could not count the number of shots which struck the *Richmond*, the lieutenant commanding the *Virginia II*, John Dunnington, kept careful account of the more than 70 shots which struck his vessel, inflicting structural damage but relatively few casualties. Beginning at 7:30 a.m., shot and shell from the 100-pound Parrott of Battery Parsons hit the starboard side and fractured timbers on the berth deck, shot away pendants for the port and starboard bows, broke the iron grating over the gun deck and crushed timbers beneath it, shot away the exhaust pipe, struck the smokestack (already riddled with small arms fire), and struck the hurricane (flush) deck and knuckle on the starboard bow. A smartly-aimed small shell passed through the starboard bow port, traveled through the starboard side of the gun carriage and exploded by the bow gun, wounding Lt. William Pinckney Mason and seven other men.[21]

At 10:45 a.m., as the *Virginia* floated free and prepared to head upriver, Parker finally brought up the *Onondaga*, along with the gunboats *Hunchback* and *Massassoit*, and torpedo boat *Spuyten Duyvil*, to the obstructions and opened fire from a distance he estimated at a half-mile. So effective were her powerful 15-inch guns that even Parker must have wished he had gotten into action sooner. Two solid shots struck the *Virginia II*. The first struck the port quarter, broke through the four-inch iron armor, crushed the two-foot thick woodwork and bent the stanchions. Fifteen minutes later a second shot broke entirely through the iron and wood, killing one man and wounding two others. "It became evident very soon," remembered a Confederate petty officer, "that the Virginia was no match for Ericsson's little tub." In fact, the *Virginia II* and *Richmond* were in no position to even attempt to match the double-turreted monitor. As the unequal duel continued, Confederate gunners at Battery Dantzler managed to score several hits on the *Massassoit*, which wounded five of her crew, but the ironclad flagship was able to fire only one round from an 11-inch rifle. Fortunately for the Confederates, the *Virginia II* and the *Richmond* were soon able to get out of the *Onondaga's* range, though not before Kell's *Richmond* lost part of her stern port shutter to a final parting shot.[22]

The *Virginia II* and the rest of the squadron spent the day under the cover of Battery Dantzler, while Mitchell and his commanders considered whether to renew the attempt to pass the obstructions. Despite the loss of the *Drewry* and the *Scorpion*, the damage sustained by the *Virginia II* and the slow leak in the *Fredericksburg*, the James River Squadron faced a better chance of success than it ever would again. Mitchell scheduled a second attempt to pass the barrier for 9:00 p.m. With the *Virginia II* in the lead, the squadron began anew its descent of the river. Circumstances immediately turned against Mitchell and his squadron. First, the pilots of the flagship complained smoke escaping from the perforated stack blinded them and virtually guaranteed a repeat of the previous night's navigational nightmare. Pressing on into Trent's Reach, Mitchell soon discovered the Federals had brought in what he described as "a brilliant Drummond light," situated on the south bank of the river to illuminate the obstructions and direct the fire of the shore batteries. The light, according to Mitchell, "would enable him to direct his fire almost as well at night as by day." It also had the unintended effect of blinding the Southern pilots, who were, at least on the flagship, already battling the escaping steam. Between 10:00 and 10:30 that evening, the ship commanders received orders to advance no further, and Mitchell summoned Kell, Dunnington and Shepperd for a council of war. As if the condition of the vessels and the Drummond light were not enough, the squadron had only one more hour of flood tide in which to pass through the shallow waters of Trent's Reach. The council of war made the inevitable decision not to attempt a passage of the obstructions. Adding insult to injury, as the *Hampton* turned around, she fouled her propeller in the anchor chain of the *Virginia II*. Unable to travel under her own power, the gunboat was towed upriver by her sister vessels *Nansemond* and *Torpedo*. The much-anticipated movement against Grant's supply base at City Point was over.[23]

Returning upriver to the anchorage at Chaffin's Bluff was fraught with the same dangers as the passage downriver. The men of the 1st Connecticut Artillery at Fort Brady were happy for another opportunity to drop iron on the Confederate ships. The *Richmond* and the *Virginia II* each suffered two more hits but suffered no casualties, while Federal infantry and sharpshooters on both banks maintained a steady fire on the passing vessels. Lieutenant Wilson of the *Hampton* counted 810 balls and slugs on the deck of his ship when she returned to the safety of

Chaffin's Bluff. "It seems almost miraculous," observed Lieutenant Butt of the *Nansemond*, "that we should have passed through this fiery ordeal unharmed." He attributed the survival of his vessel—and of the dependent *Hampton*—to his pilot's skill in negotiating the channel. With her smokestack belching smoke toward the pilot house, the *Virginia II* was a challenge for any pilot. At 5:30 a.m., she grounded just beyond Fort Brady at Devil's Reach. Freed within a half-hour, she then struck the Confederate obstructions at Kingsland Reach. Between 4:30 and 7:30 on the morning of January 25, the surviving ships of the James River Squadron—looking "roughly handled" to marine officer Edward Crenshaw—dropped anchor at Chaffin's Bluff. The opportunity "rarely presented to a naval officer," as Secretary Mallory had earlier described it, was lost forever.[24]

Much to his credit, Mitchell gave a forthright assessment of the fiasco to his superior. He shifted blame from himself only to point out the obvious deficiencies of the river pilots which so crippled the expedition. If not for the grounding of the two ironclads, Mitchell concluded, "the whole squadron would have passed below that night, and, as the enemy was unprepared for the movement, there was every reason to indulge the hope that it would have been successful." The result of the expedition proved so "unfortunate for the public interests," continued Mitchell, "I invite the closest scrutiny into the manner of conducting the enterprise committed to me." A month later, on February 18, Mitchell was removed from command of the James River Squadron. Mitchell did not challenge the right, "nay, the duty," of the navy to remove him. Since, however, his removal suggested "misconduct or mismanagement" of the affair at Trent's Reach, Mitchell requested that he be informed of any complaints against him so that he had an opportunity to vindicate himself. Meanwhile, he offered himself to the department in whatever capacity would best serve the interests of the navy. The evacuation of Richmond two months later found Mitchell without official duties.[25]

Mitchell's Federal counterpart, William Parker, was court martialed for his decisions in the affair that ultimately allowed the Confederate squadron to escape. While cleared on a technicality from arrest and conviction, U.S. Navy officers believed Parker was at least guilty of "an error in judgment" in not engaging the enemy fleet. Squadron commander Porter explained to Parker's successor just how serious he believed that "error in judgment" to have been. If Parker had acted properly, Porter wrote on February 14, "we should now be in possession of the whole Rebel Navy and on our way to Richmond. The ONONDAGA I consider a match for the whole Rebel fleet, and I feel mortified that I failed to impress the late commander of the Division with the importance of acting cooly and energetically if any occasion offered."[26]

Learning from Parker's failure, dismissal and court martial, his successors determined to avoid his fate. Anticipating yet another attempt to pass the obstructions, Lt. Cdr. Homer Blake issued detailed instructions on defending the river. Each ship was to provide one boat for nightly picket duty, and each boat was to carry a red lantern as a danger signal. A vessel anchored in front of each ironclad was to be kept armed with a gun loaded with grape and canister. Never again would enemy torpedo boats get close enough to cut away obstructions. The circular charged commanders with "doing everything in their power even to the sacrifice of our vessels, to prevent [the enemy] getting down the river." Blake's successor, Capt. William Radford, issued similar orders in February and March.[27] The Federal squadron, however, did not believe it necessary to attack the Confederate squadron. It was necessary only to stand ready against a desperate Confederate attempt to break through, and if it came, to be ready to destroy the Confederate fleet. The opportunity never presented itself.

The Trent's Reach debacle proved to be the first and only grand offensive undertaken by the James River Squadron. It was both a lost opportunity and a crippling blow. The squadron's *raison d 'etre* was the defense of Richmond, and it rarely had any chance of doing more than protecting the capital. The strategic situation of January 1865, however, afforded the squadron an opportunity to do much more. The destruction of the City Point depot was probably the last best hope of breaking Grant's stranglehold on Petersburg.

But was it a realistic hope? Commander Parker's failure to assemble all available Federal warships near the obstructions gave the Confederates the illusion of possibility. Mitchell's ships were able to reach the obstructions with only shore batteries and the river bottom to stop them.

The river alone proved a formidable opponent that paralyzed most of the Confederate squadron. Could the two ships that did make it through the obstructions have achieved the goals of the mission? Although he was not part of the Trent's Reach affair, Confederate Naval Academy superintendent William H. Parker later observed that had his old Annapolis colleague, Frank Shepperd, been allowed to take his ship on to City Point alone, that "dashing" officer "could have accomplished as much as it lay in the power of any man to do."[28] Perhaps Shepperd could have led the *Fredericksburg* and the *Hampton* on what amounted to a suicide run against City Point. After all, Shepperd had told Mitchell in June 1864 that he was "ready and willing to run. . . a risk for the sake of our cause," and complained when the other officers declined to run such a risk. Explaining to Mallory why he and his fellow officers decided against an attack, Mitchell declared that if necessary, he would "most cheerfully" attack the enemy, "even though our entire squadron may be sacrificed, either for the good of the country or the honor of the Navy." There was at least one precedent for such suicidal action. In July 1862, the Confederate ironclad *Arkansas* had steamed out of the Yazoo River into the Mississippi and through a host of Federal gunboats to Vicksburg, proving it possible for an ironclad to survive a terrible mauling by a numerically superior enemy. The *Arkansas* suffered considerable structural damage and human carnage. The *Fredericksburg* would likely have suffered even more. As the *Onondaga* demonstrated with just a few shots, naval ordnance in 1865 was better able to penetrate iron ships than in 1862. The damage the *Onondaga* inflicted almost effortlessly on the *Virginia II* suggests Admiral Porter—and Admiral Lee before him—and Grant were right: any duel between Federal and Confederate vessels would prove fatal to the Southerners.

In retrospect, a suicide run was the best chance the James River Squadron had to affect the outcome of the war in Virginia. Mitchell's 1864 bravado nothwithstanding, few naval officers in 1865 would have ordered such a mission, and few gamblers would have put money on its success.

The Final Days of the James River Squadron

The disaster at Trent's Reach essentially sealed the fate of the James River Squadron and dramatized its failures. The ironclads, vessels that were the pride of Richmond's naval-industrial complex and the waterborn defense of the Confederate capital, had proven unequal to all but their most simple role. Although constructed lighter than the original *Virginia*, they were still too heavy to navigate the shallow waters of the James safely and reliably. Even then their armor was too thin for the enemy's heavy ordnance. Whatever their actual deficiencies, their potential ability to run downriver against enemy vessels and facilities was enough of a concern to paralyze Federal vessels in the river. They were most effective as floating batteries, as formidable obstacles to the advance of enemy vessels. On the James, as in other Southern rivers and ports, that role was at best tenuous, for success of Federal land forces doomed one squadron of floating batteries after another. By the late winter of 1865, the Army of the Potomac had extended its lines around Petersburg and stretched Lee's Army of Northern Virginia to the breaking point. By then it was merely a matter of time before Lee could no longer hold his lines around Petersburg and Richmond. The days of the capital navy were numbered.

In the meantime, the squadron could only assess the damage from Trent's Reach. The human toll was relatively light: only five killed and 14 wounded. Damage to the ships, however, was far greater. The *Drewry* and *Scorpion* were lost, while each ironclad required a long list of repairs. Most seriously crippled was the *Virginia II*. Her iron shield was cracked and shattered and so, too, in places was the thick wooden framing underneath. In addition, her engines proved faulty, and her smokestack, riddled with shot, shell and small arms fire, needed replacement. The run through the obstructions had torn a hole in the port side of the *Fredericksburg*, causing her to leak at the rate of two to three inches an hour. She also lost her anchor in the expedition. Much like the *Virginia II*, the smokestack of the *Richmond* was also effectively destroyed. While her armor withstood the January 24 bombardment better than that of the flagship, the *Richmond's* mailed sides were cracked and dented in several places. Finally, the propeller of the *Hampton* was rendered useless in her eleventh hour collision with the flagship.

The condition of the squadron only grew worse in the wake of the failed expedition. The day after it returned to its anchorage, the torpedo boat *Hornet* collided with the transport *Allison* and sank. Although Mitchell was confident she could be recovered, Federal shore batteries and the continuing severe weather rendered any salvage operation difficult. Then on February 17, the James River steamer and excursion ship *Schultz*, which, according to newspaper reports, "had lately undergone extensive repairs at the hands of the Government," struck a Confederate contact mine and sank. Although not part of the squadron, the government used the *Schultz* as a flag-of-truce transport; she had gone down river to pick up exchanged Confederate prisoners who, fortunately, failed to arrive.[29]

Two days later, John Mitchell summarized for his successor the condition of the fleet: the *Virginia II* was undergoing repairs until about April 1; the *Richmond* and the *Fredericksburg* each required refitting of its torpedo defenses; the *Beaufort* was "not serviceable, except in emergencies; should be sent to navy yard to go on the ways as soon as possible to examine propeller and rudder"; the *Roanoke* was "undergoing repairs on the ways at the navy yard, Richmond"; the *Nansemond*, though serviceable, required caulking; only the *Hampton* was fully serviceable, but its commander was sick at the hospital. One of the fire boats was still sunk, and the other three were at the navy yard to be caulked. "They are all rotten and in such bad condition that they require the utmost care and watching to be kept afloat."[30]

Such was the condition of the James River Squadron upon the arrival of its last and most famous commander, Rear Adm. Raphael Semmes. "Old Beeswax," as he was affectionately known because of his elaborate twisted mustache, was an international celebrity by the time he succeeded Mitchell. Born in 1809 in Maryland, Semmes attended West Point and studied law before entering the United States Navy in 1837. In Confederate service, Semmes drew the glamorous assignments of commanding two commerce raiders, the *Sumter* and the *Alabama*, and spent much of the war in foreign ports. The *Sumter* captured 18 Northern vessels before being transformed into a blockade runner. The most celebrated Confederate vessel, the *Alabama*, captured or sank 69 U.S. commercial vessels during her two-year voyage around the globe. Semmes' warship was sunk by the *U.S.S. Kearsage* off the coast of Cherbourg, France in 1864, but its commander nevertheless returned to the Confederacy a bona fide hero.[31]

An Irish visitor to Richmond in March 1865 described Semmes as "looking hard & determined as flint with his pointed mustache & well weather-beaten thin cut face. . . ." Semmes relieved Mitchell on February 18. "He was received with all the customary honors, the marines presenting arms, etc.," wrote Marine Capt. Edward Crenshaw. Another marine, Lt. E.T. Eggleston, stationed on board the *Fredericksburg*, described Semmes as "a small man, nothing particularly striking in his appearance except his eye, which is very fine and piercing. I think his reputation will suffer with the country in having accepted this command, for he has not room here to fight as large vessels as these are," Eggleston not unreasonably predicted.[32]

After paying social calls on President Jefferson Davis and Robert E. Lee, Semmes took command of the squadron from Mitchell, whom he described as his "old and valued friend." Within days of his arrival in Richmond, Semmes came down with the prevalent illness—the same illness that forced his former *Alabama* first officer, John Kell, to relinquish command of the *Richmond*. "I came down from Richmond quite unwell with cold & fever & took possession of my gloomy, candle lighted apartment on board the iron-clad Virginia," Semmes wrote in his diary on March 18. The following day he "[w]ent ashore on Chaffin's Bluff for a walk, but found nothing but mud, water, & a dreary scenery. Returned in half an hour!" he exclaimed in disgust.[33] In his 1869 memoir Semmes described in more detail the condition of the squadron in its waning days:

> I soon had the mortification to find that the fleet was as much demoralized as the army. Indeed, with the exception of its principal officers, and about half a dozen sailors in each ship, its personnel was drawn almost entirely from the army. The movements of the ships being confined to the headwaters of a narrow river, they were but little better than prison-ships. Both men and officers were crowded into close and uncomfortable quarters, without the requisite space for exercise. I remedied this, as much as possi-

> ble, by sending squads on shore, to drill and march on the river-bank. They were on half rations, and with but a scanty supply of clothing. Great discontent and restlessness prevailed. Constant applications were coming to me for leaves of absence—almost every one having some story to tell of a sick or destitute family. I was obliged, of course, to resist all these appeals. 'The enemy was thundering at the gates,' and not a man could be spared. Desertion was the consequence. Sometimes an entire boat's crew would run off, leaving the officer to find his way on board the best he might. . . . The general understanding, that the collapse of the Confederacy was at hand, had its influence with some of the more honorable of them. They reasoned that their desertion would be but an anticipation of the event by a few weeks.[34]

Semmes had little good news to record in the "dreary, weary, lonely" days that followed. The torpedo boat *Wasp* collided with the *Richmond* and capsized. A sailor aboard the *Virginia II* committed suicide. Ice and high water posed constant dangers to the ships.[35]

Semmes did not exaggerate the effects of sickness and desertion in the squadron. The senior command was so decimated by illness that every vessel in the squadron was commanded by a lieutenant or men of lower rank. Illness among Naval Academy midshipmen became so severe that they were quartered in a tobacco factory at the corner of 24th and Franklin streets in Richmond. A week before Semmes assumed command, the entire 12-man crew of a picket boat from the *Virginia II* mutinied against its two officers and took the boat to the north bank, where the men promptly deserted to the Federal army.[36]

Desertion not only sapped the morale of the squadron, but also provided the enemy with a steady stream of remarkably accurate intelligence about Confederate river defenses and affairs in the Confederate capital. Daniel Smith, a Brooklyn-born sailor who happened to be in the South at the outbreak of war and joined the Confederate navy, deserted to the U.S. Navy after the Battle of Trent's Reach. He offered his interrogators details on damage to the Confederate ships and on the "very slow" progress of the *Texas*. Overall, he reported, the mood in Richmond as "bleak" and "it is said among the Richmond people that it will probably be evacuated in the spring." Edmund Ruffin told in his diary of a naval lieutenant who had been "for some time playing the traitor, &

aiding others to escape to the enemy's lines. . . ." The lieutenant was arrested, but, inexplicably, allowed to remain at large and escaped.[37]

Appropriately, it was a deserter who sealed the fate of a far-fetched scheme which proved the last assault planned against the Federal fleet in the James River. After the squadron's failure to break through the obstructions on January 23-24, Mitchell authorized an expedition that had been planned weeks earlier. Between 90 and 120 sailors and marines, commanded by the daring Lt. Charles W. Read, marched off from Drewry's Bluff on February 3, 1865, accompanied by wagons carrying whaleboats and torpedoes.[38] The mission, as described by one participant, was quite similar to the James River Squadron's breakout attempt: to "blow up the Federal iron-clads, clear a passage for our fleet and force the abandonment of City Point, or compel Grant to fall back or bring his supplies from Norfolk."[39] The expedition was to accomplish that goal, however, by traveling on land—from Drewry's Bluff on a broad southwesterly sweep around the flank of Grant's army facing Petersburg, then eastward to the James River in Surry County, downriver from City Point. The Confederates would then sally out and capture a passing tug boat, arm it with a spar torpedo, and use it to sink and capture enemy warships. It was a plan born and nurtured in desperation.

The officer assigned to lead the expedition was well-suited for such an unlikely mission. An 1860 graduate of the U.S. Naval Academy, "Savez" Read was a throwback to a traditional style naval adventurer. To one admirer he "embodied the most dashing type of naval officer that the nation has produced since Decatur." His friend, Midshipman "Jimmie" Morgan, wrote that Read "had such an adventurous career that anyone reading an account of it would be justified in thinking that he was a creature of the imagination who had stepped bodily out of the pages of one of Dumas' novels." Before coming to Virginia waters in 1864, Read had distinguished himself as an officer aboard the short-lived and much-bloodied Mississippi River ironclad *Arkansas*, and as commander of the successful commerce raiders *Clarence* and *Tacony*. Arriving in Virginia as an exchanged prisoner in October 1864, he had been assigned to command the naval guns at Battery Wood, and thereafter and more suitable to his temperament, command of the James River torpedo boats. His resourcefulness and courage at the obstructions had been one of the few brights spots in the Trent's Reach affair.[40]

Read never got the opportunity to add "pirate" to his already impressive military resume. Five cold, wet and troubled days into the march, the expedition received word that it had been betrayed and that a Federal force lay waiting in ambush. Lieutenant John Lewis was a Northern-born sailor who had been in the Confederate navy throughout the war. Despite his Northern origins, he was trusted enough to be sent ahead to reconnoiter. Lewis instead went directly to enemy lines near Norfolk. On January 26, his intelligence was passed on to U.S. Army and Navy officers in eastern Virginia. A "torpedo gang" numbering up to 500 was said to be heading toward the James. Lewis, however, was hardly alone in betraying the expedition. As early as December 27, 1864, an English born sailor who deserted from the *Virginia II* told interrogators the Confederates "are fitting out an expedition for the torpedo boats under Lieutenant Read." Either through ignorance or guile, the English sailor's account strayed from the truth: the expedition, he said, was to go overland, possibly to Point Lookout, Maryland. Further corroboration came from another deserter, Pvt. William B. Cross, 56th Virginia Infantry, who reported men from each regiment in George Pickett's Division had been recruited, armed with cutlasses, and sent to Drewry's Bluff.[41]

Read's force was spared complete disaster when a Confederate prisoner at Fort Monroe overheard Lewis' interrogation, then escaped and found his way back to Confederate lines. Miraculously, Read led the party through a closing enemy gauntlet and across the frozen Appomattox River without loss of man, mule or wagon. Three-quarters of the expedition's men, however, suffered so severely from the elements and rigors of the march that they were in the naval hospital when Richmond was evacuated two months later.[42]

From Ship to Shore: The Evacuation of Richmond

After his appointment to replace Mitchell as commander of the James River Squadron, Raphael Semmes visited the Navy Department in Richmond weekly. On Saturday, April 1, Semmes recorded in his diary: "Weather fine. Visited the City. River still very high. Dep[art]m[e]nts packing for a move! Saw Secretary of the Navy and the Secretary of the Treas[ury, George A. Trenholm]." The day proved to be the calm before the storm. Since his arrival in Richmond, Semmes anticipated the eventual evacuation of the capital, and was especially concerned with the threat of Gen. William T. Sherman's army approaching Virginia from the south. As early as March 1, John Kell, convalescing in Richmond, reported that government departments were preparing for evacuation.[43] Nevertheless, it came as a surprise to Semmes when at 4:00 p.m. on April 2, while eating dinner, he received by special messenger a note from Secretary Mallory:

> SIR:—General Lee advises the Government to withdraw from the city, and the officers will leave this evening, accordingly. I presume that General Lee has advised you of this, and of his movements, and made suggestions as to the disposition to be made of your squadron. He withdraws upon his lines toward Danville, this night; and unless otherwise directed by General Lee, upon you is devolved the duty of destroying your ships, this night, and with all the forces under your command, joining General Lee. Confer with him, if practicable, before destroying them. Let your people be rationed, as far as possible, for the march, and armed and equipped for duty in the field.[44]

The order was a cruel blow to Semmes, an old-fashioned warrior who, as commander of the *Alabama*, had gamely challenged the *Kearsage* to mortal combat rather than remain sealed up in a foreign port. He was now ordered to preside over the destruction of a squadron of small wooden gunboats and crippled ironclads reduced to floating batteries. Before joining his squadron, Semmes found time to go to Rocketts to inspect the powerful, but unfinished, ironclad *Texas*.[45]

Another officer whom the evacuation order caught off guard was Cdr. William H. Parker, commander of the *Patrick Henry*. As early as February 28, 1865, Parker broached the subject of evacuation with Secretary Mallory. Parker inquired hopefully whether Mallory intended "to remove the Naval School to some other locality," such as Lynchburg, Virginia, or Charlotte, North Carolina. If so, Parker assured him, "Most of the material belonging to it can be taken away in one canal boat or six freight cars—this includes provisions for two months and some of the rigging of the ship."[46]

Parker, too, was in the city on April 1 and called on Secretary Mallory, who told him the news from Lee was good. With Mallory's assurance no emergency was in the offing, Parker spent the night in Richmond. On Sunday, April 2, Parker boarded his ship, which had been moored at Rocketts since early that year. The midshipmen went through the "customary Sunday muster and inspection" before Parker received a message from Mallory: "Have the corps of midshipmen, with the proper officers, at the Danville depot to-day at 6 P.M., the commanding officer to report to the Quartermaster General of the Army." Still not grasping the gravity of the situation, Parker made arrangements to carry out the orders based on the assumption the men would return in three days. Not until hours later did he realize Richmond was to be evacuated. He ordered the men to the Danville depot at the foot of 14th Street and left one officer and ten men on board the *Patrick Henry* to fire the ship. The *Patrick Henry*, the last surviving ship from the Virginia State Navy, was sunk in the channel facing north at the foot of Louisiana St. in Rocketts, just below the navy yard.[47]

Aside from the *Patrick Henry* at Rocketts, all the ships of the squadron were at Chaffin's Bluff. Semmes determined to sink the ships quietly, so as not to alert the enemy of the evacuation. Returning to the squadron's anchorage, Semmes gave the orders to abandon the ships. All afternoon and evening the crews of the ironclads prepared for evacuation. "My officers and men worked like beavers," Semmes recalled,

> There were a thousand things to be done. The sailor was leaving the homestead which he had inhabited for several months. Arms had to be served out, provisions gotten up out of the hold, and broken into such packages, as the sailors could carry. Hammocks had to be unlashed, and the blankets taken out, and rolled up as compactly as possible. Haversacks and canteens had to be improvised.[48]

In the capital city, however, secrecy was not the priority of the evacuation. The Confederate army implemented a long-standing plan (drafted when McClellan's army threatened Richmond in 1862) to burn the tobacco warehouses. At dusk, as the last units of the city's garrison left the city, the warehouses were fired. Predictably—and as city officials had warned three years before—the fires spread. Before dawn, conflagrations burned out of control in the Shockoe Valley warehouse district and in the downtown financial district. The fire that raged through downtown licked at the southern gates of Capitol Square, threatening the heart of the city and several of its proud new structures. The Spotswood Hotel and the Customs House survived. The Mechanics Institute—home of the Confederate Navy and War Departments—did not.[49]

The Navy Department did not destroy systematically all the facilities associated with Richmond's naval-industrial complex. The public buildings at the Rocketts shipyard were set afire, but Richard Haskins' adjacent warehouse and the riverfront sheds survived the flames. At the yard opposite Rocketts, William Graves' unfinished ironclad and two torpedo boats (still under construction) at the navy yards were burned, but at Rocketts, the partially-clad *Texas* was not destroyed. Nor were her engines and boilers at the Naval Works, which survived intact. Chief of the Office of Ordnance and Hydrography Cdr. John Brooke and Naval Ordnance Works superintendent Lt. Robert Minor, left the city at 1:00 p.m. in an old ambulance and were traveling south through Chesterfield County when the sun fell on April 2.[50]

The fires illuminated Richmond's skyline and changed Semmes' plans for destroying the capital navy. Instead of sinking the vessels where they were, the squadron commander decided to move them from Chaffin's upriver to the obstructions at Drewry's Bluff. There the crews of the ironclads would transfer to the wooden gunboats and set ablaze the ponderous rams. The gunboat *Roanoke* sank in attempting to pass the Confederate obstructions at Drewry's Bluff, perhaps the one time an accident involving a vessel made the squadron's mission easier.[51]

While the officers and men packed their trunks and blankets, the man in charge of the Confederate States Navy packed his bags and cleared his office at the Mechanics Hall. After learning of the evacuation order, Stephen Mallory and the other department heads met in the afternoon with President Davis in his office. At 8:30 p.m., the cabinet members gathered at the waterfront depot of the Richmond & Danville Railroad to catch the last train out of the city. All the cars were not ready, so the train waited for several hours. Stephen Mallory waited on the train. At last, at 11:00 p.m., the president took his seat and the train began moving "in gloomy silence," Mallory recalled. Crossing over the James afforded Mallory and his compatriots "[a] commanding view of the river front of the city. . . and as the fugitives receded from its flickering lights, many and sad commentaries they made upon the Confederate cause." It was at this time the ironclads, of which Mallory had been so proud, seemed to him "like chained and sulky bulldogs," fierce enough to prevent the enemy from ascending the river, but unable to strike. Their imminent destruction, he realized, spelled the end of Confederate naval operations east of the Mississippi River.[52]

Between 1:00 and 2:00 a.m. on April 3, the wooden gunboats moved upstream, and the ironclads were fired. Before long, Semmes wrote, the ships in the melancholy procession were shocked by an explosion. The flagship *Virginia II* had blown up. "The spectacle was grand beyond description," Semmes recounted. "Her shell-rooms had been full of loaded shells. The explosion of the magazine threw all these shells, with their fuses lighted, into air. . . .The explosion shook the houses in Richmond, and must have waked the echoes of the night for forty miles around."[53]

The gunboats steamed upriver toward Richmond as the first rays of the morning sun reflected in the windows of city buildings. Semmes described the sight that greeted the men of the squadron:

> In the lower part of the city, the School-ship *Patrick Henry* was burning, and some of the houses near the Navy Yard were on fire. But higher up was the principal scene of the conflagration. Entire blocks were on fire here, and a dense canopy of smoke, rising high in the still morning air, was covering the city as with a pall. The rear-guard of our army had just crossed, as I landed my fleet at Manchester, and the bridges were burning in their rear.[54]

After disembarking, the crews set the gunboats ablaze and cast them downstream. The *Beaufort* failed to sink, and along with the unfinished *Texas*, fell into Federal hands.[55] The last ships of the James River Squadron were destroyed along the Richmond waterfront.

"Our Navy," John McIntosh Kell had complained weeks earlier, "has been destroyed piece meal by the evacuation of first one and then another of our seaports." Following the evacuation of Savannah, Georgia, in December, army ordnance chief Josiah Gorgas observed in his dairy, "The Navy is always foremost in misfortune."[56] The officers and sailors of the Confederate States Navy in Richmond—many of them veterans of the Savannah, Wilmington and Charleston Squadrons which had been similarly destroyed in December 1864 and January and February 1865—had no other fleets to join, and instead became infantrymen in the Confederate States Army. The last crews of the James River Squadron accompanied Semmes by train to Danville, Virginia. Captain John Randolph Tucker, commander of the marines and sailors who had been serving at Drewry's Bluff and at the James River land batteries, received no word at all about the evacuation. "I am without instructions as to what course to pursue," he wrote to General Lee on the evening of April 2. "Have recd [sic] no orders. Shall be happy to learn your wishes concerning this post and garrison." Late that night, having received no reply from Lee, Tucker blew up his magazines and marched his force into Richmond. On the morning of the 3rd, his men marched off to join Lee's embattled Army of Northern Virginia on the road to Appomattox.[57]

Upon arrival in the new temporary capital at Danville, Admiral Semmes became Brigadier General Semmes (though his naval rank entitled him to be a major general). Sidney Smith Lee, himself former commander of the late squadron, assisted Semmes in transforming the squadron's crews into a brigade of artillery. Lieutenant John W. Dunnington, former commander of the *Virginia II*, became colonel of one of the "regiments," while Lt. Oscar F. Johnston, of the *Richmond*, commanded the other. Semmes appointed his son, Midshipman Raphael Semmes, Jr., as staff officer and made Lt. Walter Butt, late commander of the *Nansemond*, adjutant general of his staff.[58]

Not all of the 500 men who boarded the train in Richmond arrived in Danville. "On the trip from Richmond to Danville the men who lived in the vicinity we passed through left the train and went home," recalled John Bondurant Gardner, an infantryman turned gunner on the *Richmond* and at Battery Semmes. Gardner lived in Danville, and thus was more than willing to ride all the way to the new destination. Rather than join Lee, Semmes' force manned the defenses of Danville before cooperating with Joseph E. Johnston's army in resisting Sherman's march northward through North Carolina. Under the direction of his superior, Gen. P. G. T. Beauregard, Semmes dispersed his men along the Danville–Greensboro, North Carolina, railroad that had become the lifeline of the Confederate government. When Semmes' force moved out of Danville, John Gardner remained behind in his home town.[59]

Semmes received orders on April 25 to join Johnston's army and arrived the next day to find that Johnston had surrendered to Sherman. A week later, on May 1, Semmes surrendered his force—which had dwindled through desertion to 250 men—to the Federal army. Among the officers surrendering with Semmes was his predecessor, John Mitchell, who had accompanied Semmes on the flight from Richmond.[60]

John Randolph Tucker's command, a battalion-sized unit of 400 former sailors from Charleston and Wilmington dubbed the "Naval Brigade," was not as fortunate as Semmes'. Tucker's men had constituted a land force for several months, and had been stationed previously at Fayetteville, North Carolina, and at Drewry's Bluff. Tucker's battalion joined Lee's rearguard, and despite its experience and frequent drill in small arms, the "Naval Brigade" presented a comical sight to army veterans. Officers reportedly ordered their men to face "port" and "starboard" (or "starboard" and "larboard"), while the men responded "aye-aye, sir!"[61]

Incorporated into the division of Maj. Gen. George Washington Custis Lee (R.E. Lee's eldest son), the Naval Brigade appropriately fought its first and last battle at Sailor's (or Sayler's) Creek on April 6, 1865. The former sailors presented a far-from-comical sight to the Federals, and in fact won grudging respect from their enemy. Custis Lee's Division was part of the Confederate rearguard cut off by the Federal pursuit. Before attacking, the Federals brought up several artillery batteries and opened up on the Confederate line behind Sayler's Creek, which was, according to one Northern officer, "cut up terribly by our plunging fire of shell and case-shot." Major General Horatio G. Wright, commander of the Federal Sixth Corps, described in his report what happened next:

> The First and Third Divisions charged the enemy's position, carrying it handsomely, except at a point on our right of the road crossing the creek, where a column said to be composed exclusively of the Marine Brigade [sic.] and other troops which had held the lines of Richmond previous to the evacuation, made a counter-charge upon that part of our lines on their front. I was never more astonished. These troops were surrounded—the First and Third Divisions of this corps were on either flank, my artillery and a fresh division in their front, and some three divisions of Major-General Sheridan's cavalry in their rear. Looking upon them as already our prisoners, I had ordered the artillery to cease firing as a dictate of humanity; my surprise therefore was extreme when this force charged our front.[62]

Despite fighting hard and winning the admiration of its enemy, most of the brigade, along with most of the army's Second Corps, was forced to surrender to the Federals. Three days later the remnants of Lee's army surrendered at Appomattox. With the Confederate army were many former sailors, including three black sailors formerly assigned to the ironclad *Chicora* of the Charleston Squadron. Midshipman Daniel M. Lee, nephew of the commanding general, refused to surrender at Sayler's Creek and instead became a staff officer for his brother, Maj. Gen. Fitzhugh Lee, commander of the Confederate cavalry. After again avoiding surrender at Appomattox, Midshipman Lee finally surrendered to the Federal army, along with his brother, on April 14.[63]

The midshipmen of the Naval Academy drew the most important assignment in the waning days of the Confederacy—escorting the Confederate treasury on the flight from Richmond. From April 2 to May 2, remembered Lt. William Parker, the midshipmen had one "watchword: 'guard the treasure.'"[64] The initial destination of the treasury—an estimated half-million dollars in gold and silver coin—was the mint at Charlotte, North Carolina. Arriving in Charlotte via Greensboro on the 11th, the midshipmen learned that the approach of Federal cavalry made it necessary to go further south. Ultimately, the 40 midshipmen escorted the treasury on train, wagon, and foot as far south as Washington, Georgia. Parker received orders from Secretary Mallory to disband the midshipmen but ignored the orders until he could deposit the treasury in safe hands. Backtracking to Abbeville, South Carolina, Parker met the party of President Jefferson Davis and turned over his burden to the accompanying Confederate cavalry. On May 2, 1865, Parker issued orders to the midshipmen, detaching them from the Academy and granting them "leave" to visit their homes. Before turning the midshipmen away, Parker received authorization to distribute to them a total of $1,500, or $40 for each man. This modest draw from the treasury was, insisted the midshipmen and their historians, the only money taken from the treasury. Once out of their hands, the treasury disappeared from the historical record, and its fate remains one of the great unsolved mysteries of the Civil War.[65]

The same day the midshipmen disbanded, Navy Secretary Stephen Mallory tendered his resignation to President Jefferson Davis. Mallory and other members of the president's cabinet had accompanied Davis on his flight from Richmond through Danville, Greensboro, Charlotte, and into Georgia. Davis traveled on and was captured near Irwinville, Georgia, on May 10. Mallory went to LaGrange, Georgia, to await the arrival of Federal forces. He was arrested soon afterward. The man who had presided over the birth and the death of the Confederate navy was imprisoned at Fort Lafayette, New York.[66]

Two Views of the Rebel Ironclads...

With the dashing and impetuous Lt. Francis E. Shepperd in command, the Fredericksburg passed through the enemy river obstructions just after midnight on January 24, 1865. It was the only time that a Confederate, Richmond-built, ironclad passed that far downriver. In many respects, Shepperd's thrust represented the "high tide" of the James River Squadron. Joined only by the Gunboat Hampton, the Fredericksburg was called back through the obstructions to join here grounded sibling ironclads. *Harpers Weekly*, February 11, 1865.

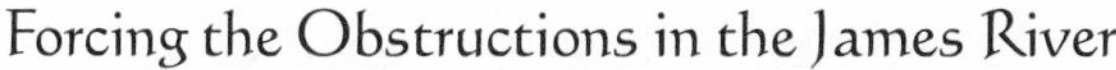

Forcing the Obstructions in the James River

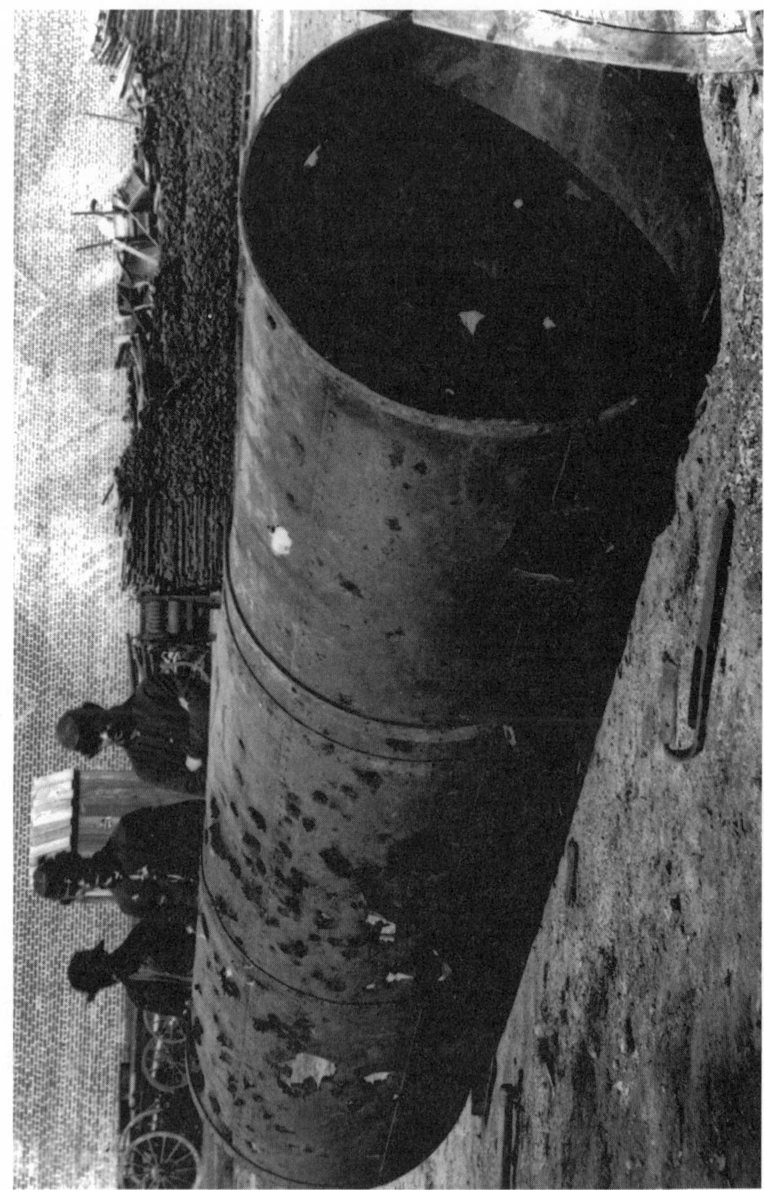

Smokestack of the C.S.S. Virginia II at Rocketts, April 1865

After the fall of Richmond in April 1865, Federal soldiers posed in the Rocketts shipyard beside the smokestack of the Virginia II. The stack had been riddled by enemy fire during the Battle of Trent's Reach on January 23-24, 1865. The Virginia II had just finished undergoing extensive repairs at Rocketts when Richmond was evacuated. Courtesy of the Library of Congress.

Rear Adm. Raphael Semmes

The best known officer in the Confederate navy, Raphael Semmes (1809-1877) arrived in Richmond to assume command of the James River Squadron in early February 1865. A marine officer described him as "a small man, nothing particularly striking in his appearance except his eye, which is very fine and piercing." Semmes' piercing eye is particularly evident in this photograph, which was taken the day after his ship, the *C.S.S. Alabama*, was sunk in action off the coast of Cherbourg, France. Carte-de-visite by S. J. Wiseman's Art Repository, 15 Above Bar, Southampton, England, June 20, 1864. Courtesy of Charles V. Peery.

Lt. Charles W. Read

Charles Read (1840-1890), wrote a friend, "had such an adventurous career that anyone reading an account of it would be justified in thinking that he was the creature of the imagination who had stepped bodily out of the pages of one of Dumas' novels." In 1863, while serving aboard the commerce raider *Florida*, Read was given command of a captured sailing vessel, *Clarence*, which he used to prey on U.S. commercial ships. He subsequently burned that ship and transferred his crew to another captured vessel, *Tacony* (also called *Florida II*), and continued to prey on enemy vessels until forced to surrender—in still another captured ship—off the coast of Maine. Called "Savez" at the Naval Academy because it was the only French word he knew, Read became known during the war as "Tacony." Arriving in Richmond in October 1864 as an exchanged prisoner, he received a variety of appropriately-daring assignments while in command of the James River torpedo boats. Salt print from Class of 1860 U.S. Naval Academy album. Courtesy of Charles V. Peery.

"The Blowing Up of the James River Fleet"

"The spectacle was grand beyond description," Admiral Semmes remarked about the blowing up of the *Virginia II* and the rest of the James River Squadron. "The explosion shook the houses of Richmond, and must have waked the echoes of the night for forty miles around." Etching by Allen C. Redwood, lithographed and published by A. Hoen & Co., Baltimore. Raphael Semmes, *Memoirs of Service Afloat.*

Sailors turned soldiers

Officers and sailors of the Confederate navy concentrated in Richmond as the Confederacy's remaining ports fell to Federal forces in early 1865. With the fall of Richmond, the sailors became soldiers. Some of them to joined Robert E. Lee's Army of Northern Virginia in its retreat to Appomattox, while others traveled south to Joseph E. Johnston's army in time for its surrender in North Carolina in late April. All of the junior officers pictured in this gallery arrived in Richmond in late 1864 or early 1865 from either recently-abandoned Atlantic port stations or were exchanged prisoners. Each of them either surrendered with John Randolph Tucker's "Naval Brigade," or with Brig. Gen. (Adm.) Raphael Semmes's command of former sailors.

Robert Foute was one of the men who traveled up the eastern seaboard as port after port fell to the Federals. He was stationed with the James River shore batteries at the time Richmond was evacuated in April 1865. A member of the U.S. Naval Academy class of 1862, the Tennessee-born sailor was the first Southern midshipman to resign from the Academy in December 1860. After an initial assignment in Savannah, Foute saw his first action as a gunner on the crew of the *Virginia* during the Battle of Hampton Roads. He was transferred back to Savannah to serve on the floating battery *Georgia*, then went abroad. He was back in Savannah when that city was evacuated in December 1864, and in Charleston when it was evacuated two months later. Foute surrendered with the Army of Northern Virginia at Appomattox. Carte-de-visite by F. Blin, 16, Rue Bannier, 16 Orleans. Courtesy of Charles V. Peery.

Lt. Robert Chester Foute

Lts. Joseph P. Claybrook,
Robert Alexander Camm and William Pinckney Mason

Photographed together in France where they waited (in vain) for the commissioning of the *C.S.S. Rappahannock*, Claybrook, Camm and Mason spent the final months of the war in Richmond. Camm and Claybrook came to Richmond from Wilmington and Charleston, respectively, served with the James River batteries, then surrendered with Tucker's Naval Brigade at Sayler's Creek. Mason had served at Drewry's Bluff and on the *Jamestown* in 1862, and returned from Europe in 1864 directly to his native Virginia. As an officer aboard the *Virginia II*, Mason was wounded in the action at Trent's Reach and did not return to active duty. Carte-de-visite by M. De La Chaperonniere, Calais, France, ca. 1863-1864.

Asst. Engineer Eugene H. Brown

Engineer Brown served with "Savez" Read aboard the *Arkansas* and on the *Clarence-Tacony* adventure and, with Read, was imprisoned at Fort Warren, Boston, and returned to Richmond in October 1864. He served with the James River Squadron and with Semmes's army command until its surrender in North Carolina. Carte-de-visite by J. W. Black, Boston, Massachusetts, ca. 1863-1864.

Master William B. Cox

Photographed in the uniform of a Confederate navy lieutenant, Cox was stationed on the *Patrick Henry* in 1864 and was promoted subsequently to master. He was captured and paroled in Charlotte, North Carolina, in 1865. Carte-de-visite by C. E. Jones & Van[n]erson, Richmond, Virginia.

Lts. Hilary Cenas, Thomas Lardner Dornin, and John F. Ramsey

Photographed while enjoying leisurely months in Europe, Cenas, Dornin and Ramsey were young officers aboard the never-commissioned *Rappahannock* and the commerce raider *Florida*. Cenas and Dornin (but not Ramsay) ended their naval service on the James River. Cenas left Richmond with Tucker's Naval Brigade and surrendered at Appomattox, while Dornin was part of Semmes' command and ended the war in North Carolina. Carte-de-visite by M. De La Chaperonniere, Calais, France, ca. 1863-1864, in *Belles, Beaux & Brains of the '60s*, part XVIII.

Matthew Fontaine Maury Monument, Richmond

Dedicated in November 1929, the monument to Matthew Fontaine Maury is the western-most Confederate statue on Monument Avenue. The Virginia-born naval scientist stands as the naval counterpart to army generals R. E. Lee, Thomas J. "Stonewall" Jackson, J. E. B. Stuart, and the Confederate government represented by President Jefferson Davis. Unlike the other monuments along the avenue, the statue of the world-renowned "Pathfinder of the Seas" does not emphasize Maury's role in Confederate service. Courtesy of The Valentine Museum

The Capital Navy, the Navy Capital, & the Men Who Made it

Richmond's Naval Heritage

The physical evidence of Richmond's four-year life as capital of the Confederate States Navy disappeared quickly after the war. What the Confederate navy did not destroy, the U.S. Navy confiscated. The biggest prize was the partially-clad *Texas*, which Federals declared to be among the finest Confederate vessels. Her engines, boilers and remaining armor were seized at the Naval Works, and she was towed downriver to Norfolk to be completed. The *Texas* served in the U.S. Navy until sold to a private shipping company in 1867. In early June, the Federals restored the Naval Works—Shockoe Foundry to its owners, Charles and James Madison Talbott. The latter Talbott eventually left the business and became partner in the firm of Ettenger and Edmond, formerly the Naval Ordnance Works.[1]

Just as the Confederate navy took over Richmond waterfront in 1862, the city's commercial and transportation industries reclaimed the area around Rocketts in 1865. The shipbuilding facilities may have been burned, but the sheds, warehouses and the businesses along the dock remained. Within weeks, the Federal navy cleared the river of torpedoes, and packets and schooners were moored at the wharves as they had been before the war. "The hum of trade is again heard where so recently nothing was audible but the occasional rumble of a Confederate wagon and the slow clanking hammers on those absurd institutions, Mr. Mallory's iron-clads," bragged the Northern-run Richmond *Whig* on April 13, 1865.[2]

As peace time pursuits reclaimed Rocketts, its wartime role as nerve center for the capital navy faded into history and was all but forgotten. Today, on a grassy island between a busy stretch of East Main St. and a railroad trestle, there is only a small bronze tablet stating matter-of-factly that a few feet away was the site of a major Civil War shipyard. There is no tangible, visible, evidence of the Confederate naval facilities at Rocketts. In fact, the "rickety suburb" of Rocketts was leveled by 1900 during the construction of the Chesapeake and Ohio Railroad. A successor working class neighborhood, known as Fulton, grew up where Rocketts had once been until it, too, was leveled during the "urban renewal" of the early 1970s. The major thoroughfare of the new Fulton neighborhood is Admiral Gravely Blvd., named for Adm. Samuel Gravely, a Richmonder who in 1972 became the first black American to reach the rank of rear admiral.[3]

Although the cruise ship, *Anabel Lee*, still docks there, Rocketts long ago ceased to be the port of Richmond. Thirty years after the Civil War, however, the Richmond waterfront was again the site of a major shipbuilding operation. William R. Trigg, of the Richmond Locomotive Works, opened the Trigg Shipyard in 1898 near the great ship lock. Building literally on the foundations of Richmond's naval history, Trigg purchased the Talbott Brothers' Shockoe Foundry, formerly the Confederate Naval Works, which he made the center of his operation. Between 1898 and 1903, the Trigg yard constructed nearly 20 ships, including a cruiser, two destroyers, three torpedo boats, two revenue cutters, a dredge, two passenger ships, an oil tanker, four tug boats, and a stern wheel river boat, for the United States Navy, the revenue cutter service, the Army Corps of Engineers, and Standard Oil Company. Three of Trigg's ships saw action in World War I. The yard also repaired John P.

Holland's experimental submarine, *Plunger*, the first modern submarine in the U.S. Navy.[4]

The ebb and flow of industrial development has left Rocketts with old power plants and oil storage terminals, but the area is still relatively unspoiled and there is strong reason to believe that evidence of its naval history remains below the surface. Archaeologists from Virginia Commonwealth University's Archaeological Research Center recently excavated several lots of the old settlement of Rocketts, and discovered evidence of eighteenth-century structures and plumbing. Rocketts, asserted chief archaeologist Dan Mouer, is "one of the more important sites we have had excavated." A long-term comprehensive excavation of the Rocketts area would not only provide further knowledge about the area's rich history, but would also be in itself an object of public interest. Other evidence of Richmond's naval history turned up during the construction of the James River flood wall, where work crews found Civil War-era cannon balls at 17th and Dock Streets. Archaeologists realized the former site was the Confederate Naval Works and the Trigg Shipyard.[5]

Directly across the James from Rocketts is the site of William Graves' shipyard, where the *Virginia II* was constructed. The site was for a time in the 1960s and 1970s home to Newton Ancarrow's speedboat yard. A devoted environmentalist and historian of the James, Ancarrow found on his property oak timbers (some curved), and wrought iron nails, and thus "rediscovered" the existence of the southside shipyard. After years of neglect, the site recently became the city boat landing. Like Rocketts, important as both a Confederate shipyard and one of Richmond's oldest neighborhoods, the southside shipyard site has an historical importance that transcends the centuries. In 1991, while searching for evidence of William Byrd's seventeenth-century trading post, archaeologists (sponsored by the William Byrd Branch of the Association for the Preservation of Virginia Antiquities) found on the site the foundations of a three-story stone structure visible in nineteenth-century photographs of the southside shipyard. Though the building predated the war, archaeologists believe that it was "the central structure" of the navy yard.[6]

The discoveries of "archaeological treasures of the Richmond's waterfront" coincide with a shifting of downtown Richmond from Broad Street to the river. The revival of the waterfront between the Mayo and Lee bridges has been anchored in large part upon the river front's historical resources—Brown's Island, the James River and Kanawha Canal and the Tidewater Connection locks, Tredegar Iron Works, and Belle Isle—and has benefited from the contributions of such groups as the Historic Richmond Foundation. The next stage of Richmond's downtown revitalization similarly involves reconstruction of the Haxall mill canal and part of the James River and Kanawha Canal (though not in its original path) along the waterfront. Planners expect the reconstructed canal to become the centerpiece of a thriving downtown commercial district. The wealth of history—especially that associated with the Confederate States Navy—lying further downriver between Shockoe Bottom and Rocketts presents an attractive opportunity for reviving another part of downtown Richmond.[7]

At present, the most secure and accessible site associated with the Confederate Navy is Drewry's Bluff, the site of a "little village" of cabins once occupied by Southern sailors, midshipmen, and marines. Owned by the National Park Service and administered by the Richmond National Battlefield Park, Drewry's Bluff interprets the role of the men who were stationed there in the defense of Richmond, especially the battle of May 15, 1862. Thanks to the preservation efforts of the Chesterfield County Historical Society, the site of Battery Dantzler (along with inland segments of the Howlett Line) downriver from Drewry's Bluff, is also accessible to the public. The society has published a small self-guided tour book for those site.[8]

The largest and most interesting artifacts of the capital navy will likely never be seen by the general public, since they lie just off Drewry's Bluff on the bottom of the James River. Although the ships sunk near Rocketts, most notably the *Patrick Henry*, were blown up and cleared out immediately after the war, the hulks of the ironclads *Virginia II*, *Fredericksburg*, and *Richmond*, along with three ships sunk by the Confederates as obstructions in 1862—the steamers *Jamestown*, *Northampton*, and *Curtis Peck*—remain. The wrecks survived channel-clearing operations begun soon after the war as well as a major dredging in

1939, during which salvage crews used explosives to remove obstructions. The crews brought up souvenirs, including anchors, anchor chains, blocks, tackle, copper-sheeted wood, copper and brass spikes, bayonets, shells, and boots; a few artifacts were donated to the Confederate Museum.[9]

Working from a detailed 1881 map, underwater archaeologists in 1981 and 1985 discovered the precise locations of the vessels, covered and preserved under thick layers of sediment. The most tangible remains of Richmond's Confederate naval history, the wrecks are, the archaeologists warned, "precariously in harm's way, potential victims of plans to deepen and widen the James for commercial purposes." The wrecks continue to vex Richmond port officials. Interest in the sunken vessels among underwater archaeologists and historians is growing. The desire to widen the river channel continues to run afoul the legally-protected status of the wrecks. Responsible disposition of the wrecks is in the best interests of all concerned parties. Although raising one or more of the ironclads would be a difficult, expensive, and risky venture, the successful preservation of a James River ironclad could give the city a large and tangible centerpiece for marketing the history of the Confederate navy as a tourist attraction. Yet undiscovered is the final resting place of the "submarine boat" built under the direction of William G. Cheeney at Tredegar in late 1861 and early 1862.[10]

Even without the ships, physical evidence of the capital navy and the men who served it survives in Richmond area museums. On permanent display in the courtyard outside The Museum of the Confederacy are the propeller shaft and anchor of the Confederacy's most famous ironclad vessel, the *Virginia*, dredged from the James River. The Museum also has a small section of the iron plate from the *Virginia* donated by a clerk at Tredegar Iron Works, the firm that produced it in 1861. A signal flag from the flagship, *Virginia II*, pieces of Confederate navy china used on the *Patrick Henry*, a midshipman's bench from the school ship, and a silver butter knife from the *Jamestown* are among the few objects surviving from the wreckage of the James River Squadron vessels. Personal possessions of such important figures as Matthew Fontaine Maury, Raphael Semmes, Robert Dabney Minor and Robert Pegram are in the Museum's collections. The Virginia Historical Society houses a valuable collection of Confederate artifacts, images and, especially, manuscripts. The papers of John K. Mitchell and Robert Dabney Minor are among the most valuable collections for historians of the Confederate States Navy.

Men Without A Navy

The men who had made the capital navy found themselves without a country in May 1865. Not only were the tangible products of their labor on the bottom the James, but their careers were destroyed and their lives in disarray. They devoted their final years to coping with defeat and to chronicling and defending their wartime deeds.

Two Confederate midshipmen who had spent part of the war aboard the school ship *Patrick Henry* were among the first historians of the Confederate navy. Marylander John Thomas Scharf published the authoritative *History of the Confederate States Navy* in 1887, a volume that is still the bedrock of any serious study of the Southern navy. Georgian William F. Clayton followed Scharf's study twenty years later with a shorter, serialized history. Their former comrade, Hardin Littlepage, who served on the *Virginia* and fought at Drewry's Bluff, played an important role in preserving the history of the Confederate navy. In 1889, the Naval War Records Office hired him to supervise the collection and publication of Confederate navy documents.[11]

Aside from Littlepage, all officers who had "gone south" to join the Confederacy sacrificed forever their careers with the United States Navy. Many Confederate officers sacrificed not only their careers, but also their property, and returned home to ruined estates. Several of the senior officers—Ebenezer Farrand, French Forrest, William F. Lynch, and Sidney Smith Lee—died shortly after the close of the war.

Some officers managed to pursue naval careers outside military service. Consistent with his service as superintendent of the Confederate States Naval Academy, Lt. William Harwar Parker wrote textbooks on naval tactics and seamanship. Before becoming a United States consul to Korea, Parker commanded vessels in the Pacific Mail Steamship Company.[12] Lieutenant John Parker, formerly head of the Office of Special

Services, after the war founded the Steamship & Packet Company, of Richmond, and was captain of the ship *City of Richmond*.[13]

Virginia's—and the country's—most distinguished naval personality found himself literally a man without a country at the end of the war. On his way back to the Confederacy from his foreign assignment when he learned of his nation's collapse, Matthew Fontaine Maury decided to return to England rather than live in the occupied South. In late 1865, Maury journeyed to Mexico, where he accepted a post as commissioner of colonization in the cabinet of Emperor Maximilian, the puppet of French emperor Louis Napoleon. Similar to his service in the United States, Maury's primary contribution to Mexico was scientific. He subsequently became director of Mexico's astronomical observatory, but left Mexico before the overthrow and execution of Maximilian in 1867. He returned to Virginia and settled in Lexington, where he spent the remainder of his life as a professor of meteorology at the Virginia Military Institute. The "pathfinder of the seas" died on February 1, 1873.[14]

South America and the Middle East were popular destinations for the more adventurous former Confederates. John Randolph Tucker, captain of the *Patrick Henry* during the 1862 crisis and of the "Naval Brigade" in 1865, became caught up in the efforts of the South American states to resist domination by Spain. For eight frustrating months in 1866-1867, he commanded the combined navies of Peru and Chile against Spain. During that time, he introduced Confederate technological and organizational innovations to the South American countries, which assisted them in fighting off Spanish aggression. Afterward he served seven years as president of the Hydrographic Commission of the Amazon, exploring and mapping that river. He finally returned to Petersburg, Virginia, late in life and died there in 1883.[15]

Among Tucker's hand-picked associates in South America were three who had seen service on the James River: David Porter McCorkle, Walter Butt and James Rochelle. In 1861, McCorkle was in Richmond working with Joseph Pierce to transform the *Patrick Henry* into a warship. Like John Brooke, McCorkle was a one-time protégé of Matthew Maury. Leaving Richmond in 1861, he created and commanded the naval ordnance works in Atlanta. Butt, the baby-faced commander of the *Nansemond* during the Trent's Reach fiasco, was Tucker's chief of staff and the only man who remained with Tucker throughout his South American adventures. Butt returned to his home city of Portsmouth, Virginia, could not find productive work, then traveled to the west coast, where he had been raised. He joined former Confederate colleagues, James I. Waddell (commander of the *Shenandoah*) and William H. Parker as an officer of the Pacific Mail Steamship *City of San Francisco*. Butt died at the age of 45 in 1885. Rochelle was Tucker's former executive officer on the *Patrick Henry* and future biographer. The Virginia-born officer had also served in the James River as commander of the *Teaser* and the *Nansemond* and commandant of midshipmen of the Naval Academy. During his prewar service in the United States Navy, Rochelle had visited South America on the Paraguay survey. Following the war, he accepted a Peruvian invitation to join the Amazon Hydrographical Commission. Rochelle served for a time as president of the commission, then as a subordinate to Tucker. When the commission dissolved in 1877, Rochelle returned home to Southampton County, Virginia, where he died in 1889.[16]

Lieutenant Hunter Davidson, head of the Submarine Battery Service for most of the war, traveled to England at the suggestion of his last Confederate commander, Thomas Jefferson Page, of the *C.S.S. Stonewall*, to contract ships for the Argentine navy. At the invitation of Argentina's president, Davidson went on to spend 11 years as head of that country's Department of Torpedo Defense and Naval Construction. After the death of his first wife, Davidson married a Paraguayan woman and settled in Paraguay where he lived until his death in 1913. Though geographically distant from the United States, Davidson was an active participant in postwar debates over interpretation of the war. Bitter at the inadequate credit which naval historians and former Confederates gave to the Submarine Battery Service, Davidson wrote and later published indignant letters to President Jefferson Davis.[17]

One of Davidson's successors in command of the James River torpedo boats, Charles W. Read, accepted a lucrative offer to meddle in Colombia's civil war. At the request of that country's president, Read slipped a wooden gunboat out of New York harbor, navigated her down the coast and delivered her to Porto Caballos. Remaining in Colombia, Read contacted the rebel commander and offered to steal the ship for him. Rounding up a dozen volunteers, Read boarded the gunboat and delivered her to the insurgents. The Colombian president declined Read's offer to "recapture" his lost gunboat. The swashbuckling ex-Confederate sailor returned to the United States and spent his remaining years as a Mississippi River pilot.[18] He is still awaiting the scholarly biography he so richly deserves.

Lieutenant Beverly Kennon, the Virginia naval officer who deployed the James River torpedoes in late 1864, went after the war to Egypt, where he was among many former Confederate and Federal officers to serve in the Khedive's army. The youthful and well-connected Confederate midshipman, "Jimmie" Morgan, was also with the Egyptian army from 1870 to 1872. At the ripe age of 27, Morgan went on to other adventures, including a controversial appointment as U.S. consul-general to Australia, all of which he chronicled in *Recollections of a Rebel Reefer*.[19]

John Kirkwood Mitchell, the luckless commander of the James River Squadron in 1864-1865, returned to Richmond after his surrender to the Federal army in North Carolina. He settled in the former Confederate capital, building a house at 303 West Grace St. He never resumed an active career or wrote a memoir, but watched vigilantly for attacks on his record and defended his wartime actions—especially at New Orleans. Mitchell died in December 1889 and was buried in Hollywood Cemetery. Upon his death, a Richmond newspaper observed: "Though he had won distinction in the navies of the United and Confederate States and had resided Richmond ever since the war, comparatively few people knew him, so seldom did he appear in public."[20]

Raphael Semmes, whose glorious naval career ended ingloriously with the destruction of the James River Squadron, paid for his glory after the war. After surrendering himself and his "brigade" in North Carolina, Semmes returned home to Alabama, where in December 1865, he was arrested and taken to Washington, D.C. Accused of war crimes while in command of the commerce raider *Alabama*, Semmes was imprisoned for six months. He eventually convinced the government to drop the charges, but was still prevented from serving in elected office and did not recover his United States citizenship until December 1868. Restoration of citizenship did not make Semmes repent his devotion to the

Confederacy. In 1869, he published his *Memoirs of Service Afloat*, which not only detailed, but defended, the exploits of the *Sumter* and the *Alabama*, and reasserted the righteousness of the Southern cause. Semmes tried two short-lived careers, one as a professor of moral philosophy at the Louisiana Military Institute and the other as an editor of the *Memphis Daily Bulletin*, but soon returned home to Mobile. He died there of ptomaine poisoning on August 30, 1877. His service in Richmond is barely a footnote in the city's history or his own career, but Semmes looms large in the history of the Confederate navy and in Mobile.[21]

John McIntosh Kell, Semmes' first officer aboard the *Alabama* and commander of the *Richmond* in the winter of 1865, was compelled by his chronic fever to return home to his native Georgia even before war's end. Upon Semmes' death, Kell became the primary defender of the *Alabama's* historical reputation. He never returned to the sea, making his living instead in agriculture. In recognition of his wartime naval accomplishments, Georgia appointed him state adjutant general in 1886. Although often incapacitated by sickness and little more than a figurehead, Kell served in that post until his death in 1900, the same year that the citizens in Mobile, Alabama, dedicated a bronze statue of his former superior.[22]

The men who supervised construction of ships in wartime Richmond returned to the Norfolk area to pursue their trades after the war. John L. Porter, the Confederate navy's chief constructor, did so with the Atlantic works and the Baker shipyards, and was superintendent of the Norfolk and Portsmouth ferry service. He died in Portsmouth in 1893.[23] William Graves resurrected his shipbuilding business and did not retire until his 70th year in 1890. Already well-established in Norfolk before the war, Graves became one of that city's leading citizens. He served for years on Norfolk city council and as a director of a Norfolk bank. He was a member of the United Confederate Veterans and, at the time of his death in 1894, director of the Virginia Pilots' Association.[24]

The men most instrumental in Confederate technological innovation continued their work after the war. The wizards of the Office of Ordnance and Hydrography, Cdr. John Brooke and Lt. Robert Dabney Minor, along with Lt. Catesby Jones, who had supervised the Selma ordnance works, formed in 1866 what Brooke referred to as a "Civil Bureau of Supply." They sought to build a profitable business on a solid foundation of expertise and national and international contacts. Each of the men salvaged papers and drawings from his respective office and were free to market their own inventions and act as brokers for the sale of other ordnance and machinery to foreign governments, most notably Japan. The business never got off the ground and dissolved in 1869. A year later the three joined together again in an effort to sell torpedo defenses to the North German Confederation for use in its war against France. They asked another former colleague, Hunter Davidson (already in Europe to observe the war for the U.S. government), to negotiate the contract. The opportunity was lost, however, when the German army overwhelmed the French at Sedan and the urgency of submarine defense disappeared. The government of Egypt in 1870 offered Brooke and Minor five-year contracts as colonels of ordnance but, unlike many of their former colleagues, the two ordnance experts declined the invitation to work for a foreign government.[25]

Brooke and Minor best represent Richmond's role as a wartime naval city—a role more industrial and technological than military. Respected and renowned in wide circles in their own day, they have been largely forgotten in the writing of Civil War history. The two men left Richmond together, crossing Mayo's Bridge in an old ambulance at 1:00 p.m. on the fateful 2nd of April 1865. Separated at Farmville, Virginia, on the flight from Richmond, Brooke and Minor were reunited in Charlotte, North Carolina. Both were paroled with Semmes' force at Greensboro. Brooke's postwar life began unhappily as he endured financial worries and continued to grieve the 1863 death of his wife and infant daughter. He joined the faculty at the Virginia Military Institute but was not content until he remarried in 1871 and came to thrive in his life in Lexington. A member of the faculty for 40 years, Brooke was a V.M.I. institution when he died of a stroke in 1906.[26] Kate Mason Rowland, an unreconstructed amateur historian of the Confederacy, met Brooke after the war at the home of Lavonia Minor, Robert Dabney Minor's widow. Rowland wrote that Minor's daughter, Bessie, "laughingly declared that she was going to 'set her cap'" for Brooke, whom Rowland incorrectly remembered to have been widowed a second time. Brooke was, however, "amusingly impervious to coquetry and smiles and soft glances were quite unnoticed by the grave and dignified old gentleman." Frustrated in flirtation, Bessie instead settled for listening to her father's friend's wartime stories. So amused was Rowland by the incident that she wrote for Bessie a playful poem about it:

> With the 'Captains' and the 'Majors' of the dear Confederate day
> Our modern maiden Bessie would try her winning ways;
> Her eyes were lifted lovingly, her smile was rare and sweet,
> Her chair was moved up eagerly to the hero's very feet.
> But alas the great inventor of warship and of gun,
> Was oblivious alike of beauty and of fun.
> His introverted eye scanned the ocean's shoreless main
> As he sped the Shenandoah on her fearless cruise again,
> His thoughts were with the victory He won that glorious day
> when the wooden ships went down, and the iron one ran away!
> And the Maid's chivalrous father—the gallant and the brave,
> Carried the gen'rous true-flag the sinking foe to save.
> The flag the craven Bluecoats fired on with treach'rous spite,
> While their wounded, dying comrades lay drowning within sight.
> Bessie! Your pulses tingle as you hear the tale anew
> Of the ironclad Virginia and her deeds of derring-do
> But sad to say no prospect can the frolic maiden see,
> of herself succeeding of the second Mrs. B.
> So I send her here my handkerchief to wipe her weeping eye,
> And recall to her the truce-flag of the gallant years gone by.[27]

Bessie's "chivalrous father" and Brooke's close friend, Robert Minor, did not live long after the war. Returning to Virginia after surrendering at Greensboro, Minor tried to put the war behind him. He took the oath of allegiance to the U.S. government and applied (successfully) for a pardon to President Andrew Johnson. "During my service in the Southern Navy I have done nothing which an honorable seaman could not have done," he wrote the president, "and occasionally I have had it in my power to render some acts of kindness to Union prisoners." He served briefly as an agent for a New York life insurance company before embarking upon the business previously described with Brooke and Jones. After the failure of the ordnance venture, Minor was elected engineer of the James River Improvement Company and settled in Richmond. Among his accomplishments was the completion of a project begun by the Federal army in 1864—the excavation of a canal across Dutch Gap. "[T]he present condition of our river and harbor is largely due to his unremitting attention," the Richmond *Enquirer* noted in late 1871. On Saturday, November 25, 1871, Minor "danced and frolicked at a children's party which was held at his residence [6th between Leigh and Clay] that evening and seemed to be overflowing with humor and animation." Later that night he complained of pain in the back of his head and, at the suggestion of his wife, wrapped himself in blankets and rested. He was found dead at 2:00 a.m. The cause of death was "apoplexy," or stroke. He was 44 years old. Buried originally at his prewar home in Fauquier County, Minor in 1913 was reinterred beside his wife in Richmond's Hollywood Cemetery.[28]

Stephen Mallory, the personification of the Confederate navy, was released from Fort Lafayette in April 1866 and returned home to Pensacola, Florida. Effectively prohibited from again entering politics, Mallory nevertheless spoke and wrote on issues such as Reconstruction and American expansion into the Caribbean. While he corresponded with former Confederate navy associates, he unfortunately declined to write a memoir or history of the department he had created and overseen until the end of the war. To James Rochelle, Mallory summarized what he believed to be the contribution of the Confederate navy:

> I am satisfied that, with the means at our control, and in view of the overwhelming force of the enemy at the outset of the struggle, our little navy accomplished so much. Our Navy alone kept that of the U.S. from reaching Richmond by the James River, and from reaching Savannah and Charleston; and yet not ten men in ten thousand of the country know or appreciate these facts.[29]

The former navy secretary died at home after a short illness on November 12, 1872. It fell to others to make the American people appreciate the accomplishments of which Mallory was so proud and to assess critically the limit to those accomplishments.

One of the most critical assessments of the Confederate navy on the James came from Federal Adm. David D. Porter, the officer who commanded the fleet that witnessed its destruction. Describing the pyrotechnic end of the capital navy, Porter was tempted to call it a "blaze of glory." But the fact is, he noted, "the James River fleet had been the most useless force the Confederates had ever put afloat." The investment in ironclads was wasted, Porter believed, because "the forts, torpedoes and obstructions on the river" were "far more formidable adversaries, and quite sufficient, if properly managed, to keep any hostile vessels from ascending the narrow channel."[30] Porter conveniently forgot what he had told Abraham Lincoln on April 2, 1865 (and recounted in his memoir in 1885), that if the Confederate ironclads "'should get down to City Point they would commit great havoc.'"

Porter and his comrade-in-arms, Ulysses Grant, recognized the potential of the Richmond ironclads for affecting the war on the James, but Porter was not wrong in dismissing their actual impact. Similarly, he was not in error in concluding the Confederate navy's primary contribution to the war on the Richmond front was in erecting torpedo barriers and serving shore batteries that kept the Federal navy at bay. Even a Confederate officer, Frank Shepperd, wondered aloud in June 1864 whether it had been a worthy investment to build ironclads which could barely navigate the river.

Whether torpedoes, shore batteries and obstructions alone could have checked Federal vessels is a question that historians cannot answer.

A Partial List of Office Chiefs, Squadron and Ship Commanders in Richmond[1]

I. Administration of the Confederate Navy Department

Secretary of the Navy

Stephen R. Mallory (March 4, 1861-end of war)

Office of Orders and Detail

Capt. Samuel Barron (June 11-July 20, 1861)
Capt. Lawrence L. Rousseau (August 1-23, 1861)
Capt. William F. Lynch (August 23-September 4, 1861)
Capt. Franklin Buchanan (September 24, 1861-February 24, 1862)
Capt. French Forrest (March 1862-March 16,1863)
Capt. John K. Mitchell (March 16, 1863-May 6, 1864)
Capt. Sidney Smith Lee (May 6, 1864-end of war)

Office of Ordnance and Hydrography

(includes Confederate States Naval Academy and
Office of Special Services)
Capt. Duncan N. Ingraham (June 10, 1861-November 1861)
Cdr. George B. Minor (December 1861-March 1863)
Cdr. John Mercer Brooke (March 1863-end of war)

Confederate States Naval Academy

Superintendent: Lt. William H. Parker (May 1863-end of war)
Commandant of Midshipmen: Lt. Benjamin
P. Loyall (May 1863-Fall 1864)
Lt. James H. Rochelle (February 1865-end of war)

Office of Special Services

Cdr. Matthew Fontaine Maury (1862)
Cdr. Thomas R. Rootes (1862-1863)
Lt. John H. Parker (1863-end of war)

Office of Provisions and Clothing

Paymaster John DeBree (1861-April 1864)
Paymaster James A. Semple (April 1864-April 1865)

Office of Medicine and Surgery

William A. W. Spotswood, Surgeon in Charge (entire war)

Chief Constructors office

Chief Constructor John L. Porter (April 1863-end of war)
Acting Constructor William A. Graves (March 1862-end of war)

Chief Engineers office

Chief Engineer William P. Williamson (April 21, 1862-end of war)

Submarine Battery Service

Commander Hunter Davidson (1862-September 1864)
Lt. John Pembroke Jones (September 1864-end of war)

II. Confederate Naval Facilities in Richmond

Drewry's Bluff

Commander Ebenezer Farrand (May 6-19, 1862)
Capt. Sidney Smith Lee (May 1862-March 1864)
Colonel George H. Terrett, CSMC (March 1864-end of war)

Rocketts Navy Yard

Commandant Cdr. Ebenezer Farrand (1862)
Commandant Cdr. Robert Gilchrist Robb (1862-end of war)

Navy Yard Opposite Rocketts

Acting Master Maxwell T. Clarke (1862)
Lt. John H. Parker (1863-end of war)

Richmond Naval Ordnance Works

Superintendent: Lt. Robert Dabney Minor (1862-end of war)
Acting Superintendents: Lt. Alexander M. DeBree (1863)
Richard B. Wright (1864)

Richmond Naval Works

Superintendent: Thomas W. Smith (1862-end of war)

III. James River Squadron

Commanders of the James River Squadron

Captain French Forrest (July 10, 1861-February 27, 1862)
Capt. Franklin Buchanan (February 27-March 29, 1862)
Capt. Josiah Tattnall (March 29-May 15, 1862)
Capt. John Randolph Tucker (squadron detachment in James River April 19-May 1862)
Capt. Sidney Smith Lee (May 15, 1862-November 3, 1862)
Capt. Samuel Barron (November 3, 1862-March 1863)
Capt. French Forrest (March 24, 1863-May 6, 1864)
Capt. John K. Mitchell (May 6, 1864-February 18, 1865)
Rear Admiral Raphael Semmes (February 18, 1865-end of war)

Commanders of Vessels in James River Squadron
(May 1862-end of war)

C.S.S. Beaufort
Lieutenant William H. Parker (1862)
Lt. William Sharp (October 1863)
Lt. Edward J. Means (November 1863-June 1864)
Lt. J. M. Gardner (June 1864)
Lt. William Pinckney Mason (October 1864)
Lt. Joseph W. Alexander (December 19, 1864-February 1865)
Lt. George Henry Arledge (in charge February 12, 1865-?)[2]

C.S.S. Drewry
William H. Parker (May-fall 1862)
Master Lewis Parrish (ca. October 1863-May 1864)
Lt. William B. Hall (May 19-21, 1864)
Lt. William H. Wall (June 1864-January 23,1865)

C.S.S. Fredericksburg
Commander Thomas R. Rootes (March 1864-February 1865 [absent ill December 1864-February 1865])
Lt. Francis E. Shepperd (?-December 28, 1864; January 14-25, 1865)
Lt. Alphonse Barbot (exec. ofc., in charge, February 1865)[3]

C.S.S. Hampton
Lt. George W. Harrison (as of May 1862)
Lt. Hunter Davidson (possibly; 1862)
Lt. John S. Maury (1863-July 6, 1864; October 26-29, 1864)
Lt. John W. Murdaugh (July 6-October 26, 1864)
Lt. Ivey Foreman (October 29-November 18, 1864)
Lt. Walter R. Butt (November 18, 1864-)
Lt. Francis E. Shepperd (December 28, 1864-January 14, 1865)
Lt. Joseph David Wilson (January-February 1865)
Lt. Francis E. Shepperd (February 1865-[in hospital as of February 19])

C.S.S. Jamestown (aka *Thomas Jefferson*)
Lt. Joseph N. Barney (1861-1862)
Lt. George W. Harrison (May 1862, temporarily in charge)

C.S.S. Nansemond

Lieutenant James H. Rochelle (May 1862–late 1863)
Lt. John Pembroke Jones (January 1864)
Master W. W. Read (–May 18, 1864)
Lt. John W. Murdaugh (May 18, 1864-June 8, 1864)
Lt. Charles W. Hays (June 8-October 11, 1864; October 26-November 17, 1864)
Lt. Thomas L. Skinner (October 12-26, 1864)
Lt. Thomas P. Bell (November 17-December 1, 1864)
Lt. Walter R. Butt (December 1, 1864-end of war)

C.S.S. Patrick Henry (aka *Yorktown*)

Capt. John Randolph Tucker (1861-June 1862)
Lt. William H. Parker (1863-end of war)

C.S.S. Raleigh (*Roanoke*)

Lt. Joseph W. Alexander (1861-1862)
Lt. Maxwell T. Clarke (1863-June 1864)
Lt. Mortimer Murray Benton (during June 1864)
Masters Mate A. E. Albertson (July 31, 1864-)
Acting Master W. Frank Shippey (October-December 1864)
Lt. William Winder Pollock (January 1865-end of war)

C.S.S. Richmond

Cdr. Robert B. Pegram (November 1862-May 1864)
Cdr. William H. Parker (May-June 1864)
Lt. John S. Maury (July-October 26, 1864)
Cdr. William A. Webb (October-November 1864))
John McIntosh Kell (December 30, 1864-February 1865)
Lt. Hamilton Henderson Dalton (February 1865-)[4]
Passed Midshipman J.A. Peters (during February 1865)

C.S.S. Teaser

Lt. James H. Rocelle (May-June 1861)
Lt. Robert Randolph Carter (June-July 1861)
Boatswain [Master] William H. Face (June 1861-January 1862)
Lt. William A. Webb (February 1862-)
Lt. Hunter Davidson (June-July 1862)

C.S.S. Virginia II
Commander Robert B. Pegram (May 1864-ca. August 1864)
Lt. Oscar F. Johnston (August 1864, commanding *pro tem*)
Lt. Francis E. Shepperd (September 24, 1864-ca. December 1864)
Lt. John W. Dunnington (December 1864-end of war)

C.S.S. Torpedo
Cdr.. Hunter Davidson (1862-1864)
Lt. John Pembroke Jones (as of November 1864)
Lt. Ivey Foreman (November 18, 1864-)
Lt. William P. Bell (January 1865)
Acting Master Peter W. Smith (January 22-25, 1865)
Lt. William W. Roberts (February 1865-end of war)

Torpedo Boats
Cdr. Hunter Davidson (1863-1864)
Lt. Beverly Kennon (late 1864)
Lt. Charles W. Read (January 1865)

Appendix 2

Ironclads of the James River Squadron

No photographs and no complete set of blueprints survive for the ironclad vessels of the James River Squadron, and the finished vessels may have diverged from the original plans. Nevertheless, enough is known about them to make reasonably accurate and detailed drawings. The set of measured drawings that grace the following pages are based on the few surviving plans made by Confederate naval constructors (including John L. Porter's profile view of the *Fredericksburg*, sectional view of the *Texas*, and William A. Graves' profile and sectional view of the *Virginia II*); on draftsman John W. H. Porter's postwar watercolor of the *Texas*; on more detailed drawings and photographs of vessels in the same class, such as the *Savannah*, which closely resembled the *Richmond*; and on critical evaluation of the drawings made in the 1950s-1960s by William E. Geoghegan.

The drawings included on the following pages are top, profile and sectional views of each of the James River ironclads, and are intended to show the evolution of size and shape. The cutaway profile and top views of the *CSS Fredericksburg* is intended to show the deck arrangement and gun placement typical for all James River ironclads. Although they are necessarily speculative in some details, these drawings document the most formidable ships built by the Confederate States Navy in Richmond.

About the draftsman

David J. Meagher, a former United States Marine and U.S. Army officer, works at Northrop/Grumman in Huntsville, Alabama. He has combined his drafting talent with his passion for naval history in creating measured drawings of dozens of Civil War ironclads. Posters and individual plans of these ironclads are available for distribution. For additional information, write to Mr. Meagher at: 208 Thach Lane, Huntsville, Alabama 35759.

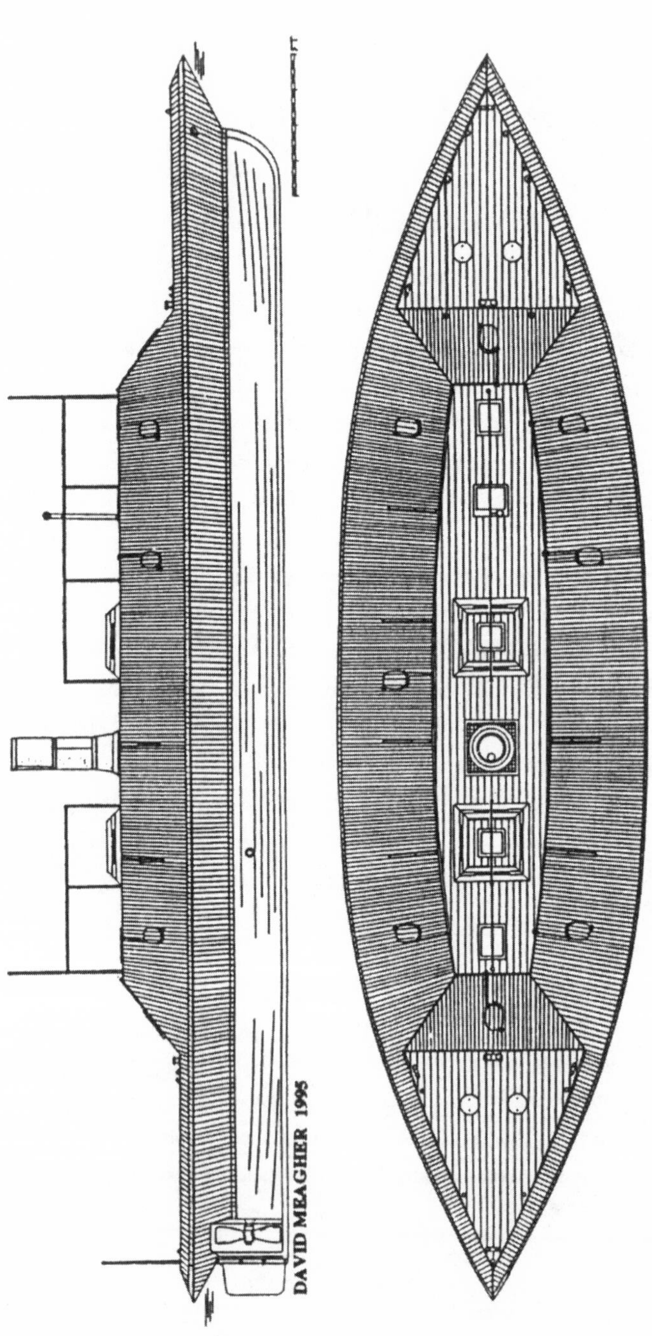

C. S. S. Richmond

Length overall: 180' - Beam: 45' - Draft: 13'

Armament: 3 single-banded 7 Inch Brooke rifles (bow and broadsides); 1 double-banded 7 Inch Brooke rifle (stern)

Launched: May 5, 1862 - Commissioned: November 1862

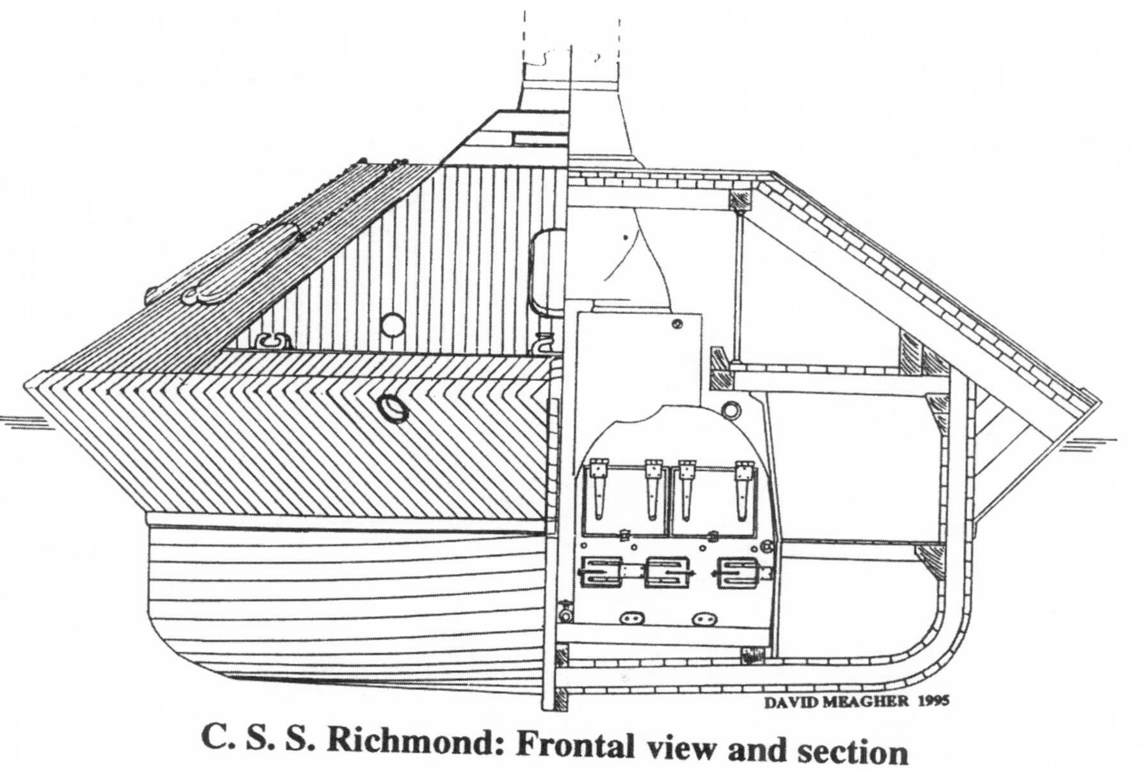

C. S. S. Richmond: Frontal view and section

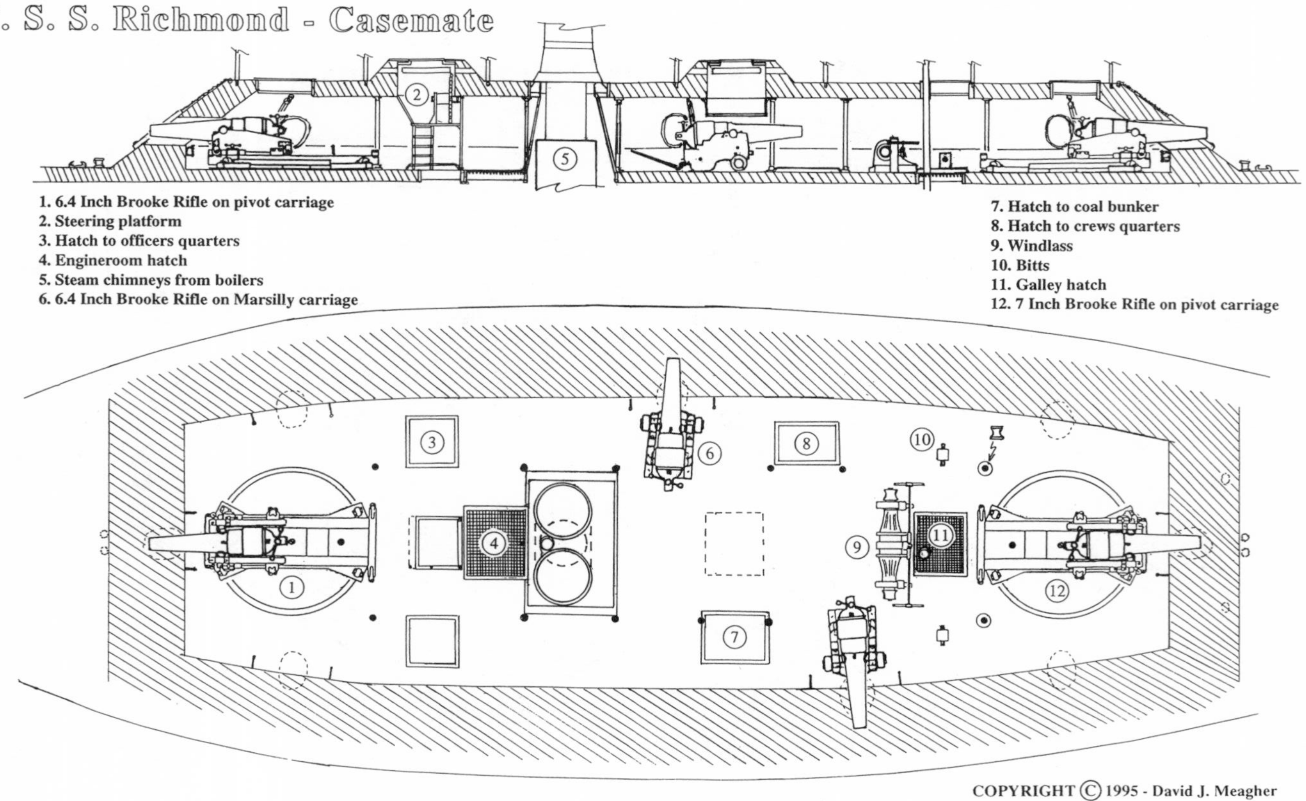
C. S. S. Richmond - Casemate
1. 6.4 Inch Brooke Rifle on pivot carriage
2. Steering platform
3. Hatch to officers quarters
4. Engineroom hatch
5. Steam chimneys from boilers
6. 6.4 Inch Brooke Rifle on Marsilly carriage
7. Hatch to coal bunker
8. Hatch to crews quarters
9. Windlass
10. Bitts
11. Galley hatch
12. 7 Inch Brooke Rifle on pivot carriage
COPYRIGHT © 1995 - David J. Meagher

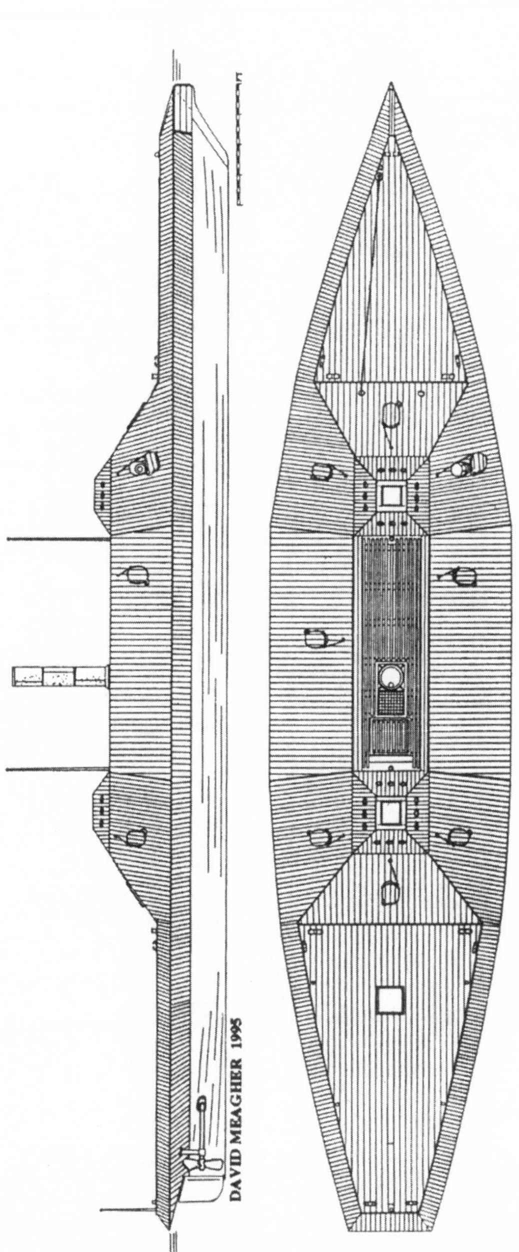

C. S. S. Fredericksburg
Length overall: 188' - Beam: 40' - Draft: 9 to 10'
Armament: 1 double-banded 7 Inch Brooke rifle (bow); 2 6.4 Inch Brooke rifles (broadsides);
1 double-banded Brooke smoothbore (stern) (replaced in October 1864 with 11 Inch smoothbore)
Launched: June 11, 1863 - Commissioned : March 1863 (completed May 12, 1863)

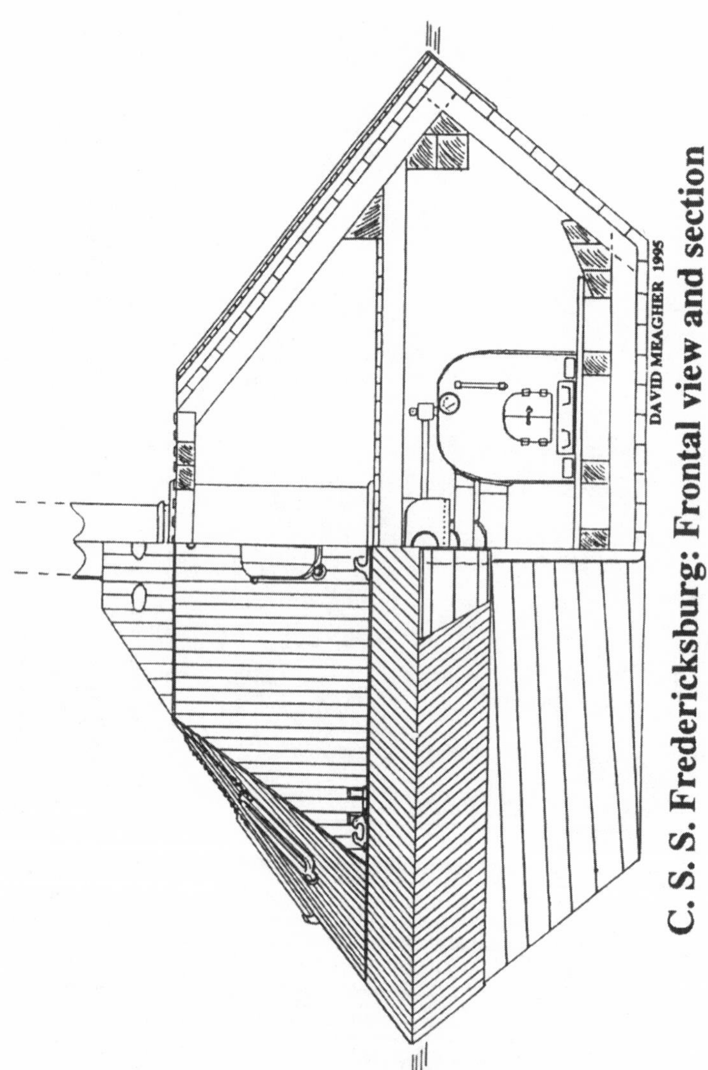

C. S. S. Fredericksburg: Frontal view and section

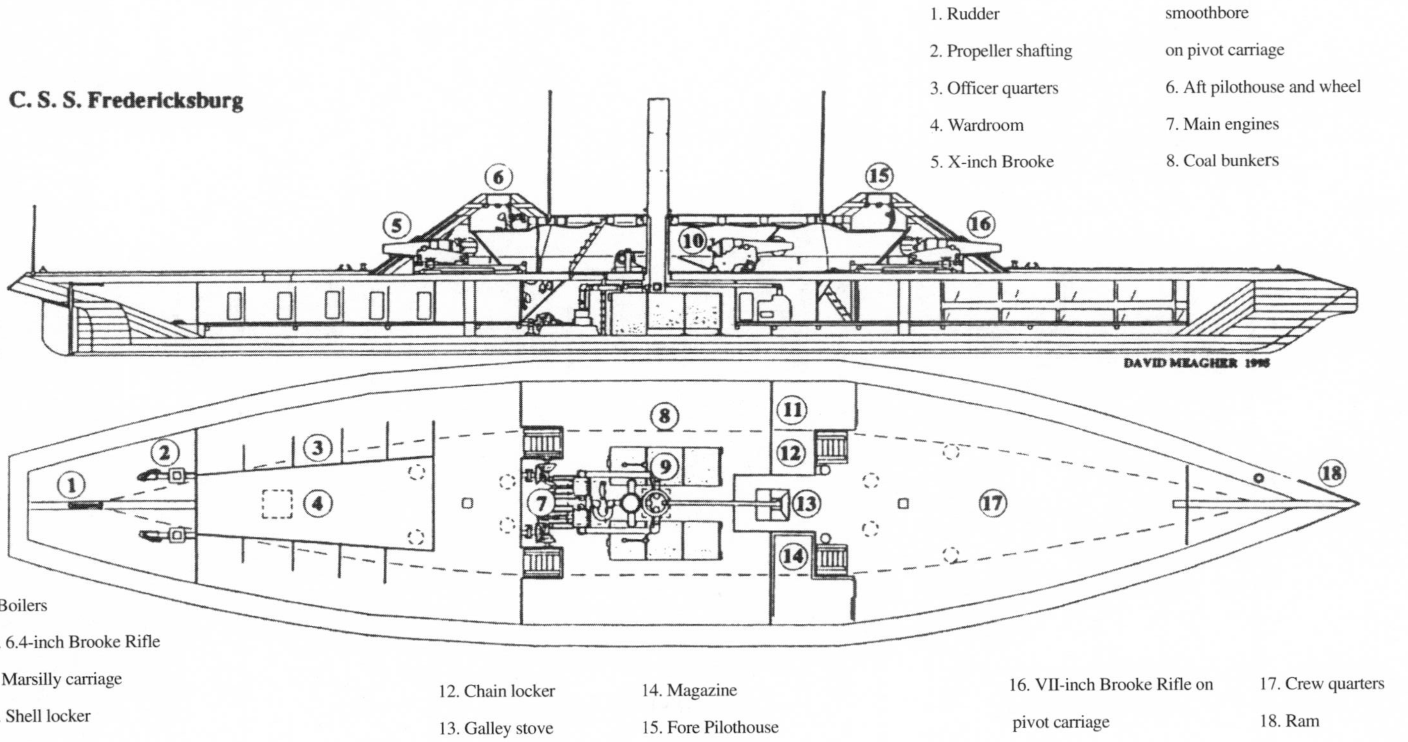
C. S. S. Fredericksburg
DAVID MEAGHER 1998
1. Rudder
2. Propeller shafting
3. Officer quarters
4. Wardroom
5. X-inch Brooke smoothbore on pivot carriage
6. Aft pilothouse and wheel
7. Main engines
8. Coal bunkers
9. Boilers
10. 6.4-inch Brooke Rifle on Marsilly carriage
11. Shell locker
12. Chain locker
13. Galley stove
14. Magazine
15. Fore Pilothouse
16. VII-inch Brooke Rifle on pivot carriage
17. Crew quarters
18. Ram

Gun Deck of C. S. S. Fredericksburg
1. VII Inch Brooke rifle in pivot carriage (Fore)
2. Air vents
3. Bitt (port side only)
4. Chain navel
5. Hatchways
6. 6.4 Inch Brooke rifle in Marsilly carriage
7. Smokestack and casing
8. Windlass (Offset to port side)
9. Engine room hatch
10. X Inch Brooke smoothbore in pivot carriage (Aft)

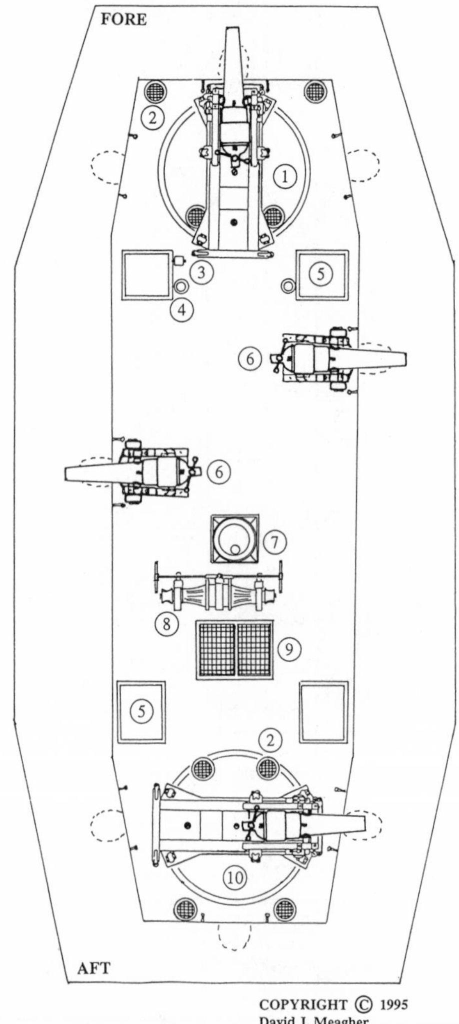

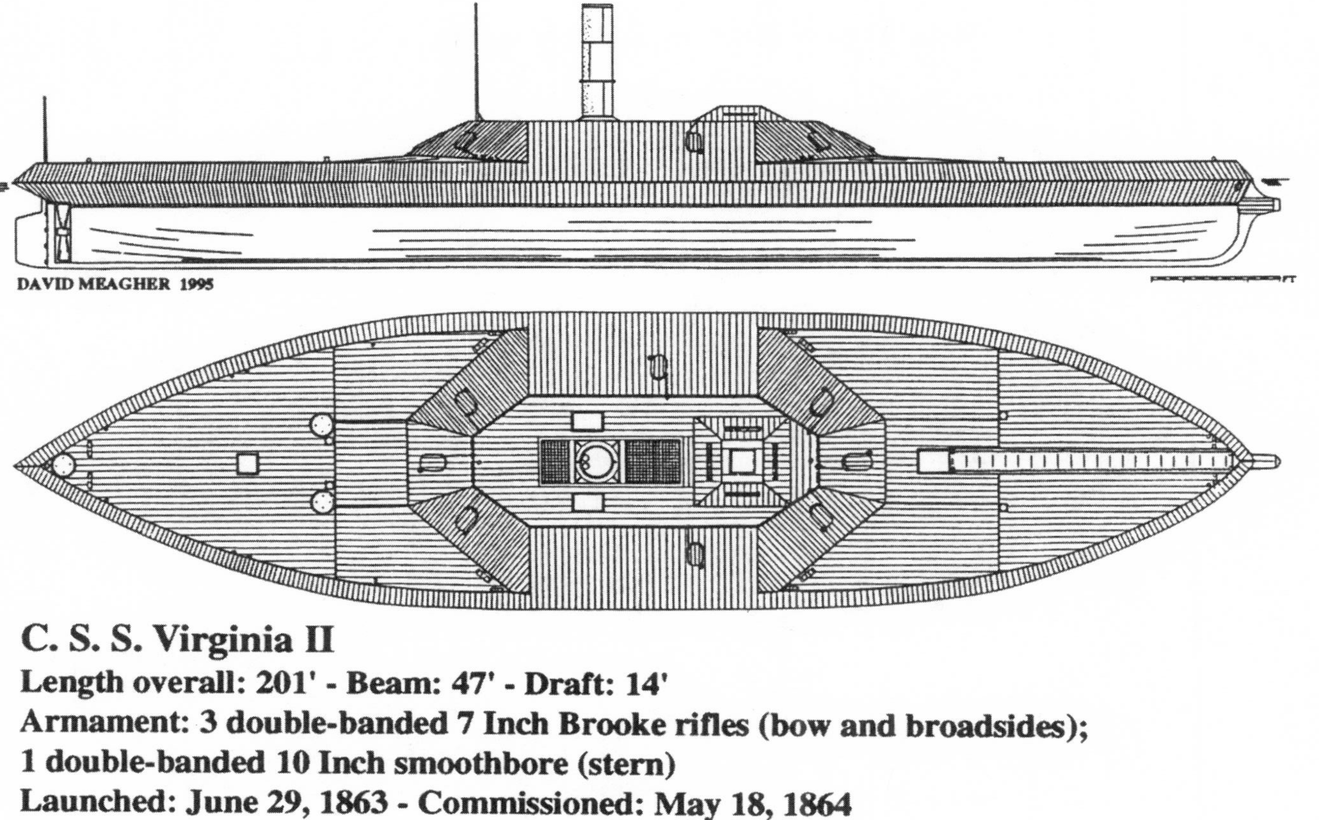

C. S. S. Virginia II

Length overall: 201' - Beam: 47' - Draft: 14'

Armament: 3 double-banded 7 Inch Brooke rifles (bow and broadsides);
1 double-banded 10 Inch smoothbore (stern)

Launched: June 29, 1863 - Commissioned: May 18, 1864

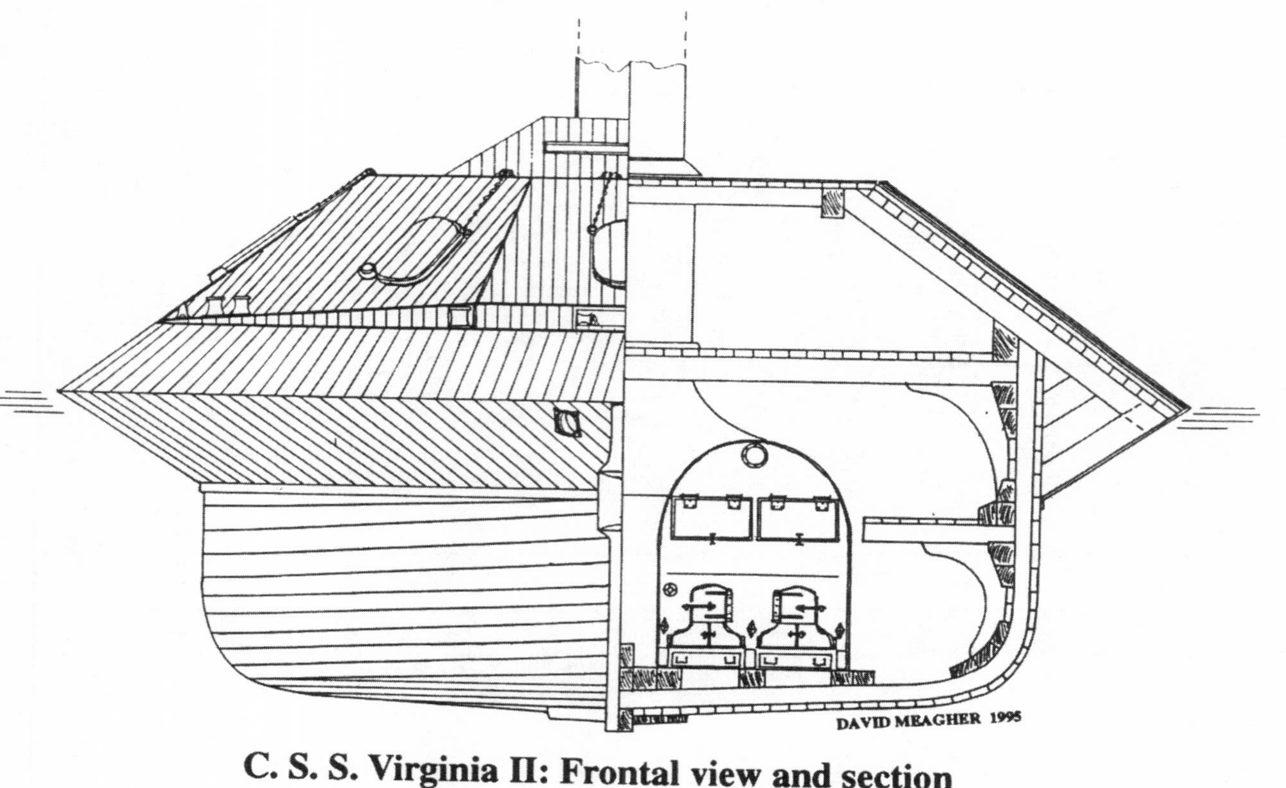

C. S. S. Virginia II: Frontal view and section

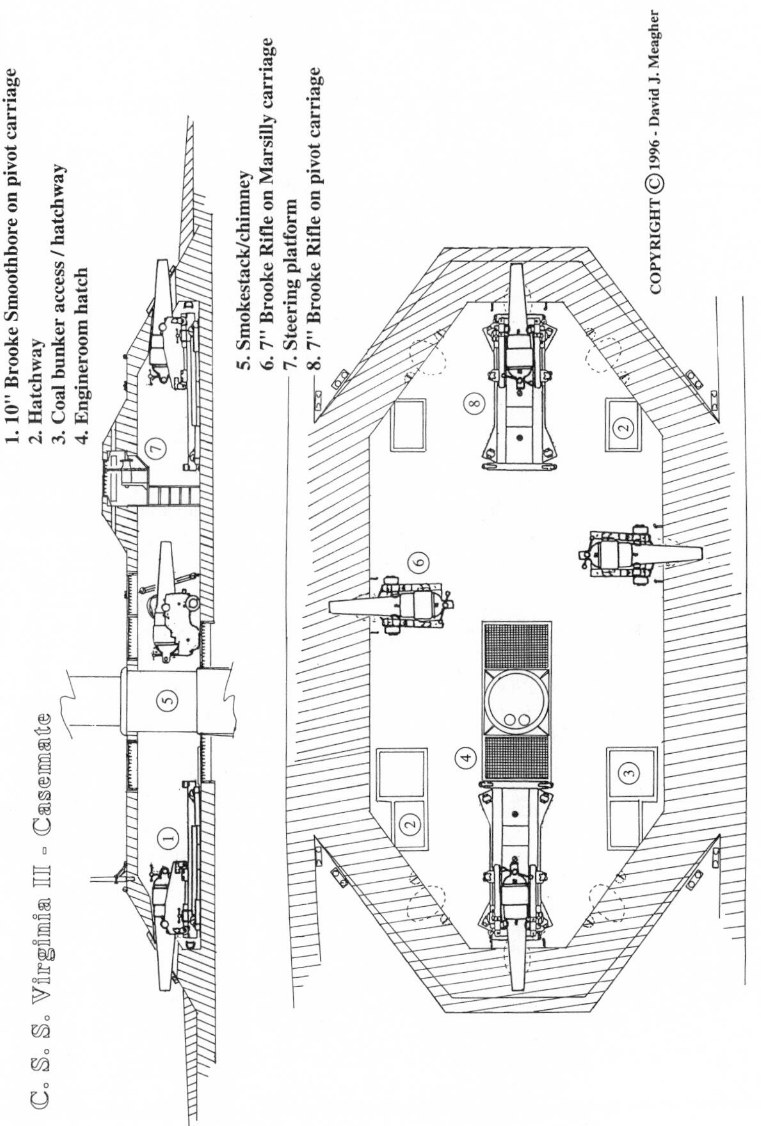
C. S. S. Virginia III - Casemate
1. 10" Brooke Smoothbore on pivot carriage
2. Hatchway
3. Coal bunker access / hatchway
4. Engineroom hatch
5. Smokestack/chimney
6. 7" Brooke Rifle on Marsilly carriage
7. Steering platform
8. 7" Brooke Rifle on pivot carriage
COPYRIGHT © 1996 - David J. Meagher

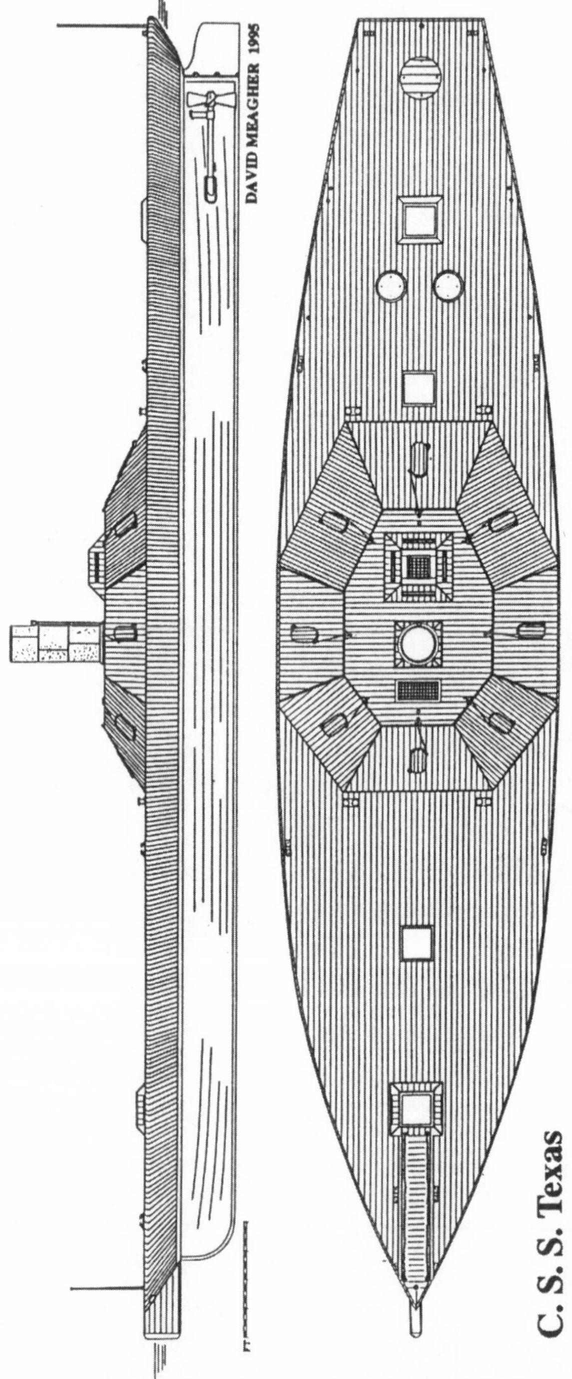

C. S. S. Texas

Length overall: 217' - Beam: 48'6" - Draft: 16 or 17'

Armament: 4 or 6 guns

Launched: Circa October 1864 or January 1865; Never commissioned or completed

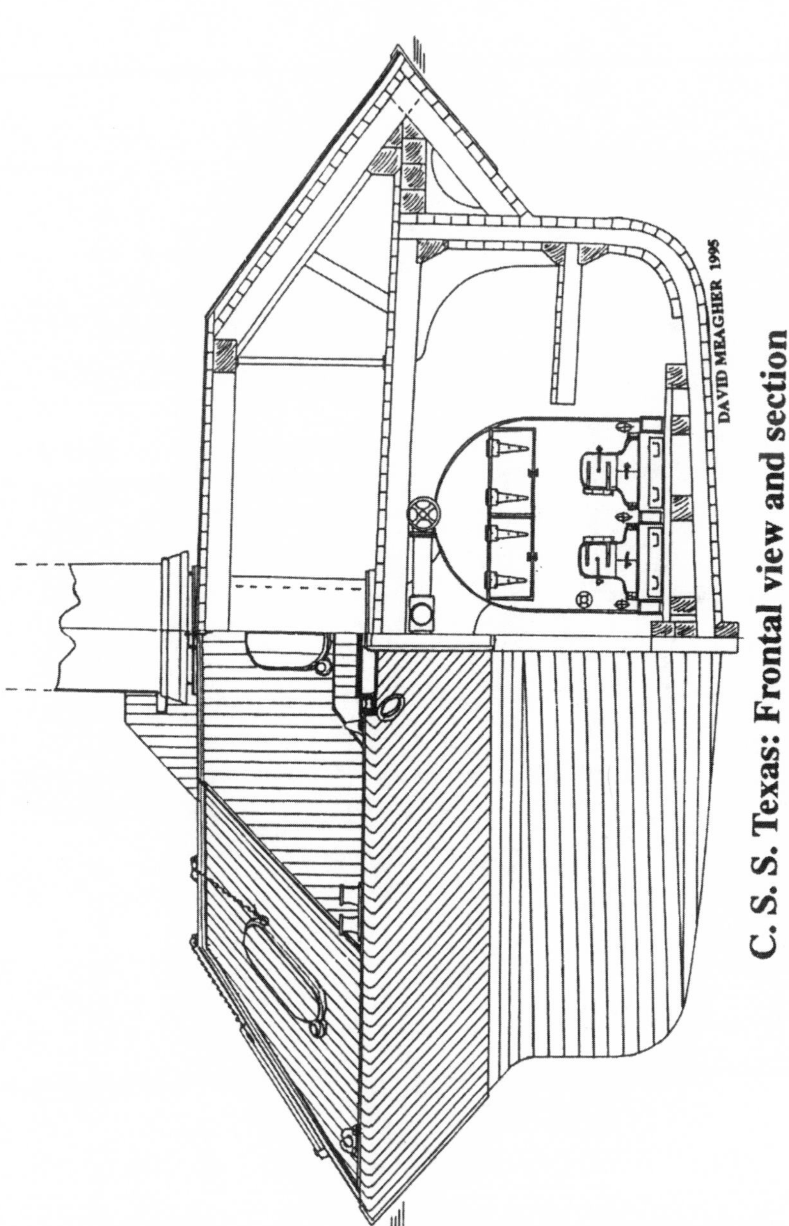

C. S. S. Texas: Frontal view and section

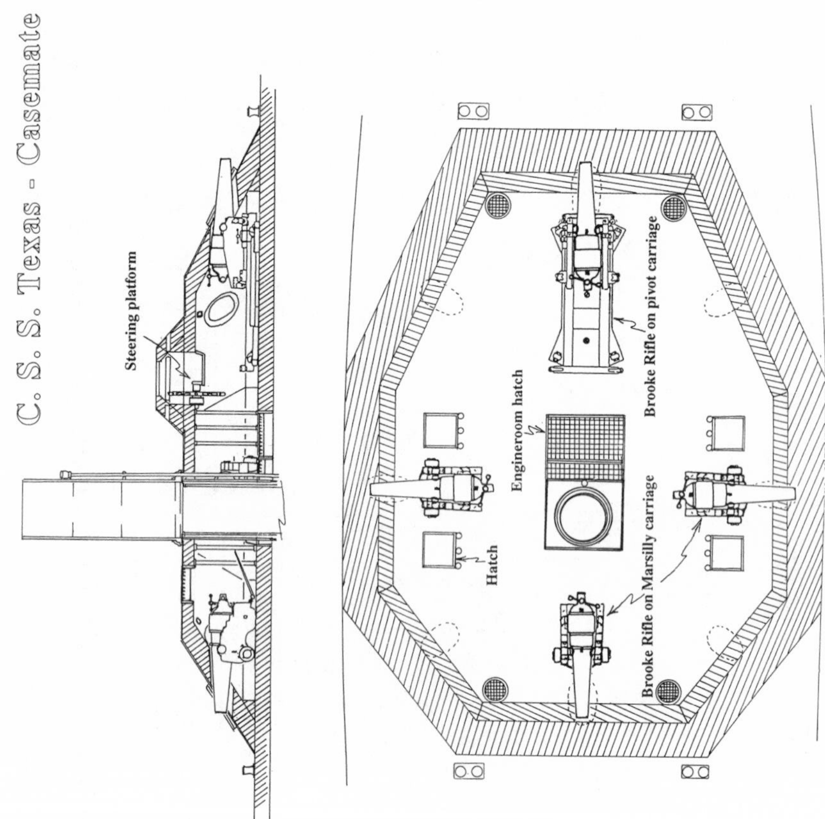
C. S. S. Texas - Casemate
Steering platform
Engineroom hatch
Hatch
Brooke Rifle on pivot carriage
Brooke Rifle on Marsilly carriage

Endnotes

Preface

1. Stanley Kimmel, *Mr. Davis's City* (New York, 1958); Richard M. Lee, *General Lee's City* (McLean, 1987).

2. The history of Civil War Richmond is recounted in many sources, most notably in Emory M. Thomas, *The Confederate State of Richmond: A Biography of the Capital* (Austin, 1971); Alfred Hoyt Bill, *The Beleaguered City: Richmond 1861-1865* (New York, 1946); Mike Wright, *City Under Siege: Richmond in the Civil War* (Lanham, 1995); E. B. Furgurson, *The Ashes of Glory: Richmond in the Civil War* (to be published); David D. Ryan, *Four Days in 1865: The Fall of Richmond* (Richmond, 1993); David D. Ryan, *Cornbread and Maggots, Cloak and Dagger: Union Prisoners and Spies in Civil War Richmond* (Richmond, 1994). Three of the best standard secondary works on Civil War navies include: J. Thomas Scharf, *History of the Confederate States Navy* (New York, 1887); Virgil Carrington Jones, *The Civil War at Sea*, 3 vols. (New York, 1960-1962); and Ivan Musicant, *Divided Waters: The Naval History of the Civil War* (New York, 1995). Italian historian Raimando Luraghi's highly-acclaimed *A History of the Confederate Navy* (Annapolis, 1996), was not available in translation when *Capital Navy* went to press. At least one other historian has written a study of the Confederate

navy in a defined geographic area. See, Maxine Turner, *Navy Gray: A Story of the Civil War on the Chattahoochee and Apalachicola Rivers* (Tuscaloosa, 1988).

Introduction

1. David Dixon Porter, *Incidents and Anecdotes of the Civil War* (New York, 1885), pp. 292-293.

2. David Dixon Porter, "Private Journal," David Dixon Porter Papers, Library of Congress Manuscripts Division, Washington, D.C., box 23. Hereinafter cited as Porter Papers.

3. *The World* [New York], April 10, 1865, p. 1, c. 4; *New York Times*, Hereinafter cited as *NYT*; April 10, 1865, p. 1., c. 2; Porter, *Incidents and Anecdotes*, p. 309.

4 *New York Herald*, p. 5, c. 2; *NYT*, April 10, 1865, p.1, c. 2; *New York Herald*, April 8, 1865, p. 5, c. 1.

5. *NYT*, April 10, 1865, p. 1., c. 2.

6.. New York *World*, April 8, 1865.

7. *New York Herald*, April 13, 1865, p. 5, c. 3.

8. *The World* [New York], April 7, 1865, p.1, c. 3.

9. Report of Alexander Henderson, April 25, 1865, Record Group 45, Confederate States Navy subject files (PN), National Archives and Records Administration, Washington, D.C., microfilm series M-1091, roll 42. Hereinafter cited as RG 45, subject files (file code), roll number; U.S. War Department. *War of the Rebellion: Official Records of the Union and Confederate Navies* (Washington, DC, 1894-1921), Series I, Volume 12, p. 101. Hereinafter cited as *ORN*.

Chapter One

1. Stephen R. Mallory Diary, Southern Historical Collection, University of North Carolina, Chapel Hill, North Carolina, entries of June 4, 12, 14, 1861. Hereinafter cited as Mallory Diary, entry date; Joseph T. Durkin, *Confederate Navy Chief: Stephen R. Mallory* (Columbia, 1987), pp. 160-164. Much to the dignified navy secretary's distress, he found himself caught in what he described as a "a perpetual cross fire of sharpshooting" between the president's wife and sister-in-law and a social rival, Charlotte Wigfall,

wife of Senator Louis T. Wigfall. John B. Jones, *A Rebel War Clerk's Diary*, 2 vols. (New York, 1935), vol. 1, p. 44.

2. William C. Davis, *"A Government of our Own": The Making of the Confederacy* (New York, 1994), is a comprehensive history of the Montgomery government.

3. William N. Still, Jr. *Iron Afloat: The Story of the Confederate Armorclads* (Columbia, 1985), pp. 6-7; James Barron Hope to wife, May 8, 1862, in James Barron Hope Papers, Special Collections, Earl Gregg Swem Library, College of William and Mary, box 1, file 86. Hereinafter cited as James Barron Hope Papers, box, file; T. C. DeLeon, "Belles, Beaux, & Brains of the '60's" *Town Topics* (1907-1908), part 7; Frank E. Vandiver, ed., *The Civil War Diary of General Josiah Gorgas* (Tuscaloosa, 1947), p. 59.

4. Scharf, *Confederate States Navy*, pp. 14-26; William S. Dudley, *Going South* (Washington, D.C., 1981), pp. ii, 33-55.

5. Mallory described the early squadron composition in his February 27, 1862 report to the President, in *ORN* II, 2, pp.149-150.

6. The story of Confederate ship acquisition abroad is told in James D. Bulloch, *The Secret Service of the Confederate States in Europe*, 2 volumes (London, 1883); Frank J. Merli, *Great Britain and the Confederate Navy, 1861-1865* (Bloomington, 1970); and Warren F. Spencer, *The Confederate Navy in Europe* (Tuscaloosa, 1983).

7. United States Congress, *Journal of the Congress of the Confederate States, 1861-1865*, 7 volumes (Washington, 1904), vol. 2, p. 189; Jerrill H. Shofner and William Warren Rogers, "Montgomery to Richmond: The Confederacy Selects a Capital," *Civil War History*, 10 (June 1964), pp. 155-166.

8. James I. Robertson, Jr., ed., *Proceedings of the Advisory Council of the State of Virginia, April 21-June 19, 1861* (Richmond, 1977), pp. 9,13.

9. Ibid., passim; Scharf, *Confederate States Navy*, p. 40.

10. Biographical sketches from Scharf, *Confederate States Navy*, pp. 371, 377, 710-711 and "Forrest, French," entry in Allen Johnson and Dumas Malone, eds., *Dictionary of American Biography*, 20 volumes (New York, 1943), vol. 6, p. 532. The biographical sketches in Scharf's out-of-print work have been reprinted in Thomas Truxtun Moebs, *Confederate Navy Research Guide* (Williamsburg, VA, 1991); James Henry Rochelle, *Life of Rear Admiral John Randolph Tucker* (Washington, D.C.: Neale Publishing Company, 1903), pp. 19-22; Robertson, *Proceedings*, pp. 42, 46.

11. *ORN* I, 5, pp. 803, 806.

12. Ibid., pp. 806, 808; II, 2, pp. 77-78. John T. Mason's letters, written between October 1861 and March 1862, describe life aboard the receiving ship *Confederate States*

at Norfolk. John T. Mason Papers, Eleanor S. Brockenbrough Library, The Museum of the Confederacy, Richmond, VA, file M-615, hereinafter cited as John T. Mason Papers.

13. Ibid., I, 5, p. 804; 4, p. 306.

14. U.S. Navy Department, Navy History Division, *Civil War Naval Chronology 1861-1865* (Washington, 1971), part 6, p. 311; Paul H. Silverstone, *Warships of the Civil War Navies* (Annapolis, 1989), p. 242, speculates the *Teaser*'s former identity was the *Wide Awake*; Report of Master William H. Face to H.H. Cocke, June 4, 1861, Face to Cocke, July 8, 1861, Cocke to Samuel Barron, July 11, 1861, Cocke to Stephen Mallory, June 15, 1861, Cocke Family Papers, Virginia Historical Society. Hereinafter cited as Cocke Papers. Biographical information on William H. Face in ZB files (Early Record Biographies), Naval Historical Center, Navy Yard, Washington, D.C., box 75. Hereinafter cited as ZB files, box number.

15. Records indicate that Lt. George W. Harrison was the lieutenant commanding the *Jamestown* and the *Hampton* during the squadron's ascent up the James River in May 1862. See *ORN* I, 7, p. 786.

16. *ORN* I, 5, p. 802; French Forrest to Joseph Pierce, July 3, 1861, Gosport Navy Yard Order Book, French Forrest Papers, Southern Historical Collection, University of North Carolina, Chapel Hill, NC. Hereinafter cited as Gosport Navy Yard Order Book; Claims dated July and August 1861 in the Executive Papers of Gov. John Letcher, Library of Virginia, reproduced in John Mark Joseph, "Confederate Naval Installations at Richmond, Virginia: an Independent Study" (unpublished paper, Virginia Commonwealth University, 1993); *ORN* I, 5, 803; James H. Rochelle, "The Confederate Steamship '*Patrick Henry*,'" *Southern Historical Society Papers*, vol. 14 (1886), pp. 128. Hereinafter cited as *SHSP*.

17. *ORN* I, 5, p. 812; I, 6, p. 715; 6, pp. 207-210, 457-459. For details on Confederate preparations and actions in the lower James in 1861-1862, see Edwin C. Bearss, *River of Lost Opportunities: The Civil War on the James River 1861-1862* (Lynchburg, 1995), pp. 1-14.

18. *ORN* I, 5, p. 804-806 (quote p. 803); .

19. "Commodore Harrison Henry Cocke," *Confederate Veteran*, vol. 14 (February 1906), pp. 76-77; Robertson, *Proceedings*, p. 42; Barron to Cocke, May 2, 1861; Cocke to Pegram, May 12, 1861, Cocke Family Papers; William Kauffman Scarborough, ed., *The Diary of Edmund Ruffin*, 3 vols. (Baton Rouge, 1966-1989), vol. 2, pp. 25-26.

20. William H. Parker, *Recollections of a Naval Officer, 1841-1865* (New York, 1883), pp. 206-209; *ORN* I, 5, pp. 803, 804.

21. Ransom B. True, *Up and Down the Noble James* (Jamestown, 1984), pp. 7-14; David D. Ryan, *The Falls of the James* (Richmond, 1975).

22. "Preliminary Chart of JAMES RIVER Virginia From Richmond to City Point. . ." Prepared under direction of A.D. Bache, Superintendent of the Survey of the Coast of the United States, 1855, Virginia Historical Society map collection, map # F232 J2 J855:1.

23. Wayland Fuller Dunaway, *History of the James River and Kanawha Canal Company* (New York, 1922), pp. 145-146; *Richmond Daily Dispatch*, February 3, 1864, p. 1, c. 4, hereinafter cited as *RDD*.

24. *Richmond Daily Whig*, February 1, 1860, p. 3, c. 2. Hereinafter cited as *RDW*.

25. Thomas S. Berry, "The Rise of Milling in Richmond," *Virginia Magazine of History and Biography*, vol. 78 (October 1970), pp. 387-408; Marie Tyler-McGraw, *At the Falls: Richmond, Virginia, & Its People* (Chapel Hill, 1994), p. 123; Michael B. Chesson, *Richmond After the War 1865-1900* (Richmond, 1981), pp. 7-10; Thomas, *Confederate State of Richmond*, pp. 21-25; Myrtle Elizabeth Callahan, "History of Richmond As a Port City," (M.A. Thesis, Department of Economics, University of Richmond, 1952), pp. 15-16; Dunaway, *History*, 165; *RDD*, January 7, 1862, p. 2, c. 3.

26. For an introduction to the history of the Richmond waterfront, see Paul Murphy, compiler, *Richmond's Historic Waterfront: Rockett's Landing to Tredegar, 1607-1865* (Richmond, [1989]).

27. *Richmond City Directory, 1860* (Richmond, 1860), passim; biographies in Louis H. Manarin, ed., *Richmond at War: The Minutes of the City Council , 1861-1865* (Chapel Hill, 1973), p. 630.

28. *RDD*, November 18, 1861, p. 3, c. 4; Daniel L. Mouer, et. al., "The Archaeology of the Rocketts Number 1 Site," 3 volumes (unpublished report prepared for the Virginia Department of Transportation, 1992), pp. 11, 72-77, 105-108, 124-126, 289-291; *Richmond City Directory*, passim. The house of one early nineteenth-century Richmond ship captain, John Woodward, survives today on the outer edge of the old Rocketts neighborhood, Calder Loth, ed., *The Virginia Landmarks Register* (Charlottesville, 1986), 394.

29. Thomas, *Confederate State of Richmond*, pp. 15-31; Tyler-McGraw, *At the Falls*, pp. 103-113.

30. V&C, *The City Intelligencer; or, Stranger's Guide* (Richmond, 1862; facsimile reprint: Richmond, 1960), p. 4; *The Stranger's Guide and Official Directory for the City of Richmond* (Richmond, 1863), p. 14.

31. *Richmond City Directory*, pp. 80, business directory, pp. 2, 49; C. A. Vanfelson, *The Little Red Book or Department Directory* (Richmond, 1861), p. 18; *City Intelligencer*, pp. 4, 23.

32. The thousands of important decisions regarding construction, provisions and supply, and personnel made in the Navy Department offices constitute the most important aspect of Richmond's Confederate naval history. This book, however, is not a history of bureaucracy and administration. The structure and processes of the Navy Department bureaucracy are described in Thomas Henderson Wells, *The Confederate Navy: A Study in Organization* (Tuscaloosa, 1971). The ideal structure and processes of the department are detailed in *Regulations for the Navy of the Confederate States 1862* (Richmond, 1862). The description of Tidball is in Durkin, *Mallory*, p. 136.

33. Wells, *Confederate Navy*, p. 74 and Chapters 12-15, passim.

34. Vanfelson, *Little Red Book*, p. 18; Wells, *Confederate Navy*, pp. 91-92; W.R. Chitwood, "Doctor Spotswood and the Confederate Navy," *Virginia Medical*, October 1976, pp. 729-730.

35. Invoices of work performed at naval hospital in RG 45, subject files (MA), roll 14; City of Richmond Hustings Court Deeds, deed book 63, pages 45-46, 406, microfilm roll 32, Library of Virginia; Wyndham B. Blanton, *Medicine in Virginia in the Nineteenth Century* (Richmond, 1933), pp. 28, 404.

36. *ORN* II, 2, pp. 52, 153, 534, 545, 640, 754; Wells, *Confederate Navy*, pp. 30-31.

37. *RDD*, May 16, 1861, p. 2, c. 6; January 16, 1864, p. 1, c. 2; March 19, 1864, p. 3, c. 3; *City Intelligencer*, p. 19; *Stranger's Guide*, p. 14.

38. On establishment of office, see Wells, *Confederate Navy*, pp. 45-46.

39. Biographical information on Brooke from George M. Brooke, Jr., *John M. Brooke: Naval Scientist and Educator* (Charlottesville, 1980), passim; John Wakelyn, ed., *Biographical Dictionary of the Confederacy* (Westport, 1977), pp. 110-111.

40. Brooke, *John M. Brooke*, 237; John M. Brooke Diaries, entries of June 23 and 28, 1861. Hereinafter cited as Brooke Diaries, date of entry.

41. Richard Harwell, ed., "Diary of Captain Edward Crenshaw of the Confederate States Army," *Alabama Historical Quarterly*, part 4, vol. 2 (1940), p. 233. Parker, *Recollections*, p. 346, later claimed the politicians stole this observation from him. Parker had escorted the party from Richmond to the bluff.

42. For background on ironclads before the American Civil War, see James Phinney Baxter, *The Introduction of the Ironclad Warship* (Cambridge, 1933).

43. *ORN* II, 1, p. 742.

44. William N. Still, Jr. *Confederate Shipbuilding* (Columbia, 1987), pp. 10-12.

45. Wells, *Confederate Navy*, pp. 95-117; Virginius Hall, *Portraits in the Collection of the Virginia Historical Society* (Charlottesville, 1981), p. 198.

46. Brooke Diary, June 23, 1861; testimony of Brooke and Porter in *ORN* II, 1, pp. 783-784, 802-803; John Brooke, "The Virginia, or Merrimac: Her Real Projector," *SHSP*, vol. 19 (1901), pp. 3-34; John L. Porter, "*C.S.S. Virginia* (*Merrimack*) Story of Her Construction, Batteries, &tc By John L. Porter Naval Constructor," [1874] in Porter file, Eleanor S. Brockenbrough Library, The Museum of the Confederacy, file P-689; John L. Porter to Rev. J. S. Moore, November 4, 1861, ibid. Both Brooke and Porter subsequently claimed credit as the primary designer of the *Virginia*. Mallory's March 29, 1862 report on the conversion of the *Virginia*, found in *ORN* II, 2 , pp. 174-176, gave high praise to Brooke, Porter and Williamson.

47. *Records of Movements, Vessels of the United States Coast Guard, 1790-December 31, 1933* (Washington, 1934). Source courtesy of Patrick D. Harris.

48. Charles B. Dew, *Ironmaker to the Confederacy: Joseph R. Anderson and the Tredegar Iron Works* (New Haven, 1966), pp. 106, 140-141, 147-148.

49. Ibid., pp. 87, 115-118.

50. Wakelyn, *Biographical Dictionary*, pp. 315-316; Francis Leigh Williams, *Matthew Fontaine Maury: Scientist of the Seas* (New Brunswick, 1963), passim.

51. Maury to John Letcher, October 8, 1861, and Maury to Franklin Minor, October 8, 1861, Matthew Fontaine Maury Papers, Library of Congress Manuscripts Division, volume 15. Hereinafter cited as Maury Papers.

52. *ORN* I, 6, p. 632; *Civil War Naval Chronology* , part VI, pp. 246-247. Still, *Confederate Shipbuilding*, p. 13, asserts that Mallory also supported the construction of small wooden gunboats.

53. Accounts of battle in William C. Davis, *Duel Between the First Ironclads* (Garden City, 1975), chapter 7; A.A. Hoehling, *Thunder at Hampton Roads* (Englewood Cliffs, 1976), part II.

54. Accounts of the first battle between ironclad warships are legion. The best narrative is Davis, *First Duel*, Chapters 8 and 9.

55. John Taylor Wood, "The First Fight of the Ironclads," in Robert U. Johnson and Clarence C. Buel, eds. *Battles and Leaders of the Civil War*, 4 vols. (New York, 1884-1889), vol. 1, pp. 703-704.

56. Betty Herndon Maury Diary, Library of Congress Manuscripts Division, volume II, entry of March 18, 1862. Hereinafter cited as Betty Maury Diary, date of entry; *Journal of the Confederate Congress*, vol. I, pp. 606, 621; Williams, *Maury*, pp. 389-390.

57. *ORN* I, 7, pp. 736-737, 794-797.

Chapter Two

1. See the relevant reports in *ORN* I, 7, pp. 328-335, 787.

2. Ibid., pp. 354-355.

3. Thomas, *Confederate State of Richmond*, pp. 34-35; *RDD*, May 13, 1862, p. 2, c. 1; see also *RDD*, May 19, 1862, p. 2, c. 1; *Richmond Daily Enquirer*, May 14, 1862, p. 1, c.1 and p. 3, c. 1. Hereinafter cited as *RDE*.

4. Scarborough, ed. *Diary of Edmund Ruffin*, vol. 2, p. 99; *ORN* I, 7, p. 437, 461.

5. *Journal of the House of Delegates for the State of Virginia for the Session of 1861-1862* (Richmond, 1861 [sic.]), p. 198; Rives to Mason, February 22, 1862, Charles T. Mason Papers, Virginia Historical Society, sect. 1, file 5. Hereinafter cited as Charles T. Mason Papers; *Journal of the Confederate Congress*, vol. 5, pp. 19-20; *ORN* II, 2, p. 169; I:7, pp. 742-743.

6. *ORN* I, 7, p. 768; ibid., I, 6, pp. 774, 775; William M. Robinson, Jr., "Drewry's Bluff: Naval Defense of Richmond, 1862," *Civil War History*, vol. 7 (June 1961), p. 71.

7. Letter from A. H. Drewry, November 17, 1901, reprinted in *SHSP*, vol. 29 (1901), p. 284; William I. Clopton, "New Light on the Great Drewry's Bluff Fight," ibid., vol. 34 (1906), pp. 83-85; Account by Samuel Mann, of the Southside Artillery, in ibid., pp. 85-87. See Bearss, *River of Lost Opportunities*, Chapter 2, for details.

8. *ORN* I, 6, p. 575; Record for payment, undated, to Haskins for schooners *Wythe* and *Gallego*, National Archives and Records Administration, RG 109, microfilm series M-347, Records Relating to Confederate Citizens and Business Firms, roll 419; *ORN* I, 7, pp. 781, 784; Tucker to Farrand, May 8, 1862, Charles T. Mason Papers, sect. 2, file 2.

9. Although Barney never commanded another ship in the James River Squadron, he was given command of the commerce raider *Florida*, which he commanded until illness forced him to resign. ZB files, box 11; [Robert Wright], "Sinking of the Jamestown," *SHSP*, vol. 29 (1901), p. 372.

10. *ORN* II, 1, p. 636; Edwin C. Bearss, "Battle of Drewry's Bluff" (unpublished research report, National Park Service, 1961), sect. V, pp. 8-12. This research report has been published as *River of Lost Opportunities*. Subsequent citations will be from the published version.

11. John Taylor Wood to wife, May 24, 1862, John Taylor Wood Papers, Southern Historical Collection, University of North Carolina, Chapel Hill, NC, file 3. Hereinafter cited as Wood Papers; Robinson, "Naval Defense," 172; U.S. War Department, *War of the Rebellion: Official Records of the Union and Confederate Armies*, 128 vols. (Washington, DC, 1880-1901), series I, volume 11, part 3, p. 514, hereinafter cited as *OR*;

Royce Gordon Shingleton, *John Taylor Wood: Sea Ghost of the Confederacy* (Athens, 1979), pp. 49-51; Ralph W. Donnelly, *The History of the Confederate Marine Corps* (privately printed), reprinted as *The Confederate States Marine Corps: The Rebel Leathernecks* (Shippensburg, 1989), pp. 31-32 (references are to original edition); William A. Young, Jr. and Patricia C. Young, *56th Virginia Infantry* (Lynchburg, 1990), pp. 38-41.

12. Robinson, "Drewry's Bluff," p. 172; Jeff Johnston, "The Naval Battle at Drewry's Bluff, May 15, 1862," (unpublished article, 1993); Rear Adm. John D. Hayes, "Decision at Drewry's Bluff," *Civil War Times Illustrated*, vol. 2 (May 1961), p. 6. Some accounts claim that officers from the *Virginia* also worked another gun, variously described as a 9-inch Dahlgren or 10-inch Columbiad, the source of which is not clear. Drewry letter, p. 285; Hardin B. Littlepage, "With the Crew of the Virginia," *Civil War Times Illustrated* vol. 13 (May 1974), p. 40; Robert W. Daly, in his annotations of the letters of William Frederick Keeler, *Aboard the U.S.S. Monitor: 1862* (Annapolis, 1964), p. 127, wrote that the crew of the *Patrick Henry* worked a IX-inch gun protected by the log casemate and that the *Virginia's* crew worked a second IX-inch gun near the entrance to the fort. William J. Miller, "The Battle of Drewry's Bluff," *Civil War*, June 1995, pp. 40-41, accepts Daly's numbers. Catesby Ap. R. Jones, "Services of the 'Virginia' (Merrimac), *SHSP* 11 (March 1883), p. 74, was silent on the role of the gun he was supposed to have commanded. Scharf, *Confederate States Navy*, p. 711, claims a total of nine guns on the bluff.

13. Rochelle to J. Thomas Scharf, January 12, 1887, typescript in Rochelle's file in ZB files, box 191; Bearss, *River of Lost Opportunities*, Chapter 6, pp. 16, 52-53, describes the guns placed to the left of the fort; Robinson, "Drewry's Bluff," p. 172, describes the guns on a "lower level" from the fort; Drewry letter, p. 285.

14. Lieutenant Commanding Thos. Phelps to Capt. William Smith, May 5, 1862, in National Archives and Records Administration, RG 45, microfilm publication M-625, U.S. Navy Area Files (area 7), roll 86, hereinafter cited as RG 45.

15. Joseph Smith to John Rodgers, May 3, 1862, and John Rodgers to Ann Rodgers, April 25, 1862 and virtually daily through May 9, 1862, Rodgers Family Papers, Naval Historical Foundation Collection, Library of Congress Manuscripts Division, Washington, D.C., boxes 9 and 21. Hereinafter cited as Rodgers Papers. Kurt Hackemer, in "The Other Union Ironclad: The USS *Galena*" *Civil War History*, vol. 40 (September, 1994), pp. 226-247, offers a more favorable estimate of the *Galena*.

16. *ORN* I, 7, pp. 357, 362; Parker, *Recollections*, pp. 279-280; Littlepage, "With the Crew," p. 39; Charles Hasker quoted in James Soley, "The Navy in the Peninsula

Campaign," *Battles and Leaders of the Civil War*, vol. 2: *North to Antietam* (New York, 1956), p. 269.

17. Henry St. George Tucker Brooke, "Monitor and Merrimac," *Richmond Times-Dispatch*, March 15, 1903, CMLS Scrapbook, 1902-1907, p. 180, Eleanor S. Brockenbrough Library, The Museum of the Confederacy. Brooke's account is neither corroborated nor disputed in other sources, but Scharf, *Confederate States Navy*, p. 713, also claimed that the squadron waited behind the obstructions; Edwin C. Bearss, *River of Lost Opportunities*, draws almost exclusively from the *Official Records* and other published sources, and is the most thorough account of the battle.

18. Clopton, "New Light," p. 96; *ORN* I, 7, p. 370; Shingleton, *Sea Ghost*, p. 51.

19. Keeler, pp. 126-128, 130.

20. John Rodgers to wife, May 17, 1862, Rodgers Papers, box 21; *ORN* I, 7, pp. 357, 359-360, 362-363; Report of May 16, 1862 in RG 45, area files, roll 86.

21. Letter of William A. Heirs to "Dear Cousin," May 17, 1862, in *Civil War Times Illustrated* Collection, U.S. Army Military History Institute, copy in files of Richmond National Battlefield Park, Richmond, VA, hereinafter cited as Heirs letter; *ORN* I, 7, p. 370. L. M. Ironmonger, of Company H, 6th Virginia Infantry, Mahone's brigade, writing in "Our Confederate Column," *Richmond Times-Dispatch*, May 3, 1903 (CMLS Scrapbook, 1902-1907, p. 81, Eleanor S. Brockenbrough Library, The Museum of the Confederacy), described the casualties in very similar language.

22. Jones, *A Rebel War Clerk's Diary*, vol. 1, p. 125; *RDD*, May 16, 1862, p. 3, c. 1 and p. 3, c. 2; *RDE*, May 16, 1862, p. 3, c.1; Littlepage, "With the Crew," p. 42; W.F. Clayton, "The Confederate Navy," serialized in *Richmond Times-Dispatch*, Chapter 7, June 28, 1908, in CMLS Scrapbook, 1908-1911, p. 13, Eleanor S. Brockenbrough Library, The Museum of the Confederacy.

23. Clopton, "New Light," p. 95.

24. Heirs letter. The men who fled were probably the "laborers, mechanics, and companies of unorganized regiments" described by Robert E. Lee in *OR*, I, 11, part 3, p. 521, and in Littlepage, "With the Crew," pp. 39-41; quote in letter to *RDW*, May 21, 1862, p. 2, c. 2.

25. Ibid.; ibid., May 22, 1862, p. 2, c. 1 and 2.

26. T. C. DeLeon, *Four Years in Rebel Capitals* (Chicago, 1983), pp. 270, 267 (emphasis in original); Mann in Clopton, "New Light," p. 90; *ORN* I, 7, pp. 359-360.

27. Clopton, "New Light," pp. 84 (quote), 90, 96. Compounding the issue is a discrepancy in the identity of the gun the naval officers helped direct. Drewry, in "New Light," p. 90, claims that Jones and Farrand helped direct gun no. 2, and 8-inch

Columbiad, while Littlepage, in "With the Crew," p. 40, recalled working a 10-inch Columbiad, which he also identified as gun no. 2.

28. Drewry letter, p. 285; Clopton, "New Light," p. 90 (emphasis added); Bearss, *River of Lost Opportunities*, p. 61; Rochelle, "The Confederate Steamship 'Patrick Henry,'" p. 136. Rochelle later recalled the names of some of the officers present on the bluff during the battle: Capt. Tucker, Lt. Francis L. Hoge, and Midshipman Daniel Carroll, of the *Patrick Henry*, Lt. Barney and Acting Master Samuel Barron, Jr., of the *Jamestown*, and lieutenants Catesby Jones, Hunter Davidson, Walter Butt and John Taylor Wood, of the *Virginia*. Rochelle to Scharf, January 12, 1887, ZB files, box 191; Scharf, *Confederate States Navy*, p. 711. Rochelle's memory was mistaken on at least one count, since Wood was with the sharpshooters below Chaffin's Bluff; L. M. Ironmonger, "Our Confederate Column."

29. *OR* I,11, pt. 3, pp. 574, 610, 615; Dew, *Ironmaker*, p. 183; Brooke, *John M. Brooke*, p. 259; *OR*, I, 11, pt. 2, pp. 717-718.

30. Gary W. Gallagher, ed., *Fighting for the Confederacy: The Personal Recollections of General Edward Porter Alexander* (Chapel Hill, 1989), p. 117; Judith Anthis and Richard M. McMurry, "The Confederate Balloon Corps," *Blue & Gray Magazine* (August 1991), pp. 20-24; David Page, *Ships versus Shore: Civil War Engagements Along Southern Rivers and Shores* (Nashville, 1994), p. 40; *ORN* 1, p. 543.

31. *RDE*, July 14, 1862, p. 1, c. 3; see also Rodgers letters to wife, Rodgers Papers, box 21. Between early July and late August, Federal ships in the James comprised a specially-designated James River Flotilla, commanded by Rodgers' successor, Capt. Charles Wilkes.

32. Mallory Diary, May 15, 1862.

33. *ORN* I, 7, p. 800; *OR*, 11, pt. 3, pp. 519, 521, 528; Scarborough, ed., *Diary of Edmund Ruffin*, vol. 2, p. 309.

34. *ORN* I, 7, p. 789, 801; *ORN* I, 7, p. 801; Lee to Johnston, May 22, 1862, in Clifford Dowdey and Louis H. Manarin, ed., *The Wartime Papers of R.E. Lee* (Boston, 1961), p. 177; Scharf, *Confederate States Navy*, p. 718.

35. Smith to Boyd, January 19, 1863, typescript in Francis W. Smith Papers, Virginia Historical Society, hereinafter cited as Smith Papers; ibid., Smith to Jackson, March 30, 1863. Commander Frederick Chatard succeeded Page later in 1862.

36. William Kennon Kay, "Drewry's Bluff or Fort Darling?" *Virginia Magazine of History and Biography*, vol. 77 (April 1969), pp. 191-200.

37. Scarborough, *Diary of Edmund Ruffin*, vol. 2, p. 309; *ORN* I, 8, pp. 68-69. According to a claim filed by R. O. Haskins, the *Curtis Peck* was sunk as early as May

13, 1862. Records Relating to Confederate Citizens and Business Firms, M-347, roll 419.

38. Mason to Rives, June 25, 1862, Charles T. Mason Papers, sect. 1, file 5; Mason to Walter H. Stevens, August 5, 1863, ibid., file 7. See especially Stevens to Mason, November 14, 1863, ibid. Aside from the *Currie*, the engineers also used the schooner, *James Buchanan*, sloops *Olivia*, *Townes*, *Seabord*, and *Tom Farity*, and towing vessel, *Falconer*. See sundry correspondence in ibid., sect. 1. Obstructions are described also by Federal informants in *ORN* I, 8, pp. 68-70, 10, pp. 466-467.

39. William W. Blackford, *War Years With JEB Stuart* (New York, 1945), pp. 63-68.

40. Richard B. Harwell, ed., *A Confederate Marine: A Sketch of Henry Lea Graves, With Excerpts from the Graves Family Correspondence, 1861-1865* (Tuscaloosa, 1963), p. 54. Hardin Littlepage, "With the Crew," pp. 40, 43, echoed Lea, describing Drewry's Bluff as "a second Gibraltar"; Confederate Engineers Map of Drewry's Bluff, Virginia Historical Society map collection, map #F232 C47 1864:2; Confederate Engineers Map of Drewry's Bluff, January 1863, Jeremy F. Gilmer Papers, Southern Historical Collection, University of North Carolina, Chapel Hill, NC, map #521. I am indebted to Clifford Dickinson for the Gilmer maps. Mason to Thomas Tully Lynch Snead, February 11, 1864, Mason Papers, sect. 1, file 6; Mason to David Bullock Harris, June 14,1864, Charles T. Mason Papers, sect. 1, file 3, describes in detail the bridges near Drewry's Bluff.

Chapter Three

1. Francis W. Dawson, *Reminiscences of Confederate Service 1861-1865* (Baton Rouge, 1980), pp. 3-41; *ORN* 1, p. 748. The *Drewry's* first commander, William H. Parker, noted that the vessel was without its engines for several months. Parker, *Recollections*, p. 286.

2. Dawson, *Reminiscences*, pp. 43-44; Parker, *Recollections*, pp. 214, 286. Dawson remained in the Confederacy, married James Morgan's sister Sarah, and became an influential newspaper editor in North Carolina.

3. Data on vessels in *Civil War Navy Chronology*, part 6, pp. 189-326, passim, and *ORN*, I, 1, pp. 247-272; and Silverstone, *Warships*, passim; description of *Beaufort* in Parker, *Recollections*, pp. 214, 286.

4. Joseph N. Barney to Franklin Buchanan, December 28, 1861, Joseph N. Barney Letterbook, 1861-1863, RG 45 (entry 430), National Archives.

5. Still, *Confederate Shipbuilding*, pp. 23-46. Excellent accounts of the operation of other inland shipyards can be found in Turner, *Navy Gray*, and Robert G. Elliott, *Ironclad of the Roanoke: Gilbert Elliott's Albemarle* (Shippensburg, 1994), pp. 88-117.

6. Dawson quote in Still, *Confederate Shipbuilding*, p. 33.

7. *Regulations*, p. 193. For the duties of the commandant and other navy yard personnel, see ibid., pp. 193-225.

8. Benjamin B. Weisiger, III, *The Parker Family of Port Royal and Richmond* Virginia (Richmond, 1990), p. 31; Beers, *Confederacy*, pp. 29-30; *The Stranger's Guide*, p. 14; *City Intelligencer*, p. 19. Clarke signed the payrolls for the Yard Opposite Rocketts from July-October 1862, but later recalled being "given charge" of the yard in early 1863. See Maxwell T. Clarke to Children, October 25, 1890, p. 4, Maxwell T. Clarke Papers, Southern Historical Collection, University of North Carolina, Chapel Hill, NC, hereinafter cited as Clarke Papers. Clarke subsequently commanded the Naval Rope Walk (Works) in Petersburg, Virginia.

9. Payrolls for Rocketts, July 1862-December 1863, RG 45 (Richmond payrolls files), National Archives, hereinafter cited as Payroll(s), installation, date(s), RG 45; Wells, *Confederate Navy*, pp. 95-97. See Mead's file in ZB files, box 151. Among the other highly-paid skilled employees at Rocketts was draughtsman John W. H. Porter, the son of John L. Porter. Payrolls, Rocketts, July 1862-December 1863, RG 45. See transfer orders in papers of Porter and Graves in ZB files, boxes 182 and 92; Payrolls, Yard Opposite Rocketts, July 1862-December 1863, RG 45.

10. *RDD*, April 18, 1863, p. 2, c. 3; February 11, 1864, p. 2, c. 4; *ORN* II, 2, p. 152. A detailed listing of those men employed at Rocketts in November of 1863 is both interesting and instructional. Specifically, the men as they appear on the payroll, include: a "superintendant" [sic.], James Meads; a master carpenter; a superintendent of riggers; a draughtsman; nine quartermen; 49 1st-class carpenters; 32 2nd-class carpenters; a master smith; a blacksmith foreman; six 1st-class smiths; two 2nd-class smiths; two engineers; six strikers; three 1st-class boat builders; six 2nd-class boat builders; four boys; one watchman; seven bolt drivers; three 1st-class caulkers; one reamer; nine 1st-class riggers; three 1st-class painters; two coopers; a naval storekeeper; a foreman of laborers; two white laborers; four black caulkers; one white washer; one colored smith; 28 black laborers (all hired slaves); 19 helpers; a master joiner; a foreman of joiners; 11 1st-class joiners; 28 2nd-class joiners and two 3rd-class joiners. Payroll, Rocketts, November 1863, RG 45. Those workers earned an aggregate of almost $30,000 for that month.

11. Lee A. Wallace, Jr. *1st Virginia Infantry* (Lynchburg, 1984), pp. 82, 89, 100, 102, 105; William D. Henderson, *12th Virginia Infantry* (Lynchburg, 1984), pp. 118, 121,

122, 136, 137. The regiments from which the 21 carpenters and joiners were drawn included the 15th, 26th, 30th, 47th, 53rd, 55th, and 61st Virginia Infantry regiments, the 6th Georgia Infantry, 13th Alabama Infantry, and 1st Louisiana Battery. Payrolls for Rocketts, July and August 1862; payroll, Yard Opposite Rocketts, July 1862, RG 45; Mallory Diary, August 15, 1862.

12. James H. Brewer, *The Confederate Negro: Virginia's Craftsmen and Military Laborers, 1861-1865* (Durham, 1969), pp. 31-34; payrolls, Rocketts and Yard Opposite Rocketts, July 1862-December 1863, RG 45.

13. Slave payrolls and "extra time" rolls, Rocketts, July 1862-February 1863, RG 45; Brewer, *The Confederate Negro*, pp. 33-34. In the final months of the war, Secretary Mallory reported that the navy required 120 negroes (and 100 white men between ages 18 and 45) for construction and repair of vessels in Virginia, 43 negroes (and 48 white men) for construction and repair of steam machinery in Richmond and 42 negroes (and 115 white men) for ordnance work in Virginia. Stephen R. Mallory, "Communication from Secretary of the Navy," February 7, 1865 in Message of the President to the Senate of the Confederate States, February 15, 1865 (Richmond, 1865), pp. 2-3.

14. William H. Parker, in *Elements of Seamanship* (Richmond, 1864), pp. 26-34, described in detail the process and technical terminology of nineteenth-century shipbuilding; J. B. MacBride, *A Handbook of Practical Shipbuilding with a Glossary of Terms*, second revised ed. (New York, 1921), pp. 79-80; *RDD*, April 1, 1862, p. 3, c. 2 and p. 4., c. 4; Mallory to H.H. Lewis, April 26, 1862, RG 45, subject files (AC), roll 5; payrolls, "Mr. [J.H.] Wyatt's party" of axemen and carpenters, November-December 1863, RG 45; Thomas R. Rootes expense account papers for travel to Fluvanna and Goochland counties, November 1862, March 1863 in ZB files, box 193.

15. Parker, *Elements*, pp. 35-36, described the process in detail; W. A. McEwen and A. H. Lewis, *Encyclopedia of Nautical Knowledge* (Cambridge, 1953), pp. 280-281.

16. Dew, *Ironmaker*, pp. 128, 134-136, 265-267.

17. Anderson to Mallory, March 25, 1863 and March 31, 1863, Tredegar Iron Works Records, Library of Virginia, Richmond, VA, letterbook #23, pp. 174-176, 208, hereinafter cited as Tredegar Records.

18. McEwen and Lewis, *Encyclopedia*, p. 170.

19. *ORN* II, 2, p. 269; Dew, *Ironmaker*, 122, 265; A. Robert Holcombe to author, October 28, 1992.

20. The government optimistically renewed the lease on March 1, 1865 for another two years at the rate of $5,000 per month. Both leases mentioned are in Talbott Brothers Papers, Virginia Historical Society, Richmond, VA; advertisement in *RDW*, February 1,

1860, p. 4, c. 7; Still, *Confederate Shipbuilding*, p. 38; payrolls (semi-monthly), Naval Works, 1862-1863, RG 45.

21. Spencer Tucker, "Confederate Naval Ordnance," *Journal of Confederate History*, vol. 4 (1989), pp. 135-136, 147; *Civil War Naval Chronology*, 6, pp. 229, 293, 313, 321.

22. Tucker, "Confederate Naval Ordnance," p. 147.

23. Brooke, *John M. Brooke*, chapters 8 and 9; Tucker, "Confederate Naval Ordnance," pp. 141-146. Brooke and Dahlgren guns customarily were described by their bore size in Roman numerals. Thus a "7-inch" gun was routinely referred to as a "VII-inch," but this book will use arabic numerals for consistency. Brooke Diary, February 6, 1863. Once prototypes of guns and projectiles were finished, Brooke supervised their testing, usually at Drewry's Bluff. In November 1862, he tested a 7-inch rifle along the Richmond waterfront. Lieutenant Alexander M. DeBree set up a target on Belle Isle (which was not yet in use as a prisoner-of-war camp) at which were fired three bolts from a gun at Tredegar. Two of the bolts missed the target and buried themselves in the bank. Ibid., November 18, 1862, December 7, 1862 and February 25, 1863.

24. Obituary in *RDE*, November 27, 1871, p. 3, c. 1; biographical sketch by daughter, Mary W. B. Minor Lightfoot, in Minor Family Papers, Virginia Historical Society, Richmond, VA, hereinafter cited as Minor Papers, sect. 36, roll B29; John McIntosh Kell to wife, January 1, 1865, John McIntosh Kell Papers, William R. Perkins Library, Duke University, Durham, NC, box 4, hereinafter cited as Kell Papers; James Barron Hope to wife, August 8, 1863, James Barron Hope Papers, box 1, file 110; Francis W. Smith to wife, March 9, 1862, Smith Papers; Brooke, *John M. Brooke*, pp. 301, 329. Even War Department clerk and diarist John B. Jones counted Minor as "my friend." *A Rebel War Clerk's Diary*, 1, p. 115. Receipts in the Minor Papers, VHS (items c. 2977-3194) indicate Minor roomed at the boarding houses of Mrs. F. W. Tabb, on Grace St. between 8th and 9th streets, and P. M. Tabb, Jr., at the corner of Broad and 11th; rented rooms with E. B. Spence on Main St. between 3rd and 4th streets; and rented a house from Joseph P. Winston at the corner of 2nd and Franklin streets; He dined frequently with guests at Mrs. Bass' boarding house. John Brooke noted on January 6, 1865 (Brooke Diaries) that "Lt. Minor is shifting his quarters to 4th & Franklin."

25. Scharf, *Confederate States Navy*, pp. 111-117. For Minor's handwritten list of men and officers on the *St. Nicholas*, see Minor Papers, sect. 34, roll B29. Details of Minor's work can be found in comonplace book, ibid., item C3197; Minor to Brooke, March 11, 1862 in Brooke, "Virginia or Merrimac," pp. 5-8.

26. George Minor to Robert Minor, September 1, 1862, Minor Papers, sect. 8; Robert D. Minor to son, July 20, 1863 and Robert D. Minor to wife, August 23, 1862, ibid., roll B27; *Richmond City Directory*, p. 62. The Navy Department paid Ettenger and Edmond rent of $1,000 per month for the facility. Vouchers of December 1, 1862 and April 1, 1863 in RG 45, subject files (AC), roll 42.

27. *ORN* II, 2, pp. 250-251.

28. Ibid., p. 548; Beers, *The Confederacy*, 383, summarizes component parts of ordnance works; payrolls, Naval Ordnance Works, September 1862-November 1863, RG 45. When the Confederate government began conscripting free blacks in 1864, black machinists Henry Lewis, John Nickens and Thomas Cole were assigned to the Naval Ordnance Works. Brewer, *Confederate Negro*, p. 33.

29. Brooke Diary, November 1, 1862; Robert D. Minor to wife, May 16, 1863, Minor Papers, roll B27.

30. Bill for rent, November 21, 1862, RG 45, subject files (AC), roll 5. Those Richmond businesses and artisans listed in the Navy Department's records included: Dunlap, Moncure & Company, commission merchants at Cary and 11th, furnished kegs of gin and boat spikes for "Navy Yard at Rocketts & Navy Store"; blacksmith Samuel Banks sold barrels of charcoal to the navy for the blacksmiths shop at Rocketts; the OSS purchased from Richard England an iron brace for use at both ship yards; R. Wendenburgh provided tracing cloth to the "Yard opp[osite] Rocketts" and varnish and turpentine for ordnance purposes; John D. Quarles, a bricklayer, was hired to rebuild furnaces and repair walls at Shockoe Foundry; J.W. Ratcliffe's Broad Street hardware store sold wood and a saw to the OSS; Thomas Weldon and J. M. McFarland sold iron boxes, patterns, etc., to the government for the construction of ironclad vessels; and the Lester St. firm of Faherty & Walsh provided materials for repair of the *Jamestown* and the *Teaser* at Rocketts. Sundry vouchers in ibid., (AC and PN), rolls 5 and 42; *Richmond City Directory*, passim. The office also maintained a naval ordnance store near the ordnance works, on 13th St. between Cary St. and the canal. *City Intelligencer*, p. 19.

31. For an interpretation of this theme, see Emory M. Thomas, *The Confederacy as a Revolutionary Experience* (Englewood Cliffs, 1971); and Emory M. Thomas, *The Confederate Nation* (New York, 1979), pp. 206-214.

32. Holcombe's thesis is the authoritative work on this subject, from which this discussion is drawn. A. Robert Holcombe, Jr., "The Evolution of Confederate Ironclad Design" (Master's Thesis, East Carolina University, 1993), pp. 65, 75-77, 78, 80-81, 103. Holcombe, "Evolution," pp. 65, 75-77, 78, 103. The *Virginia II* was originally to have a casemate of slightly over 100 feet in length, but it was altered to reduce her weight and

the amount of iron required to cloak her. The measurements offered in other sources, *ORN* II, 1, *Civil War Navy Chronology*, and Silverstone, *Warships*, vary slightly, often because they rely on different criteria for defining length and beam.

33. Holcombe, "Evolution," p. 65; A. Robert Holcombe, Response to Query on Richmond class Confederate ironclads in "Insofer," *Warship International*, vol. 29 (1983), p. 309; *ORN* I, 9, p. 801; I, 10, p. 652.

34. *ORN* I, 7, p. 786; ibid, I, 7, pp. 549, 569, 624-627; Keeler, *Aboard the Monitor*, p. 199; *Harper's Weekly*, July 26, 1862, p. 1.

35. *OR* 11, pt. 3, p. 335; *ORN* I, 7, pp. 336, 624-625.

36. J. P. McKinstry to John Rodgers, August 1, 1862, Rodgers Papers, box 9; *ORN* I, 7, pp. 583, 620-621; H. L. P. King Diary, August 20, 1862, in Thomas Butler King Papers, Southern Historical Collection, Wilson Library, University of North Carolina, Chapel Hill, NC; Richard B. Harwell, ed., *A Confederate Marine*, p. 85.

37. *ORN* II, 2, p. 256; George Weber to brother, August 1862, George Weber Letters, Library of Virginia, Richmond, VA, hereinafter cited as Weber Letters.

38. *OR* 11, pt. 3, pp. 335, 336.

39. Holcombe, "Insofer," p. 309; Quarterly inspection report, dated June 18, 1864, Minor Papers, sect. 26, roll B29.

40. *ORN* I, 7, pp. 620-621.

41. *RDD*, April 1, 1862, p. 3, c. 2, p. 4, c. 4; Brooke Diary, March 28, 1862; Chesterfield County Plat Book No. 1, p. 79, Chesterfield County Clerk's Office, Chesterfield, VA; Payment to James Rogers "For Building 2 Forges for Black Smith's Shop" for "use of yard," signed by Graves, January 24, 1863, and sundry vouchers endorsed by Graves, 1862-1863, RG 45, subject files (AC), roll 5.

42. Obituaries in *Norfolk Landmark* and *Norfolk Virginian*, February 18, 1894 (copies courtesy of A. Robert Holcombe); Voucher, August-September 1861, in RG 45, subject files (OL), roll 24; orders of August 30 and August 31, 1861, Forrest to Nash and Graves, November 4, 1861, and Forrest to John L. Porter, December 11, 1861 and January 3, 1862, in Gosport Navy Yard Order Books, April-October 1861 and October 1861-March 1862, in Douglas French Forrest Papers, Southern Historical Collection, Wilson Library, University of North Carolina, Chapel Hill, NC, hereinafter cited as Forrest Papers. For the identity of the ship destroyed (*Dixie*), see Parker, *Recollections*, p. 278; Stephen Mallory to John DeBree, October 2, 1862, RG 45, subject files (AC), roll 5.

43. Compiled Service Records of Soldiers Serving in the Army of the Confederate States of America, National Archives, Record Group 109, Soldiers from Virginia, micro-

film publication M-324, roll 959. Henceforth cited as Service Records, roll number; Brooke Diaries, entry of November 1, 1862.

44. Still, *Iron Afloat*, pp. 84-88; Scharf, *Confederate States Navy*, pp. 726-727; *RDD*, March 18, 1862, p. 2, c. 2; ibid., April 4, 1862, p. 3, c. 1; April 11, 1862, p. 3, c. 2; April 17, 1862, p. 2, c. 3.

45. Manarin, ed., *Richmond at War*, p. 139.

46. Ibid., March 25, 1862, p. 2, c. 4; March 26, 1862, p. 2, c. 4; Ladies Defense Association Minute Book, March 25, 1862, Ladies Defense Association Papers, Eleanor S. Brockenbrough Library, The Museum of the Confederacy, Richmond, VA, box V-8-3-1, hereinafter cited as Ladies Defense Association Papers. The biographical sketch on Mrs. Clopton was prepared by her descendants, "Where Mercy Dwelt," clipping from Richmond newspaper, April 19, 1936, and pass for Mrs. Clopton and family, July 7, 1864, in Clopton Hospital Letters, Eleanor S. Brockenbrough Library, The Museum of the Confederacy, Richmond, VA, box V-9-2-2, hereinafter cited as Clopton Hospital Letters; Minute Book, March 27, 1862, Ladies Defense Association Papers; *RDD*, April 1, 1862, p. 2, c. 5; , April 5, 1862, p. 3, c. 1; Maria G. Clopton to Stephen Mallory, undated [probably early April 1862], in Clopton Hospital Letters.

47. *RDD*, April 11, 1862, p. 1, c. 4.

48. Ibid., April 21, 1862, p. 3, c. 1. Definitive evidence that the *Virginia II*, not the *Fredericksburg*, was the "ladies gunboats" is in *RDW*, July 1, 1863, p. 2, c. 1; Robert D. Minor to wife, April 1, 1864 and May 15, 1864, Minor Papers, roll B27; Maria G. Clopton to daughter, April 8, 1862, Clopton Papers, Special Collections, William R. Perkins Library, Duke University, Durham, NC, hereinafter cited as Clopton Papers.

49. Sundry notes and receipts in Ladies Defense Association Papers; *RDD*, April 11, 1862, p. 1, c. 4; April 21, 1862, p. 3, c. 1.

50. Minute book, April 9, 1863, April ?, 1863 and May 24, 1863, Ladies Defense Association Papers; Still, *Iron Afloat*, pp. 86-87.

51. B. W. Jones, *Under the Stars and Bars: A History of the Surry Light Artillery* (Richmond, 1909), p. 86.

52. Minor to wife, June 6, 1863, Minor Papers, roll B27; ibid., June 11, 1863.

53. *RDW*, July 1, 1863, p. 2, c. 1; Dan Blair, "The CSS Virginia II" (unpublished paper, East Carolina University, 1993).

54. *ORN* I, 9, p. 116; Sundry entries in Tredegar Journals, January 1862-November 1864, Tredegar Records; bill for iron furnished by J.R. Anderson & Co., to "Capt. Graves" for "Ladies Gunboat," June 30, 1862-January 26, 1863, RG 45, subject files (AC), roll 5; *ORN* II, 2, pp. 531-532.

55. Statement of deserter, Benjamin F. Thomas, February 1, 1864, RG 45, subject files (NZ), roll 22; J. R. Anderson to Mallory, March 9, 1864, Letterbook (February 20, 1964-March 1, 1864), Tredegar Records; *RDD*, April 1, 1865, p. 1, c. 5; Minor to wife, April 13, 1864.

56. Maurice Melton, *The Confederate Ironclads* (New York, 1968), p. 249; *ORN* II, 2, p. 750. Some sources suggest that the *Texas* was to carry a battery of six guns. See Silverstone, *Warships*, p. 208; *Civil War Naval Chronology*, p. 314.

57. Virginia Service Records, rolls 416-417; Lee A. Wallace, *A Guide to Virginia Military Organizations, 1861-1865*, 2nd edition (Lynchburg, 1986), p. 183. Company A consisted of Navy Department and Naval Ordnance Works employees; Company B of employees from the yard opposite Rocketts; Company C of Naval Works employees; Companies D and E of Rocketts yard employees and detailed army soldiers. Ibid. When he was assigned temporarily to supervise ship construction in North Carolina in February 1864, Minor tried without success to resign his infantry command. He returned to Richmond in March 1864 just in time to find that his battalion had been called into service during the infamous Kilpatrick-Dahlgren cavalry raid against the capital. Minor quickly rejoined his unit in the Richmond defense works. Minor to wife, March 3, 1864, Minor Papers, roll B27; *ORN* II, 2, p. 750.

58. Still, *Iron Afloat*, pp. 227-228.

59. T. C. DeLeon, "Belles, Beaux, & Brains of the '60's," in *Town Topics* (1907-1908), sect. 29. Mallory had acquired a great distaste for Maggie Howell early in the war when they shared a dining table at the Spotswood Hotel. Mallory disapproved of her "ill-timed and tart remarks" and marveled at the president's patience at her indiscretion. See Mallory Diary, July 10, 1861.

60. *Regulations*, pp. 190-191; Wells, *Confederate Navy*, pp. 29-30, 141-143; Samuel Barron, General Orders issued from flagship *Patrick Henry*, December 12, 1862, letterbook of Samuel Barron, July 26, 1861–March 4, 1865, p. 13, Samuel Barron Papers, Special Collections, Earl Gregg Swem Library, College of William and Mary, Williamsburg, VA, box IV, file 68, suggest squadron commander Barron also handled logistical concerns associated with the station commander. The James River Squadron letterbook kept by Adm. French Forrest, 1863-1864, leaves no doubt he held command simultaneously of both the station and the squadron during a year in which the squadron saw virtually no active service. James River Squadron Letterbook, 1863-1864, Library of Virginia, Richmond, VA., hereinafter cited as James River Squadron Letterbook. Several junior officers assigned to the *Richmond* were ordered to report to Robb. See files of Lt. Benjamin Loyall and Midshipman James W. Pegram, ZB files, boxes 137 and 175.

61. John Horry Dent, Jr., to John Horry Dent, Sr., July 8, 1863, John Horry Dent Papers, W.S. Hoole Special Collections, Amelia Gayle Gorgas Library, University of Alabama, Tuscaloosa, hereinafter cited as Dent Papers.

62. Sidney Smith Lee to James H. Rochelle, September 11, 1862, James H. Rochelle Papers, William R. Perkins Library, Duke University, Durham, NC, hereinafter cited as Rochelle Papers; John T. Mason to Kate Mason Rowland, June 15, 1862, John T. Mason Papers.

63. Mary Custis Lee to Mildred Lee, November 15, 1862, Lee Family Papers, Virginia Historical Society, Richmond, VA; Robert Garlick Hill Kean, *Inside the Confederate Government: The Diary of Robert Garlick Hill Kean*, ed. Edward Younger (New York, 1957), p. 52.

64. Edward F. Heite, "Captain Robert B. Pegram: Hero Under Four Flags," *Virginia Cavalcade*, vol. 14 (Autumn 1965), pp. 39-40. The sword is now in the collection of The Museum of the Confederacy.

65. John Horry Dent, Jr. to John Horry Dent, Sr., June 30, 1863, Dent Papers.

66. Most of the letters in the James River Squadron Letterbook #1, written in late 1863 and early 1864, concern details about such assignments; John T. Mason to mother, June 25, 1862, John T. Mason Papers; John Horry Dent, Jr., to John Horry Dent, Sr., July 8, 1863, Dent Papers.

67. James H. Lynch to James H. Rochelle, June 13, 1862, Rochelle Papers; John DeBree to James H. Rochelle, June 16, 1862, ibid.; RG 45, subject files (PN), roll 42.

68. *Uniform and Dress of the Army and Navy of the Confederate States* (Richmond, 1861); Brooke Diary, December 20, 1861. Uniform standards are reprinted also in Wells, *Confederate Navy*, pp. 153-160.

69. James Morris Morgan, *Recollections of a Rebel Reefer* (Boston, 1917), pp. 52-53; Dawson letter to Mother, June 20, 1862, reprinted in Dawson, *Reminiscences*, p. 184; Morgan, *Recollections*, pp. 79-80; circular of February 25, 1863 from Flag Officer Samuel Barron to James H. Rochelle, Rochelle Papers; Order ca. April 21, 1863, signed by John K. Mitchell, in Rochelle Papers.

70. General Order, August 7, 1862, Rochelle Papers; Stephen Mallory to French Forrest, April 3, 1863, copy in ibid.; surviving quarterly inspection reports for the *Nansemond*, *Hampton* and *Richmond* in the Minor Papers (sect. 26, roll B29) indicate that inspections were made in July and October 1863; John Horry Dent, Jr., to John Horry Dent, Sr., July 8, 1863, Dent Papers; *Regulations*, pp. 60-94.

71. Undated report in RG 45, subject files (BR), roll 12; Mason to mother, July 27, 1862, John T. Mason Papers. The Confederate fleet at Galveston further proved the

deficiencies of "cotton-clads" later that year. See Scharf, *Confederate States Navy*, pp. 498-503. After the test firing the *Richmond*'s guns in November 1863, Brooke suggested the erection of an "experimental battery" at Chaffin's Bluff. Brooke to Capt. W. H. Stevens, November 24, 1863, and C. A. McElvoy to Brooke, November 23, 1863, RG 45, subject files (BG), roll 11.

72. Sundry correspondence between Mason and Stevens in Charles T. Mason Papers, sect. 1, file 7. For a period in late 1863, the gunboat *Roanoke* (*Raleigh*) spelled the *Schultz* as the "flag-of-truce" ship transporting prisoners to and from the designated exchange point at Aiken's Landing near City Point. Maxwell Clarke to Children, Clarke Papers, p. 5; *ORN* I, 9, pp. 798-799.

73. *ORN* I, 8, pp. 841-842. No doubt with the same "disasters" in mind—especially the senseless loss of the *Arkansas* on the Mississippi in August 1862—Sen. James D. Phelan, of Mississippi, wrote to President Jefferson Davis in great distress at the rumored opening of the obstructions: "I would prefer that the James River should, for the time being, be dried up" than remove the obstructions and lose the *Richmond.* Softening his own determination to open a passage, Secretary Mallory assured Phelan that a passage would be opened only when and if it were "expedient." Ibid., pp. 842-843.

74. Ibid., I, 8, pp. 868-869; 1, 10, pp. 654-655; Mason to Stevens, August 5, 1863, Charles T. Mason Papers, sect. 1, file 7.

75. *ORN* I, 9, p. 799, 802.; William A. Graves to Mason, February 3, 1864, Charles T. Mason Papers, sect. 1, file 2; Stevens to Mason, March 27, 1864, and Stevens to Mason, April 14, 1864, ibid., file 7.

Chapter Four

1. Donnelly, *Confederate States Marine Corps,* pp. 8, 33.

2. Ibid., pp. 33, 39. Many of the marines in Company F transferred to Richmond from Mobile, Alabama, in 1864.

3. Harwell, ed. *A Confederate Marine*, pp. 85-87; *ORN* I, 8, p. 842; Hubbard T. Minor, "Diary of a Confederate Naval Cadet," *Civil War Times Illustrated*, 2 parts, vol. 13 (November and December 1974), part 1, p. 29; James O. Harrison to father, February 11, 1864, James O. Harrison Papers, Library of Congress Manuscript Division, Washington, D.C. Hereinafter cited as Harrison Papers; Donnelly, *Confederate States Marine Corps*, pp. 39-40, 124; Harwell, "Diary of Edward Crenshaw," part 2, p. 448; David M. Sullivan, "From Hampton Roads to Appomattox: Virginia and the Confederate State

Marine Corps," *Virginia Country's Civil War Quarterly*, vol. 8 (March 1987), p. 22; *ORN*, 1, 9, p. 806. Sketches of the cabins and works are in the Charles T. Mason Papers, Sect. 6, folders 1-3.

4. Donnelly, *Confederate States Marine Corps*, pp. 27, 38, 39, 128, 215. In early 1864, when Confederate sailors stationed at the bluff were ordered aboard the ships of the James River Squadron, Maj. George H. Terrett, C.S.M.C., assumed command of the inter-service garrison. See also Ralph W. Donnelly, *Biographical Sketches of the Commissioned Officers of the Confederate States Marin Corps* (Privately printed, 1973), pp. 4, 22, 34, 45-46, 55.

5. Donnelly, *Confederate States Marine Corps*, pp. 26-28, 37-38.

6. Quoted in Dean Snyder, "Torpedoes for the Confederacy," *Civil War Times Illustrated*, vol. 24 (March 1985), p. 42.

7. Williams, *Maury*, p. 612; Maury to Franklin Minor, July 19, 1861, Maury Papers, volume 14.

8. Williams, *Maury*, pp. 376-377; Ralph W. Donnelly, "Scientists of the Confederate Nitre and Mining Bureau," *Civil War History*, vol. 2 (1956), pp. 66-92.

9. Richard L. Maury, "The First Marine Torpedoes Were Made in Richmond, Va., and Used in James River," *SHSP*, vol. 31 (1901), p. 328; Williams, *Maury*, pp. 379, 381.

10. Milton F. Perry, *Infernal Machines: The Story of Confederate Submarine and Mine Warfare* (Baton Rouge, 1965); Snyder, "Torpedoes," pp. 41-45; Lewis Williams Taggart, "Technology and the Confederate Navy" (unpublished M.A. Thesis, University of Tulsa, 1991), Chapter VIII. Americans used wooden kegs filled with gunpowder against British ships-of-war in the Delaware River during the American Revolution. Steamboat pioneer Robert Fulton is usually credited with perfecting the general design of torpedoes. Russian troops used them in the harbors of the Crimean peninsula in the 1850s.

11. *ORN* I, 4, p. 567.

12. Maury to Franklin Minor, November 5, 1861, Maury Papers, vol. 15; Betty Maury Diary, June 19, 1861; Williams, *Maury*, pp. 377-378.

13. *ORN* I, 6, pp. 4a-b. Maury's cousin, Isabel, recalled Minor being present during the washtub experiments. Handwritten note in Confederate Memorial Literary Society [CMLS] scrapbook, 1908-1911, p. 8; Betty Maury Diary, October 12, 1861.

14. The career of the *Hunley* is documented in Mark K. Ragan, *The Hunley: Submarines, Sacrifice, & Success in the Civil War* (Miami, 1995), and in an overview of the submarine's history in Mark M. Newell, "The *CSS H. L. Hunley*: Solving a 131-Year-Old Mystery," *Civil War Regiments: A Journal of the American Civil War*, vol. 4, No. 3

(1995), pp. 77-87. The submarine was recently discovered intact off Sullivan's Island, South Carolina.

15. Perry, *Infernal Machines*, chapters 8 and 9; Tredegar Order Book (September, October, and November, 1861), pp. 1166, 1192, 1212, Tredegar Records; sketch in Minor Papers, copy courtesy of Patrick D. Harris; Brooke Diary, November 8, 1861 and July 25, 1861. Maury could not lead the expeditions himself because of his pre-war injury, and the fact that he was too valuable as a scientist and thus not expendable.

16. Allan Pinkerton, *Spy of the Rebellion* (Kansas City, 1883), pp. 399-401, 402-403. The Pinkerton Papers at the Library of Congress contain no (legible) original documents from Mrs. Baker in Richmond.

17. "A Rebel Infernal Machine," *Harper's Weekly*, November 2, 1861, p. 701.

18. Perry, *Infernal Machines*, pp. 93-94, debates whether there was a submarine built on the James. Goldsborough to Welles, October 17, 1861, RG 45, area files (area 7), roll 81; *ORN* I, 6, pp. 392-393, 363.

19. *ORN* I, 6, pp. 346-350; Peery, *Infernal Machines*, pp. 91-92.

20. The materials and services at least *suggest* that the submarine may have been steam powered (as unlikely as that may have been), and that it was completed to the point of being painted. "Pay Roll of Workmen on Submarine Batteries," RG 45, subject files (BM), roll 11; entry for B.B. Brooke, Richmond City Directory, 1860, p. 56; Invoice from Tredegar Iron Works, May 13,1862, RG 45, subject files (BM), roll 11.

21. *OR* II, 7, p. 343. This document is dated September 1861, but internal evidence suggests that it must be September 1862. One student of Confederate submarines, Frank Furman, of Rolla, Missouri, is pursuing the intriguing and credible theory that the James River submarine was transported (along with the drive shaft of the *CSS Louisiana*) from Tredegar to New Orleans in the spring of 1862, arrived just before the fall of the city, was scuttled, later recovered, and is the small submarine now on display outside the Louisiana State Museum on Jackson Square in New Orleans. Francis Chandler Furman to author, January 14, 1996.

22. *ORN* I, 7, p. 780.

23. Ibid., pp. 545-546; Hunter Davidson to Jefferson Davis, December 5, 1881 in *SHSP*, vol. 24 (1896), p. 285.

24. *ORN* I, 7, p. 543. Letters in RG 45, subject files (BM), dated as early as August 1862 were written on stationery bearing the letterhead, "C.S. Steamer Torpedo."

25. Perry, *Infernal Machines*, pp. 26-27.

26. R. O. Crowley, "Making the 'Infernal Machines,' " *Century Magazine*, 56 (June 1898), reprinted in *Civil War Times Illustrated*, vol. 12 (June 1973), p. 25.

27. Facsimile of "Enlisting Articles" reprinted in William J. Morgan, "Torpedoes In The James," *The Iron Worker*, vol. 26 (Summer 1962), p. 9; also see *ORN* I, 10, pp. 10-11.

28. Williams, *Maury*, chapters 18-20.

29. Biographical sketch of Davidson in ZB files, box 60.

30. *ORN* 1, 8, pp. 849-850; ibid., I, 7, p. 61.

31. Ibid., 1, 9, pp. 111-112, 146.

32. Crowley, "Making the 'Infernal Machines,'" pp. 26-28; *ORN* I, 9, p. 146.

33. *Civil War Naval Chronology*, pt. 6, pp. 187, 317; John Curtis, a crew member of the *Squib*, (in Reminiscences, Library of Virginia, Richmond, VA), described the vessel's torpedo apparatus and specified her dimensions as 35 feet long and five feet wide; *ORN* I, 12, p. 115; Parker, *Recollections*, pp. 328-329.

34. Curtis, Reminiscences; *ORN* I, 9, pp. 599-603; Hunter Davidson, "The Electrical Submarine Mine—1861-65," *Confederate Veteran*, vol. 16 (September 1908), p. 459.

35. *ORN* I, 11, pp. 759, 811; II, 2, 688, 724-725, 739, 790-791.

36. Crowley, "Making the 'Infernal Machines,'" pp. 30-31; Perry, *Infernal Machines*, pp. 83, 165; Scharf, *Confederate States Navy*, p. 594; Perry, pp. 199-201.

37. Parker, *Recollections*, pp. 117-118, 174-175; Park Benjamin, *The United States Naval Academy* (New York, 1900), Chapters 1-15.

38. Melville Herndon, "The Confederate States Naval Academy," *Virginia Magazine of History and Biography*, vol. 69 (July 1961), pp. 304-306.

39. Parker, *Recollections*, p. 287; George Hollins to James Barron Hope, June 25, 1862, James Barron Hope Papers, box 1, file 91; John Brooke to Samuel Barron, November 19, 1863, Barron Papers, box IV, file 36; John Brooke to J. L. M. Curry, November 30, 1863, Miscellaneous Papers, Eleanor S. Brockenbrough Library, The Museum of the Confederacy, Richmond, VA, file C-259; John Thompson Mason to mother, June 25, 1862, John T. Mason Papers.

40. Parker, *Recollections*, pp. 117-125, 322; Scharf, *Confederate States Navy*, p. 773; [William H. Parker], *Regulations of the Confederate States School-Ship Patrick Henry* (Richmond, 1863 [Confederate Imprint, Parrish & Willingham #1711]). The biographical sketch of Parker is taken from Richard Current, ed., *Encyclopedia of the Confederacy*, 4 vols. (New York, 1994), vol. 3, p. 1180.

41. Herndon, "Confederate States Naval Academy," pp. 307-309; *ORN* II, 2, p. 635; Roster in Herndon, "Confederate States Naval Academy," pp. 317-319; standards specified in [Parker], *Regulations for the School-Ship*, pp. 16-20.

42. Mason to mother, July 29, 1862, John T. Mason Papers; William F. Clayton, *A Narrative of the Confederate States Navy* (Weldon, NC, 1910), p. 113.

43. Ibid, p. 102; J. Stevens Mason to Robert D. Minor, September 24, 1863, Minor Papers, roll B26; Minor, "Diary of a Confederate Naval Cadet," part I, p. 28.

44. Morgan, *Recollections*, pp. 204, 200-203, and chapters I-XXIV, passim. General Josiah Gorgas, chief of the Army's Ordnance Bureau, attended the examinations in July 1863 and dismissed them as "very cursory in navigation, firing, making sail and broad-sword exercises." Vandiver, ed., *Gorgas Diary*, p. 130.

45. *ORN* II, 2, p. 744. For a detailed and popular account of Wood's New Bern *Underwriter* raid, see generally, chapter 6 of Shingleton, *Sea Ghost*; Scharf, *Confederate States Navy*, pp. 395-401; Morgan, *Recollections*, p. 206; Loyall's file in ZB files, box 137.

46. Parker, *Elements*; [Parker], *Regulations for the School-Ship*," pp. 10-11, 25; Parker, *Recollections*, pp. 324-325; Herndon, "Confederate States Naval Academy," pp. 307-309; James M. Morgan, "A Realistic War College." *U.S. Naval Institute Proceedings*, vol. 42 (March-April 1916), p. 543; *ORN* II, 2, p. 533.

47. Scharf, *Confederate States Navy*, p. 775; Morgan, "Realistic," p. 546, described the food as "scanty and unappetizing."

48. James Oliver Harrison to Ellen, October 30, 1864, and Harrison to father, February 9, 1864, James Oliver Harrison, Sr., to wife, December 12, 1864, Harrison Papers.

49. Minor, "Diary of a Confederate Naval Cadet," part 1, p. 29; part 2, pp. 24-28; Scharf, *Confederate States Navy*, p. 776.

50. Ibid., p. 775; Morgan, *Recollections*, pp. 204-206.

51. *ORN* II, 2, pp. 634-635.

Chapter Five

1. *ORN* I, 10, p. 11.

2. For background on Butler's campaign, see William Glenn Robertson, *Back Door to Richmond: The Bermuda Hundred Campaign, April-June 1864* (Cranbury, 1987), and Herbert M. Schiller, M.D., *The Bermuda Hundred Campaign* (Dayton, 1988).

3. *ORN* I, 9, p. 725.

4. Davidson, "Submarine Battery Service," p. 285; Payroll, James River Submarine Battery Service, May 1864 in Payroll file of James River Squadron, RG 45, National

Archives; Dr. Carthon Archer to the editor of the *Richmond Dispatch*, February 20, 1904, manuscript copy in James River Submarine Battery Service file of Dr. Carthon Archer, Eleanor S. Brockenbrough Library, The Museum of the Confederacy, Richmond, VA, file A-21; Crowley, "Making the 'Infernal Machines,'" p. 28. Archer spelled Johnson's first name "Jeffries," but payroll records for April-June 1864 indicate it as "Jervise" or "Jervies." The payroll of May 1864 indicated that John Britton was killed on May 7, and thus was the unnamed third man mentioned by Archer. *ORN* I, 10, pp. 9-10.

5. Quoted in Herbert M. Schiller, "Confederate Submarine Battery Service in the James River," *Blue & Gray Magazine*, vol. 7 (October 1989), p. 18; *ORN* I, 10, p. 9.

6. Ibid., pp. 10-11; Archer to editor of *Richmond Dispatch*; Crowley, "Making the 'Infernal Machines,'" p. 29; Morgan, "Torpedoes in the James," pp. 8-10. Smith apparently suffered no undue punishment from Confederate or Federal authorities. He was exchanged and subsequently put in command of the *Torpedo*. *ORN* I, 10, p. 16; 11, p. 807.

7. *ORN* I, 10, pp. 52, 27-30. While searching upriver for torpedoes, the tug gunboat *Shawsheen* was at anchor near at Turkey Island Creek. Confederate infantry and army artillery pieces opened up on her, killing her commander and exploding her magazine. Most of the sailors survived the explosion, but were taken prisoner. According to a Confederate soldier, *Shawsheen* fired at a house on Turkey Island. "What a quick retribution came to her," the soldier wrote to his brother. "There were two fires close to each other. The destroyer and his prey. Soon the shell in the boat commenced to burst and soon after her magazine blew up with a terrific sound." C. H. Carlton to Walter Raleigh Carlton, May 9, 1864, Library of Virginia, Richmond, VA.

8. *ORN* I, 9 p. 809.

9. Ibid., II, 2, p. 531.

10. Ibid., I, 9, pp. 806, 810, 805.

11. Ibid., pp. 624-625; Wayne Dixon Lett, "John Kirkwood Mitchell and Confederate Naval Defeat" (unpublished M.A.Thesis, Old Dominion University, 1972), Chapter 1; Scharf, *Confederate States Navy*, pp. 293-295; Chester G. Hearn, *The Capture of New Orleans 1862* (Baton Rouge, 1995).

12. Quarterly inspection reports of *Fredericksburg* and *Virginia II*, July 6 and July 9,1864, respectively, in Minor Papers, items c. 3238 and c. 3240, roll B29; 21; Mitchell to Mallory, May 7, 1864, Drewry's Bluff telegrams, May 1864, Eleanor S. Brockenbrough Library, The Museum of the Confederacy, file T-806; *ORN* I, 10, pp. 626, 628-629.

13. Mitchell to S.S. Lee, May 10, 18, 24, and June 20 and 28, 1864, RG 45, subject files (NA), roll 17.

14. *ORN*, pp. 634-635; 642-643; Robert D. Minor to wife, May 18 and May 20, 1864, Minor Papers, roll B27. Minor referred to *Patrick Henry* as flagship, probably because the men of the *Virginia II* were boarded temporarily on the school ship.

15. By the fall of 1864, Pegram had left Richmond for England to serve as agent for a joint stock venture called the Virginia Volunteer Navy Association. See Heite, "Captain Robert B. Pegram," p. 43; *RDD*, January 18, 1864, p. 1, c. 1; April 20, 1864, p. 2, c. 2; Scharf, *History*, pp. 91-92; *ORN* II, 2, p. 772. Other command changes in *ORN* I, 10, pp. 624ff. See the appendix of this book for details.

16. Scharf, *Confederate States Navy*, p. 726; Moebs, *Confederate States Navy Research Guide*, pp. 199, 206, 217, 240, 253, 260, 277; ZB files for each of the officers named; *ORN* I, 10, p. 677.

17 *ORN* I, 10, p. 64.

18 Ibid., pp. 51-52.

19. Quoted in Still, *Iron Afloat*, p.173; *ORN* I, 10, pp. 625-626, 644-645, 655-656. The army engineers warned in May the Navy Department was "going to make an issue" of the failure to clear the obstructions. See Stevens to Mason, May 18, 1864, Charles T. Mason Papers, sect. 1, file 7.

20. Stephen R. Mallory, "Last Days of the Confederate Government [account written in 1865 and published by Mallory's daughter], *McClure's Magazine*, vol. 16 (December 1900), p. 103; *ORN* I, 10, pp 651-652.

21. *ORN* I, 10, pp. 648-651.

22. Ibid., pp. 662-664, 666.

23. Ibid., pp. 671, 678, 682; 666, 667, 673-674, 675; 667-668, 673-675. Federal officers learned on May 30 [ibid., p. 105] from a deserter of the plans to use fire ships.

24. Robert D. Minor to wife, May 15, 1864, James H. Rochelle to Robert D. Minor, June 23, 1864, Minor Papers, roll B27.

25. *ORN* I, 10, pp. 678-679.

26. Ibid., p. 692.

27. Ibid., p. 694.

28. Ibid., pp. 129,129-132.

29. Ibid., p. 149.

30. Ibid., pp. 184, 464; 372-374; 315-316.

31. Robert D. Minor to John McIntosh Kell, August 8, 1864, Private Collection.

32. *ORN* I, 10, pp. 706, 739-740.

33. Ibid., 192. Confederate reports of this action in ibid., pp. 185-192 and pp. 705-706; Federal reports, ibid., pp. 176-184; Parker, *Recollections*, p. 338. The Federal deserter probably mistook the fire from Battery Dantzler as fire from the Confederate ships.

34. John C. Taylor, *History of the First Connecticut Artillery and of the Siege Trains of the Armies Operating Against Richmond, 1862-1865* (Hartford, 1893), pp. 48-88, 108-115; *ORN* I, 11, p. 400.

35. *Ibid.*, pp. 350-355; *OR* I, 42, pt. 2, pp.147, 150, 162; Rootes to Minor, August 16, 1864, Minor Papers, file c. 2644-2651. Jefferson Davis expressed concern over the Dutch Gap Canal. See Vandiver, ed., *Gorgas Diary*, p. 134.

36. Minor to wife, August 19, 1864, Minor Papers, roll B27; Rootes to Lee, copy of report of August 19, 1864, in Lee Headquarters Papers, Virginia Historical Society, Richmond, VA.

37. *ORN* I, 10, pp. 761-762, 762-763, 757; 753-754. For exhaustive detail on the military operations of September 29-October 1, 1864, see Richard Sommers, *Richmond Redeemed: The Siege at Petersburg* (Garden City, 1981).

38. ORN I, 10, pp. 755; 761-762, 753-765.

39. Ibid., pp. 744, 745; 777, 779, 780, 781-782, 785, 802-803; 788 (quote), 789-790; 804-805.

40. Ibid., pp. 768-769; also pp. 720, 725; 776, 784, 799. The navy was, of course, patrolling the river even before the fall of Fort Harrison. See for example *OR* I, 42, pt. 2, p. 1290; notes on lookouts and patrols, June 12, 14, 1864, R. D. Minor's commonplace book, Minor Papers, item c. 3199, roll B29.

41. *ORN* I, 10, pp. 586, 589, 585, 585-592; Taylor, *First Connecticut*, pp. 116-119.

42. Ibid., p. 587; inspection reports of *Fredericksburg*, July 6, 1864; *Hampton*, August 3, 1864; *Nansemond*, July 5, 1864; *Richmond*, June 18, 1864 and *Virginia II*, July 9, 1864, in Minor Papers, items c3236-3240, roll B29; chief engineer's report of *Virginia II*, July 7, 1864, in *ORN* I, 10, pp. 718-719.

43. Parker, *Recollections*, p. 348; *ORN* I, 10, p. 590, pp. 750-751; 722. The yards also worked on the *Gallego* and the wooden vessels reserved as fire ships in the event of an attack against the Federal fleet. See ibid., I, 11, pp. 761, 763, 768-769; John K. Mitchell Diary, entries of December 17, 18, 1864, John K. Mitchell Papers, Virginia Historical Society, Richmond, VA, folder 10. Hereinafter cited as Mitchell Papers.

44. *ORN* I, 11, pp. 586, 588-589, 798, 662-663. The *Fredericksburg's* shield deck (the roof of the casemate) had been left unarmored to make the vessel lighter in draft.

45 Interrogation of deserter Henry B. Craft in ibid., I, 11, p. 102; "List of Torpedo Stores Received and Expended in James River Squadron," ca. July 1864, RG 45, subject files (BM), roll 11.

46 *ORN* I, 10, pp. 795-799, 803.

47. Ibid., I, 11. p. 102; 749, 753, 761; 748, 777-779; Diary of John Mitchell, entries of December 4, 14, 1864, Mitchell Papers, folder 10. For a recent detailed examination of this incident, see Elliott, *Ironclad of the Roanoke,* chapter 15, "Noble to the End."

48. Rootes to Minor, November 21, 1864, Minor Papers, file c. 2644-2651.

49. Mitchell Diary, entries of December 17, 22, 1864, with crude drawings, Mitchell Papers, folder 10.

50 *ORN* I, 11, p. 752; Parker, *Elements*, pp. 168-178; Wells, *Confederate Navy*, p. 145. Ranks and responsibilities are detailed in *Regulations*, pp. 4-7, ff; Confederate muster roll (specifying rank and grade) are reprinted in *ORN* II, 1, pp. 273-323.

51. Quoted in J. W. Harris, "Some Notes of the Confederate States Navy," *SHSP*, vol. 28 (1900), p. 307; Quarterly reports of provisions of the *C.S.S. Richmond*, June 30, September 30 and October 31, 1864, Marsden Bellamy Papers, Southern Historical Collection, University of North Carolina, Chapel Hill, NC. Hereinafter cited as Bellamy Papers; John M. Kell to wife, January 6, 1865, Kell Papers, box 4.

52 *ORN* I, 11, p. 383; Oliver Hamilton to father, April 10, 1864, Eli Spinks Hamilton Papers, Southern Historical Collection, University of North Carolina, Chapel Hill, NC. Hereinafter cited as Hamilton Papers; George Weber to brother Louis, August 11, 1861, Weber letters. For background on Civil War sailor life see William N. Still, Jr., "The Civil War's Uncommon Man: The Common Sailor," pt. 2: "Confederate Tars," *Civil War Times Illustrated*, vol. 24 (March 1985), pp. 13-19.

53. *Regulations*, pp. 163, 173; Ralph W. Donnelly, "Blacks in the Confederate Navy," unpublished manuscript in the files of Richmond National Battlefield Park.

54. Les Jensen, *32nd Virginia Infantry* (Lynchburg, 1990), pp. 56, 173, 177, 180, 194, 197; Compiled Service Records of Confederate Soldiers Who Served in organizations From Virginia, Record Group 109, Microfilm publication M-324, National Archives and Records Administration, Washington, D.C., roll 860, copies in Library of Virginia, Richmond, VA; *OR* IV, pt. 1, p. 1092, pt. 2, pp. 138, 191-192, 705.

55. Gideon Fellers to John H. Winder, July 24, 1863, William Jones to Winder, July 3, 1863; and Murray Mason to Winder, January 8, 1864, Correspondence of John H. Winder, 1863-1864, Records of C.S.A. Department of Henrico, Virginia Historical Society, Richmond, VA, files 5-8, 9.

56. Hamilton to father, April 10, 1864, Hamilton Papers; *ORN* I, 11, pp. 382, 380-383; Hamilton to father, April 10, 1864, Hamilton Papers.

57. Quarterly reports of provisions and small stores, in Bellamy Papers; rations issued at Gosport Navy Yard in order of May 5, 1861, Gosport Navy Yard Order Book, April-October 1861, Forrest Papers. A deserter told Federal authorities on November 1, 1864, that sailors on the ships and at the batteries had "enough to eat." Taylor, *First Connecticut*, p. 120.

58. Parker, *Recollections*, 338; *ORN* I, 10, p.743.

59. *ORN* I, 10, p. 779.

60. Taylor, *First Connecticut*, p. 120; Undated statement of Daniel Smith, in NA, RG 45, area files (area 7), roll 93; Kell, *Recollections*, p. 268; quarterly reports of clothing, 1864, Bellamy Papers. For evidence of gray cloth shortages even before the fall of Wilmington, see Wells, *Confederate Navy*, pp. 84-87; Raphael Semmes, *Memoirs of Service Afloat during the War Between the States* (New York, 1869), pp. 803-804.

61 Minor to wife, July 8, 1864, Minor Papers, roll B27; *ORN* I, 10, p. 710; 11, p. 383; Harwell, ed., "Diary of Captain Edward Crenshaw," entry of January 13, 1865, part 5, p. 377.

62. Parker, *Elements*, p. 164.

63. Nelson D. Lankford, ed. *An Irishman in Dixie: Thomas Conolly's Diary of the Fall of the Confederacy* (Columbia, 1988), pp. 65-66. In his description of the gundeck, Conolly obviously mistook gun *ports* for the guns themselves. See blueprint drawing in Appendix Two.

64. *ORN* II, 2, p. 759; I, 10, p. 736.

65. Morgan, *Recollections*, p. 205; *ORN* I, 10, pp. 734-735; II, 2, p. 759.

66. *ORN* I, 10, p. 785.

67. Mitchell Diary, December 25, 1864, Mitchell Papers, folder 10; Kell to wife, January 8 and 20, 1865, Kell Papers, box 4.

68. *RDD*., December 24, 1864, p. 1, c. 2.

69. Hubbard T. Minor, "Diary," pt. II, p. 32.

70. Morgan, *Recollections*, p. 85; Clayton, "Confederate Navy," Chapter VII; James O. Harrison to Ellen, March 31, 1864, Harrison Papers; C. Vann Woodward, ed., *Mary Chesnut's Civil War* (New Haven, 1981), pp. 441, 479-481; Hubbard T. Minor, "Diary," part II, p. 31; invitation to Midshipman's Hop, Minor Papers, item c.3233, roll B29.

71. Harwell, ed., "Diary of Captain Edward Crenshaw," March 18, 1865, part 5, pp. 383-384.

72. Hubbard T. Minor, "Diary," pt. I, p. 30. Minor's matter-of-fact reference to intoxication is significant since, according to the school ship regulations, intoxication was grounds for dismissal from the Academy.

73. *RDD.*, February 3, 1864, p. 1, c. 4; Forrest to Mallory, February 3, 1864, James River Squadron Letterbook.

74. *RDD.*, February 17, 1864, p. 1, c. 6.

75. Clayton, *Narrative*, pp. 102-103.

76. John T. Chappell, "'Buddies' of 1865," Samuel Chappell Papers, Library of Virginia, Richmond, VA.

Chapter Six

1. Morgan, *Recollections*, p. 215; Harwell, ed., "Diary of Captain Edward Crenshaw," pt. 5, pp. 370-371; Jones, *Rebel War Clerk's Diary*, 2, pp. 371-378; Kell to wife, January 6, 1864, Kell Papers, box 4.

2. *ORN* I, 11, p. 797.

3. Ibid., p. 798.

4. Ibid., pp. 792, 795-796, 798-799, 803.

5. Ibid., pp. 636, 186, 195; ship data from ibid., II, 1, passim.

6. Rawlins to Parker, January 21, 1865, in NA, RG 45, area file (area 7), roll 93; also in *ORN* I, 11, p. 632; ibid., pp. 412-413, 633.

7. The Battle of Trent's Reach has been described in Still, *Iron Afloat*, chapter 11; Theodore P. Savas, "Last Clash of the Ironclads: The Bungled Affair at Trent's Reach," *Civil War*, February 1989, pp. 15-22; Dale S. Snair, "Lt. Thomas P. Bell, C.S.N., and the Action at Trent's Reach," *Blue & Gray Magazine*, vol. 3, (February-March 1986), pp. 23-27. Each of these accounts draws primarily from reports in the *Official Records*. The account offered here is similarly based on the official reports.

8. *ORN* I, 11, pp. 664-665, 669; "Preliminary chart of the JAMES RIVER."

9. *ORN* I, 11, p. 677.

10. Ibid., pp. 673, 674.

11. *OR* 46, pt. 1, p. 176.

12. *ORN* I, 11, pp. 659-661. Detailed reports and correspondence is also in John C. Taylor, *First Connecticut Artillery* (Hartford, 1893), pp. 133-139.

13. Ibid., pp. 672, 678, 681, 686-687.

14. Ibid., pp. 671, 677, 683-684. Shepperd reported that his ship's outriggers were torn off by the spar, while Read insisted that the *Fredericksburg* did not strike the spar. Perhaps in a gesture of mediation, Mitchell reported that the outriggers were sheared off by one of the sunken hulks. The three reports also obscure exactly when the flag officer was in a small boat at the obstructions and when he was on the *Fredericksburg*.

15. Ibid., pp. 683-684, 677.

16. Ibid., pp. 669, 673, 684.

17. Ibid., pp. 667, 678, 680, 681-682, 687-688. Lt. James W. Alexander reported that his vessel, the *Beaufort*, spent the night anchored at Osborne's Landing, upstream from Dantzler.

18. Ibid., pp. 659, 673-674, 670, 684, 688-689.

19. Ibid., pp. 635, 636, 656-657, 653-654, 656.

20. Ibid., pp. 637-638; 650-651, 635, 639-643.

21. Ibid., p. 675.

22. Ibid., pp. 647, 649, 656, 675-676, 674; Memoir of John T. Chappell, Chappell Papers. The Confederate commanders estimated the distance of the *Onondaga* at closer to a mile.

23. *ORN* I, 11, pp. 689-690, 671, 674, 678, 683.

24. Ibid., pp. 674, 676, 682-683; Harwell, ed., "Diary of Captain Edward Crenshaw," pt. 5, pp. 374-375.

25. *ORN* I, 11, pp. 672-673; ibid., 12, pp. 184-185.

26. Ibid., 11, pp. 662-663; Porter to Homer C. Blake, February 14, 1865, NA, RG 45, area files (area 7), roll 93. A few days after the battle, Parker confessed that his decision not to move up to the obstructions was wrong. *ORN* I, 11, p. 656.

27. Circular of January 28, 1865, General Order, James River Flotilla, February 28, 1865, and Blake (approved by Radford), order of March 16, 1865, in NA, RG 45, area files (area 7), roll 93.

28. Parker, *Recollections*, p. 344.

29. *ORN* I, 12, p. 185; *RDD*, February 20, 1865, p. 4, c. 1.

30. *ORN* I, 12, pp. 185-186.

31. Wakelyn, ed., *Biographical Dictionary*, p. 380. The careers of the *Sumter* and *Alabama* are detailed in Semmes, *Memoirs*.

32. Lankford, ed., *An Irishman in Dixie*, p. 65; Harwell, ed., "Diary of Captain Edward Crenshaw," February 18, 1865, pt. 5, p. 378; *ORN* I, 12, p. 190.

33. Semmes, *Memoirs*, p. 803; W. Stanley Hoole, ed., "Admiral on Horseback: The Diary of Brigadier General Raphael Semmes, February-May 1865," *The Alabama Review*, vol. 28 (April 1975), note, p. 132.

34. Semmes, *Memoirs*, pp. 803-804.

35. Hoole, ed., "Admiral," pp. 134-136.

36. Harris, "Confederate Naval Cadets," p. 170; Harwell, ed., "Diary of Captain Edward Crenshaw," pt. 5, pp. 381-382.

37. Undated statement of Daniel Smith, in NA, RG 45, area files (area 7), roll 93. Scarborough, *Ruffin Diary*, vol. 3, p. 761. Although Scarborough casts doubt on this story, it is credible in every respect, and the unnamed sailor in question may even have been Daniel Smith.

38. The definitive account of the expedition is Ralph W. Donnelly, "A Confederate Navy Forlorn Hope," *Military Affairs*, vol. 28 (Summer 1964), pp. 73-78; details of the expedition are drawn from this account unless noted otherwise. See especially *ORN* I, 11, pp. 380-383.

39. W. F. Shippey, "A Leaf from my Log-Book," *SHSP*, vol. 12 (1884), p. 417.

40. Julia Porter Wickham, "Commanders of the Confederate Navy: Charles Read of Mississippi," *Confederate Veteran*, vol. 37 (February 1929), p. 61. Read earned the name "Savez" at the U.S. Naval Academy because he claimed it was the only French word he knew; James Morris Morgan and John Philip Marquand, *Prince and Boatswain: Sea tales from the recollection of Rear-Admiral Charles E. Clark* (Greenfield, 1915), pp. 31, 60-62; *ORN* I, 11, pp. 683-684, 747; Charles W. Read file in ZB files, box 186.

41. NA, RG 45, area files (area 7), roll 93; Statement of George Henry Dunnett in *ORN* I, 11, p. 382; Undated statement in NA, RG 45, area files (area 7), roll 93.

42. Shippey, "A Leaf," 421.

43. Semmes, *Memoir*, p. 805; Hoole, ed., "Admiral," p. 138; Kell to wife, March 1, 1865, Kell Papers, box 4.

44. Semmes, *Memoirs*, pp. 809-810.

45. Hoole, ed., "Admiral," p. 138.

46. Parker to Mallory, February 28, 1865, RG 45, subject file (NE), roll 19.

47. Parker, *Recollections*, pp. 349-350; John F. Mayer to Mrs. F. Powell Hartenstein, August 30, 1915, Miscellaneous documents, Eleanor S. Brockenbrough Library, The Museum of the Confederacy, file M-623; Hoole, ed., "Admiral," p. 138.

48. Semmes, *Memoirs*, p. 811.

49. Manarin, ed., *Richmond at War*, pp. 169, 174, 180-184; A.A. Hoehling & Mary Hoehling, *The Day Richmond Died* (New York, 1981); Ryan, *Four Days*.

50. Richmond *Evening Whig*, April 4, 1865, p. 2, c. 3; undated page insert in Brooke diaries.

51. Semmes, *Memoirs*, p. 811.

52. Mallory, "Last Days," p. 102.

53. Semmes, *Memoirs*, p. 811.

54. Ibid.

55. Lieutenant Commander James Parker to Admiral Radford, April 24, 1865, RG 45, area files (area 7), roll 94. Fiction writer Clive Cussler made the Federal capture of the *Texas* the starting point for his 1992 novel *Sahara*.

56. Kell to wife, March 18, 1865, in Kell, *Recollections*, p. 272; Vandiver, *Gorgas Diary*, p. 156.

57. Werlich, *Admiral*, p. 68; Rochelle, *Life of Tucker*, p. 53; J. B. Gardner, Letter in "Our Confederate Column," *Richmond Times-Dispatch*, April 5, 1914, in CMLS Scrapbook, 1912-1915, p. 131, Eleanor S. Brockenbrough Library, The Museum of the Confederacy. Captain William T. Alexander and Col. Joseph H. Alexander, "From Ironclads to Infantry," *Naval History*, vol. 5 (summer 1991), p. 15, claim (without corroboration) that the sailors spiked the guns of the batteries and tumbled them down the bluff.

58. Semmes, *Memoirs*, pp. 818-819. According to documents in the ZB files, box 16, Lt. Mortimer M. Benton commanded a company in Semmes' brigade; Record of John Bondurant Gardner in Admiral A.O. Wright Collection of Confederate Navy Service Records, Library of Virginia, Richmond, VA; Gardner, Letter.

60. Hoole, ed., "Admiral," pp. 140-143; Semmes, *Memoirs*, pp. 817-823; Mitchell's oath in John K. Mitchell file, box 155, ZB files.

61. Werlich, *Admiral*, pp. 67-70; Rochelle, *Life of Tucker*, pp. 51-54; Donnelly, *Confederate States Marine Corps*, pp. 42-45. Tucker's navy rank entitled him to hold the army rank of brigadier general.

62. *OR* I, 46, pt. 1, pp. 652, 906.

63. Donnelly, "Blacks in the Confederate Navy," p.1; Appomattox Paroles published in *SHSP*, vol. 15 (1887), p. 460; D.M. Lee, CSN, "Last Fight of the Confederate States Navy," *Richmond Times Dispatch*, March 7, 1909, in Scrapbook # 120, p. 42, Eleanor S. Brockenbrough Library, The Museum of the Confederacy; Richmond, VA; D. M. Lee's file in ZB files, box 131.

64. Parker, *Recollections*, p. 352, 351-372.

65. Harris, "Confederate Naval Cadets," p. 171; Scharf, *Confederate States Navy*, pp. 778-779.

66. Durkin, *Stephen R. Mallory*, pp. 342-343 and chapter 14, passim.

Epilogue

1. *Civil War Naval Chronology*, pt. 4, p. 314; *ORN* I, 12, p. 115; II, 1, pp. 222, 269; Lt. James H. Parker, USN, report of June 2, 1865, on Talbott & Bros., in Talbott & Bros. Papers, file a71-75; Manarin, ed., *Richmond at War*, pp. 634-635.

2. *Richmond Whig*, April 13, 1865, p. 1, c. 2; also May 25, 1865, p. 2, c. 5.

3. Patrick D. Harris, "Richmond's Maritime and Naval Heritage" (unpublished paper, 1992), p. 5.

4. Patrick D. Harris, "Richmond—Submarine Capital of the World" (unpublished paper, 1992); Paul Murphy, "The Richmond Dock and the Trigg Shipyard, 1898-1903" (unpublished paper for Historic Richmond Foundation, August 1992); "SHIPBUILDING, Richmond,Va.: Trigg Shipbuilding Co.," Valentine Museum clippings files.

5. Claude Burrows, "Excavation yields surprises about city's past," *RTD*, September 4, 1990, pp. A1, A8; Mouer, *The Archaeology of the Rocketts Number 1 Site*.

6. James Hanscom, "Confederate Shipyard Rises Again," *Richmond News-Leader*, April 18, 1962 and Clyde Wilson, "Ship Yard Remains Found?" ibid., June 30, 1964 in "CONFEDERATE STATES OF AMERICA NAVY: Navy Yard-Richmond," Valentine Museum clippings files. L. Daniel Mouer, "Confederate Navy Yard Discovered on Richmond's Waterfront," *APVA Newsletter*, vol. 11 (Spring 1992), pp. 11-13.

7. Paul Murphy, comp. *Richmond's Historic Waterfront: Rockett's Landing to Tredegar, 1607-1865* (Richmond, 1989).

8. George L. Fickett, Jr., "The Bermuda Hundred Tour" (Chesterfield, 1990). Members of the "James River Squadron," a Tidewater-based reenactment and volunteer group have constructed models and display them at special events at Drewry's Bluff and elsewhere in the Richmond area. The group has also constructed accurate replicas of Confederate torpedoes and portrays a station of the Submarine Battery Service. A description of the group's activities appeared in *Naval History*, vol. 8 (August 1994), p. 60. The group publishes an occasional newsletter.

9. Pat Jones, "New Thunder Along the James," *Richmond Times Dispatch Magazine*, September 24, 1961, pp. 8-10. Chesson, *Richmond After the War*, p. 69; cites sources claiming that the wrecks were blown to little pieces in the year after the war.

10. Ron Sauder, "Hulks found in river," *Richmond Times-Dispatch*, December 1, 1982, in "CONFEDERATE STATES OF AMERICA NAVY: Navy Yard-Richmond,"

Valentine Museum clippings files; Sam Margolin, "Preserving Virginia's Civil War Naval Heritage, Part I: History and Archaeology of the Wreck Sites" (unpublished conference paper, 1990); [John N. Townley], "Saved! C.S.S. Richmond, C.S.S. Virginia II, C.S.S. Fredricksburg [sic.] and Many More. . . " *The Confederate Naval Historical Society Newsletter*, vol. 1 (June 1989), pp. 1-5. Rick Sauder, "Dredging Up History: Ghost fleet of the James haunts Port of Richmond," *Richmond Times-Dispatch*, March 15, 1993, pp. E16-E18.

11. Beers, ed., *The Confederacy*, p. 339.

12. Scharf, *Confederate States Navy*, p. 773.

13. Weisiger, *The Parker Family*, p. 32.

14. Williams, *Maury*, chapters 21-23.

15. Werlich, *Admiral*; and Rochelle, *Life of Tucker*, passim.

16. Werlich, *Admiral*, pp. 89-90, 90-91, 107, 252-253; Butt's file in ZB files, box 35; Scharf, *Confederate States Navy*, pp. 702-703.

17. "Capt. Hunter Davidson," obituary in *Confederate Veteran*, vol. 21 (June 1913), 307; biographical sketch in box 60, ZB files. Letters of 1881-1882 published in "Davis and Davidson," *SHSP*, vol. 24 (1896), pp. 285-289.

18. Morris and Marquand, *Prince and Boatswain*, pp. 70-71.

19. Morgan, *Recollections*, pp. 207-208, 266-315, and passim.

20. Obituary from unidentified newspaper in Mitchell Papers, sect. 4.

21. Wakelyn, ed., *Biographical Dictionary*, p. 380; Adolphe W. Roberts, *Semmes of Alabama* (Indianapolis, 1938).

22. Norman C. Delaney, *John McIntosh Kell of the Raider Alabama* (Tuscaloosa, 1973), chapter 17; Kell, *Recollections*, pp. 273-274, 296, 306.

23. Hall, *Portraits*, p. 198.

24. "Capt. W.A. Graves Dead." *Norfolk Virginian*, February 18, 1894; "The Death Roll. Mr. W.A. Graves, Sr. Passes Away At His Residence," *Norfolk Landmark*, February 18, 1894.

25. Brooke, *John M. Brooke*, pp. 299-310, 319-320.

26. One-page memorandum in Brooke Diary, 1865; Brooke, *John M. Brooke*, p. 287, Chapter 12.

27. Poem written, June 15, 1894 in scrapbook #6, Kate Mason Rowland Papers.

28. Minor to Andrew Johnson, June 3, 1865, in ZB files, box 154; obituary in *RDE*, November 27, 1871; Virginia Department of Vital Statistics, Deaths, City of Richmond, microfilm roll 35, Library of Virginia, Richmond, VA.

29. Durkin, *Stephen R. Mallory*, chapter 15 (quoted from pp. 409-410).

30. David D. Porter, *The Naval History of the Civil War* (New York, 1886), p. 797.

Appendix One

1. Compiled from *ORN*, I, vols. 7-12; Wells, *Confederate Navy*, passim; and Beer, ed., *The Confederacy*, passim; ZB files.

2. Semmes, *Memoir*, p. 803, listed "Capt. Wyatt" as commander of the vessel in February 1865, but surviving documents do not corroborate his recollection.

3. Ibid., lists a "Capt. Glassel" as commander of the vessel in February 1865, but surviving documents do not corroborate his recollection. Lieutenant William T. Glassel was apparently not in Richmond in February 1865.

4. Ibid., lists a "Capt. Johnson" in command of the vessel as of February 1865. This could have been Lt. Oscar F. Johnston, but other documents suggest that Dalton, not Johnston, was in command when Semmes arrived.

Note on Sources and Bibliography

Because *Capital Navy* attempts to offer a coherent and interesting narrative history of the subject, I consciously chose not to incorporate the thousands of details that can be gleaned from surviving records and documents. Readers desiring more detailed information about particular facets of Richmond's naval history, or a particular individual, vessel or business in some way related to this story, have many sources available to them.

The most important source of documentation is the Confederate Naval Records section of Record Group 45 (microfilm publication M-1091) at the National Archives in Washington, D.C. Those records are available on microfilm at the Archives and through interlibrary loan. A small published guide to the record group is available for sale. Henry Putney Beers' *The Confederacy*, is an invaluable guide to National Archives collections, to the records in other collections, and to the structure and processes of the Confederate government and armed services. Consulting Beers' guide and the guide to RG 45 before traveling to the Archives will save researchers (and the Archives' staff) an enormous amount of time and trouble.

Officers and Sailors of the Confederate States Navy

While comprehensive records, such as the compiled service records of Confederate soldiers, are not available for naval personnel, scattered (and usually superficial) information is available. Lists of crews and officers for vessels of the James River Squadron and Richmond Station are published in series II, vol. 1 of the *Official Records* of the Navies. Abstracts of officer's service records were published in 1931 in *Register of Officers*. The National Archives contains seven rolls of microfilmed Confederate Navy personnel records (Record Group 45, microfilm series 260), which consist almost entirely of hospital and prison records. The National Archives also has *Abstracts of U.S. Service Records of Naval Officers, 1798-1893*, which is a good source of information on the many Confederates who began their careers wearing blue. Documents relating to the service of officers are also available in the ZB files (Early Records Biographies) at the Naval Historical Center located at the Washington, D.C. Navy Yard. Most of those files contain only routine documents providing skeletal service information, and most of the valuable information was published in the *Official Records*. Nevertheless, the ZB files contain enough gems to warrant consultation. A navy committee of the United Confederate Veterans compiled "service records" for the navy. The result is a drawer of index cards (the Admiral A. O. Wright Collection at the Library of Virginia) containing very basic information. Thomas T. Moebs's *Confederate Navy Research Guide* includes a convenient compendium of promotion dates and commands for officers. More detailed information on a few officers and sailors is available in the *Confederate Veteran* magazine (published 1893-1932). This invaluable set has since been republished, and Broadfoot Publishers, of Wilmington, N.C., has published a comprehensive three-volume index to the *Veteran*, which has made its wealth of information accessible for researchers.

Laborers employed by the Confederate Navy

Pay vouchers and payrolls for laborers, enslaved and free, appear in many different files of Record Group 45 (especially three thick files of payrolls exclusively from Richmond facilities) and in manuscript collections. Consult James Brewer's *The Confederate Negro* for a guide to those resources. The Charles T. Mason Papers at the Virginia Historical Society (sect. 4) are especially rich in documents relating to laborers employed at Drewry's Bluff.

Vessels in the Confederate Navy

Basic technical data (and dates for warships and a few other vessels) is available in series II, vol. 1 of the *Official Records* of the navies, part 6, of the extremely valuable *Civil War Naval Chronology*, and Moebs's *Research Guide*. Blueprints and measured drawings of a few warships survive in Record Group 19 (Bureau of Ships) of the National Archives. The National Museum of American History (Smithsonian) has blueprints produced in the 1950s by W. E. Geoghegan. Documents relating to the construction of Confederate ships are in the subject files (file AC) of the Navy Department records, Record Group 45, of the National Archives. A few documents relating to other specific features of vessels are in the Engineering series (E files) of the subject files. A "Vessels" series in the National Archives (microfilm publication M-909) contains information primarily on some of the civilian vessels employed by the Confederate navy.

Richmond-Area Businesses Involved With the Confederate Navy

Scores, probably hundreds, of Richmond businesses and artisans dealt in some way with the Confederate navy. Thousands of vouchers, receipts, bills, invoices and other documents detailing the extent and nature of the "naval-industrial complex" survive in the subject files (M-1091) of RG 45 (files AC and PN in particular), and in a huge and underappreciated series of records known as Records Relating to Confederate Citizens and Business Firms, Record Group 109 (microfilm publication M-346). The latter is arranged alphabetically by the name of business or proprietor. Thus, Tredegar Ironworks is under its formal name: Anderson, J.R. & Co., and so forth. This series also includes documents similar to those in RG 45. For those interested in quantifying the naval-industrial complex (material, labor, dollar value, etc.), the records are available to do so.

Ordnance and Torpedo Technology

Details on the scientific and technical aspects of the Confederate Navy's technological innovation are available in several sources. The ordnance and armament series (B files) of the RG 45 subject files contain valuable documents for activities on the James River. Record Group 74 of the National Archives (Records of the Bureau of Ordnance), which this study did not consult, contain details on the work of John Brooke. George Brooke's published biography of his grandfather, John Mercer Brooke, is a good introduction and source guide to Confederate technological experiments. The papers of Robert Dabney Minor (in the collections of the Virginia Historical Society) and John Mercer Brooke include notebook entries and drawings regarding the field testing of ordnance and armor. The Matthew Fontaine Maury Papers at the Library of Congress Manuscripts Division, and the Gabriel Rains "Torpedo Book" in the Eleanor S. Brockenbrough Library, contain similar details for torpedo technology.

Bibliography

Manuscripts and Archives

University of Alabama, Tuscaloosa, Alabama, William Stanley Hoole Special Collections, Amelia Gayle Gorgas Library

John Horry Dent Papers

Scrapbooks

Private Collections.

John Mercer Brooke Diaries.

Letter of Robert Dabney Minor to John McIntosh Kell, August 8, 1864.

Chesterfield County Clerk's Office, Chesterfield, VA.

Chesterfield County Plat Books and Deed Books.

Colonial Williamsburg Foundation Research Library, Williamsburg, VA.

Robert Randolph Carter Papers in "Records of Ante-Bellum Southern Plantations from the Revolution through the Civil War, series K: Selections from the Colonial Williamsburg Foundation Library, The Shirley Plantation Collection, 1650-1888. Microfilm publication by University Publications of America, 1993.

Duke University, Durham, NC, Special Collections, William R. Perkins Library

Clopton Family Papers.

John McIntosh Kell Papers.

James Henry Rochelle Papers.

Hampton Roads Naval Museum, Norfolk, VA.

Photograph collections.

Library of Congress, Manuscripts Division, Washington, D.C.

Daniel B. Conrad Diaries.

James O. Harrison Papers.

Betty Herndon Maury Diaries.

Matthew Fontaine Maury Papers.

David Dixon Porter Papers.

Rodgers Family Papers.

The Museum of the Confederacy, Richmond, VA, Eleanor S. Brockenbrough Library

Confederate Memorial Literary Society [CMLS] Scrapbooks, 1902-1944.

Records and Register of the Clopton Hospital, Richmond, Virginia (box V-9-2-2).

Drewry's Bluff telegrams, May 1864 (files T-806, 807, 808).

Correspondence of Mrs. James W. Harris, Gunboat Association of Columbus, Mississippi (V-6-1-2)

James River Submarine Battery Service file of Dr. Carthon Archer (file A-21).

Ladies Defense Association Minute Book (V-8-3-1).

Ladies Defense Association Papers (file L-542).

John Thompson Mason Papers (file M-615).

Miscellaneous Papers.

John L. Porter file (file P-689).

Photograph Collection.

Gabriel Rains "Torpedo Book."

Kate Mason Rowland Papers.

National Archives, Washington, D.C.

Record Group 45 (entry 430), Lt. Joseph N. Barney Letterbook, December 3, 1861-April 20, 1863.

Record Group 45, Confederate States Navy Payroll files.

Record Group 45 (M-1091), Confederate States Navy subject files.

Record Group 45 (M-625), United States Navy area files, area 7.

Record Group 109 (M-346), Records Relating to Confederate Citizens and Business Firms.

Record Group 109 (M-260) Records Relating to Confederate Naval and Marine Personnel.

Record Group 109 (M-324) Compiled Service Records of Confederate Soldiers Who Served in Organizations From Virginia [copies in Virginia State Library and Archives]

Record Group 109 (M-909) Papers Pertaining to Vessels of or Involved with the Confederate States of America.

Naval Historical Center, U.S. Navy Department, Navy Yard, Washington, D.C.

Early Records Biographies (ZB) files.

Photograph collection.

Richmond National Battlefield Park, Richmond, VA.

Drewry's Bluff research files.

University of North Carolina at Chapel Hill, NC, Southern Historical Collection, Louis Round Wilson Library

Marsden Bellamy Papers.

John M. Brooke Papers.

Franklin Buchanan Letterbook, 1862-1863.

Maxwell T. Clarke Papers.

Eli Spinks Hamilton Papers.

Thomas Locke Harrison Papers.

Henry Lord Page King Diary in Thomas Butler King Papers.

Stephen R. Mallory Diary.

James Morris Morgan Papers.

John Taylor Wood Papers.

United States Army Military History Institute, Carlisle Barracks, PA.

William A. Heirs letter in Civil War Times Illustrated Collection [photocopy of transcript in manuscript collections of Richmond National Battlefield Park].

Photograph collections.

Valentine Museum, Richmond, VA.

Clippings files.

Virginia Historical Society, Richmond, VA.

Correspondence of Isaac Howell Carrington, 1863-1864, in Records of Confederate States Army, Department of Henrico.

Hamilton Henry Cocke Papers.

Lee Family Papers.

Map collection.

Charles T. Mason Papers.

Matthew Fontaine Maury Monument Association Papers.

Robert Dabney Minor Papers in Minor Family Papers.

John Kirkwood Mitchell Papers.

Isaac Sterrett Diary.

Francis W. Smith Papers.

Talbott & Brother Papers.

John H. Winder Correspondence, 1863-1864 in Records of Confederate States Army, Department of Henrico.

Library of Virginia, Archives Division, Richmond, VA.

Anderson Family Papers.

Bureau of Vital statistics, Deaths, Richmond City.

St. George Tucker Brooke Autobiography.

C. H. Carlton letter, May 9, 1864

John T. Chappell personal papers.

John A. Curtis Reminiscences, 1864.

Douglas French Forrest Papers.

Hustings Court Deeds, Richmond City.

James River Squadron Letterbook, 1863-1864.

Picture Collection.

Tredegar Iron Works Papers.

George Weber Letters, 1861-1862.

Admiral A. O. Wright Collection of Confederate Navy Service Records.

College of William and Mary, Williamsburg, VA, Special Collections, Earl Gregg Swem Library

Barron Family Papers.

James Barron Hope Papers.

Civil War-era Newspapers and Directories

New York Herald, April 1865.

Richmond City Directory, 1860. Richmond: W. Eugene Ferslew, 1860.

Richmond Daily Dispatch, 1861-1865.

Richmond Daily Enquirer, 1861-1865.

Richmond Daily Whig, 1861-1865.

The Stranger's Guide and Official Directory for the City of Richmond. Richmond: George P. Evans & Co., Printers, 1863.

Vanfelson, C.A. *The Little Red Book or Department Directory*. Richmond: Tyler, Wise & Allegre Printers, 1861.

V&C. *The City Intelligencer; or, Stranger's Guide*. Richmond: MacFarlane & Fergusson, Printers, 1862; facsimile: Richmond: The Confederate Museum, 1960.

Other Published Primary Sources

(Includes Autobiographies, Diaries, Journals, Memoirs, Reminiscences and Unit Histories)

"A Rebel Infernal Machine." *Harper's Weekly*, November 2, 1861, p. 701.

Blackford, William W. *War Years With JEB Stuart*. New York: Charles Scribner's Sons, 1946.

Brooke, Henry St. George Tucker, "Monitor and Merrimac." *Richmond Times-Dispatch*, March 15, 1903.

Brooke, John M. "The Virginia, or Merrimac: Her Real Projector." *Southern Historical Society Papers*, vol. 19(1901), 3-34.

Bulloch, James D. *The Secret Service of the Confederate States in Europe*, 2 volumes. London: Richard Bentley & Son, 1883.

"Capt. W. A. Graves Dead." *Norfolk Virginian*, February 18, 1894.

Clayton, W. F. *A Narrative of the Confederate States Navy.* Weldon, NC: Harrell's Printing House, 1910.

— "The Confederate Navy," serialized in "Our Confederate Column," *Richmond Times-Dispatch*, 1908.

"Commissioned And Warrant Officers Of The Navy Of The Confederate States January 1, 1864." *Southern Historical Society Papers*, vol. 3 (1877), A106-107.

Crowley, R.O. "'Making the Infernal Machines': A Memoir of the Confederate Torpedo Service," *Century Magazine*, vol. 56 (June 1898) reprinted in *Civil War Times Illustrated*, vol. 12 (June 1973), pp. 24-35.

Davidson, Hunter. "The Electrical Submarine Mine—1861-65. *Confederate Veteran*, vol. 16 (September 1908), pp. 456-459.

— "Electrical Torpedoes as a System of Defence." *Southern Historical Society Papers*, vol. 2 (1876), pp. 1-6.

"Davis and Davidson,." *Southern Historical Society Papers*, vol. 24 (1896-1897), pp. 284-291.

Dawson, Francis W. *Reminiscences of Confederate Service 1861-1865*. Charleston, SC: The News & Courier Book Press, 1882; reprint, Baton Rouge: Louisiana State University Press, 1980.

"The Death Roll. Mr. W. A. Graves, Sr. Passes Away At His Residence." *Norfolk Landmark*, February 18, 1894.

Dedication of the Soldiers' and Sailors' Monument Richmond, Va.. Richmond: Confederate Soldiers' and Sailors' Monument Association, [1894].

DeLeon, T.C. "Belles, Beaux, and Brains of the '60s" in *Town Topics*, vol. 58 (1907-1908).

East, Charles, ed. *The Civil War Diary of Sarah Morgan*. Athens: University of Georgia Press, 1991.

Gallagher, Gary W., ed. *Fighting For the Confederacy: The Personal Recollections of Edward Porter Alexander*. Chapel Hill: University of North Carolina Press, 1989.

Gardner, J[ohn] B[ondurant]. Letter in "Our Confederate Column." *Richmond Times-Dispatch*, April 5, 1914.

Harris, J. W. "Confederate Naval Cadets." *Confederate Veteran*, vol. 12 (April 1904), pp. 170-171.

Harris, J. W. "Some Notes of the Confederate States Navy. Unofficial Letter from Lieutenant Minor." *Southern Historical Society Papers*, vol. 28 (1900), p. 307.

Harwell, Richard, ed. *A Confederate Marine: A Sketch of Henry Lea Graves, With Excerpts from the Graves Family Correspondence, 1861-1865.* Tuscaloosa: Confederate Publishing Co., 1963.

[Harwell, Richard, ed.] "Diary of Captain Edward Crenshaw of the Confederate States Army." *Alabama Historical Quarterly*, vol. 1 (1930): pp. 261-270 [part 1], pp. 438-452 [part 2]; 2 (1940): pp. 52-68 [part 3], pp. 221-238 [part 4], pp. 365-385 [part 5], pp. 465-482 [part 6].

Hoole, W. Stanley, ed. "Admiral on Horseback: The Diary of Brigadier General Raphael Semmes, February-May 1865," *The Alabama Review* 28 (April 1975): pp. 129-150.

Ironmonger, L[emuel] M[anning]. Article on Drewry's Bluff, 1862 in "Our Confederate Column." *Richmond Times-Dispatch*, May 3, 1903.

Jones, B. W., *Under the Stars and Bars: A History of the Surry Light Artillery*. Richmond: Everett Waddey, 1909; reprinted with notes by Lee A. Wallace, Jr., Dayton, OH: Press of the Morningside Bookshop, 1975.

Jones, J. B. *A Rebel War Clerk's Diary at the Confederate States Capital*, 2 volumes. Philadelphia: J.B. Lippincott & Company, 1866; reprinted New York: Old Hickory Bookshop, 1935.

Journal of the House of Delegates for the State of Virginia for the Session of 1861-1862. Richmond: Public Printer, 1861 [sic.].

Kean, Robert Garlick Hill. *Inside the Confederate Government: The Diary of Robert Garlick Hill Kean*, ed., Edward Younger. New York: Oxford University Press, 1957.

Keeler, William Frederick. *Aboard the U.S.S. Monitor: 1862*, ed. Robert W. Daly. Annapolis: U.S. Naval Institute Press, 1964.

Kell, John McIntosh. *Recollections of a Naval Life*. Washington, D.C: Neale Publishing Co., 1900.

Lankford, Nelson D., ed. *An Irishman in Dixie: Thomas Conolly's Diary of the Fall of the Confederacy.* Columbia: University of South Carolina Press, 1988.

Littlepage, Hardin B. "With the Crew of the Virginia," Part II. *Civil War Times Illustrated*, vol. 13 (May 1974), pp. 36-43.

Mallory, Stephen R. "Communication from Secretary of the Navy," February 7, 1865, in Message of the President to Senate of the Confederate States, February 15, 1865, in response to resolution of January 24, 1865 [Confederate Imprint, Crandall 866].

Mallory, Stephen R. "Last Days of the Confederate Government" [account written in 1865 and published by Mallory's daughter]. *McClure's Magazine,* vol. 16 (December 1900), pp. 100-107.

Manarin, Louis H., ed. *Richmond at War: The Minutes of the City Council, 1861-1865.* Chapel Hill: University of North Carolina Press, 1973.

Maury, Richard L. "The First Marine Torpedoes Were Made in Richmond, Va., and Used in James River," *Southern Historical Society Papers*, vol. 31 (1901), pp. 326-333.

Minor, Hubbard T. "Diary of a Confederate Naval Cadet." *Civil War Times Illustrated,* vol. 13 (November 1974), pp. 25-32; (December 1974), pp. 24-28+.

Morgan, James M. "A Realistic War College." *U.S. Naval Institute Proceedings*, 42 (March-April 1916), pp. 543-554.

—*Recollections of a Rebel Reefer*. Boston: Houghton Mifflin, 1917.

Parker, William Harwar. "The Confederate States Navy," in *Confederate Military History*, volume 12. Atlanta: Confederate Publishing Company, 1899.

—*Elements of Seamanship: Prepared as a Textbook for the Midshipman of the C.S. Navy.* Richmond: M cFarlane & Fergusson, Printers, 1864.

—*Recollections of a Naval Officer*. New York: Scribner's, 1883.

— *Regulations for the School-Ship Patrick Henry*. [Richmond, 1863; Confederate Imprint, Parrish & Willingham #1712]

Pinkerton, Allan. *The Spy of the Rebellion*. Kansas City: Kansas City Publishing Company, 1883.

Porter, David Dixon. The Naval History of the Civil War. New York: Sherman Publishing Co., 1886.

—*Incidents and Anecdotes of the Civil War*. New York: D. Appleton & Co., 1885.

Rains, Gabriel J. "Torpedoes." *Southern Historical Society Papers*, vol. 3 (1877), pp. 255-260.

Regulations for the Navy of the Confederate States 1862. Richmond: MacFarlane & Fergusson, Printers, 1862 [Confederate Imprint, Parrish & Willingham #1711].

Robertson, James I., Jr., ed. *Proceedings of the Advisory Council of the State of Virginia, April 21-June 19, 1861*. Richmond: Virginia State Library, 1977.

Rochelle, James H. "The Confederate Steamship 'Patrick Henry,'" *Southern Historical Society Papers*, vol. 14 (1886), pp. 126-136.

Scarborough, William Kauffman, ed. *The Diary of Edmund Ruffin*, 3 volumes. Baton Rouge: Louisiana State University Press, 1966-1989.

Semmes, Raphael. *Memoirs of Service Afloat during the War Between the States*. New York: J. P. Kennedy & Sons, 1869.

Shippey, W.F. "A Leaf from my Log-Book." *Southern Historical Society Papers*, vol. 12 (1884), pp. 416-421.

Spotswood, W. A. W. *Report of the Office of Medicine and Surgery, November 1, 1864, in Report of the Secretary of the Navy, 1864*. Richmond: G.P. Evans & Co., 1864, pp. 43-46.

Taylor, John C. *History of the First Connecticut Artillery and of the Siege Trains of the Armies Operating Against Richmond.* Hartford, CT: Case, Lockwood & Brainard, 1893.

Uniform and Dress of the Army and Navy of the Confederate States. Richmond: Charles H. Wynne, Printer, 1861; facsimile reprint: New Hope, PA: River House, 1952.

United States Congress, *Journal of the Congress of the Confederate States, 1861-1865*, 7 volumes. Washington, DC: Government Printing Office, 1904.

Walthall, Ernest Taylor. *Hidden Things Brought to Light*. Richmond: Dietz Press, 1933.

Waterman, George S. "Notable Events of the Civil War," *Confederate Veteran*, vol. 6 (January 1898), pp. 20-21.

Wood, John Taylor. "The First Fight of the Ironclads" in *Battles and Leaders of the Civil War*, edited by Robert Underwood Johnson and Clarence C. Buel. New York: Century, 1887.

Woodward, C. Vann, ed. *Mary Chesnut's Civil War*. New Haven, CT: Yale University Press, 1981.

Wright, Robert. "Sinking of the Jamestown," *Southern Historical Society Papers*, vol. 29 (1901), p. 372.

Reference Works

Beers, Henry Putney. *The Confederacy: A Guide to the Archives of the Government of the Confederate States of America*. Washington: National Archives, [1986].

Current, Richard, et. al., eds. *Encyclopedia of the Confederacy*, 4 volumes. New York: Simon & Schuster, 1993.

Faust, Patricia L., et. al., eds. *Historical Times Illustrated Encyclopedia of the American Civil War*. New York: Harper, 1986.

Johnson, Allen & Dumas Malone, eds. *Dictionary of American Biography*, 20 volumes. New York: Charles Scribner's Sons, 1943.

McEwen, W.A. and A.H. Lewis. *Encyclopedia of Nautical Knowledge*. Cambridge, MD: Cornell Maritime Press, 1953.

Moebs, Thomas Truxtun. *Confederate Navy Research Guide* Williamsburg, VA: Moebs Publishing Co., 1991.

Register of Officers of the Confederate States Navy 1861-1865. Washington, DC: Government Printing Office, 1931.

United States Naval Academy Graduates Association. *8th, 9th, 10th, and 11th Annual Reunions and Register of Graduates*. Baltimore: Deutsch Lithographic & Printing Co., 1897.

U.S. Navy Department, Navy History Division. *Civil War Naval Chronology*. Washington: Government Printing Office, 1971.

U.S. War Department. *War of the Rebellion: Official Records of the Union and Confederate Armies*, 129 volumes. Washington, DC: Government Printing Office, 1880-1900.

U.S. War Department. *War of the Rebellion: Official Records of the Union and Confederate Navies*, 29 volumes. Washington, DC: Government Printing Office, 1894-1921.

Wallace, Lee A. *A Guide to Virginia Military Organizations, 1861-1865*, 2d revised edition. Lynchburg: H.E. Howard, Inc., 1986.

Wakelyn, John, ed. *Biographical Dictionary of the Confederacy*. Westport, CT: Greenwood Press, 1977.

Secondary Sources

Alexander, Captain William T. and Col. Joseph H. Alexander. "From Ironclads to Infantry," *Naval History*, vol. 5 (summer 1991), pp. 9-15.

Anthis, Judith and Richard M. McMurry, "The Confederate Balloon Corps," *Blue and Gray Magazine*, vol. 9 (August 1991), pp. 20-24.

Ballard, Michael B. *A Long Shadow: Jefferson Davis and the Final Days of the Confederacy*. Jackson: University Press of Mississippi, [1988].

Baxter, James Phinney, 3rd. *The Introduction of the Ironclad Warship*. Cambridge: Harvard University Press, 1933.

Bearss, Edwin C. *River of Lost Opportunities: The Civil War on the James River 1861-1862*. Lynchburg, VA: H. E. Howard, Inc., 1995.

Benjamin, Park. *The United States Naval Academy.* New York: G. P. Putnam's Sons, 1900.

Berry, Thomas S. "The Rise of Milling in Richmond." *Virginia Magazine of History and Biography* vol. 78 (October 1970), pp. 387-408.

Besse, Sumner B. *C.S. Ironclad Virginia and U.S. Ironclad Monitor.* Newport News: The Mariners Museum, 1978.

Bill, Alfred Hoyt. *The Beleaguered City: Richmond 1861-65.* New York: Alfred A. Knopf, 1946.

Blair, Dan. "The CSS Virginia II." Unpublished term paper, East Carolina University, 1993.

Blanton, Wyndham B., M.D. *Medicine in Virginia in the Nineteenth Century.* Richmond: Garrett & Massie, 1933.

Brewer, James H. *The Confederate Negro: Virginia's Craftsmen and Military Laborers, 1861-1865.* Durham: Duke University Press, 1969.

Brooke, George M., Jr. *John M. Brooke: Naval Scientist and Educator.* Charlottesville: University Press of Virginia, 1980.

Browning, Robert M., Jr. *From Cape Charles to Cape Fear: The North Atlantic Blockading Squadron during the Civil War.* Tuscaloosa: University of Alabama Press, 1993.

Burrows, Claude. "Excavation yields surprises about city's past." *Richmond Times-Dispatch* September 4, 1990, pp. A1, A8.

Burton, David L. "Richmond's Great Homefront Disaster: Friday the 13th." *Civil War Times Illustrated*, October 1982, pp. 36-40.

Callahan, Myrtle Elizabeth. "History of Richmond as a Port City." M.A. Thesis, Department of Economics, University of Richmond, 1952.

Canfield, Eugene. *Notes on Naval Ordnance in the American Civil War.* Washington, D.C.: American Naval Ordnance Asociation, 1960.

Cavanaugh, Michael A. *6th Virginia Infantry.* Lynchburg, VA: H.E. Howard, Inc., 1988.

Chesson, Michael B. *Richmond After the War 1865-1900.* Richmond: Virginia State Library, 1981.

Chitwood, W. R. "Doctor Spotswood and the Confederate Navy," *Virginia Medical*, October 1976, pp. 728-33.

"Col. John W. Dunnington." *Confederate Veteran*, vol. 4 (April 1896), p. 100.

Cunningham, H. H. *Doctors in Gray: The Confederate Medical* Service. Baton Rouge: LSU Press, 1958.

Davis, William C. *"A Government of Our Own": The Making of the Confederacy.* New York: The Free Press, 1994.

— *Duel Between the First Ironclads*. Garden City, NY: Doubleday, 1975.

Delaney, Norman C. *John McIntosh Kell of the Raider Alabama*. Tuscaloosa: University of Alabama Press, 1973.

Dew, Charles B. *Ironmaker to the Confederacy: Joseph R. Anderson and the Tredegar Iron Works*. New Haven: Yale University Press, 1966.

Donnelly, Ralph W. "A Confederate Navy Forlorn Hope." *Military Affairs,* vol. 28 (Summer 1964), pp. 74-78.

— *Biographical Sketches of the Commissioned Officers of the Confederate States Marine Corps*. Privately Published, 1973.

— "Blacks in the Confederate Navy." Unpublished paper, courtesy Richmond National Battlefield Park.

— *The History of the Confederate States Marine Corps. Privately published* [Reprinted as *The Confederate States Marine Corps: The Rebel Leatherneck*s, Shippensburg, PA: White Mane Publishing Co., 1989].

— "Scientists of the Confederate Nitre and Mining Bureau." *Civil War History*, vol. 2 (1956), pp. 69-92.

— *Service Records of Confederate Enlisted Marines*. Privately Published, 1979.

Dudley, William S. *Going South: U.S. Navy Officer Resignations and Dismissals on the Eve of the Civil War*. Washington: Naval Historical Foundation, 1981.

Dunaway, Wayland Fuller. *History of the James River and Kanawha Canal Company*. New York: Columbia University Press, 1922.

Durkin, Joseph T. *Stephen R. Mallory: Confederate Navy Chief.* Chapel Hill: University of North Carolina Press, 1954; reprint, Columbia: University of South Carolina, 1987.

Elliott, Robert G. *Ironclad of the Roanoke: Gilbert Elliott's Albemarle*. Shippensburg, PA: White Mane, 1994.

Fickett, George L., Jr. "The Bermuda Hundred Tour." Chesterfield, VA: Chesterfield Historical Society, 1990.

Folk, Lt. Winston. "The Confederate States Naval Academy." *U.S. Naval Institute Proceedings*, vol. 60 (September 1934), pp. 1235-1240.

Hackemer, Kurt. "The Other Union Ironclad: The USS *Galena* and the Critical Summer of 1862." *Civil War History*, vol. 40 (September 1994), pp. 226-247.

Hall, Virginius. *Portraits in the Collection of the Virginia Historical Society*. Charlottesville: University Press of Virginia, 1981.

Harris, Patrick D. "Richmond's Maritime and Naval Heritage." unpublished manuscript, August 1992.

—"Richmond—Submarine Capital of the World." unpublished manuscript, August 1992.

Hearns, Chester G. *The Capture of New Orleans, 1862.* Baton Rouge: Louisiana State University, 1995.

Heite, Edward F. "Captain Robert B. Pegram: Hero Under Four Flags." *Virginia Cavalcade*, vol. 14 (Autumn 1965), pp. 38-43.

Henderson, William D. *12th Virginia Infantry*. Lynchburg, VA: H.E Howard, Inc., 1984.

Herndon, G. Melville. "The Confederate States Naval Academy," *Virginia Magazine of History and Biography*, vol. 69 (July 1961), pp. 300-323.

Hoehling, A. A. *Thunder at Hampton Roads*. Englewood Cliffs, NJ: Prentice-Hall, 1976.

Hoehling, A.A. and Mary. *The Day Richmond Died.* New York: A.S. Barnes & Co., 1981.

Holcombe, A. Robert, Jr. "The Evolution of Confederate Ironclad Design." M.A. Thesis, East Carolina University, 1993.

— Response to Query on *Richmond* class Confederate ironclads in "Insofer," *Warship International*, vol. 20 (1983), pp. 309-314.

Jahns, Patricia. *Matthew Fontaine Maury & Joseph Henry Scientists of the Civil War.* New York: Hastings House, 1961.

Jensen, Les D. *32nd Virginia Infantry* . Lynchburg: H. E. Howard, Inc., 1990.

Johnston, Jeff. "The Naval Battle at Drewry's Bluff, May 15, 1862." (unpublished article, [1993]).

Jones, Virgil Carrington. *The Civil War at Sea*, 3 volumes. New York: Holt, Rinehart & Co., 1960-1962.

— "New Thunder Along the James." *Richmond Times-Dispatch Magazine*, September 24, 1939, pp. 8-10.

Jones, Wilbur Devereux. *The Confederate Rams at Birkenhead: A Chapter in Anglo-American Relations*. Tuscaloosa, AL: Confederate Publishing Co., Inc., 1961.

Jordan, Ervin L., Jr. *Black Confederates and Afro-Yankees in Civil War Virginia*. Charlottesville: University Press of Virginia, 1995.

Joseph, John Mark. "Confederate Naval Installations at Richmond, Virginia: an independent study." Unpublished paper, Virginia Commonwealth University, 1993.

Lee, Richard M. *General Lee's City*. McLean, VA: EPM Publishing Co., 1987.

Lett, Wayne Dixon. "John Kirkwood Mitchell and Confederate Naval Defeat." M.A. thesis, Old Dominion University, 1972.

Loth, Calder, ed. *The Virginia Landmarks Register*. Charlottesville: University Press of Virginia, 1986.

MacBride, J. D. *A Handbook of Practical Shipbuilding with a Glossary of Terms*, second revised edition. New York: D. Van Nostrand Co., 1921.

MacBride, Robert. *Civil War Ironclads: The Dawn of Naval Armor*. Philadelphia: Chilton Books, 1962.

Madison, Dennis W. "A Brief History of Drewry's Bluff and Naval Actions on the James River." *Blue & Gray Magazine*, vol. 7 (October 1989), pp. 59-61.

Margolin, Sam. "Preserving Virginia's Civil War Naval Heritage, Part I: History and Archaeology of the Wreck Sites." Unpublished Conference Paper, 1990.

Melton, Maurice. *The Confederate Ironclads*. New York: Thomas Yoseloff, 1968.

Merli, Frank J. *Great Britain and the Confederate Navy, 1861-1865*. Bloomington: Indiana University Press, 1970.

Miller, William J. "The Battle of Drewry's Bluff." *Civil War*, vol. 51 (June 1995), pp. 39-43.

Minor, John B. *The Minor Family of Virginia*. Lynchburg: J. Bell Co., 1923.

Monroe, Alexander G. Unpublished Memoranda on James River Wrecks, June 28, 1989 and July 28, 1989.

Morgan, William J. "Torpedoes In The James." *The Iron Worker*, vol. 26 (Summer 1962), pp. 1-11.

Mouer, L. Daniel. "Confederate Navy Yard Discovered on Richmond's Waterfront." *APVA Newsletter,* vol. 11 (spring 1992), pp. 11-13.

Mouer, L. Daniel, et. al. The Archaeology of the Rocketts Number 1 Site, 3 volumes. Unpublished report prepared for the Virginia Department of Transportation, 1992.

Murphy, Paul. "The Richmond Dock and the Trigg Shipyard, 1898-1903." Unpublished paper submitted to Historic Richmond Foundation, August 1992.

— compiler. Richmond's Historic Waterfront: Rockett's Landing to Tredegar, 1607-1865. Richond: Historic Richmond Foundation, [1989].

Musicant, Ivan. *Divided Waters: The Naval History of the Civil War.* New York: Harper Collins, 1995.

Newell, Mark M. "The *C.S.S. H. L. Hunley*: Solving a 131-Year-Old Mystery," *Civil War Regiments*, vol. 4, No. 3, pp. 77-87.

Page, Dave. *Ships versus Shore: Civil War Engagements Along Southern Shores and Rivers*. Nashville: Rutledge Hill Press, 1994.

Perry, Milton F. *Infernal Machines: The Story of Confederate Submarine and Mine Warfare*. Baton Rouge: LSU Press, 1965.

Ragan, Mark K. *The Hunley: Submarines, Sacrifice, & Success in the Civil War* Miami and Charleston: Narwhal Press, 1995.

Roberts, W. Adolphe. *Semmes of the Alabama*. Indianapolis: Bobbs-Merrill, 1938.

Robertson, William Glenn, *Back Door to Richmond: The Bermuda Hundred Campaign, April-June, 1864*. Newark: University of Deleware Press, 1987.

Rochelle, James Henry. *Life of Rear Admiral John Randolph Tucker.* Washington, D.C.: Neale Publishing Co., 1903.

Ryan, David D. *Cornbread and Maggots, Cloack and Dagger: Union Prisoners and Spies in Civil War Richmond.* Richmond: Dietz Press, 1994.

— *The Falls of the James*. Richmond: William Byrd Press, 1975.

Sauder, Rick. "Dredging Up History: Ghost fleet of the James haunts Port of Richmond." *Richmond Times-Dispatch*, March 15, 1993, pp. E16-E18.

Savas, Theodore P. "Last Clash of the Ironclads: The Bungled Affair at Trent's Reach." *Civil War*, vol. 16 (February 1989), pp. 15-22.

Scharf, J. Thomas. *History of the Confederate States Navy*. New York: Rogers & Sherwood, 1887.

Schiller, Herbert M. *The Bermuda Hundred Campaign.* Dayton: Press of Morningside, 1988.

— "Confederate Submarine Battery Service on the James River." *Blue & Gray Magazine*, vol. 7 (October 1989), p.18.

Sheppard, J. L. "Confederate States Naval Academy," *Confederate Veteran*, vol. 2 (1995), pp. 12-17.

Shingleton, Royce Gordon. *John Taylor Wood: Sea Ghost of the Confederacy*. Athens: University of Georgia Press, 1979.

Shofner, Jerrell H. And William Warren Rogers, "Montgomery to Richmond: The Confederacy Selects a Capital," *Civil War History*, vol. 10 (June 1864), pp. 155-166.

Silverstone, Paul H. *Warships of the Civil War Navies*. Annapolis: Naval Institute Press, 1989.

Snair, Dale S. "Lt. Thomas P. Bell, C.S.N., and the Action at Trent's Reach." *Blue & Gray Magazine*, vol. 3 (February-March 1986), pp. 23-27.

Snyder, Dean. "Torpedoes for the Confederacy." *Civil War Times Illustrated*, vol. 24 (March 1986), pp. 41-45.

Soley, James Russell. "The Navy in the Peninsular Campaign." *Battles and Leaders of the Civil War*, volume II: *North to Antietam*. New York: Thomas Yoseloff, 1956, pp. 264-270.

Soley, James Russell. "The Union and Confederate Navies." *Battles and Leaders of the Civil War*, volume I: *From Sumter to Shiloh*. New York: Thomas Yoseloff, 1956, pp. 611-631.

Spencer, Warren F. *The Confederate Navy in Europe*. Tuscaloosa: University of Alabama Press, 1983.

Still, William N., Jr. "Confederate Naval Strategy: The Ironclad." *The Journal of Southern History*, vol. 9 (June 1963), pp. 331-343.

— "The Civil War's Uncommon Man The Common Sailor, part II: Confederate Tars." *Civil War Times Illustrated*, vol. 24 (March 1985), pp. 13-19+.

— *Confederate Shipbuilding*. Athens: University of Georgia, 1969; reprint, Columbia: University of South Carolina, 1987.

— *Iron Afloat: The Story of the Confederate Armorclads*. Nashville: Vanderbilt University, 1971; reprint, Columbia: University of South Carolina, 1985.

—ed., *Odyssey in Gray: A Diary of Confederate Service 1863-1865*. Richmond: Virginia State Library, 1979.

Sullivan, David M. "From Hampton Roads to Appomattox: Virginia and the Confederate States Marine Corps." *Virginia Country's Civil War Quarterly*, vol. 8 (March 1987), pp. 15-27.

Taggart, Lewis Williams. "Technology and the Confederate Navy." M.A. thesis, University of Tulsa, 1991.

Thomas, Emory M. *The Confederacy as a Revolutionary Experience*. Englewood Cliffs, NJ: Prentice-Hall, 1971.

— *The Confederate Nation: 1861-1865*. New York: Harper, 1979.

— *The Confederate State of Richmond: A Biography of the Capital*. Austin: University of Texas Press, 1971.

[Townley, John N.] "Saved!! C.S.S. Richmond, C.S.S. Virginia II, C.S.S. Fredricksburg [sic], and Many More. . . " *The Confederate Naval Historical Society Newsletter*, vol. 1 (June 1989), pp. 1-5.

True, Ransom B. *Up and Down the Noble James*. Jamestown: Association for the Preservation of Virginia Antiquities, 1984.

Tucker, Spencer. "Confederate Naval Ordnance," *Journal of Confederate History*, vol. 4 (1989), pp. 141-146.

Turner, Maxine. *Navy Gray: A Story of the Confederate Navy on the Chattahoochee and Appalachicola Rivers* Tuscaloosa: University of Alabama Press, 1989.

Tyler-McGraw, Marie. *At the Falls: Richmond, Virginia, & Its People*. Chapel Hill: University of North Carolina Press, 1994.

United States, Department of the Army. James River, Virginia. . . Washington, D.C: Government Printing Office, 1962.

Vandiver, Frank E., ed. *The Civil War Diary of General Josiah Gorgas*. Tuscaloosa: University of Alabama Press, 1947.

Wallace, Lee A., Jr. *1st Virginia Infantry*. Lynchburg: H.E. Howard, Inc., 1984.

Weisiger, Benjamin B., III. *The Parker Family of Port Royal and Richmond, Virginia*. Richmond: privately published, 1990.

Wells, Thomas Henderson. *The Confederate Navy: A Study in Organization*. Tuscaloosa: University of Alabama Press, 1971.

Werlich, David P. *Admiral of the Amazon: John Randolph Tucker His Confederate Colleagues, and Peru*. Charlottesville: University Press of Virginia, 1990.

White, Frank R., III. "The Confederate States Navy in Richmond, Virginia." Unpublished paper, Virginia Commonwealth University, 1990.

Wickham, Julia Porter. "Commanders of the Confederate Navy: Charles Read of Mississippi." *Confederate Veteran*, vol. 37(February 1929), pp. 58-61.

Williams, Frances Leigh. *Matthew Fontaine Maury, Scientist of the Seas*. New Brunswick, Rutgers University Press, 1963.

Young, William A., Jr. and Patricia C. *56th Virginia Infantry*. Lynchburg, VA: H. E. Howard, Inc., 1990.

Index